Bloom's Classic Critical Views

WILLIAM WORDSWORTH

Bloom's Classic Critical Views

Alfred, Lord Tennyson

Benjamin Franklin

The Brontës

Charles Dickens

Edgar Allan Poe

Geoffrey Chaucer

George Eliot

George Gordon, Lord Byron

Henry David Thoreau

Herman Melville

Jane Austen

John Donne and the Metaphysical Poets

John Milton

Jonathan Swift

Mark Twain

Mary Shelley

Nathaniel Hawthorne

Oscar Wilde

Percy Shelley

Ralph Waldo Emerson

Robert Browning

Samuel Taylor Coleridge

Stephen Crane

Walt Whitman

William Blake

William Shakespeare

William Wordsworth

WILLIAM WORDSWORTH

Edited and with an Introduction by
Harold Bloom
Sterling Professor of the Humanities
Yale University

BLOOM'S
LITERARY CRITICISM
An imprint of Infobase Publishing

Bloom's Literary Criticism
An imprint of Infobase Publishing
132 West 31st Street
New York NY 10001

Library of Congress Cataloging-in-Publication Data
William Wordsworth / edited and with an introduction by Harold Bloom; Janyce Marson, volume editor.
   p. cm.—(Bloom's classic critical views)
   Includes bibliographical references and index.
   ISBN 978-1-60413-427-8
   1. Wordsworth, William, 1770–1850—Criticism and interpretation.   I. Bloom, Harold.   II. Marson, Janyce.   III. Title.   IV. Series.
   PR5881.W465 2009
   821'.7—dc22   2009011465

Bloom's Literary Criticism books are available at special discounts when purchased in bulk quantities for businesses, associations, institutions, or sales promotions. Please call our Special Sales Department in New York at (212) 967-8800 or (800) 322-8755.

You can find Bloom's Literary Criticism on the World Wide Web at
http://www.chelseahouse.com

Volume editor: Janyce Marson
Series design by Erika K. Arroyo
Cover designed by Takeshi Takahashi
Printed in the United States of America
IBT IBT 10 9 8 7 6 5 4 3 2 1

This book is printed on acid-free paper.

All links and Web addresses were checked and verified to be correct at the time of publication. Because of the dynamic nature of the Web, some addresses and links may have changed since publication and may no longer be valid.

Contents

Series Introduction	ix
Introduction by Harold Bloom	xi
Biography	1
Personal	3
Dorothy Wordsworth (1802)	5
Henry Crabb Robinson (1812)	5
Robert Southey (1814)	6
John Gibson Lockhart "Letters from the Lakes" (1819)	7
George Ticknor (1819)	9
Charles Mayne Young (1828)	10
Thomas De Quincey "The Lake Poets: William Wordsworth" (1839)	13
Robert Browning "The Lost Leader" (1845)	14
Leigh Hunt (1850)	15
Ralph Waldo Emerson "First Visit to England" (1856)	17
Thomas Carlyle (1867)	21
Émile Legouis (1922)	23
General	59
Charles Burney (1799)	61
Robert Southey (1804)	62
George Gordon, Lord Byron (1809)	62
Charles Lamb "Wordsworth's *Excursion*" (1814)	63
Sydney Smith (1814)	64
John Keats "Addressed to Haydon" (1816)	64
William Hazlitt (1818)	64
Thomas Love Peacock "The Four Ages of Poetry" (1820)	66
Walter Scott (1820)	66

Henry Wadsworth Longfellow (1829)   66
Thomas Babington Macaulay "Moore's Life of
    Lord Byron" (1831)   67
Henry Taylor "Wordsworth's *Poetical Works*" (1834)   67
George Eliot (1839)   72
Elizabeth Barrett Browning (1842)   72
Margaret Fuller "Modern British Poets" (1846)   74
Leigh Hunt (1848)   76
Matthew Arnold "Memorial Verses" (1850)   77
George Meredith "The Poetry of Wordsworth" (1851)   79
John Stuart Mill (1873)   79
Harriet Martineau (1877)   81
Matthew Arnold "Preface" (1879)   83
Edmond Scherer "Wordsworth and Modern Poetry
    in England" (1882)   85
Aubrey De Vere "Remarks on the Personal Character of
    Wordsworth's Poetry" (1883)   86
William Watson "Wordsworth's Grave" (1890)   87
Edward Dowden (1897)   88
David Watson Rannie "Fellow-Workers in
    Romanticism" (1907)   90
A.C. Bradley "Wordsworth" (1909)   108

WORKS   119

Descriptive Sketches   121
H.W. Garrod "Descriptive Sketches" (1923)   121

The Lyrical Ballads   133
William Wordsworth "Preface" (1798)   133
Vida D. Scudder "Wordsworth and New Democracy" (1895)   135
Arthur Symons "Wordsworth" (1902)   138
Charles Wharton Stork "The Influence of the
    Popular Ballad on Wordsworth and Coleridge" (1914) 150

The Prelude   169
Samuel Taylor Coleridge (1807)   169
Walter Pater "Wordsworth" (1874)   173
Thomas Babington Macaulay (1850)   188
F.W.H. Myers (1881)   188

Ode: Intimations of Immortality   190
George McLean Harper "The 'Intimations Ode'" (1916)   190

H.W. Garrod "The 'Immortal Ode'" (1923)   196

The White Doe of Rylstone   206
John Wilson (1815)   206
Francis Jeffrey, Lord Jeffrey "Wordsworth's
    White Doe" (1815)   207
John Campbell Shairp "The White Doe of Rylstone" (1881)   208

The Excursion   210
William Hazlitt "Observations on Mr. Wordsworth's
    Poem the *Excursion*" (1814)   211
Francis Jeffrey, Lord Jeffrey "Wordsworth's
    Excursion" (1814)   213
Henry Crabb Robinson (1814)   220
Robert Southey (1814)   221
Samuel Taylor Coleridge (1817)   221
George Gordon, Lord Byron "Dedication" (1819)   236
William Hazlitt "Mr. Wordsworth" (1825)   236
John Wilson "An Hour's Talk about Poetry" (1831)   246
Leslie Stephen "Wordsworth's Ethics" (1876)   247
T.E. Brown (1894)   268

The Patriotic and Political Sonnets   268
William Wordsworth (1807)   268
W.J. Dawson "Patriotic and Political Poems" (1908)   274

The River Duddon Sonnets   281
Unsigned (1820)   281

The Ecclesiastical Sonnets   298
Abbie Findlay Potts "Introduction" (1922)   298

Peter Bell   321
Percy Bysshe Shelley "Peter Bell the Third" (1819)   321
William Wordsworth (1819)   322

Chronology   325

Index   327

Series Introduction

Bloom's Classic Critical Views is a new series presenting a selection of the most important older literary criticism on the greatest authors commonly read in high school and college classes today. Unlike the Bloom's Modern Critical Views series, which for more than 20 years has provided the best contemporary criticism on great authors, Bloom's Classic Critical Views attempts to present the authors in the context of their time and to provide criticism that has proved over the years to be the most valuable to readers and writers. Selections range from contemporary reviews in popular magazines, which demonstrate how a work was received in its own era, to profound essays by some of the strongest critics in the British and American tradition, including Henry James, G.K. Chesterton, Matthew Arnold, and many more.

Some of the critical essays and extracts presented here have appeared previously in other titles edited by Harold Bloom, such as the New Moulton's Library of Literary Criticism. Other selections appear here for the first time in any book by this publisher. All were selected under Harold Bloom's guidance.

In addition, each volume in this series contains a series of essays by a contemporary expert, who comments on the most important critical selections, putting them in context and suggesting how they might be used by a student writer to influence his or her own writing. This series is intended above all for students, to help them think more deeply and write more powerfully about great writers and their works.

Introduction by Harold Bloom

Wordsworth invented modern poetry in English. Before him, the poet could cultivate subjects outside the self. After Wordsworth, the poem is the man or woman who composes it.

Byron, influenced by Wordsworth through the mediation of Shelley, broke through to his own new mode in *Don Juan*, but this was an exploit of individual genius and has no progeny. Hazlitt remarked that with Wordworth we begin anew on a *tabula rasa* of poetry. The classical tradition had gone from Homer to Goethe, with Byron as an aristocratic last stand. With Wordsworth, the democratic phase of literature began and is with us still as we approach the end of the first decade of the twenty-first century. T.S. Eliot's attempt to consolidate neoclassicism, neofascism, and neo-Christianity failed, and today Eliot is clearly seen as an amalgam of Tennyson and Walt Whitman, another late romantic.

Wordsworthian "nature" is the center of his enterprise and now is little understood. Though he regarded himself as "the poet of nature," his sense of nature was transcendent, in the mode of Spinoza, Coleridge, and German philosophical idealism. Like his American disciple, Emerson, Wordsworth said "nature" and meant "man." He sought in nature something strikingly akin to what his older contemporary William Blake called "the Human Form Divine."

All of Wordsworth turns upon his vision of "intimations of immortality." A transcendental naturalism, whether in Wordsworth or Emerson, is now difficult to comprehend, as we are post-Darwinian, post-Freudian, and postquantum mechanics. The simplest and perhaps most accurate sense we can give to Wordsworthian "immortality" is its return to the childlike condition of having no consciousness of death.

Inwardness is the Wordsworthian legacy that no poet coming after him has been able to evade. Whitman, Emily Dickinson, Wallace Stevens, Robert Frost, Hart Crane, John Ashbery: the great tradition of American poetry is Wordsworthian at its core.

BIOGRAPHY

WILLIAM WORDSWORTH
(1770–1850)

William Wordsworth was born on April 7, 1770, at Cockermouth, Cumberland, to John Wordsworth, an attorney, and Anne Cookson Wordsworth; he had three brothers and one sister, Dorothy. Wordsworth grew up in the Lake District and lost both his mother and his father in early youth, in 1778 and 1783 respectively. He was educated at Hawkshead Grammar School (1779–83) and at St. John's College, Cambridge (1787–91). Wordsworth went on a European tour in 1790 and, after graduating from Cambridge, spent a year (1791–92) in France. While in France, Wordsworth became an enthusiastic republican, although later developments gradually turned him against the revolution. He became friendly with some of the Girondists and had an affair with Annette Vallon, the daughter of a French surgeon. Vallon gave birth to Wordsworth's daughter, Caroline, in December 1792, but Wordsworth returned alone to England when war broke out between his country and France in 1793.

In that year Wordsworth published two highly descriptive and relatively conventional poems, *An Evening Walk* and *Descriptive Sketches*, both in heroic couplets. In 1794 he inherited £900, which temporarily freed him of financial worries and allowed him to settle at Racedown in Dorset, where he was joined by his sister, Dorothy; she was to be his close companion and an influence on his poetry for the rest of his life. In 1797 the two moved to Alforden, Somerset, to be nearer Samuel Taylor Coleridge, whom Wordsworth had first met in 1795 and with whom he now entered into an artistic partnership. Under Coleridge's influence Wordsworth's poetry became more metaphysical, and for both poets the next several years were to be a period of intense creativity. A selection of their poetry was published as *Lyrical Ballads,* which included Wordsworth's "Tintern Abbey" and "The Idiot Boy"; the first edition appeared in 1798, and a second, with the addition of new poems and the famous "Preface," on January 1, 1801 (although it is known as the 1800 edition). Between 1798 and 1805, Wordsworth worked on his long autobiographical poem

The Prelude; or, Growth of a Poet's Mind, which he frequently revised and which was not published until 1850, shortly after his death. Together with *The Excursion* (1814), it was to have been part of a long but never-completed philosophical poem, *The Recluse.*

In 1799, Wordsworth and Dorothy returned to the Lake District, where they settled permanently at Grasmere, living first at Dove Cottage, then at nearby Rydal Mount. In 1802 Wordsworth married Mary Hutchinson, by whom he had five children between 1803 and 1810. *Poems in Two Volumes,* containing many of his most celebrated lyrics, such as "Resolution and Independence" and "Intimations of Immortality from Recollections of Early Childhood," was published in 1807 but received poor reviews. In 1813 Wordsworth was appointed stamp distributor, a sinecure which until 1842 brought him some £400 a year. Although his productivity continued and his popularity as one of the so-called Lake Poets gradually increased, Wordsworth wrote little of value, in the opinion of modern critics, after the publication of his *Collected Works* in 1815. His later works include *The White Doe of Rylstone* (1815), *Peter Bell* (1819), and *The Waggoner* (1819). In 1842 Wordsworth was awarded a pension of £300 a year, and in 1843 he succeeded Southey as poet laureate. By this point the young radical of the 1790s had long since become a politically conservative patriot and had received over the years a great deal of criticism from Byron, Shelley, Keats, Hazlitt, and others. Wordsworth lived out his last years at Grasmere and died at Rydal Mount on April 23, 1850.

PERSONAL

DOROTHY WORDSWORTH (1802)

Wm. was very unwell. Worn out with his bad night's rest. He went to bed—I read to him, to endeavour to make him sleep. Then I came into the other room, and read the first book of *Paradise Lost*. After dinner we walked to Ambleside—found Lloyds at Luff's—we stayed and drank tea by ourselves. A heart-rending letter from Coleridge—we were sad as we could be. Wm. wrote to him. We talked about Wm.'s going to London. It was a mild afternoon—there was an unusual softness in the prospects as we went, a rich yellow upon the fields, and a soft grave purple on the waters. When we returned many stars were out, the clouds were moveless, in the sky soft purple, the Lake of Rydale calm; Jupiter behind, Jupiter at least *we* call him, but William says we always call the largest star Jupiter. When we came home we both wrote to C. I was stupefied.

—DOROTHY WORDSWORTH, *Journal*, Jan. 29, 1802

HENRY CRABB ROBINSON (1812)

Henry Crabb Robinson reports that Wordsworth speaks confidently of his poems but does not expect to profit from them, settling instead for the improvement of society vis-à-vis his work. According to this journal entry, Wordsworth was consoling himself with approval from those in a position to judge rather than worrying about his waning popularity, admitting that his "unpoetical" language takes time to appreciate. Wordsworth also sets forth the condition for appreciating his work, which is—"happiness"—a state he associates with the life of an independent and reflective thinker: "no man who does not partake of that happiness, who lives a life of constant bustle, and whose felicity depends on the opinions of others, can possibly comprehend the best of my poems."

<hr />

A visit from Wordsworth, who stayed with me from between twelve and one till past three. I then walked with him to Newman Street. His conversation was long and interesting. He spoke of his own poems with the just feeling of confidence which a sense of his own excellence gives him. He is now convinced that he never can derive emolument from them; but, being independent, he willingly gives up all idea of doing so. He is persuaded that if men are to become better and wiser, the poems will sooner or later make their way. But if we are to perish, and society is not to advance in civilization, "it would be," said he, "wretched selfishness to deplore the want of any personal reputation." The approbation he has met with from some superior persons compensates for the loss of popularity, though no man has completely understood him, not excepting Coleridge, who is not happy enough to enter into his feelings. "I am myself," said Wordsworth, "one of the happiest of men; and no man who does not partake of that happiness, who lives a life of constant bustle, and whose felicity depends on the opinions of others, can possibly comprehend the best of my poems." I urged an excuse for those who can really enjoy the better pieces, and who yet are offended by a language they have by early instruction been taught to consider unpoetical; and Wordsworth seemed to tolerate this class, and to allow that his admirers should undergo a sort of education to his works.

—HENRY CRABB ROBINSON, *Diary,* May 8, 1812

ROBERT SOUTHEY (1814)

Robert Southey attests to Wordsworth's fine, exemplary character, similarly strong to the way he represents himself in *The Excursion.* Summoning impartiality, Southey also contends that Wordsworth's poetic gifts rival those of John Milton.

<hr />

Wordsworth's residence and mine are fifteen miles asunder, a sufficient distance to preclude any frequent interchange of visits. I have known him nearly twenty years, and, for about half that time, intimately. The strength and the character of his mind you see in the *Excursion,* and his life does not belie his writings, for, in every relation of life, and every point of view, he is a truly exemplary and admirable man. In conversation he is powerful beyond any of his contemporaries; and, as a poet,—I speak not from the partiality of friendship, nor because we have been so absurdly held up as both writing upon one concerted system of poetry, but with the most deliberate exercise of impartial judgment whereof I am capable, when I declare my full conviction that posterity will rank him with Milton.

—ROBERT SOUTHEY, letter to Bernard Barton,
December 19, 1814

JOHN GIBSON LOCKHART
"LETTER FROM THE LAKES" (1819)

John Gibson Lockhart is humble, even awed to be in Wordsworth's company, in his introduction to his impressions of the poet. He remarks that Wordsworth is anything but a simple pastoral poet but, rather, a sobering individual, even "grave" in his demeanor, all enhanced by a deep voice. This impression stands in contrast to Southey's praise of Wordsworth's easy-going manner in the previous selection in this volume, though Lockhart at least asserts that Wordsworth is kind to his family and household. As to the poet's physiognomy, Lockhart remarks that his features are severe, so that when he smiles it is all the more striking for its unexpectedness, conveying an image of a carved figure, permanently fixed in its features, over which a smile appears as the result of the momentary effects of the sun passing by. As to Wordsworth's skill at dinner conversation, Lockhart found him unremarkable.

I soon entered the house, and was shewn into the parlour, where Mr Wordsworth and his family were assembled to breakfast. The name of Southey acted like a talisman in my favour, and I also found that my name was not unknown to the family as that of a foreigner resident in Ambleside. Their kind and affable reception of me soon relieved me from any temporary embarrassment, and when I told the circuit I had made, they seemed pleased that a foreigner should feel so enthusiastically the beauties of their country. I soon found that even the ladies well knew every step I had taken, and that the poet's wife and sister had trodden with him the mountains and cliffs I had just traversed. Our conversation became every moment more kind and animated, and the room was filled with gentle voices and bright smiles. I know not how to describe to you the great Poet himself. They who have formed to themselves, as many have foolishly done, the idea of a simple pastoral poet, who writes sweet and touching verses, would be somewhat astounded to find themselves in the presence of William Wordsworth. There seemed to me, in his first appearance, something grave almost to austerity, and the deep tones of his voice added strength to that impression of him. There was not visible about him the same easy and disengaged air that so immediately charmed me in Southey—his mind seemed to require an effort to awaken itself thoroughly from some brooding train of thought, and his manner, as I felt at least, at first reluctantly relaxed into blandness and urbanity. There was, however, nothing of vulgar pride in all this, although perhaps it might have seemed so, in an ordinary person. It was the dignity of a mind habitually conversant with high and abstracted thoughts—and unable to divest itself wholly, even in common hours, of the stateliness inspired by the loftiest studies of humanity. No wonder if at first I felt somewhat abashed before such a man—especially when the solemnity of his manner was rendered more striking by the mild simplicity of his wife, and the affectionate earnestness of his sister. But I soon saw how finely characteristic all this was of the man. By degrees he became more lively and careless—and he shewed his politeness towards me his guest and a stranger, by a number of familiar and playful remarks addressed to the members of his own family. I could not help feeling that there was something extremely delicate in this. Often have I been oppressed and almost disgusted with the attention heaped and forced upon me because a stranger, to the utter neglect and seeming forgetfulness of the master of the house towards his own family. But here the kind affections continued in full play—I did not act as a dam to stop the current of domestic enjoyment—and when I saw Mr Wordsworth so kind, so attentive, and so affectionate, to his own happy family, I felt assured that the sunshine of his heart would not fail also to visit me, and that he was disposed to think well of a man before whom he thus freely indulged the best feelings of his human nature.

The features of Wordsworth's face are strong and high, almost harsh and severe—and his eyes have, when he is silent, a dim, thoughtful, I had nearly said melancholy expression—so that when a smile takes possession of his countenance, it is indeed the most powerful smile I ever saw—gives a new character to the whole man, and renders him, who before seemed rather a being for us to respect and venerate, an object to win our love and affection. Smiles are, assuredly, not the abiding light on that grand countenance; but at times they pass finely over it, like playful sunbeams chasing each other over the features of some stern and solemn scene of external nature, that seems willingly to yield itself for a while to the illumination. Never saw I a countenance in which Contemplation so reigns. His brow is very lofty—and his dark brown hair seems worn away, as it were, by thought, so thinly is it spread over his temples. The colour of his face is almost sallow; but it is not the sallowness of confinement or ill health, it speaks rather of the rude and boisterous greeting of the mountain-weather. He does not seem a recluse philosopher, who pores over the midnight oil in his study; but rather a hermit who converses with nature in his silent cell, whose food is roots and herbs, and whose drink is from wherever fountain or fresh current flowed Against the eastern ray, translucent pure, With touch ethereal of Heaven's fiery rod. I at once beheld, in his calm and confident voice—his stedfast and untroubled eyes—the serene expansion of his forehead—and the settled dignity of his demeanour—that original poet, who, in an age of poetry, has walked alone through a world almost exclusively his own, and who has cleared out for himself, by his own labour, a wide and magnificent path through the solitary forests of the human imagination.

—JOHN GIBSON LOCKHART, "Letters from the Lakes," *Blackwood's Edinburgh Magazine,* March 1819, pp. 739–740

GEORGE TICKNOR (1819)

George Ticknor (1791–1871) was a Harvard professor who specialized in French and Spanish literature. Here he describes a pleasant drive he took to the countryside of Rydal to visit Wordsworth. Wordsworth was about fifty-three years old at the time, tall and again described as having a rather somber aspect, with a chiseled appearance, resembling a classical statue, of "Roman dignity and simplicity." Ticknor also describes his meeting with Wordsworth's wife and sister and states that he felt immediately comfortable in their presence. When the dinner conversation, which was otherwise lackluster, turned to the topic of poetry, Ticknor reports that Wordsworth came alive, speaking "metaphysically and extravagantly," and Ticknor compares him to "the Khan of Tartary"—a reference to Ghengis Khan (1162–1227), the ruler of the Mongol Empire, whose aggressive foreign policy and military campaigns enabled him to conquer vast parts of Asia. Most impressive to Ticknor, however, is Wordsworth's reputation as a family man and the respect accorded to him by his neighbors; the poet is portrayed as a man whose counsel is sought after and revered.

An extremely pleasant drive of sixteen miles brought me to Wordsworth's door, on a little elevation, commanding a view of Rydal water. . . . It is claimed to be the most beautiful spot and the finest prospect in the lake country, and, even if there be finer, it would be an ungrateful thing to remember them here, where, if anywhere, the eye and the heart ought to be satisfied. Wordsworth knew from Southey that I was coming, and therefore met me at the door and received me heartily. He is about fifty three or four, with a tall, ample, well-proportioned frame, a grave and tranquil manner, a Roman cast of appearance, and Roman dignity and simplicity. He presented me to his wife, a good, very plain woman, who seems to regard him with reverence and affection, and to his sister, not much younger than himself, with a good deal of spirit and, I should think, more than common talent and knowledge. I was at home with them at once, and we went out like friends together to scramble up the mountains, and enjoy the prospects and scenery. We returned to dinner, which was very simple, for, though he has an office under the government and a patrimony besides, yet each is inconsiderable.

His conversation surprised me by being so different from all I had anticipated. It was exceedingly simple, strictly confined to subjects he understood familiarly, and more marked by plain good-sense than by anything else. When, however, he came upon poetry and reviews, he was the Khan of Tartary again, and talked as metaphysically and extravagantly as ever Coleridge wrote; but, excepting this, it was really a consolation to hear him. It was best of all, though, to see how he is loved and respected in his family and neighborhood. The peasantry treated him with marked respect, the children took off their hats to him, and a poor widow in the neighborhood sent to him to come and talk to her son, who had been behaving ill.

—GEORGE TICKNOR, *Journal,* March 21, 1819,
Life, Letters, and Journals of George Ticknor, ed.
Anna Ticknor, 1876, vol. 1, p. 287

CHARLES MAYNE YOUNG (1828)

Charles Mayne Young, an actor specializing in tragedy, speaks dramatically of being transported to a privileged realm in the company of Wordsworth and Coleridge, admitting at the same time to feeling somewhat intimidated when they spoke of metaphysical subjects. "Sometimes I was in pure aether—much oftener *in the clouds.*" When the topic turned to history, politics, or literature, however, Mayne felt much more at ease. With respect to his observations concerning the relationship between Wordsworth and Coleridge, Young can detect no rivalry or competitiveness, though he remarks that Wordsworth appeared to be less imaginative than Coleridge though certainly more stable emotionally. Young feels much more comfortable with Wordsworth, while Coleridge projected an aura of superiority that left the young actor feeling unworthy and diminished. Young also makes a distinction between the two poets in their respective stance toward nature. While Wordsworth had a passionate, almost religious relationship with nature. Coleridge studied it from a distance to learn all that he could, maintaining a studious remove. Young reports that Coleridge would never be deterred or stop expressing his admiration of nature but instead would get caught up in his own fanciful imagination, seeing in the "rolling mist, as it hung suspended over the valley, and partially revealed the jagged tower and crag of Drachenfels, . . . the presence of elemental power, as exhibited in the thunderstorm, the waterfall, or the avalanche. [These] were stimulus enough to stir the pulses of his teeming brain." Wordsworth is described as possessing a more Rasselas-like mind in his retreat to nature, as being one who "loved the life removed," preferring to investigate the minute details of nature, to "dilate with exquisite sensibility and microscopic power of analysis on the construction of the humblest grasses, or on the modest seclusion of some virgin wild-flower nestling in the bosom." While Wordsworth was calmed by nature, Coleridge would become animated by it.

I observed that, as a rule, Wordsworth allowed Coleridge to have all the talk to himself; but once or twice Coleridge would succeed in entangling Wordsworth in a discussion on some abstract metaphysical question: when I would sit by, reverently attending, and trying hard to look intelligent, though I did not feel so; for at such times a leaden stupor weighed down my faculties. I seemed as if I had been transported by two malignant genii into an atmosphere too rarefied for me to live in. I was soaring, as it were, against my will, 'twixt heaven and the lower parts of the earth. Sometimes I was in pure aether—much oftener *in the clouds.* When, however, these potent spirits descended to a lower level, and deigned to treat of history or politics, theology or belles lettres, I breathed again; and, imbibing fresh ideas from them, felt invigorated.

I must say I never saw any manifestation of small jealousy between Coleridge and Wordsworth; which, considering the vanity possessed by each, I thought uncommonly to the credit of both. I am sure they entertained a thorough respect for each other's intellectual endowments.

Coleridge appeared to me a living refutation of Bacon's axiom, 'that a full man is never a ready man, nor the ready man the full one:' for he was both a full man and a ready man.

Wordsworth was a single-minded man; with less imagination than Coleridge, but with a more harmonious judgment, and better balanced principles. Coleridge, conscious of his transcendent powers, rioted in a license of tongue which no man could tame.

Wordsworth, though he could discourse most eloquent music, was never unwilling to sit still in Coleridge's presence, yet could be as happy in prattling with a child as in communing with a sage.

If Wordsworth condescended to converse with me, he spoke to me as if I were his equal in mind, and made me pleased and proud in consequence. If Coleridge held me by the button, for lack of fitter audience, he had a talent for making me feel his wisdom and my own stupidity: so that I was miserable and humiliated by the sense of it. . . .

Idolatry of nature seemed with Wordsworth both a passion and a principle. She seemed a deity enshrined within his heart. Coleridge studied her rather as a mighty storehouse for poetical imagery than from innate love of her, for her own sweet sake. If once embarked in lecturing, no landscape, however grand, detained his notice for a second: whereas, let Wordsworth have been ever so absorbed in argument, he would drop it without hesitation to feast his eyes on some combination of new scenery. The union of the great and the small, so wonderfully ordered by the Creator, and so wondrously exemplified on the banks of the great German river, had little attraction for the author of *The Ancient Mariner*. The grander features of a landscape he took in at a glance; and he would, with signal power of adaptation, dispose them into a magic world of his own. The rolling mist, as it hung suspended over the valley, and partially revealed the jagged tower and crag of Drachenfels, the river shooting out of sight the burden on its bosom with the velocity and force of an arrow; the presence of elemental power, as exhibited in the thunderstorm, the waterfall, or the avalanche, were stimulus enough to stir the pulses of his teeming brain, and set his imagination afloat with colossal speculations of hereafter. With him terrestrial objects soon expanded into immensity, and were quickly elevated above the stars. The more Rasselas-like mind of the recluse of the Lakes, on the other hand, who 'loved the life removed,' would direct itself to the painstaking investigation of nature's smallest secrets, prompt him to halt by the wayside bank, and dilate with exquisite sensibility and microscopic power of analysis on the construction of the humblest grasses, or on the modest seclusion of some virgin wild-flower nestling in the bosom, or diffidently peering from out the privacy of a shady nook composed of plumes of verdant ferns. In that same stroll to Heisterbach, he pointed out to me such beauty of design in objects I had used to trample under foot, that I felt as if almost every spot on which I trod was holy ground, and that I had rudely desecrated it. His eyes would fill with tears and his voice falter as he dwelt on the benevolent adaptation of means to ends discernible by reverential observation. Nor did his reflections die out in mawkish sentiment; they lay 'too deep for tears,' and, as they crowded thickly on him, his gentle spirit, subdued by the sense of the Divine goodness towards his creature, became attuned to better thoughts; the love of nature inspired his heart with a gratitude to nature's God, and found its most suitable expression in numbers.

—CHARLES MAYNE YOUNG, *Journal*, July 6,
1828, cited in Julian Charles Young, *A Memoir of
Charles Mayne Young*, 1871, pp. 112–115

THOMAS DE QUINCEY "THE LAKE POETS: WILLIAM WORDSWORTH" (1839)

De Quincey offers a somewhat humorous description of Wordsworth's physical being, a portrait of a man rather unattractive to women, whose highly irregular legs were at least useful for walking enormous distances to contemplate nature, an activity more cherished than alcohol or other available excitation. To this great love of nature De Quincey attributes Wordsworth's inner peace, happiness, and the beauty of his writing. "But, useful as they have proved themselves," he writes, "the Wordsworthian legs were certainly not ornamental; and it was really a pity . . . that he had not another pair for evening dress parties."

He was, upon the whole, not a well-made man. His legs were pointedly condemned by all female connoisseurs in legs; not that they were bad in any way which *would* force itself upon your notice—there was no absolute deformity about them; and undoubtedly they had been serviceable legs beyond the average standard of human requisition; for I calculate, upon good data, that with these identical legs Wordsworth must have traversed a distance of 175,000 to 180,000 English miles—a mode of exertion which, to him, stood in the stead of alcohol and all other stimulants whatsoever to the animal spirits; to which, indeed, he was indebted for a life of unclouded happiness, and we for much of what is most excellent in his writings. But, useful as they have proved themselves, the Wordsworthian legs were certainly not ornamental; and it was really a pity, as I agreed with a lady in thinking, that he had not another pair for evening dress parties—when no boots lend their friendly aid to mask our imperfections from the eyes of female rigorists—those *elegantes formarum spectatrices.* A sculptor would certainly have disapproved of their contour. But the worst part of Wordsworth's person was the bust; there was a narrowness and a droop about the shoulders which became striking, and had an effect of meanness, when brought into close juxtaposition with a figure of a more statuesque build. Once on a summer evening, walking in the Vale of Langdale with Wordsworth, his sister, and Mr. J, a native Westmoreland clergyman, I remember that Miss Wordsworth was positively mortified by the peculiar illustration which settled upon this defective conformation. Mr. J, a fine towering figure, six feet high, massy and columnar in his proportions, happened to be walking, a little in advance, with Wordsworth; Miss Wordsworth and myself being in the rear; and from the nature of the conversation which then prevailed in our front rank, something or other about money, devises, buying and selling, we of the rear-guard thought it requisite to preserve this arrangement for a space of three miles or more; during which time, at intervals, Miss Wordsworth would exclaim, in a tone of vexation, "Is it possible,—can that be William? How very mean he looks!" And she did not conceal a mortification that seemed really painful, until I, for my part, could not forbear laughing outright at the serious interest which she carried into this trifle. She was, however, right, as regarded the mere visual judgment. Wordsworth's figure, with all its defects, was brought into powerful relief by one which had been cast in a more square and massy mould; and in such a case it impressed a spectator with a sense of absolute meanness, more especially when viewed from behind and not counteracted by his countenance; and yet Wordsworth was of a good height (five feet ten), and not a slender man; on the contrary, by the side of Southey, his limbs looked thick, almost in a disproportionate degree. But the total effect of Wordsworth's person was always worst in a state of motion. Meantime, his face—that was one which would have made amends for greater defects of figure. Many such, and finer, I have seen amongst the portraits of Titian, and, in a later period, amongst those of Vandyke, from the great era of Charles I, as also from the court of Elizabeth and of Charles II, but none which has more impressed me in my own time.

—THOMAS DE QUINCEY, "The Lake Poets:
William Wordsworth," 1839, *Collected Writings*,
ed. David Masson, vol. 2, pp. 242–243

ROBERT BROWNING "THE LOST LEADER" (1845)

Although Browning does not mention Wordsworth in his poem "The Lost Leader," he nevertheless expresses his profound disappointment in Wordsworth for abandoning his former radical politics and becoming instead a supporter of the conservative Tory Party. In the following excerpt, Browning accuses the poet of selling out in his later years, when he accepted a stipend from the government and became poet laureate, "for a riband to stick in his coat." Browning, who clearly loved and admired Wordsworth's early poetry and looked up to him as a beacon of hope, feels deserted and betrayed, so much so that he sees Wordsworth's transformation from one who spoke to the common human existence in a new language to one who has become enslaved by his choices.

Just for a handful of silver he left us,
Just for a riband to stick in his coat—
Found the one gift of which fortune bereft us,
Lost all the others she lets us devote;
They, with the gold to give, doled him out silver,
So much was theirs who so little allowed:
How all our copper had gone for his service!
Rags—were they purple, his heart had been proud!
We that had loved him so, followed him, honoured him,
Lived in his mild and magnificent eye,
Learned his great language, caught his clear accents,
Made him our pattern to live and to die!
Shakespeare was of us, Milton was for us,
Burns, Shelley, were with us,—they watch from their graves!
He alone breaks from the van and the freemen,
—He alone sinks to the rear and the slaves!

—ROBERT BROWNING, "The Lost Leader,"
Dramatic Romances and Lyrics, 1845

LEIGH HUNT (1850)

Leigh Hunt's essay compares his first meeting with Wordsworth, when Hunt concluded he was in the company of a venerable and reserved man, to a subsequent audience with the poet, some thirty years later, when Hunt detects a change in the man, noting both an improved and cheerful humor and a marked self-esteem. This latter quality reminds Hunt of the impression he received of the duke of Wellington, nicknamed "the iron duke," with his soldier's taste for discipline and order and the aristocrat's distrust of democratic institutions. Wordsworth's demeanor is described as dignified and his manner of speaking eloquent. Hunt likewise asserts that Wordsworth's self-assurance had evolved to the point to which he no longer felt the need to deprecate other poets and, instead, adopted an air of reticence. After listening to Milton's impassioned description of Satan descending the stairway from heaven, aided and abetted by angels in his irreversible plunge from the celestial realm, Hunt finds Wordsworth's silence remarkable.

—⟨·/·/·⟩—   —⟨·/·/·⟩—   —⟨·/·/·⟩—

Mr. Wordsworth, whom Mr. Hazlitt designated as one that would have had the wide circle of his humanities made still wider, and a good deal more pleasant, by dividing a little more of his time between his lakes in Westmoreland and the hotels of the metropolis, had a dignified manner, with a deep and roughish but not unpleasing voice, and an exalted mode of speaking. He had a habit of keeping his left hand in the bosom of his waistcoat; and in this attitude, except when he turned round to take one of the subjects of his criticism from the shelves (for his contemporaries were there also), he sat dealing forth his eloquent but hardly catholic judgments. In his "father's house" there were not "many mansions" He was as sceptical on the merits of all kinds of poetry but one, as Richardson was on those of the novels of Fielding.

Under the study in which my visitor and I were sitting was an archway, leading to a nursery ground; a cart happened to go through it while I was inquiring whether he would take any refreshment; and he uttered, in so lofty a voice, the words, "Anything which is *going forward*," that I felt inclined to ask him whether he would take a piece of the cart. Lamb would certainly have done it. But this was a levity which would neither have been so proper on my part, after so short an acquaintance, nor very intelligible, perhaps, in any sense of the word, to the serious poet. There are good-humoured warrants for smiling, which lie deeper even than Mr. Wordsworth's thoughts for tears.

I did not see this distinguished person again till thirty years afterwards; when, I should venture to say, his manner was greatly superior to what it was in the former instance; indeed, quite natural and noble, with a cheerful air of animal as well as spiritual confidence; a gallant bearing, curiously reminding me of the Duke of Wellington, as I saw him walking some eighteen years ago by a lady's side, with no unbecoming oblivion of his time of life. I observed, also, that the poet no longer committed himself in scornful criticisms, or, indeed, in any criticisms whatever, at least as far as I knew. He had found out that he could, at least, afford to be silent. Indeed, he spoke very little of anything. The conversation turned upon Milton, and I fancied I had opened a subject that would have "brought him out," by remarking, that the most diabolical thing in all *Paradise Lost* was a feeling attributed to the angels. "Ay!" said Mr. Wordsworth, and inquired what it was. I said it was the passage in which the angels, when they observed Satan journeying through the empyrean, let down a set of steps out of heaven, on purpose to add to his misery—to his despair of ever being able to re-ascend them; they being angels in a state of bliss, and he a fallen spirit doomed to eternal punishment. The passage is as follows:

Each stair was meant mysteriously, nor stood
There always, but, drawn up to heaven, sometimes
Viewless; and underneath a bright sea flow'd
Of jasper, or of liquid pearl, whereon
Who after came from earth sailing arriv'd
Wafted by angels, or flew o'er the lake
Rapt in a chariot drawn by fiery steeds.
The stairs were then let down, whether to dare
The fiend by easy ascent, or *aggravate*
His sad exclusion from the doors of bliss.

Mr. Wordsworth pondered, and said nothing. I thought to myself, what pity for the poor devil would not good Uncle Toby have expressed! Into what indignation would not Burns have exploded! What knowledge of themselves would not have been forced upon those same coxcombical and malignant angels by Fielding or Shakspeare!

Walter Scott said that the eyes of Burns were the finest he ever saw. I cannot say the same of Mr. Wordsworth's; that is, not in the sense of the beautiful, or even of the profound. But certainly I never beheld eyes that looked so inspired or supernatural. They were like fires half burning, half smouldering, with a sort of acrid fixture of regard, and seated at the further end of two caverns. One might imagine Ezekiel or Isaiah to have had such eyes. The finest eyes, in every sense of the word, which I have ever seen in a man's head (and I have seen many fine ones) are those of Thomas Carlyle.

—Leigh Hunt, *Autobiography*, 1850, chapter 15

Ralph Waldo Emerson
"First Visit to England" (1856)

Ralph Waldo Emerson writes of his visit to the elderly and quite conservative poet at Rydal Mount. Emerson relates what Wordsworth had to say in regard to the United States, that its system of education and its culture are based on a poor set of values, namely a preoccupation with making money, and that the nation valorizes political distinction as an end rather than a means to a higher purpose. Emerson also reports that Wordsworth found the United States sorely lacking in a leisure class capable of bringing nobility to its society. When their conversation turned to literary matters, Wordsworth expressed disdain for Goethe's *Wilhelm Meister* as "full of all manner of fornication," while declaring Carlyle to be insane. At the time of Emerson's visit, Wordsworth recited three sonnets he had just written on Fingal's Cave, a sea cave on the uninhabited island of Staffa, located in the Inner Hebrides of Scotland and discovered by the eighteenth-century naturalist Joseph Banks in 1772. The location susequently became known as Fingal's Cave after the eponymous hero of an epic poem by the eighteenth-century Scottish poet-historian James Macpherson. Overall, Emerson was not impressed by Wordsworth and concludes his commentary by pointing out a fundamental hypocrisy on the poet's part: He was a man who set himself apart from others while reverting to conformity in all other ways. "Off his own beat, his opinions were of no value," Emerson writes. "It is not very rare to find persons loving sympathy and ease, who expiate their departure from the common in one direction, by their conformity in every other."

<hr />

On the 28th August I went to Rydal Mount, to pay my respects to Mr. Wordsworth. His daughters called in their father, a plain, elderly, white-haired man, not prepossessing, and disfigured by green goggles. He sat down, and talked with great simplicity. He had just returned from a journey. His health was good, but he had broken a tooth by a fall, when walking with two lawyers, and had said that he was glad it did not happen forty years ago; whereupon they had praised his philosophy.

He had much to say of America, the more that it gave occasion for his favorite topic,—that society is being enlightened by a superficial tuition, out of all proportion to its being restrained by moral culture. Schools do no good. Tuition is not education. He thinks more of the education of circumstances than of tuition. 'Tis not question whether there are offences of which the law takes cognizance, but whether there are offences of which the law does not take cognizance. Sin is what he fears,—and how society is to escape without gravest mischiefs from this source. He has even said, what seemed a paradox, that they needed a civil war in America, to teach the necessity of knitting the social ties stronger. "There may be," he said, "in America some vulgarity in manner, but that's not important. That comes of the pioneer state of things. But I fear they are too much given to the making of money; and secondly, to politics; that they make political distinction the end and not the means. And I fear they lack a class of men of leisure,—in short, of gentlemen,—to give a tone of honor to the community. I am told that things are boasted of in the second class of society there, which, in England,—God knows, are done

in England every day, but would never be spoken of. In America I wish to
know not how many churches or schools, but what newspapers? My friend
Colonel Hamilton, at the foot of the hill, who was a year in America, assures
me that the newspapers are atrocious, and accuse members of Congress
of stealing spoons!" He was against taking off the tax on newspapers in
England,—which the reformers represent as a tax upon knowledge,—for this
reason, that they would be inundated with base prints. He said he talked on
political aspects, for he wished to impress on me and all good Americans to
cultivate the moral, the conservative, etc., etc., and never to call into action
the physical strength of the people, as had just now been done in England in
the Reform Bill,—a thing prophesied by Delolme. He alluded once or twice
to his conversation with Dr. Channing, who had recently visited him (laying
his hand on a particular chair in which the Doctor had sat).

The conversation turned on books. Lucretius he esteems a far higher
poet than Virgil; not in his system, which is nothing, but in his power of
illustration. Faith is necessary to explain anything and to reconcile the
foreknowledge of God with human evil. Of Cousin (whose lectures we had
all been reading in Boston), he knew only the name.

I inquired if he had read Carlyle's critical articles and translations. He said
he thought him sometimes insane. He proceeded to abuse Goethe's *Wilhelm
Meister* heartily. It was full of all manner of fornication. It was like the crossing
of flies in the air. He had never gone farther than the first part; so disgusted
was he that he threw the book across the room. I deprecated this wrath, and
said what I could for the better parts of the book, and he courteously promised
to look at it again. Carlyle he said wrote most obscurely. He was clever and
deep, but he defied the sympathies of every body. Even Mr. Coleridge wrote
more clearly, though he had always wished Coleridge would write more to be
understood. He led me out into his garden, and showed me the gravel walk
in which thousands of his lines were composed. His eyes are much inflamed.
This is no loss except for reading, because he never writes prose, and of
poetry he carries even hundreds of lines in his head before writing them. He
had just returned from a visit to Staffa, and within three days he had made
three sonnets on Fingal's Cave, and was composing a fourth when he was
called in to see me. He said, "If you are interested in my verses perhaps you
will like to hear these lines." I gladly assented, and he recollected himself for
a few moments and then stood forth and repeated, one after the other, the
three entire sonnets with great animation. I fancied the second and third
more beautiful than his poems are wont to be. The third is addressed to the
flowers, which, he said, especially the ox-eye daisy, are very abundant on the
top of the rock. The second alludes to the name of the cave, which is "Cave of

Music;" the first to the circumstance of its being visited by the promiscuous company of the steamboat.

This recitation was so unlooked for and surprising,—he, the old Wordsworth, standing apart, and reciting to me in a garden-walk, like a school-boy declaiming,—that I at first was near to laugh; but recollecting myself, that I had come thus far to see a poet and he was chanting poems to me, I saw that he was right and I was wrong, and gladly gave myself up to hear. I told him how much the few printed extracts had quickened the desire to possess his unpublished poems. He replied he never was in haste to publish; partly because he corrected a good deal, and every alteration is ungraciously received after printing; but what he had written would be printed, whether he lived or died. I said "Tintern Abbey" appeared to be the favorite poem with the public, but more contemplative readers preferred the first books of the *Excursion,* and the Sonnets. He said, "Yes, they are better." He preferred such of his poems as touched the affections, to any others; for whatever is didactic—what theories of society, and so on—might perish quickly; but whatever combined a truth with an affection was good to-day and good forever. He cited the sonnet, "On the Feelings of a Highminded Spaniard," which he preferred to any other (I so understood him), and the "Two Voices;" and quoted, with evident pleasure, the verses addressed "To the Skylark." In this connection he said of the Newtonian theory that it might yet be superseded and forgotten; and Dalton's atomic theory.

When I prepared to depart he said he wished to show me what a common person in England could do, and he led me into the enclosure of his clerk, a young man to whom he had given this slip of ground, which was laid out, or its natural capabilities shown, with much taste. He then said he would show me a better way towards the inn; and he walked a good part of a mile, talking and ever and anon stopping short to impress the word or the verse, and finally parted from me with great kindness and returned across the fields.

Wordsworth honored himself by his simple adherence to truth, and was very willing not to shine; but he surprised by the hard limits of his thought. To judge from a single conversation, he made the impression of a narrow and very English mind; of one who paid for his rare elevation by general tameness and conformity. Off his own beat, his opinions were of no value. It is not very rare to find persons loving sympathy and ease, who expiate their departure from the common in one direction, by their conformity in every other.

—RALPH WALDO EMERSON, "First Visit
to England," *English Traits,* 1856

Thomas Carlyle (1867)

Thomas Carlyle comments on the last years of Wordsworth's life, in which the poet viewed himself as a champion among literary circles; more specifically, Carlyle turns his focus to those occasions on which Wordsworth and his wife were in London as guests of Lord Monteagle and the first Lord Stanley of Alderley. Carlyle's view of Mrs. Wordsworth is not flattering; he describes her as small, withered, and pretentious. In describing a dinner party at Lord Monteagle's house, Carlyle found Wordsworth boring, insipid, and eccentric. Because the poet's eyes were unusually sensitive to light, Carlyle reports that Wordsworth would carry around a brass candlestick with a peculiar green circle that would block out the offensive light.

During the last seven or ten years of his life, Wordsworth felt himself to be a recognised lion, in certain considerable London circles, and was in the habit of coming up to town with his wife for a month or two every season, to enjoy his quiet triumph and collect his bits of tribute *tales quales*. The places where I met him oftenest were Marshall's (the great Leeds linen manufacturer, an excellent and very opulent man), Spring-Rice's (i.e. Lord Monteagle's, who and whose house was strangely intermarried with this Marshall's), and the first Lord Stanley's of Alderley (who then, perhaps, was still Sir Thomas Stanley). Wordsworth took his bit of lionism very quietly, with a smile sardonic rather than triumphant, and certainly got no harm by it, if he got or expected little good. His wife, a small, withered, puckered, winking lady, who never spoke, seemed to be more in earnest about the affair, and was visibly and sometimes ridiculously assiduous to secure her proper place of precedence at table. One evening at Lord Monteagle's—Ah! who was it that then made me laugh as we went home together: Ah me! Wordsworth generally spoke a little with me on those occasions; sometimes, perhaps, we sat by one another; but there came from him nothing considerable, and happily at least nothing with an effort. 'If you think me dull, be it just so!'—this seemed to a most respectable extent to be his inspiring humour. Hardly above once (perhaps at the Stanleys') do I faintly recollect something of the contrary on his part for a little while, which was not pleasant or successful while it lasted. The light was always afflictive to his eyes; he carried in his pocket something like a skeleton brass candlestick, in which, setting it on the dinner-table, between him and the most afflictive or nearest of the chief lights, he touched a little spring, and there flirted out, at the top of his brass implement, a small vertical green circle which prettily enough threw his eyes into shade, and screened him from that sorrow. In proof of his equanimity as lion I remember, in connection with this green shade, one little glimpse which shall be given presently as finis. But first let me say that all these Wordsworth phenomena appear to have been indifferent to me, and have melted to steamy oblivion in a singular degree. Of his talk to others in my hearing I remember simply nothing, not even a word or gesture. To myself it seemed once or twice as if he bore suspicions, thinking I was not a real worshipper, which threw him into something of embarrassment, till I hastened to get them laid, by frank discourse on some suitable thing; nor, when we did talk, was there on his side or on mine the least utterance worth noting. The tone of his voice when I got him afloat on some Cumberland or other matter germane to him, had a braced rustic vivacity, willingness, and solid precision, which alone rings in my ear when all else is gone. Of some Druid circle, for example, he prolonged his response to me with the addition, 'And there is another some miles off, which the country people call Long Meg and her Daughters'; as to the now ownership of which 'It' etc.; 'and then it came into the hands of a Mr. Crackenthorpe;' the sound of those two phrases is still lively and present with me; meaning or sound of absolutely nothing more. Still more memorable is an ocular glimpse I had in one of these Wordsworthian lion-dinners, very symbolic to me of his general deportment there, and far clearer than the little feature of opposite sort, ambiguously given above (recollection of that viz. of unsuccessful exertion at a Stanley dinner being dubious and all but extinct, while this is still vivid to me as of yesternight). Dinner was large, luminous, sumptuous; I sat a long way from Wordsworth; dessert I think had come in, and certainly there reigned in all quarters a cackle as of Babel (only politer perhaps), which far up in Wordsworth's quarter (who was leftward on my side of the table) seemed to have taken a sententious, rather louder, logical and quasi-scientific turn, heartily unimportant to gods and men, so far as I could judge of it and of the other babble reigning. I looked upwards, leftwards, the coast being luckily for a moment clear; there, far off, beautifully screened in the shadow of his vertical green circle, which was on the farther side of him, sat Wordsworth, silent, slowly but steadily gnawing some portion of what I judged to be raisins, with his eye and attention placidly fixed on these and these alone. The sight of whom, and of his rock-like indifference to the babble, quasi-scientific and other, with attention turned on the small practical alone, was comfortable and amusing to me, who felt like him but could not eat raisins. This little glimpse I could still paint, so clear and bright is it, and this shall be symbolical of all.

In a few years, I forget in how many and when, these Wordsworth appearances in London ceased; we heard, not of ill-health perhaps, but of increasing love of rest; at length of the long sleep's coming; and never saw

Wordsworth more. One felt his death as the extinction of a public light, but not otherwise. The public itself found not much to say of him, and staggered on to meaner but more pressing objects.

—THOMAS CARLYLE, "Appendix," 1867,
Reminiscences, ed. James Anthony Froude,
1881, vol. 2, pp. 338–341

ÉMILE LEGOUIS (1922)

In the following excerpt, Legouis discusses the early relationship of William Wordsworth and Annette Vallon from their first meeting at Orléans in December 1791, including important biographical facts concerning Wordsworth's radical years as well as details pertaining to Annette Vallon and members of her family. Legouis is emphatic in pointing out that, although William lived into the reign of Queen Victoria, he was a Georgian (a romantic) throughout his best years. Legouis cites the poet's acceptance of a new and freer morality born of his Cambridge experience and his intense commitment to the French Revolution. Among the facts important to Legouis is his belief that Annette was indifferent to politics and preoccupied with her love of the poet. According to her letters, Annette appeared to be a passionate young woman "of an irrepressible, exuberant sensibility, which is a trait of her nature." Legouis also finds her to be "obliging and generous," while William was "in those years inclined to melancholy and the elegiac mood." Legouis points out that Wordsworth's poem "Vaudracour and Julia" is the story of their love affair and, based on this poem, he speculates on the circumstances surrounding their nocturnal meetings, assignations that reminded Wordsworth of Romeo and Juliet.

Later in his biography, Legouis points out that Annette left Blois and returned to Orléans once her pregnancy was visible, in order to find respite among caring friends. Wordsworth followed her there and remained for several weeks during a time marked with fear and violence. Legouis then proceeds to give an accurate description of the Reign of Terror. When Annette gave birth to Anne Caroline on December 15, 1792, Wordsworth was in Paris when he heard the news and, shortly thereafter, returned to England. Speculating on why Wordsworth left Anne in France, Legouis believes it was mostly due to his poverty and, possibly, to seek his guardians' consent, which it turned out he would never receive. Legouis further states that Wordsworth's return to England could possibly have been due to the influence of William Godwin, who saw the institution of marriage as an obstacle to happiness. What is clear is that Legouis does not want to pass judgment on the poet. He also points out that Dorothy Wordsworth became William's chief source of support and unfailing devotion, maintaining a vigorous correspondence with Annette Vallon, whose letters charted the progress of the young Anne Caroline. The passage concludes that the events of the Reign of Terror were so horrific for the Vallon family that they took precedence over Annette's problems as an unwed mother.

When William Wordsworth arrived at Orleans at the beginning of December 1791, he was twenty-one and a half years old. Though he had taken his degree in January, he still postponed, in spite of the entreaties of his uncles and guardians, the choice of his career. Yet his means were limited. At that time, his sister Dorothy estimated that she and her brothers possessed £470 each, but that the cost of William's education had to be deducted from his share.[1] He then possessed only the bare means of staying some months in France in very modest circumstances. It is true that all the orphans had one hope: that of the recovery of a considerable sum of money owed to their father by the Earl of Lonsdale whose steward he had been: a dangerous hope which induced in the young poet a tendency to idle away his time in waiting, to shirk definite tasks, and follow his wandering instincts. At the moment of his arrival in France he had found a pretext for procrastination: he was aiming, so he said, at a thorough knowledge of French so as to fit himself to be tutor to some rich young fellow-countryman, and to accompany him in his continental travels. At the back of his mind was a desire to gain time, to escape from drudgery and to write poetry. Who was to say, after all, whether the poems he was even then composing, were not to make him famous at once, sparing him the slavery of a profession? He was revising a description of his birthplace, the beautiful Lake Country,[2] and meditating another[3] of the splendid Alpine tramp he had made the year before with a Cambridge friend, on foot, his knapsack on his back.

In all these verses Nature is his theme. His dominant passion had already revealed itself, but it was still far from engrossing all his thoughts. He was curious of everything; he felt a keen appetite for life. His mood was not yet attuned to the seclusion of a country hermitage. Hardly out of college, he had settled in London where he had just spent several months, idling about, drawn thither by the varied pleasures of the crowded metropolis, and if he now turned to France, the principal attraction was the Revolution. He remembered his arrival at Calais on 13th July, 1790, the eve of the Federation, and the ecstasy of joy and hope that then possessed the whole country: a thrilling memory which long made his heart beat faster, and the traces of which he sought during his new stay. His mind still bore the imprint of those ineffable hours during which the rapture of a whole nation had accompanied with its mighty music his own mirth of a student on holiday. His mind was then stirred by no political faith, unless it were by the word Liberty in its fresh gloss, its vagueness full of infinite promise; he had, above all, been moved by the overflowing spirit of brotherhood that showed itself in a thousand acts of courtesy towards the young Englishman, the son of a free country. Decidedly the glimpse he had had of France and of the French had enchanted him.

He now returned eager to enjoy that same hearty greeting, and with his expectations of social intercourse he could not but mingle some dream of love, the scenes and circumstances of which he could not yet determine. Everything predisposed him to it. No existing attachment was there to prevent a new passion; no strict rule of conduct yet guided his steps. Austerity had been foreign to his education; for this he was grateful all his life, rejoicing to have been

> Unchecked by innocence too delicate,
> And moral notions too intolerant,
> Sympathies too contracted.[4]

He had known no rigid discipline in his native Westmorland, still less at Cambridge, loose as its morals were. He does not conceal from us that at the university he consorted with *bons vivants* rather than with earnest students. It is saying a good deal, and will suggest much to those who have read to some extent the descriptions of college life in those days.

It may not be superfluous to remind the reader that Wordsworth was born in 1770, so that he was an old man of 67 when Queen Victoria ascended the throne. He might have died before her accession without any loss to his poetry and to his glory. It is only through his latest, and weakest, effusions and chiefly owing to the tendency of his first biographers that he has assumed that Victorian air which is decidedly anachronistic. No greater mistake can be made in literary history than the confusion of the two epochs, the one in which he lived and the one in which he outlived himself and died. Wordsworth was, to all intents and purposes, a Georgian throughout his best years, and his youthful conduct should be judged according to the standard of times very widely separated from those of Victoria.

Great looseness of manners prevailed in the last decades of the eighteenth century—much corruption in the higher and much roughness in the lower ranks of society. There certainly existed even then in England, chiefly among the Evangelicals, classes of men remarkable for their entire purity—even austerity—of morals, but the general tone of the country was neither refined, nor even what would afterwards have been called simply decent.

Of the difference between those and later times, a single instance will suffice here. It puts, I think, the whole contrast in a nutshell. Dorothy Wordsworth, the poet's exquisite sister, writing to a friend in 1795—she was then twenty-three—expressed herself in this way:

> A natural daughter of Mr. Tom Myers (a cousin of mine whom I dare say you have heard me mention) is coming over to England . . . to be educated . . . and T. Myers' brother . . . has requested that I should take her under my care.[5]

Who could imagine a young lady of the Victorian era speaking with this simplicity and ingenuousness of her cousin's natural daughter? This is only a trifling example of the unconventionality of those days, but it tends to show to what an extent natural children were a normal occurrence under the Georges. The case was so usual that it scarcely provoked any comment.

There was no strain of asceticism in the young poet's nature, to make him an exception to his age. However reticent his poetry may be, we can feel in it the ardour of his blood in those years. It partly reveals what De Quincey bluntly describes as Wordsworth's "preternatural animal sensibility, diffused through *all* the animal passions (or appetites)" and considers as the basis of his "intellectual passions."[6] It would be quite idle to give proofs, had not the fact been ignored by most critics and biographers. Setting aside the mysterious Lucy whom he was to sing in his finest verse and for whom he felt among the English hills "the joy of his desire," there were daughters of Westmorland farmers whom he visited during his Cambridge vacations. With them the whole night sometimes passed in dances from which he came home with fevered brain, having felt in their company

> Slight shocks of young love-liking interspersed,
> Whose transient pleasure mounted to the head
> And tingled through the veins.[7]

And it was that very "tingling" that had favoured the birth of his poetic vocation. It was in the morning following one of those nights of rustic revelry that coming home on foot and seeing the rise of a glorious dawn, he had had the first consciousness of his genius and dedicated himself to the worship of Nature.[8] The tumult of his senses had been the means of rousing his imaginative fire. For the first time he had felt the truth of the profound maxim he uttered later on: "Feeling comes in aid of feeling."[9]

One year later, when he journeyed across the Alps, the sublimity of the mountains had not engrossed his enthusiasm to the point of blinding him to the beauty of the girls he met on his way. The dark Italian maids he passed by on the shore of Lake Como had stirred in him voluptuous desires, and he was to remember them in that very year 1792, in lines full of a sensuous exaltation which makes itself felt in spite of the awkward and old-fashioned form of the verse:

> Farewell! those forms that, in thy noon-tide shade,
> Rest, near their little plots of wheaten glade;
> Those steadfast eyes, that beating breasts inspire
> To throw the "sultry ray" of young Desire;
> Those lips, whose tides of fragrance come, and go,
> Accordant to the cheek's unquiet glow;
> Those shadowy breasts in love's soft light arrayed,
> And rising, by the moon of passion swayed.[10]

Surely the young man who wrote these lines was neither ignorant of, nor deaf to the call of the senses. He revelled in beautiful scenery but desired love;—love in its integrity, not merely the immediate satisfaction of a passing fancy, for his heart was as impetuous as his senses. He carried into his attachments the "violence of affection"[11] that endeared him to his sister Dorothy. There were in his disposition all the elements which make for a great passion.

II

This, then, was the young man who on his arrival at Orleans alighted at "The Three Emperors" and without delay went in quest of lodgings. He finally decided on the rooms offered him by Monsieur Gellet-Duvivier, a hosier, Rue Royale, at the corner of the Rue du Tabour which is called the Coin-Maugas. There, for the moderate sum of eighty francs a month, he had both board and lodging.[12] His host was a man of 37 whose mind had been deranged by his wife's recent death, and who showed imprudent exaltation in the expression of his hatred of the Revolution,—an unfortunate whose tragic end we shall soon hear of. In his house the poet found as fellow-boarders two or three cavalry officers, and a young gentleman from Paris, who all no doubt shared the political opinions of their host. When he wrote on the 19th December to his elder brother he knew as yet no one else in the town.

Yet there was one exception: "one family which I find very agreeable, and with which I became acquainted by the circumstance of going to look at their lodgings, which I should have liked extremely to have taken, but I found them too dear for me." Here the paper is torn and we can only make out the words: "I have . . . of my evenings there." Does he mean that being unable to lodge with them he was spending his evenings at their house? And was that house the house in which Annette was living? And if such is the case, is it the house in the Rue du Poirier where lived M. André Augustin Dufour, *greffier du tribunal* of the Orleans district, who with his wife was to assist Annette in her ordeal?

Mere conjectures these, to which we are driven by the lack of authentic details. The letter to his brother Richard, in which Wordsworth gives us these few details, is cheerful. We feel that he is enjoying the novelty of the place. Everything pleases him; even the surrounding country, which no doubt seems very flat to the hill-born youth, but abounds "in agreeable walks, especially by the side of the Loire, which is a very magnificent river."

He realises that his French is not at all up to the mark, yet he does not intend to engage a teacher of the language. He has no intention of going to that expense. Had he, so soon, found Annette willing to give him free conversation lessons?

The young lady whose life was to be linked with his own, Marie Anne (or Annette) Vallon, was born at Blois on 22nd June, 1766. She was the sixth and last child of Jean Léonard, surnamed Vallon, a surgeon, and of Françoise Yvon, his wife. The father belonged to a family which, by its own tradition, traced itself back to Scotland, and in which the surgical profession was hereditary. One of Annette's brothers, writing to the Board of the Hôtel-Dieu of Blois, stated that his great-grandfather, grandfather and father had been surgeons of the same hospital in succession. In 1755, at the funeral of Joseph Léonard Vallon, formerly surgeon, aged 95, the chief mourner was the "Sieur Vallon," his son, himself *maître chirurgien*. It appears that Jean, Annette's father, was a grandson of the aged Joseph Léonard. Her two eldest brothers, Jean Jacques, born in 1758, and Charles Henry, born the following year, adopted the paternal profession. They were both attached as surgeons to the Hôtel-Dieu before 1792.

When Wordsworth made Annette's acquaintance, the girl's father had been dead for several years and her mother had married again, her second husband being a "Sieur Vergez," himself a surgeon. Fatherless, somehow morally estranged from her mother by the latter's re-marriage, Annette was hardly less left to herself than William.

In addition to the two surgeons who were the eldest sons of the family, there was yet a third—Paul, born in 1763, who had turned his thoughts to law. Also three daughters: Françoise Anne, born in 1762; Angélique Adélaïde, born in 1765; and Marie Anne, one year younger, the latest born.

Two second cousins of the children are also known to us: Charles Olivier and Claude Léonnar (*sic*) Vallon, born the first in 1728 and the other in 1729, both *curés* of the diocese of Blois, both reconciled with the Revolution and patronised by the constitutional Bishop Grégoire, who made Claude one of his *vicaires épiscopaux* in the department of Loir-et-Cher. They had taken the constitutional oath in 1791; they were in the autumn of 1792 to take the oath of *liberté-égalité*; and five years later, on 30th Fructidor of the fifth Republican year, that of hatred to monarchy. For these reasons a prefectorial report of 9th Thermidor of the ninth year of the Republic speaks highly of them. It commends Claude's "great theological science" and declares Charles to be "of perfect morals, learned and tolerant."[13]

There does not seem, then, to have prevailed from the first in the Vallon family the hostility towards the Revolution which manifested itself later on so violently in some of their members. The name of Jean Jacques, given in 1758 to the eldest of Annette's brothers, strengthens this impression. The father must have become an adept of the new creed spread by Jean Jacques Rousseau; of his worship of nature and sensibility. Yet there was a sturdy sense of tradition in that well-established family whose head had for generation after generation confined himself within his corporation as within a caste. If the two priests themselves became "constitutional," they none the less retained their loyalty to religion. Charles Olivier uttered an indignant protest when the Convention, in order to sever priests from Christianity, pledged itself to give pecuniary assistance to those who would be willing to give up the ministry. He wrote to the *Citoyen Administrateur* on 30th March, 1794, the very day on which Robespierre ordered the arrest of the *Indulgents*: "I beg you will not depend on me for help, and not take it ill if I tell you truthfully that religion, conscience and honour forbid me to take any step towards resigning my ministry, which I hold from God alone."[14] He was in the end, after the Concordat, to recant his oaths of the revolutionary period.

Finally Wordsworth's evidence, his repeated affirmation in *The Prelude* that, before knowing Captain Michel Beaupuy, he had lived among the opponents of the Revolution, induces us to think that as early as 1792 those of the Vallon family whose acquaintance he could have made, saw rather with sorrow than with satisfaction the advance of the nation towards a republic. As to Annette herself, it is probable that she remained rather indifferent to politics until the day when a tragedy that struck her home threw her into the most active opposition. If she felt the slightest disagreement with Wordsworth's opinions on monarchy and republic, it did not trouble her much, engrossed as she was by her love for him.

III

Unless we are to accept the idea that Annette became Wordsworth's mistress on their very first meeting, the birth of their child as early as 15th December, 1792, obliges us to think they made each other's acquaintance soon after the poet's arrival at Orleans where he spent the winter.[15] There is nothing astonishing in Annette having made a stay—even a prolonged stay—in that town. In Orleans lived her brother Paul, with whom she seems to have been particularly intimate, partly, perhaps, on account of their nearness in age, partly on account of a certain similarity of temperament. Paul had for some years been notary's clerk in Orleans under a Maitre Courtois, whose office was in the Rue de Bourgogne, close to the Rue du Poirier where the Dufours were living. In winter Orleans offered more attractions, being a larger and busier town. Paul had made friends there, and his worldly tastes, his sociable temper, found an echo in Annette.

We know what Paul's physical appearance was: he was a small dark man, with a thick-set neck, and large bold eyes under heavy black brows. We have a glimpse of his character in the memoirs of his grandson Amédée, a magistrate, who declares him to have been "one of the wittiest men he had the privilege of knowing," with an excellent heart. His chivalry and generosity tended to excess, and his carelessness of money was so great that his financial position suffered by it. The appearance of Annette's daughter is also known to us. It is a face which, according to its age, wears a look of frank gaiety, or a gently mischievous smile. But Annette dwells so much on her daughter's likeness to her father that it would be illusory to expect to find the expression of the mother in the face of the child. The portrait of Annette published in this volume is not well enough authenticated for us to place much reliance on it. It does not seem as if liveliness had been outstandingly characteristic of her, though kindness and generosity certainly were. In the letters of Annette that have recently been discovered the dominant note is that of an irrepressible, exuberant sensibility which is a trait of her nature and is not exclusively due to the harassing circumstances in which the letters were written. She abounded in words, was prone to effusions and tears. These emotions of a "sensitive soul" were, moreover, quite of a nature to win her the young Englishman's heart. He himself was in those years inclined to melancholy and the elegiac mood. His very first sonnet[16] had been inspired by the sight of a girl weeping at the hearing of a woeful story. At that sight, he said, his blood had stopped running in his veins:

Dim were my swimming eyes—my pulse beat slow,
And my full heart was swell'd to dear delicious pain.

The maiden's tears had made manifest her virtue. The poet's turn for sentimentality found in Annette many an opportunity of satisfying itself, while the garrulity of the young Frenchwoman fell in splendidly with his intention of learning the language.

All subsequent evidence agrees in representing Annette as obliging and generous. For economy's sake, Wordsworth had decided on not incurring the expense of a teacher. Annette, then, was his tutor. She listened kindly to the stammered sentences of the foreigner. She set him at ease by laughing goodhumouredly over his unpronounceable name. Her tender heart was filled with affection for the youth, younger than she by four and a half years, who was separated from all his friends and was living among men whose language he knew but ill. And when William allowed his budding passion to burst forth, her too charitable soul was powerless against his ardour.

His love for her was an exalted, blinding passion, in the presence of which all else vanished. The sight of Annette at her window, or even of Annette's window alone, was each day's supreme instant. He himself tells us so, though under a disguise, in the story of *Vaudracour and Julia*.

A wretched poem, said Matthew Arnold, the only one of Wordsworth's which it was impossible for him to read. The verdict is not altogether undeserved. But Arnold errs in not excepting a few very fine lines, and, on the other hand, does not take into account what we now know, that is to say the keen biographical interest of this awkward and confused poem, to which the author seems to have found some difficulty in assigning a place amongst his works, and of which he is at a loss to explain the origin.

He began by inserting it at the end of the very book of *The Prelude* in which his memories of France are related. The poem strikes the love note which is lacking elsewhere. It was at first, according to Wordsworth, a story told by his friend Captain Beaupuy, the devoted Republican, who was trying to make the young Englishman realise the evils of the old regime, and particularly the horrors of the *lettres de cachet*.

Young Vaudracour, a nobleman from Auvergne, loved a daughter of the people whom he wanted to marry. A *lettre de cachet* obtained by his father came as a barrier between him and his purpose. Imprisoned for having killed one of the men sent out to arrest him, he only recovered his freedom by pledging himself to give up his mistress. Could he be true to such an oath? The lovers met again, but were again violently separated. Julia, now a mother, was shut up in a convent. The child was left with Vaudracour, who withdrew with it to a hermitage in the woods. 1789 sounded the call of freedom; it could not rouse him from his lethargy: he had become insane.

It is easy to see that Vaudracour is not Wordsworth, nor his story that of the poet. There existed between Wordsworth and Annette no difference of caste. The surgeon's daughter was as good as the son of the Earl of Lonsdale's steward. There was no violence used in their case; no *lettre de cachet*, murder, prison, convent, nor tragic ending. But before coming to the lovers' woes, the poet described *con amore*—and it is the only place in his works where he has done so—the intoxication of passion. As invention never was his *forte*, he turned for help to the memories and exact circumstances of his own love-story in order to give some reality to the first hours of rapture broken by sudden partings. He may have been afraid lest marks of his personality should be discovered in the poem if it found a place so near his own adventures, and it is this, rather than the overburdening of the Ninth Book of *The Prelude*, and the awkwardness of its composition—he never was very sensitive to defects of this kind—which induced him to publish *Vaudracour and Julia* separately in 1804. Later on, when in his old age he started commenting upon his poems, he wrote at the head of this one a note, the object of which was to avert suspicion, rather than to give information to the public. The story, he says this time, was told him not by Beaupuy but "from the mouth of a French lady who had been an eye-and-ear-witness of all that was done and said." And he adds: "The facts are true; no invention as to these has been exercised, as none was needed."

A most astonishing French lady surely, with the eyes of a lynx, the ears of a mole, to have overheard, even to their minutest details, all the lovers' effusions, and to have been both present and invisible at their most secret meetings! One can hardly refrain from smiling, in reading the beginning of the poem, at the thought of the story-teller endowed with senses so acute behind whom the poet hides his identity.

However, no careful reader will be led astray. Professor Harper, the most thorough and best informed of his biographers, straightway proclaimed the connection between *Vaudracour and Julia* and Wordsworth's youthful love adventure. The real difficulty is to draw the line between reality and fiction, between Wordsworth's story and Vaudracour's.

To Wordsworth, the lover of Annette, no doubt belong the ecstasies of the very young man who sees, not a mere woman of flesh and blood, but rather he knows not what blinding splendour: ". . . He beheld a vision and adored the thing he saw," a vision so dazzling that its very radiance renders it indistinct. It will be observed that his attitude of wonder is more in keeping with the youth's sudden passion for the foreigner, than with Vaudracour's long and tender love for his Julia, known from the cradle, beloved since she was a child, the constant companion of his games throughout his childhood. Let us listen to the poet:

Arabian fiction never filled the world
With half the wonders that were wrought for him.
Earth breathed in one great presence of the spring;
Life turned the meanest of her implements,
Before his eyes, to price above all gold;
The house she dwelt in was a sainted shrine;
Her chamber-window did surpass in glory
The portals of the dawn; all Paradise
Could, by the simple opening of a door,
Let itself in upon him:—pathways, walks,
Swarmed with enchantment, till his spirit sank,
Surcharged, within him, overblest to move
Beneath a sun that wakes a weary world
To its dull round of ordinary cares;
A man too happy for Mortality!

These were the first days of fascination, when the lovers were still innocent.

In comparison with that—for him exceptional—outburst, the story of the consummation of their love is cold and stilted, and full of awkward explanations that seem to chill the lover's ardour:

So passed the time, till, whether through effect
Of some unguarded moment that dissolved
Virtuous restraint—oh, speak it, think it, not!
Deem rather that the fervent Youth, who saw
So many bars between his present state
And the dear haven where he wished to be
In honourable wedlock with his Love,
Was in his judgment tempted to decline
To perilous weakness, and entrust his cause
To nature for a happy end of all;
Deem that by such fond hope the Youth was swayed
And bear with their transgression, when I add
That Julia, wanting yet the name of wife,
Carried about her for a secret grief
The promise of a mother. . . .

Poor verse and wretched moral! Rather than confess to the rash thoughtlessness of an instant of passion, to the sudden exaltation of heart and senses, the poet chooses to ascribe to Vaudracour a calculated act, in the very depth of his transports. In spite of that constrained explanation, suggested with but little conviction by the author himself, we are tempted to believe that Wordsworth and Annette merely succumbed, with no preconceived design, like thousands of others, because nature prevailed over prudence, and passion over wisdom. They loved each other unreservedly from the time of their stay at Orleans; and when Annette left the town to go back to Blois, at the beginning of the spring of 1792, she already carried about her, like Julia, perhaps not knowing it, perhaps not yet being sure of it, "the promise of a mother."

IV

Shall we look in *Vaudracour and Julia* for the reason of that change of residence? Vaudracour is opposed not only by his father but also by Julia's humble parents, who are in fear of the nobleman's anger. Julia, as soon as her shame is known to them, is hurried away by them one night, in spite of her protests. When in the morning her lover realises what has happened, he does not know whither to turn for her. He

> . . . Chafed like a wild beast in the toils.

But he is soon able to find her track, follows her to the distant town where they carried and confined her:

> Easily may the sequel be divined—
> Walks to and fro—watchings at every hour;
> And the fair Captive, who, whene'er she may,
> Is busy at her casement as the swallow
> Fluttering its pinions, almost within reach,
> About the pendent nest, did thus espy
> Her Lover!—thence a stolen interview,
> Accomplished under friendly shade of night.

Was Annette in the same way taken back to Blois in spite of herself and torn from her lover by her alarmed friends? We have no reason for assuming this. Her father was dead. Her mother, who had married again, was without much power over her. Yet Blois was her native town; there stood the family house. She had no private means and had probably visited Orleans on the invitation of friends or her brother Paul, for a limited space of time. Despite her twenty-five years, she was therefore still partly dependent on her people, and it is likely that at Blois the couple's intimacy was held in greater check than at Orleans. The town was smaller and Annette better looked after.

Indeed the two lovers did wander about Blois and its surroundings. We even know that their walks often took them to the neighbourhood of the convent in which Annette had been brought up—an opportunity for them to grow sentimental over "their happy innocent years."[17] For aught we know, Wordsworth may have had some access to the Vallon family. He may have been acquainted with the two priests, the uncles of Annette, who were perhaps in his mind when he said to Ellis Yarnall in 1849, that during the Revolution "he had known many of the *abbés* and other ecclesiastics, and thought highly of them as a class; they were earnest, faithful men; being unmarried, he must say, they were the better able to fulfil their sacred duties; they were married to their flocks."[18]

But it is not certain how far the house in which Annette lived was open to the young man. We are therefore inclined to believe that Wordsworth drew from his own memories the lines—the last fine lines of the poem—in which he describes a nocturnal meeting of the lovers, invoking for the occasion the memory of Romeo and Juliet, and of the lark which gave the signal for the last embrace. This scene of passion on a summer night, which the French lady narrator could surely not have seen with her eyes nor heard with her ears, probably commemorates one of their secret meetings during the second part of their loves:

... Through all her courts
The vacant city slept; the busy winds,
That keep no certain intervals of rest,
Moved not; meanwhile the galaxy displayed
Her fires, that like mysterious pulses beat
Aloft;—momentous but uneasy bliss!
To their full hearts the universe seemed hung
On that brief meeting's slender filament!

The other striking fact of Wordsworth's stay at Blois, the town of the Vallons, is his friendship with Captain Beaupuy. Of that attachment only, he spoke abundantly and beautifully in his *Prelude*. But in omitting Annette, he at the same time did away with all that made the pathetic complexity of those summer months.

Wordsworth, who could now see Annette only by stealth, found himself thrown back upon the society of other companions. It seems that at this time he was boarding with officers of the late Bassigny regiment, all of whom, with one exception, he introduces to us as exalted aristocrats whose minds were bent on emigrating. He now made friends with the only one who was in favour of the new ideas, Captain Michel Beaupuy. Very soon, their friendship became close, and the young foreigner deferentially listened to the officer of thirty-seven who—a nobleman by birth—had abandoned all the interests of his caste and even the esteem of his colleagues for the revolutionary cause. Beaupuy's eager proselytism converted the young Englishman into a true patriot,—a *Jacobin* in the sense the word had in 1792—prompted by a zeal equal to his own. They were frequently to be seen together at the patriotic club of Blois;[19] in the town and its surroundings, among neighbouring forests and even in places as distant as Chambord or Vendäme, they would take long walks during which Beaupuy preached his gospel. From each of these talks, Wordsworth returned increasingly exalted by his republican enthusiasm, for a Republic was in the air. His ardour was like a consuming fever. In that heart already heated by love, stirred by anxiety and remorse, it soon flamed into passion. Again "feeling comes in aid of feeling." Meanwhile Annette was beginning secretly to prepare the expected baby's linen, bidding William touch and kiss all the things that were to be used for the infant, particularly "a little pink cap" intended for it. They mourned together, between two kisses, their lost innocence. Dreading the impending and inevitable revelations, they discussed, perhaps, the possibility of a marriage that would patch up matters. In these impassioned emotions, weeks passed away and the much dreaded event drew nearer.

V

Beaupuy had started for the Rhine on 27th July with his regiment, and Wordsworth still lingered at Blois. Beaupuy had not been the cause of his coming there, and he needed another departure, another invitation to go away in his turn. He stayed on till the beginning of September, and we may hazard two reasons for his new removal.

One of them may have been the sudden death of Annette's eldest brother. Jean Jacques the surgeon died at thirty-four, leaving a widow and two little daughters, one aged two years and the other a few months. According to a family tradition, he was killed one night in the forest of Blois on his way to bring urgent help to a wounded man. The precise date is missing, but would appear to be in the second half of 1792. For the benefit of his widow, three doctors from Blois offered to the town officials to take over his post as surgeon to the Hôtel-Dieu and to the hospitals of the parishes of St. Louis, St. Nicolas and St. Saturnin. One of the three was his own brother Charles Henry, who, at the widow's request, was finally appointed on 13th November.[20] Such a tragedy alone would have been sufficient to upset the family and necessitate some changes. But Annette's departure from Blois may easily be accounted for by direct motives. The state she was in could no longer be concealed. It was impossible for her to remain in her native town without her trouble becoming public. She preferred to return to Orleans where, in some quiet place near compassionate friends, she might give birth to her child. And Wordsworth again followed her thither. On 3rd September, he once more dated from Blois a letter to his elder brother, asking him for an urgently needed sum of money. The next day he was back at Orleans, where he tells us he happened to be during the September massacres.

It was indeed on the morning of 4th September that Fournier, surnamed the American, despite the orders issued by the Convention, started at the head of his gang for Versailles with the prisoners who were waiting in the prison of Orleans for the verdict of the "High Court." At Versailles, *septembrisseurs* (or assassins) from Paris were appointed to meet and butcher them. This crime, conceived and perpetrated in cold blood, caused a shudder of horror to run through the town which had witnessed the wretched creatures' departure. It left behind an inextinguishable hatred in the hearts of all those who were not among the fanatics of the Republic. It is astonishing that Wordsworth should make no allusion to this event; he speaks of the September massacres only as of a Parisian tragedy. The only event he commemorates, either in his *Descriptive Sketches* or in his *Prelude*, as having taken place during the period of his second stay at Orleans is the proclamation of the Republic. This is the occasion of a veritable paean of joy. His *Sketches* show him wandering by the source of the Loiret and seeing the river, its banks and the whole earth transformed by the magic world. It is all over with the monarchy, with all monarchies. The reign of happiness and freedom has begun for all men.[21]

Strange alternations of enthusiasm and despondency when from those delightful visions he fell back to the thought of the young girl who was on the eve of becoming a mother. Was he allowed to see her at Orleans during the few weeks he spent there? He was to leave Orleans at the end of October for Paris and stay there for about two months. We know nothing of the reasons of these comings and goings. It is certain, however, that he lingered in France beyond the appointed date. On 3rd October he again informed his elder brother of his proposed return to London in the course of the month. But what motive prompted him to leave Orleans before Annette's deliverance? Was his presence considered inadvisable in view of the secrecy that was desired? On the other hand, he could not bring himself to put the sea between himself and Annette so long as he did not know the now imminent issue.

It was in Paris that he learned the birth of his daughter. On 15th December, 1792, in the cathedral church of Sainte Croix, was baptised "Anne Caroline Wordswodsth (*sic*), daughter of Williams Wordswodsth, Anglois, and of Marie Anne Vallon." Paul Vallon stood godfather to the child and Madame Augustin Dufour stood godmother. The absent father was represented by André Augustin Dufour, with a legal power from the poet. The father owned the child as his and gave it his name, in so far at least as the episcopal *vicaire* Perrin could spell it.[22]

Some little time after, at the end of December, Wordsworth came back to England. It seems that he stayed in France to the utmost limit of his resources, and it was against his will that he went back to his country, "dragged" as he says "by a chain of harsh necessity."[23] But he suffers us to think that his revolutionary zeal alone made him wish to stay on in France. Had it been possible for him, he tells us, he would have shared the Girondins' fortune: "made common cause with some who perished."[24] He hides from us the chief reason of his unwillingness to leave the country in which his child had just been born.

VI

Why did Wordsworth leave France without marrying Annette? He had owned his daughter, why did he not legitimise her by making the mother his wife? Considering the passion which inflamed him in 1792, it seems he would have done so there and then, had it been in his power. And yet there was no marriage. There was none before Caroline's birth, as her christening certificate testifies; there was none later on, as is attested by the death certificate of Annette, who died a "spinster."

The likeliest explanation is his poverty, which was only too real. To support wife and child he needed help from his guardians, an instalment of the money that was to be his one day. Therefore it was indispensable to obtain their consent. He might perhaps disarm their opposition by showing his readiness to enter some one of the careers they pointed out to him—even the church, which, at that time, did not exact too strict a faith. He decided, therefore, to go to England, with the intention of returning shortly to bring help to the dear ones he had left in France, or to take them away with him to his own country. This plan was submitted to Annette, who accepted it resignedly. Wordsworth was to come back and marry her as soon as he had his guardians' consent and the necessary help.

Another man might have reversed the decision; married Annette straightway, then placed before his guardians the accomplished fact. Marriage first; money would come afterwards when fate should think fit. This would have been splendid imprudence, but it was made impossible by the inborn cautiousness of the young poet. His native wariness inclined to procrastination. Besides, he may have been somewhat alarmed by the force of the fascination which enchained him. To speak plainly, he had lived in France for months in an unknown, strange and feverish atmosphere in which he felt at times as though he were dreaming. Annette was fascinating, but she remained in part a mystery to him. He felt anxious at having so far resigned his will-power, and lost the control of his actions. She gave the impulse and swept him on in her wake, not merely because she was four years older than he, but because she was gifted with that natural intrepidity which was to make her a model conspirator, an "intriguer" as her political adversaries called her. Who can assert that she did not find pleasure in concealment, and in her very sorrows an exciting sensation not devoid of charm? Did Wordsworth in the depth of his heart feel a vague mistrust of the woman he loved?

VII

On coming back to London, Wordsworth's time was occupied in two directions: the publication of his first two poems in the hope that they might bring him fortune as well as fame, and the consideration of the steps that must be taken to propitiate his uncles. He hesitated to face them, knowing them to be displeased and hostile. He begged his sister Dorothy, who lived with her uncle, Dr. Cookson, a clergyman, to speak for him. He confided everything to Dorothy, who immediately conceived a warm affection for the young French mother and her child. She imagined no other issue than marriage, and she already pictured the cottage in which the newly married couple would live, and in which she would have a place.[25] Of her own accord, she started a correspondence with Annette, to whom she protested her sisterly affection. To carry on this letter-writing, she began "fagging at French again." But she trembled at the thought of telling the whole story to the Cooksons, whose anger she foresaw. She confessed her fear to Annette, who wrote to William: "I beg you to invite her not to say anything to your uncle. It will be a hard fight she will have to engage in. *But you deem it necessary.*" And Annette forgot for a time her own grief in pitying Dorothy for the trouble she caused her. She was distressed at the thought of her being deprived of all sympathy:

> You have no one to whom you might freely confide the painful state of your soul, and you must check the tears which your tender feelings force from you. I advise you to hide as long as you possibly can from your uncle and aunt the reasons which make your tears flow.

Thus did Annette express herself in a double letter written on 20th March, 1793, to William and Dorothy, a letter seized by the French police on account of the war and recently discovered in the Blois Record Office.[26]

Annette returned to Blois with her child. She lived with her family, but for fear of scandal she had to part from Caroline, who was sent to a nurse some little way off in the suburbs, so that the poor mother might see her frequently.

She carried on with Wordsworth a copious correspondence. If the letter to William dated 20th March is comparatively short, it is because she wrote "quite a long one" on the preceding Sunday, and because she is to write him another the Sunday following. It is also because she devotes hers this time chiefly to Dorothy, to whom she owes an answer and gives ample measure.

The two letters, read together, are a long and pathetic appeal to the distant friend. At every page is repeated the prayer: Come back and marry me. She suffers too much in his absence. She loves him so passionately! When she embraces her child, she thinks she holds William in her arms: "Her little heart often beats against mine; I think I am feeling her father's." She writes to Dorothy:

> I wish I could give you some comfort, but alas! I cannot. I rather should look for it from you. It is in the certainty of your friendship that I find some comfort, and in the unalterable feelings of my dear Williams (*sic*). I cannot be happy without him, I long for him every day.

Indeed she sometimes tries to call reason to her help. She wishes for her lover's return, yet fears it, for war is threatening. She contradicts herself four times in the course of ten lines:

> My distress would be lessened were we married, yet I regard it as almost impossible that you should risk yourself, if we should have war. You might be taken prisoner. But where do my wishes lead me?
> I speak as though the instant of my happiness were at hand. Write and tell me what you think, and do your very utmost to hasten your daughter's happiness and mine, but only if there is not the slightest risk to be run,—but I think the war will not last long. I should wish our two nations to be (reconciled). That is one of my most earnest wishes. But above all, find out some way by which we can write to each other in case the correspondence between the two kingdoms were stopped.

Her strongest reason for insisting on marriage is her motherly love, rather than her wifely passion. She is ready to accept that William should come only to go away again immediately afterwards, if he must. Although she needs him for her happiness she would make the sacrifice. But then her situation being regularised, her daughter could be given back to her. She writes to Dorothy:

> I can assure you that were I happy enough to have my dear Williams journey back to France and give me the title of his wife, I should

be comforted. First my daughter would have a father and her poor
mother might enjoy the delight of always having her near. I should
myself give her the care I am jealous to see her receive from other
hands. I should no longer cause my family to blush by calling her
my daughter, my Caroline; I should take her with me and go to the
country. There is no solitude in which I should not find charm,
being with her.

Her bitterest trial was on the day on which the child went out for the
first time, for the woman who carried her passed before the mother's house
without stopping: "That scene," she writes to Dorothy, "caused me a whole
day of tears. They are flowing even now."

Indeed, Caroline is the theme of almost all her letters. She speaks endlessly
about the wonderful progress achieved by the three-months-old babe. In her
mother's eyes she is a beautiful picture of her father, though she is not fair-
haired like him. Annette carries on with the child many a tender, childish
dialogue. She smothers her with kisses and bathes her in tears. She speaks of
her pride in dressing her, in putting on "that little pink cap which fits her so
well," and which she had once bidden William kiss.

The first time she had it on, I put it on her head myself after kissing it a
thousand times. I said to her, "My Caroline, kiss this bonnet. Your father is
less happy than I; he cannot see it; but it should be dear to you, for he put his
lips to it."

The impression left on us by these letters is firstly, that Annette is in every
sense a kind and passionately fond woman. No bitter word or recrimination
is to be found in all these pages. Nor is her disinterestedness less manifest.
She raises no cry of poverty, no call for material help. She is all sensibility. Too
much so for our present taste, even if we take into account the circumstances
in which she writes. We feel that her natural tenderness has been accentuated
by the reading of the novels of that time—novels in which tears flowed
abundantly, which teemed with moving apostrophes. This is the more
evident by reason of the inferiority of her education. There is no punctuation
in her letters and her spelling is eminently fanciful. Here and there, one
meets sentences with a popular turn, like "le chagrin que vous avez *rapport
à moi*"; then again we find whole paragraphs overflowing with the facile
sentimentality of the age. She writes to Dorothy:

Often when I am alone in my room with his [William's] letters, I
dream he is going to walk in. I stand ready to throw myself into his
arms and say to him: "Come, my love, come and dry these tears
which have long been flowing for you, let us fly and see Caroline,

your child and your likeness; behold your wife; sorrow has altered
her much; do you know her. Ay, by the emotion which your heart
must share with hers. If her features are altered, if her pallor makes
it impossible for you to know her, her heart is unchanged. It is still
yours. Know your Annette, Caroline's tender mother. . . ." Ah! my
dear sister, such is my habitual state of mind. But waking from my
delusion as from a dream, I do not see him, my child's father; he
is very far from me. These transports occur again and again, and
throw me into a state of extreme dejection.

Although inexhaustibly voluble when she pours out her heart, she seems
to be devoid of intellectual curiosity. She is an afflicted lover, a doting mother.
But she seems to know nothing of that William whom she longs to see again,
nor yet to want to learn anything. She does not inquire after his doings; does
she even realise that he is a poet? Of the war, of politics, of the dawning Terror
she has not a word to say, except in so far as it concerns her lover's journey.
Her sentimental absorption is absolute. The pathetic strain never relaxes.

One may imagine Wordsworth's perturbation as he received these moving
letters, which at first were frequent. Did many others come to his hand after
20th March, 1793? Were the next ones likewise intercepted? We find no trace
of another letter from Annette till the end of 1795. But one thing is sure: that
Dorothy performed without much delay her arduous mission. She spoke to her
uncle Cookson. The result was not favourable. She complains on 16th June in a
letter to her friend Jane Pollard, "of the prejudices of her two uncles against her
dear William."[27] She must have heard a thorough indictment of him, directed
not only against his political heresies, and have been somewhat shaken by it, for
she owns that "he has been somewhat to blame"; she adds, "The subject is an
unpleasant one for a letter; it will employ us more agreeably in conversation."
But her affection will take no serious alarm. She perceives in her brother's
strange and wayward nature, in his very errors, the mark of his genius.

Repulsed by his guardians, called for by Annette, what did Wordsworth
do? War, which had been officially declared on 1st February, had little by
little become a reality. The lovers who had, when they parted, hoped for a
near reunion, found themselves divided by an almost insuperable obstacle.
William could only run the risk of another journey to France at the cost of
the utmost difficulties and perils. Did he run that risk? It is an open question.
Much might be said to prove that he did or that he did not. On one point all
his readers will be unanimous: they will wish that, for chivalry's sake, he had
hastened to Annette's relief, notwithstanding his lack of money, in spite of the
war and in the teeth of danger.

Against the probability of his having shown this courage there is the silence of his *Prelude* and our general knowledge of his cautious nature. His very sister had declared the year before, that he was "wise enough to get out of the way of danger."[28] A strange combination of outward circumstances and natural wariness always kept him from dangerous extravagances. Some friendly power always held him back on the brink of the precipice. He was not the man to defy fate. He it is who thought at one time of joining his destiny to that of the Girondins, but was prevented; who in the midst of the English counter-Terror wrote a proud republican letter to the Bishop of Llandaff, but kept it in manuscript and probably never even sent it to his opponent; who in 1795 wrote satirical verses against the Court and the Regent, but decided not to publish them. His courage was of the passive rather than of the active kind. He was capable of stubbornness and silent pertinacity, not of that fiery temper that hurls itself against the cannon's mouth.

But it is never safe to generalise. Young love may have momentarily transformed his native circumspection. There are strong reasons to believe that for once he was capable of a fine imprudence. Why did he linger for a whole month towards the end of the summer of 1793 in the Isle of Wight when nothing obliged him to do so, if he was not waiting for some smack to carry him over the Channel?[29] Besides, he must have been in France again in the autumn of 1793 if he was present at the execution of Gorsas, the first Girondin sent to the scaffold, on 7th October, as he told Carlyle in 1840.[30] If we combine this statement with an anecdote related by Alaric Watts, which evidently contains some truth and much error, Wordsworth was on this occasion alarmed by a Republican named Bailey, who told him that he would surely be guillotined if he remained in France any longer, whereupon Wordsworth fled back to England.[31] The risk he had run simply by coming at all, at a time of war between the two countries, was extreme. As soon as the Terror had set in, it would have been sheer madness to stay on. As a friend of the Girondins and as an Englishman he was doubly liable to suspicion.

Even if he made that bold attempt as his admirers wish it might be proved he did—as it would perhaps be proved if the family papers relating to the Annette episode had not all been destroyed—it is quite possible that he had only been able to reach Paris on his way to Blois and had had to take flight home, not only without marrying, but also without seeing Annette.

Whether he crossed the Channel or not, we know by *The Prelude* how wretched at heart he was throughout the Terror. He was shaken with anger against the ministers of his country whom he held responsible for the war; he longed for the victory of the Republic over her enemies, over the English themselves, and refused to join in the thanksgivings with which the churches of England greeted the naval successes of their people, even rejoicing within himself at the defeat of the English armies.

At first his poetry is gloomy. He puts into it all his hatred of war and takes a delight in recounting its atrocities. He paints its sinister effects on individuals and families; he gives expression to his indignation against the whole of society, which is ill-ordered, unjust, merciless to the humble, heartless and devoid of charity (*Guilt and Sorrow*). But he is, moreover, discontented with himself, conscience-stricken. In order to face needs which are no longer his only, he ought to set resolutely to work, and yet he remains the wanderer who postpones the choice of a remunerative career. He lives from hand to mouth, as unbreakable to the yoke as when he had neither burdens nor responsibilities to bear. This is the great moral fault of these years. His excuse is that, had he enriched himself by work, he could not, during the war, have shared it with wife or child. Hence a kind of inertia compounded of sundry elements: his general disgust of a society grown odious to him, his unconquerable reluctance to enter into any regular profession, his powerlessness to help the forsaken ones, and above all, the insistent call of his genius. An ordinary man would have perceived his urgent duty more clearly than the poet, harassed as he was by the demon of verse.

Besides, whilst we can be sure that he considered it his duty to help Annette, it is less certain that he remained anxious to marry her. It was in the course of this very year 1793, or very soon after, that he became the confirmed disciple of Godwin the philosopher, who was the adversary of marriage, which he proclaimed to be an evil institution, for cohabitation provided an atmosphere too dangerous and disturbing for the intellect whose supreme need was calm. The wise man would relegate marriage to its place amongst other outworn prejudices.[32] The poet echoes the philosopher. He discards at that time every institution, law, creed, rite, and only believes in

personal Liberty,
Which, to the blind restraints of general laws
Superior, magisterially adopts
One guide, the light of circumstances, flashed
Upon an independent intellect.[33]

He may have gone further still in his enfranchisement, and fought against pity itself, a frequent source of injustice. Who knows but that he strove to harden his heart like Oswald in his *Borderers*?

The wiles of woman,
And craft of age, seducing reason, first

Made weakness a protection, and obscured
The moral shapes of things.[34]

He felt that his first duty was to keep unblemished his intellectual faculties, above all his poetic gift, threatened by the anguished appeals from Blois. His nature was too tender and passionate to allow him to fortify himself against compassion. But it is likely that he may then have tried to harden his heart and, moreover, that he held this hardening to be a higher virtue. His first biographer, his nephew Bishop Wordsworth, who had in his hands and afterwards destroyed the evidence of the case, does not conceal that his uncle's doctrines then revealed themselves in his very conduct. True, he attributes the evil thereof to France and the Revolution: "The most licentious theories were propounded, all restraints were broken, libertinism was law."[35] Young Wordsworth, emancipated by the Revolution, would for a time appear to have resembled the solitary man of his *Excursion* who did not scruple to display "unhallowed actions . . . worn as open signs of prejudice subdued."[36] He was certainly no Don Juan, but could very well be an adept of free love.

While he was endeavouring to choke the voice of his heart and conscience by taking refuge in the abstraction of his ethical theories, Annette on the other hand, roused from her plaintive sorrow by a tragedy very near to her, was little by little infected by a political fever the violence of which was to counterpoise her love.

VIII

So grievous were the misfortunes through which the Vallons were to live during the Terror that the piteous situation of the young husbandless mother soon took a secondary place amid their troubles. Annette herself ceased to be absorbed by her own cares. At the time at which she wrote to Wordsworth and Dorothy her tearful letter, the Terror was raging at Orleans, and Paul, her favourite brother, he who had stood by her in the time of her trouble, was about to come dangerously within reach of the guillotine.

Paul Vallon found himself implicated in the alleged criminal attack on the delegate of the People—Léonard Bourdon—an affair in which ludicrous and atrocious elements are inextricably mixed. Bourdon was one of the most shameless demagogues of the Revolution, previously to which he had styled himself Bourdon de la Crosnière. The founder of an Educational Home and a clever self-advertiser, he had obtained from the *Assemblée constituante* permission to lodge in his institution the famous centenarian of the Jura, so as, he said, to impress on his pupils a respect for old age. During the *Législative*, he had managed to get himself elected as deputy for Orleans, his native town. Sent to this town in August 1792 to look into the procedure employed against the prisoners of the High Court, he had given help to Fournier, known as the American, and had in consequence taken part in that butchering of the poor wretches by the *septembrisseurs,* which we mentioned above.

Although Bourdon's complicity cannot be distinctly determined, he had acquired for himself ever since that date a criminal notoriety at Orleans. However, supported by the most turbulent elements of the town, and thanks to them sent as deputy to the Convention, he delighted in defying his opponents, the aristocrats of the national guard who were suspected of reactionary feelings.

Thus it is that in March 1793, while on a mission to the *Côte d'Or,* he went out of his way to see his Jacobin friends at Orleans. Without seeing any of the local authorities, he immediately presented himself amid acclamations to the People's Society, whom he excited with incendiary talk. The meeting at the club was followed by a patriotic dinner where drunkenness was added to political excitement. From the banquet-room, there soon poured forth an intoxicated and yelling mob that insulted the aristocrats on their way, and threatened the soldier on duty at the Town Hall. The man gave the alarm, the body of the guard rushed out and a scuffle ensued, in which Bourdon got a few bayonet thrusts which merely grazed his skin. The commanding officer of the national guard was not long in liberating Bourdon. The latter was carried to his inn and there most carefully tended. Concerned about the consequences of the fray, the municipality expressed their regrets to Bourdon for a fight which they could neither foresee nor prevent.[37]

But Bourdon had made up his mind to strike the attitude of a republican martyr. He wrote to the Convention a letter in which he affects to be a victim of the aristocrats. He pictures the affair as a kind of conspiracy in which a delegate of the people hardly escaped being murdered. He was saved, he says, by nothing less than a miracle. If he is still living, he owes it to a coin, now dyed with his blood, which was in his pocket. That coin plays the part of the blessed medal in pious stories, for the blade, sliding along the face of the Goddess Liberty, was only thus prevented from penetrating more deeply.[38] Bourdon cries for revenge. At the Convention, Barrère claims to see in the assault, the news of which is brought by the same post as that of the Vendée insurrection, the proof of a huge monarchist plot: "They want," he says, "to murder the Republic, and begin with the patriot deputies." Full of indignation, the Convention declare Orleans to be in a state of rebellion, and suspend the municipal authorities. The instigators of the plot are to be arraigned before the revolutionary court.

The mayor of Orleans, however, writes to the Convention and asks that he may be held as sole culprit and sole responsible person; the reading of his generous letter instantly converts the hysterical assembly. The sentence is repealed only to be pronounced again a few days later by the influence of the Mountain. Not till a month later, on 26th April, is military law to be abrogated.

During this month, Orleans lies under the terrorist regime. Some thirty suspected persons are implicated, among whom are Wordsworth's former landlord, Gellet-Duvivier, and Annette's brother, Paul Vallon.

The Jacobins at Orleans busy themselves in gathering evidence against the aristocrats and the national guard, which they hate. One of them, who was also one of the most active supporters of Bourdon, the apothecary Besserve, writes to his good brothers and friends to assure them that the affair is being actively followed up, that the accused have grounds for some uneasiness, that his own evidence has terrified more than one of them, that he spoke with the frankness characteristic of the genuine republican and honest man, and that "he showed Truth so naked that more than one judge fell in love with her."[39]

One can with difficulty form an idea of the idleness of most of the charges gathered by the delegates of the executive power who held the inquiry at Orleans. There may be some truth as regards poor Gellet-Duvivier. Not being fully responsible for his actions, he had shown extreme excitement in the scuffle amongst the national guard, in which he was a grenadier. Not only did he hurl insults against Bourdon and the Convention, but he took the deputy by the throat, knocked him down and struck him with his sword. It is even said that he fired one shot. Thus he was the first to be arrested.

But one reads with bewilderment the charges brought against Paul Vallon, who was on special duty at the Town Hall:

> Citizen "X" gives evidence that a young citizen [told him] that having seized by the throat a young man who uttered insolent words and insulted Bourdon and the patriots, the young man thus seized cried out that he was not the man, and that citizen Vallon used every means to tear himself out of the hands of the patriots who held him.
>
> Citizen "Y" gives evidence that being at the Place de l'Étape, he heard three or four young men who were gunners, grenadiers or chasseurs, say on seeing the patriots drawing near, "Here come the knave Goullu, the rascal Besserve and the other scoundrels"; that in the same moment there came out of the courtyard of the municipal buildings some thirty young men, that three of four of the said young men surrounded the witness, that one of them called at the

top of his voice for one Vallon; and, seeing the said Vallon did not
come, they turned back to assault citizen Besserve.[40]

Paul Vallon had tried to disengage himself from the patriots' hands; he
had *not* come to the assaulters' help, but had been called to the rescue by one
of them, and this evidence was amply sufficient to lose him his head. Was he
not known in town as a friend of the old regime?

Yet some hope dawned for the accused. Other representatives of the people
passing through Orleans, gave an account to the Convention of the wretched
state of the town (11th May); by their statements the criminal attempt was
reduced to a mere scuffle, the responsibility of which was thrown on to
Bourdon. On 19th May, Noël read a report exonerating the town council and
incriminating Bourdon. The Mountain grew indignant. The Girondin Louvet
made an eloquent reply. The Convention followed Noël's lead and cancelled
their former verdict. But a fortnight later, the Mountain had the upper hand
again. The accused, transferred to Paris, to the Conciergerie du Palais, were
arraigned by Fouquier-Tinville before his tribunal.

Gellet-Duvivier's daughter—a minor—now presented a petition, in which
she explains that since his wife's death her poor father's mind is unhinged,
that the people of Orleans know him to be weak-minded, that since his arrest
his madness has become complete, that his incoherent shouting prevents his
fellow-prisoners from sleeping, that when she visits her father, he does not
recognise her, calls her his wife and offers to marry her. She demands for
him a medical examination so that his madness or weak-mindedness may
be certified.

In correct style, Fouquier-Tinville granted the examination, but poor
Gellet-Duvivier nevertheless was one of the nine accused from Orleans to
mount the scaffold on 13th July.

Nearly two years passed after 9th Thermidor before the iniquitous case
was revised. Six sections of the commune of Dijon—the town Bourdon
visited just after the scuffle at Orleans—then denounced the deputy as having
boasted that he had himself purposely provoked the fray (9th May, 1795).
Bourdon, who, in the meantime, had had his period of grandeur, who had
succeeded to Robespierre as president of the Jacobins, who had dared to
stand up against him—not indeed as a moderating factor but by virtue of his
alliance with the Hébertists or *Enragés* (maddened ones)—and who, urged
by his fear of his powerful enemy, had helped to accomplish his overthrow—
Bourdon was denounced as "infamous" by his colleagues, though they had
been witnesses to many kinds of inhumanity. Legendre, during a stance of the
Convention, Boissy d'Anglas in the Council of the Five Hundred, one after

the other called him murderer. He lasted out till the Empire, however, having returned to his educational calling and become head of a primary school.

Meanwhile, more cautious or more lucky than Gellet-Duvivier, Paul Vallon succeeded in saving his head. When they tried to arrest him on 24th April, 1793, he had disappeared. He figures among the accused, marked down as absent, whom Fouquier-Tinville indicted on 16th June, and ordered to be committed to the Conciergerie. He was in hiding at Orleans at the house of a M. Lochon-Petitbois, a merchant and a friend of the family.[41] But we may well imagine the anxiety of his friends, and of his sisters, during all these months when the least word might cause his death. No doubt he was assisted by them as far as lay in their power, with the constant fear of their very help betraying him. No doubt also that the atrocious injustice under which their brother laboured inspired these women with the hatred of the Revolution.

This miserable affair must have occupied a great part of the letters which Annette continued to send Wordsworth. But did he get them? And did his own letters reach her? The first he received, as far as we know, is that of which Dorothy speaks to a friend in November 1795: "William has had a letter from France since we came here. Annette mentions having despatched half a dozen, none of which he has received."[42] The violence of the war rendered all correspondence precarious, if not impossible. However, relations became frequent again during the preliminaries of the Peace of Amiens. Then from 21st December, 1801, to 24th March, 1802, are noted down in Dorothy's diary a series of letters exchanged between the poet and Annette. It is clear that their correspondence was as active as possible, and that circumstances alone prevented it from being carried on continuously.

IX

If, in this new series of letters, Annette has no such tragic adventures to relate, yet misfortunes and dangers have not ceased to beset her and her friends after a short period of calm. The Terror once over, Paul Vallon having come out of his hiding-place and returned to the office of Maître Courtois, it seems there was a short period during which the Vallon family could breathe in peace. The three sisters lived together at Blois, poorly enough no doubt (but who was not poor then?), but on good terms with the best society of the town. They lived with their mother and stepfather at the family house in the Rue du Pont. Sheltered by the name of Madame William that she had assumed, or of Veuve William—for one finds both in turn—Annette, protected from scandal, was bringing up Caroline. Her brother Charles Henry, who had become head of the family at the death of Jean Jacques, was in a prosperous situation as head surgeon at the Hospital of Blois.

Life, after the fall of Robespierre and throughout the Directory, in spite
of persisting troubles, in spite of war and the general impoverishment of the
country, had the sweetness of convalescence. It seems to have had at Blois a
peculiar charm, according to Dufort, Comte de Cheverny, who drew in his
Memoirs this idyllic picture:

> Thanks be rendered to the inhabitants of the town of Blois,
> who have succeeded in making of the society which gather
> there the pleasantest that may be imagined. Blois is in every
> way preferable to its three neighbours, Orleans, Vendôme and
> Tours, a distinction it has always enjoyed. The general lack of
> means has levelled all rivalry and there is no disparity in rank.
> The insignificant trade that is being carried on does not arouse
> competition. The few people who live at Blois stay by reason of its
> irresistible attraction. . . . Despite [he adds] the poverty suffered
> by all classes, there are gatherings of twenty, thirty people,
> sometimes more. The stranger admitted to these parties might
> think himself in the midst of a family. Women are elegantly
> dressed, and there are numbers of marriageable young girls,
> every one prettier than the next. Music is carried to a point of
> great perfection. [They give concerts] that would be deemed good
> even in Paris.[43]

A fine spirit of generosity prevailed towards the victims of the Revolution,
according to another witness, the wife of Doctor Chambon de Montaux, who
lived at Blois from 1793 to 1804:

> One would never end if one tried to give an account of the acts
> of kindness performed by the people of Blois on behalf of the
> unhappy proscribed. We were welcomed and helped as brothers
> by the nobility of the town—true to king and state. Our tears were
> dried by the hand of friendship.[44]

Royalists were numerous and active. Blois was "one of the most ardent
centres of the counter-revolution." The 9th of Thermidor raised great
hopes. The Vendémiaire insurrection found in Blois zealous agents who
corresponded with the Paris sections in revolt, and among these agents
men such as Guyon de Montlivault and Pardessus the younger, to whom we
constantly find reference among the friends of the Vallon sisters. These early
hopes were to be wrecked on 13th Vendémiaire (5th October, 1795) by young
Bonaparte on the steps of the church of St. Roch. At first great discouragement
ensued for the royalists. The tone of Annette's letter mentioned by Dorothy

on 30th November, must have been very different according as it was written before or after 13th Vendémiaire.

But soon the party took heart again. Without renouncing their aim, they changed their tactics. To the Parisian insurrection succeeded the provincial *chouannerie* of which Blois was to be one of the chief centres and into which Annette threw herself heart and soul. She allied herself with the most combative among the Chouans, those criticised by the Comte de Cheverny, whose own ideal was to keep himself and family safe by "an absolute nullity."[45]

Cheverny is full of recriminations against the imprudent members of his class or party, whose intrigues endanger the security of others. Yet when the occasion comes, when a clever stroke has been well struck, he is fain to applaud it. Thus he relates with relish a certain incident at Blois in which one of the three sisters bears a part.

It occurred after an anti-royalist move on the part of the Directory. The act of the 22nd of Germinal, in the fourth year of the Republic (11th April, 1796), had just prescribed new penalties against non-juring priests and emigrants. There happened to be two emigrants in the prison of Blois. A plot was formed in the town to help them to escape. One morning five persons were arrested before the prison by a patrol; among them was Lacaille the younger, aged sixteen years, gunsmith, and surgeon's apprentice under Vallon. They were accused of having planned the escape of the emigrants. On the ground by them was found a very well-made rope-ladder. And Cheverny adds here:

> A *demoiselle* Vallon, of meritorious character and of an obliging disposition, is questioned by the jury as to having ordered twenty-seven fathoms of rope to make the ladder which was to save the prisoners. She owns to having ordered the rope but says it is still in her attic, which is proved true. Thus she is pronounced not guilty.[46]

If Cheverny congratulates her, it is probably because he thinks she showed both daring in abetting the escape and skill in getting out of the difficulty. He rejoices at the happy issue of the case which, in compliance with the request of the accused, had been tried in Orleans. Once acquitted, they came back triumphantly to Blois in the carriage of Brunet the coffee-house keeper, and a scuffle ensued between their followers and the Jacobin post on duty, in which the latter got the worst of it.

Although we cannot say for certain which of the Vallon sisters Cheverny has in mind, there are many reasons to believe that it was Annette, who is always noted as the most active of the trio. She now definitely separated herself from her uncles, the constitutional priests, and went back to the old form of worship. Her signature is found to a secret Roman Catholic marriage, held in the private chapel used instead of the parish church of St. Honoré, on 14th July, 1795. This is the one and only time she signs herself William Wordsworth Vallon. It seems that her enthusiasm carried away her relations. On 29th December, 1796, her brother Charles Henry, who two years earlier had contracted a civil marriage with a girl named Charruyau, had their union secretly consecrated by a non-juring priest in a room of the house in the *Rue Pierre de Blois*, used instead of the church of St. Solenne.[47]

Annette and her sisters, but more particularly Annette, were allied to those too energetic families who fell under the displeasure of Cheverny. They were at the very heart of that *chouannerie* whose leaders were such men as Pardessus the younger, Charles de Rancogne, Guyon de Montlivault, with whom they were closely acquainted.

Guyon de Montlivault was the nominal head of the Blois chouannerie. Cheverny, who disliked him for his turbulence, speaks of him as ambitious and trusted by nobody. Montlivault certainly lacked circumspection. He ingenuously betrayed the secrets of the conspiracy to a spy who passed himself off on him as a Chouan and who, on 3rd March, 1797, sent a report on the councils of the Chouans to the Ministry of Police: "I learned through him," says the spy, "that Blois had a paid Chouan brigade, bound by the customary oath, recruited among the artisans and labourers, but of established moral character and formed only to ensure the secret execution of the Council's designs." Their procedure was to provoke the former Terrorists to make trouble so that the suspicions of the Directory might be shifted on to them. The Chouans were under oath to render every assistance to the Catholic and royal party.[48]

It was no mere affair of caste, as may be seen. The bulk of the soldiery was drawn from the people. Part of the population lightheartedly entered the fight against the Jacobins, insulted and reviled them, occasionally came to blows with them. In the ranks of the conspirators were found men of all ranks. The Vallon sisters threw their house open to noblemen such as Montlivault and Rancogne, to *bourgeois* such as Jean Marie Pardessus, to artisans such as the gunsmith Lacaille and his sons, to mention only those whose names are coupled with theirs in the police reports. Pardessus's father had been in custody during the Terror, his younger brother was killed at Savenay, fighting under Larochejaquelin, Jean Marie himself was the ordinary counsel for the Chouans of the region when brought to justice. Charles, the son of the Marquis de Rancogne, despite the entreaties of his father—as timorous as Cheverny himself—was for a time a captain under Georges Cadoudal. The younger Lacaille too, it is said, fought under the same chief. Lacaille's very apprentices were known for their extremist opinions; one of them was later shot at Brest under suspicion of espionage in English pay.

The usual meeting-place of the Chouans was, doubtless, Berruet's coffee-house, "The Three Merchants." But there were more secret haunts, used chiefly by those who were being tracked down, and the house of the Vallon sisters was one of these shelters. We do not know the name of those "numberless" French people who, as we are told by a Restoration document,[49] owed their salvation to Annette, of those who were "saved, hidden and assisted by her," of the persecuted emigrants and priests whom she helped to escape from prison and death. Among those who later testify to her devotedness, only one, the *Chevalier de la Rochemouhet*, declares that "Madame William saved his life at the peril of her own." The others are witnesses to her devotion rather than personally her debtors: Théodore de Montlivault, the Comte de Salaberry, the Vicomte de Malartic, the Baron de Tardif, etc. . . . It is just possible that the Vicomte de Montmorency-Laval owed her some direct assistance in his troubles. Formerly a staunch liberal—he had gone as far as to move, on the night of 4th August, the abolition of the aristocratic privileges—he had repented of what he termed his errors; towards the end of the century he was in the department of Loir-et-Cher under threat of arrest. When the Bourbons came back to the throne, he gave proof of his gratitude to Annette.

All those who struck at the Jacobins won Annette's sympathy, amongst others Nicolas Bailly, whom we shall meet later as her great friend. It was he who, entrusted with the public prosecutor's speech against Babeuf and his followers at Vendôme in May 1797, contributed to the condemnation of the redoubtable socialist and to the fall of his Jacobin supporters.

The activity of the Vallon sisters, and chiefly of Annette, was extreme and could not long escape the attention of the government. The police searches ranged nearer and nearer and ended in the compilation of a long list of suspected persons, whose arrest was decreed by the Minister of Justice. This vigilance began at the end of the Directory, and continued into the first months of the Consulate. From 10th October, 1799, to 31st January, 1800, were indicted: Montlivault, Montmorency-Laval, Rancogne the younger, Jean Marie Pardessus, Puzéla (Paul Vallon's future father-in-law, whom we shall meet again), among many others. Annette was one of the persons not to be arrested on the spot, but for whom "it were advisable to have an order for a domiciliary search to examine their papers and arrest them if any plotting is discovered" (police document, 31st January, 1800). She is marked down on the police paper as "Widow Williams at Blois; gives shelter to the Chouans."[50]

We do not know whether the search took place. It is certain, however, that more coherent action was being taken against the Chouans. Most of them were discovered; some were imprisoned, others placed under supervision and rendered powerless. The big fight in the West ended on 26th January, 1800, with Georges Cadoudal's defeat at Pont de Loch, followed by his submission. The Chouans were capable of nothing more than spasmodic movements in the following years.

This was a source of sadness for a zealous royalist like Annette, and personal troubles were added to it. Her eldest sister Françoise, at more than thirty-five years old, was implicated in a mysterious and painful adventure.

We must imagine the strange atmosphere in which these women conspirators moved in order to understand—there is no question of excusing— what happened to Françoise. We must consider the perturbing promiscuity of excited men and women maddened in turn with anger and with fear, the secret meetings, the long whisperings, the feverish intimacy, when pity provokes love and danger leads to unrestraint. In 1798, Françoise gave birth to a son whose father is not known. Given the extraordinary laxity of morals throughout the country during the Directory, the mad thirst for pleasure which carried away all classes, and the general discredit into which marriage had fallen, this might have been a simple occurrence enough at a time when so many men and women "followed nature." But in the house of the Vallon sisters, who were known for their devotion to Church and Throne, and who were nieces of two priests, the matter was different. It was a scandal in the very sanctuary. What jeers, what sarcasms would be levelled at the Catholic conspirators! How their adversaries would make use of the adventure to ridicule the Cause itself! Thus Françoise was induced, after having concealed her state, to abandon the child. The very day of its birth (1st November, 1798), it was exposed at the Hospital of Blois, where, on account of the date (11th Brumaire of the seventh year of the Republic), they gave it the names of Toussaint Décadi. Both calendars were thus united: Décadi, a revolutionary name, striking a strangely false note in the records of a monarchist family.

We must remember that Françoise's brother, Charles Henry, was head of the hospital. We may conclude that he connived at the plan and exercised special supervision over the disowned child. Nature had been sacrificed to the Cause, but it would be wrong to regard Françoise as devoid of all maternal feeling. She suffered and did not forget. Twenty years later, when settled away from Blois, in Paris, where she was safe from the malicious curiosity of neighbours, she owned Toussaint Décadi as her child (22nd May, 1819), and some time afterwards married him to a girl of illegitimate birth, who could not upbraid him with his own (22nd July, 1820).

At the same time, Annette was beset with other anxieties concerning her brother Paul, who suddenly left Orleans, in 1800, to lead in Paris a precarious and disorderly existence of which we shall speak further.

It is not probable that Annette related all these misfortunes in the letters received from her by Wordsworth at the beginning of 1802, but she could tell enough to justify Dorothy's exclamation, "Poor Annette!"

Notes

1. Harper's *William Wordsworth, His Life, Works and Influence*, London, 1916, Vol. I. p. 87.
2. *An Evening Walk.*
3. *Descriptive Sketches.*
4. *Prelude*, XIV. 339–41.
5. Harper's *William Wordsworth*, I. p. 275.
6. *De Quincey's Collected Writings*, Edited by David Masson, II, p. 246.
7. *Prelude*, IV. 317–19.
8. *Prelude*, IV. 319–38.
9. *Prelude*, XII. 269–70.
10. *Descriptive Sketches*, 148–56.
11. Letter of Dorothy of 16th Feb., 1793.
12. Letter to Richard Wordsworth, 19th Dec., 1791. Harper, I. p. 145.
13. I owe my information on the two priests to Abbé J. Gallerand, professor at the Seminary of Blois.
14. Letter communicated to me by Madame Lecoq-Vallon.
15. It is impossible to know the exact date of Wordsworth's change of residence from Orleans to Blois, but we know that he meant to spend the winter in the former town (Letter to Mathews of 23rd Nov., 1791, Harper, I. p. 122, and Dorothy of 7th Dec., 1791, ibid. p. 124). On the other hand, if we admit that there is a parallelism between his own story and that of *Vaudracour and Julia*, we are led to infer that Wordsworth's love had two successive towns for its scene of action.
16. Sonnet signed *Axiologus*, printed in *European Magazine* (March 1787) and ascribed to Wordsworth by Knight and Hutchinson. Professor Harper expresses some doubt as to the authorship.
17. We gather this from Annette's letter printed in Appendix II.
18. Reminiscences of Mr. Ellis Yarnall of Philadelphia: W. Knight's *Life of Wordsworth*, Vol. II. p. 334. The passage immediately preceding is amusing, read in the light of what we now know. "France," relates Yarnall, "was our next subject, and one which seemed very near his heart. He had been much in that country at the outbreak of the Revolution, and

afterwards during its wildest excesses. At the time of the September massacres he was at Orleans. *Addressing Mrs. Wordsworth, he said: 'I wonder I came to stay there so long, and at a period so exciting.'*"

19. See Harper's *Life of William Wordsworth*, Vol. I. ch. viii, and especially his "Wordsworth at Blois" in *John Morley and other Essays*, 1920.

20. Archives of the Hôtel-Dieu of Blois, Registre E3, folios 57–8.

21. On that same occasion, Wordsworth was probably present at the "Civic Feast" given at Orleans on 21st September to celebrate the suppression of monarchy, during which deputy Manuel made a speech before the Assembly. As a symbol of the fall of royalty, fire was set to a big wood-pile: "Le feu est solennellement mis à l'énorme bûcher, composé de fagots élevés en une haute pyramide couronnée d'un bouquet d'artifice qui bientôt tombe en mille flammèches étincelantes, et les citoyens se livrent à la joie qu'ils ressentent de l'établissement de la République française; dans leur enthousiasme, avec ces élans qui n'appartiennent qu'à des hommes vraiment dignes de la liberté, les cris de 'Vive la République! Vive la nation française!' éclatent de toutes parts."—Quoted in *Histoire de la ville d'Orléans*, by Bimbenet, Vol. II. p. 1225.

22. The full certificate of Caroline's birth has been printed by Professor Harper in *Wordsworth's French Daughter*, Princeton University Press, 1921.

23. *Prelude*, X. 222.

24. *Prelude*, X. 229–30.

25. We gather this from Annette's letters to William and Dorothy (Appendix II.). The dream of a retired life in a small cottage which is found both in Dorothy's letters and in Wordsworth's *Evening Walk* first makes its appearance at the beginning of 1793 when the letters were written and the poem published. It was first connected with William's determination to marry Annette. The cottage was to shelter both sister and wife. This is how we ought to read the following lines in *An Evening Walk*, addressed to Dorothy:

"Even now [Hope] decks for me a distant scene,
(For dark and broad the gulf of time between)
Gilding that cottage with her fondest ray,
(Sole bourn, sole wish, sole object of my way;
How fair its lawns and silvery woods appear!
How sweet its streamlet murmurs in mine ear!)
Where we, my Friend, to golden days shall rise,
Till our small share of hardly-paining sighs

(For sighs will ever trouble human breath)
Creep hushed into the tranquil breast of death."

26. See Appendix II.

27. Professor Harper's *Life of William Wordsworth*, I. p. 202.

28. Letter of Dorothy, 6th May, 1792. Harper II. p. 181.

29. I owe this suggestion to Mr. G. C. Smith, school inspector at Edinburgh, a keen Wordsworthian. On Wordsworth's feelings while he stayed in the Isle of Wight, see *Prelude*, X. 315–30.

30. Carlyle's Reminiscences: see Harper's *William Wordsworth*, I. p. 209 and II. p. 417.

31. Harper's *William Wordsworth*, I. 179. According to Watts, Bailey said: "He had met Wordsworth in Paris, and having warned him that his connection with the Mountain rendered his situation there at that time perilous, the poet decamped with great precipitation." There is no indication of time. Wordsworth could be in no danger at the end of 1792, a comparatively quiet period. He never was connected with the Mountain. His sympathies were all for the Girondins (Louvet against Robespierre, etc.). The anecdote is full of gross mistakes, but the fact of his being in Paris at a particularly dangerous moment, and his having decamped, can scarcely have been invented.

32. The denunciation of marriage was common at that time. Charles Lloyd's novel, *Edmund Oliver* (1798), is a defence of marriage against its then numerous enemies. The story is supposed to adumbrate a passage of Coleridge's early life.

33. *Prelude*, XI. 240–4.

34. *The Borderers*, II. 1090–3.

35. *Memoirs of William Wordsworth*, I. p. 74.

36. *The Excursion*, II. 269–72.

37. Cf. *Histoire de la Terreur*, by Mortimer Ternaux, Vol. VI. p. 479 et sqq. The author is a deadly enemy of the Terrorists, but his information is perfectly accurate, as is proved by an examination of the original documents in the *Archives nationales*.

38. Letter of Léonard Bourdon to the Convention of 19th March, 1793. All the documents relating to the Bourdon affair are found in the *Archives nationales*, BB30 87 and AF11 167.

39. Tuetey, *Répertoire général des Sources manuscrites de l'histoire de Paris pendant la Révolution française*, Vol. VIII p. 278.

40. *Archives nationales*, AF11 167, No. 137.

41. Manuscript memoirs of Amédée Vallon, Paul's son.

42. Letter of Dorothy to Mrs. Marshall of 30th November, 1795. See *Harper*, I, p. 292.

43. *Mémoires sur les Règnes de Louis XV. et Louis XVI. et sur la Révolution*, par J. N. Dufort, Comte de Cheverny, Introducteur des Ambassadeurs, Lieutenant Général du Blaisois (1732–1802), publiées par Robert de Crèvecoeur. Tome II.

44. Quoted in *Mémoires de Madame Vallon*, published by Guy Trouillard, p. 223 (note).

45. *Mémoires de Cheverny*, II. p. 128.

46. *Mémoires de Cheverny*, II. p. 295.

47. Notes furnished by Abbé J. Gallerand, professor at the Seminary of Blois.

48. *Mémoires sur les Conseils Chouans remis au Ministre de la Police générale le 13 Ventôse an V.* (3 mars, 1797): Archives nationales, F7 6200.

49. See Appendix IV.

50. Archives nationales, F7 6200.

–ÉMILE LEGOUIS, *William Wordsworth and Annette Vallon*, 1922, pp. 1–39

GENERAL

CHARLES BURNEY (1799)

Charles Burney speaks of Wordsworth's "Lines Composed a Few Miles above Tintern Abbey on Revisiting the Banks of the Wye Valley During a Tour, July 13, 1798" as a beautiful and reflective poem, but he complains that it is weighted down by pessimistic thoughts and a general retreat from the active life. Burney objects to the message of "Tintern Abbey" on social grounds, arguing that Wordsworth was somewhat elitist, for he had the benefit of education and an exchange with men of letters. As a result of his privileged background, Burney argues that Wordsworth can afford to indulge in tranquillity as an ideal way to experience nature, but the uncultivated person, busy providing the means of her or his subsistence, does not have the time or the resources to think about this aesthetic ideal.

The reflections (in "Tintern Abbey" are) of no common mind; poetical, beautiful, and philosophical: but somewhat tinctured with gloomy, narrow, and unsociable ideas of seclusion from the commerce of the world: as if men were born to live in woods and wilds, unconnected with each other! Is it not to education and the culture of the mind that we owe the raptures which the author so well describes, as arising from the view of beautiful scenery, and sublime objects of nature enjoyed in tranquillity, when contrasted with the artificial machinery and "busy hum of men" in a city? The savage sees none of the beauties which this author describes. The convenience of food and shelter, which vegetation affords him, is all his concern; he thinks not of its picturesque beauties, the course of rivers, the height of mountains, &c. He has no dizzy raptures in youth; nor does he listen in maturer age "to the still sad music of humanity."

—CHARLES BURNEY, *Monthly Review,*
June 1799, p. 210

ROBERT SOUTHEY (1804)

In 1804, Robert Southey gives Wordsworth his vote of confidence that his reputation will improve. The author of the excerpt predicts that the poet will show himself superior to all others, except of course Shakespeare.

Wordsworth will do better, and leave behind him a name, unique in his way; he will rank among the very first poets, and probably possesses a mass of merits superior to all, except only Shakspeare. This is doing much, yet would he be a happier man if he did more.

—ROBERT SOUTHEY, letter to
John Rickman, March 30, 1804

GEORGE GORDON, LORD BYRON (1809)

Byron finds Wordsworth uninspired, one who follows the precepts of poetic rule as opposed to writing verse that conveys passion and emotionalism and that delights the audience.

Next comes the dull disciple of thy school,
That mild apostate from poetic rule,
The simple Wordsworth, framer of a lay
As soft as evening in his favourite May,
Who warns his friend 'to shake off toil and trouble,
And quit his books, for fear of growing double;'
Who, both by precept and example, shows
That prose is verse, and verse is merely prose;
Convincing all, by demonstration plain,
Poetic souls delight in prose insane;
And Christmas stories tortured into rhyme
Contain the essence of the true sublime.
Thus, when he tells the tale of Betty Foy,
The idiot mother of 'an idiot boy';
A moon-struck, silly lad, who lost his way,
And, like his bard, confounded night with day;
So close on each pathetic part he dwells,
And each adventure so sublimely tells,
That all who view the 'idiot in his glory'
Conceive the bard the hero of the story.

—GEORGE GORDON, LORD BYRON, *English Bards
and Scotch Reviewers*, 1809, 11. 235–254

CHARLES LAMB
"WORDSWORTH'S *EXCURSION*" (1814)

Commenting on *The Excursion*, Charles Lamb states that Wordsworth, who never panders to popular taste, has not received the recognition he deserves because his unique vision and profound emotions are not appreciated. Lamb further believes that Wordsworth is assailed for his subject matter and reverence for simple country people, as well as for his concern for the plight of children, which others criticize as resulting in childish poetry. "If from a familiar observation of the ways of children," Lamb asserts, "and much more from a retrospect of his own mind when a child, he has gathered more reverential notions of that state than fall to the lot of ordinary observers." Sydney Smith, in the excerpt following this one, concurs with Lamb and responds to Francis Jeffrey, whom he views as having slandered and abused Wordsworth.

The causes which have prevented the poetry of Mr. Wordsworth from attaining its full share of popularity are to be found in the boldness and originality of his genius. The times are past when a poet could securely follow the direction of his own mind into whatever tracts it might lead. A writer, who would be popular, must timidly coast the shore of prescribed sentiment and sympathy. He must have just as much more of the imaginative faculty than his readers, as will serve to keep their apprehensions from stagnating, but not so much as to alarm their jealousy. He must not think or feel too deeply.

If he has had the fortune to be bred in the midst of the most magnificent objects of creation, he must not have given away his heart to them; or if he have, he must conceal his love, or not carry his expressions of it beyond that point of rapture, which the occasional tourist thinks it not overstepping decorum to betray, or the limit which that gentlemanly spy upon Nature, the picturesque traveller, has vouchsafed to countenance. He must do this, or be content to be thought an enthusiast.

If from living among simple mountaineers, from a daily intercourse with them, not upon the footing of a patron, but in the character of an equal, he has detected, or imagines that he has detected, through the cloudy medium of their unlettered discourse, thoughts and apprehensions not vulgar; traits of patience and constancy, love unwearied, and heroic endurance, not unfit (as he may judge) to be made the subject of verse, he will be deemed a man of perverted genius by the philanthropist who, conceiving of the peasantry of his country only as objects of a pecuniary sympathy, starts at finding them elevated to a level of humanity with himself, having their own loves, enmities, cravings, aspirations, &c., as much beyond his faculty to believe, as his beneficence to supply.

If from a familiar observation of the ways of children, and much more from a retrospect of his own mind when a child, he has gathered more reverential notions of that state than fall to the lot of ordinary observers, and, escaping from the dissonant wranglings of men, has tuned his lyre, though but for occasional harmonies, to the milder utterance of that soft age,—his verses shall be censured as infantile by critics who confound poetry 'having children for its subject' with poetry that is 'childish,' and who, having themselves perhaps never been children, never having possessed the tenderness and docility of that age, know not what the soul of a child is—how apprehensive! how imaginative! how religious!

—CHARLES LAMB, "Wordsworth's *Excursion*,"
Quarterly Review, October 1814, pp. 110–111

SYDNEY SMITH (1814)

I am much obliged to you for the (Edinburgh) Review, and shall exercise the privilege of an old friend in making some observations upon it. I have not read the review of Wordsworth, because the subject is to me so very uninteresting; but may I ask was it worth while to take any more notice of a man respecting whom the public opinion is completely made up? and do not such repeated attacks upon the man wear in some little degree the shape of persecution?

—SYDNEY SMITH, letter to Francis,
Lord Jeffrey, December 30, 1814

JOHN KEATS "ADDRESSED TO HAYDON" (1816)

He of the cloud, the cataract, the lake,
Who on Helvellyn's summit, wide awake,
Catches his freshness from Archangel's wing.

—JOHN KEATS, "Addressed to Haydon," 1816

WILLIAM HAZLITT (1818)

William Hazlitt praises Wordsworth for his originality, and, to substantiate this statement, he compares the poet to Walter Scott, whose work depended on tradition and local history. As to the *Lyrical Ballads*, Hazlitt has no lack of accolades for their originality and pathos, declaring Wordsworth to have achieved a profundity much greater than any poet of modern times. At the same time, Hazlitt points out that Wordsworth's artistry consists in achieving a refined tone drawing on the sights and sounds of nature, though the poet is neither a master of construction nor in full control of the meaning of his poems, the truth of this assessment confirmed by the relatively static work *The Excursion*.

Mr. Wordsworth is the most original poet now living. He is the reverse of Walter Scott in his defects and excellences. He has nearly all that the other wants, and wants all that the other possesses. His poetry is not external, but internal; it does not depend upon tradition, or story, or old song; he furnishes it from his own mind, and is his own subject. He is the poet of mere sentiment. Of many of the Lyrical Ballads, it is not possible to speak in terms of too high praise, such as 'Hart-Leap Well,' the 'Banks of the Wye,' 'Poor Susan,' parts of the 'Leech-Gatherer,' the lines 'To a Cuckoo,' 'To a Daisy,' the 'Complaint,' several of the Sonnets, and a hundred others of inconceivable beauty, of perfect originality and pathos. They open a finer and deeper vein of thought and feeling than any poet in modern times has done, or attempted. He has produced a deeper impression, and on a smaller circle, than any other of his contemporaries. His powers have been mistaken by the age, nor does he exactly understand them himself. He cannot form a whole. He has not the constructive faculty. He can give only the fine tones of thought, drawn from his mind by accident or nature, like the sounds drawn from the Eolian harp by the wandering gale.—He is totally deficient in all the machinery of poetry. His Excursion, taken as a whole, notwithstanding the noble materials thrown away in it, is a proof of this. The line labours, the sentiment moves slow, but the poem stands stock-still. The reader makes no way from the first line to the last. It is more than any thing in the world like Robinson Crusoe's boat, which would have been an excellent good boat, and would have carried him to the other side of the globe, but that he could not get it out of the sand where it stuck fast. I did what little I could to help to launch it at the time, but it would not do. I am not, however, one of those who laugh at the attempts or failures of men of genius. It is not my way to cry 'Long life to the conqueror.' Success and desert are not with me synonymous terms; and the less Mr. Wordsworth's general merits have been understood, the more necessary is it to insist upon them.

—WILLIAM HAZLITT, *Lectures on the English Poets*, 1818

Thomas Love Peacock
"The Four Ages of Poetry" (1820)

Thomas Love Peacock finds that those critics who laud Wordsworth for having returned to nature are not exactly accurate; instead Peacock detects the continued presence of a fantastic detail or element—such as "a Danish boy or the living ghost of Lucy Gray"—whose insertion into the poem contradicts the pretense of what purports to be a description of the natural world.

The descriptive poetry of the present day has been called by its cultivators a return to nature. Nothing is more impertinent than this pretension. Poetry cannot travel out of the regions of its birth, the uncultivated lands of semi-civilized men. Mr. Wordsworth, the great leader of the returners to nature, cannot describe a scene under his own eyes without putting into it the shadow of a Danish boy or the living ghost of Lucy Gray, or some similar phantastical parturition of the moods of his own mind.

—Thomas Love Peacock,
"The Four Ages of Poetry," 1820

Walter Scott (1820)

I do not know a man more to be venerated for uprightness of heart and loftiness of genius. Why he will sometimes choose to crawl upon all-fours, when God has given him so noble a countenance to lift to heaven, I am as little able to account for, as for his quarrelling (as you tell me) with the wrinkles which time and meditation have stamped his brow withal.

—Walter Scott, letter to
Allan Cunningham, December 1820

Henry Wadsworth Longfellow (1829)

Comparing Wordsworth to Byron, Longfellow declares that Wordsworth is only second in having influenced the times in which he wrote. In his metaphoric description of Wordsworth driving to Parnassas, a mountain in Greece that in classical mythology was the seat of the Muses and thus poetic inspiration, Longfellow is expressing Wordsworth's ultimate triumph despite the Englishman's slow and difficult experience with the press and his critics. Longfellow maintains that Wordsworth appealed to the moral and political convictions of his age.

Next to Byron, there is no poet whose writings have had so much influence on the taste of the age as Wordsworth. Byron drove on through the upper air till the thunder of his wheels died on the ear. Wordsworth drove to Parnassus by the lower road, got sometimes lost in bushes and lowland fogs, and was much molested by mosquito critics. In our own country the Wordsworth school has evidently the upper hand. His simple austerity and republican principle in poetry were in unison with our moral and political creed. Our modes of thought are sober and practical. So, in most instances, were his.

—HENRY WADSWORTH LONGFELLOW,
Notebook (1829), cited in *Samuel Longfellow,*
Life of Henry Wadsworth Longfellow,
1891, vol. 1, p. 172

THOMAS BABINGTON MACAULAY
"MOORE'S LIFE OF LORD BYRON" (1831)

Thomas Babington Macaulay, an English essayist, historian, and politician, here praises *The Excursion* and the *Lyrical Ballads*, both of which had been systematically attacked. Expressing an appreciation of the sacred qualities of nature both poems explore, Macaulay believes they are too profound for general popularity.

In the Lyrical Ballads and the Excursion Mr. Wordsworth appeared as the high priest of a worship, of which nature was the idol. No poems have ever indicated a more exquisite perception of the beauty of the outer world, or a more passionate love and reverence for that beauty. Yet they were not popular; and it is not likely that they ever will be popular as the poetry of Sir Walter Scott is popular. The feeling which pervaded them was too deep for general sympathy. Their style was often too mysterious for general comprehension. They made a few esoteric disciples, and many scoffers.

—THOMAS BABINGTON MACAULAY, "Moore's Life
of Lord Byron," 1831, *Critical, Historical, and*
Miscellaneous Essays, 1860, vol. 2, p. 356

HENRY TAYLOR "WORDSWORTH'S
POETICAL WORKS" (1834)

Sir Henry Taylor lauds Wordsworth as a philosophical poet with a vast and expansive analytical mind possessing an ability to articulate the general. However, Taylor points out that Wordsworth does not offer any new perspective, ethical or metaphysical, nor is he a creative genius like Shakespeare. According to Taylor, who offers specific criteria for judging a poet's worth, Wordsworth's true value is in his ability to look into "the particulars of life" and formulate a general truth based on that observation, for the proper arena for judging individual philosophy is the particular poet's character. Furthermore, Taylor asserts that poetry can reveal only minute aspects of the truth and that a poet should not be faulted for this. Most impressive in Wordsworth's character is not only his humility—both in regard to himself and toward the subjects of his poems—but his spirit of independence without any thought of public gain or glory. Taylor declares Wordsworth as a man "who writes from the impulses of an ardent mind, and throws light upon human nature, less by the depth of his investigations, than by the liveliness of his sympathies; exhibiting, in truth, a subject for a philosopher to contemplate, rather than the spirit of philosophical contemplation."

The poem included here, which refers to Wordsworth's poem "Lines Left upon a Seat in a Yew-tree," is an interpretation of his moral teaching. Taylor presents that lesson as a caveat that the sin of pride and superiority against any living thing is a sin against nature, and that true nobility resides in one who is humble and receptive to its truth. "Oh be wiser, thou! / Instructed that true knowledge leads to love, / True dignity abides with him alone / Who, in the silent hour of inward thought, / Can still suspect, and still revere himself, / In lowliness of heart." Taylor continues with an analysis of what he believes to be the man of dignity, mainly one who eschews personal gain and praise from others, one who holds fast to his independence while living in the world. He maintains that the man in the "Yew Tree" is not really free of thoughts of himself and what others think, for if he had achieved a security of independence he would not have had to remove himself from society and live his life in solitude. In comparison to the poet Robert Burns, Wordsworth is the poet who wrote of the need to contemplate nature in tranquillity. From here, Taylor seeks to define Wordsworth's particular prescription for governing human emotions and contends that feelings such as anger, resentment, and contempt have their place in Wordsworth's perspective but must be controlled and used in situations in which they are justified.

⸗ɪ/ɪ/ɪ⸗   ⸗ɪ/ɪ/ɪ⸗   ⸗ɪ/ɪ/ɪ⸗

Mr. Wordsworth ... in our estimation, is a philosophic writer in the sense in which any man must be so, who writes from the impulses of a capacious and powerful mind, habituated to observe, to analyse, and to generalise. So far forth was Shakspeare likewise a philosopher. But it does not follow from this that he should be supposed to have invented any peculiar ethical or metaphysical system, or to have discovered any new principles upon which such a system could be built. What is new and peculiar in him as a philosophic thinker is not his view of the primary principles of psychological philosophy, nor the trains of ratiocination by which he descends to those which are secondary and derivative: it consists not so much in reasoning as in judgment; not so much in the exposition of abstract truths, as in his manner of regarding the particulars of life as they arise, and of generalising them into one truth or another, according as the one or the other harmonises with his moral temperament and habitual and cherished states of feeling.

If a poet have any peculiar philosophy of his own, it must be mainly through this modification of the judgment by individual temperament; the affinities of such temperament drawing round him and giving predominant influence to some truths, whilst others are merely not rejected in deference to the reason. Nor is it to be supposed that a judgment so modified, and a philosophy into which sensibility thus enters, are therefore fallacious. Such a supposition will be entertained, we are aware, by those who have imagined to themselves such a mere fiction as the contemporaneous discernment of all moral truth. The real state of the case being, however, that truth can only be shown piecemeal in its component parts, and that poetry, at all events, can do no more than cast partial lights upon it, it is saying nothing in derogation of any man's philosophy, still less of his poetical philosophy, to affirm, that, in so far as it is peculiar to himself, it is so by dealing with that portion of truth of which his temperament gives him the most lively consciousness. By his individual temperament it is that Mr. Wordsworth's philosophic perceptions of truth, various and composite as they are, come to have a certain unity of drift, which has given to his writings the character of embodying a peculiar system of philosophy. We shall best explain our view of what that philosophy is, by a commentary upon some of the passages in which it comes to light.

The lines left upon a yew-tree seat, after describing the life of
    mortification led by a neglected man of genius—
Who with the food of pride sustained his soul
In solitude—
conclude with the following moral:—
If thou be one whose heart the holy forms
Of young imagination have kept pure,
Stranger! henceforth be warned; and know that pride,
Howe'er disguised in its own majesty,
Is littleness; that he who feels contempt

For any living thing, hath faculties
Which he has never used; that thought with him
Is in its infancy. The man whose eye
Is ever on himself, doth look on one,
The least of Nature's works, one who might move
The wise man to that scorn which wisdom holds
Unlawful ever. Oh be wiser, thou!
Instructed that true knowledge leads to love,
True dignity abides with him alone
Who, in the silent hour of inward thought,
Can still suspect, and still revere himself,
In lowliness of heart.

Let the stranger who is addressed in this passage be supposed to be another Wordsworth, another philosophic poet, or rather a pupil apt for becoming such, and then the injunctions which it contains are admirably calculated to train him in the way that he should go, although it may be possible to represent them as requiring to be received with some qualification by others. The nature of these qualifications will present a key to some of the peculiarities of Mr. Wordsworth's moral views.

It is undoubtedly essential not only to the philosophic character, but to the moral elevation of any man, that he should regard every atom of pride which he may detect in his nature as something which detracts from his dignity, inasmuch as it evinces some want of independence and of natural strength. When Burns breaks out into fiery expressions of contempt for the rich and the great, we recognise the man of genius, but not the man of an independent nature. If in his real feelings he had been independent of the rich and the great, they might have gone their way and he would have gone his, and we should have heard nothing of his scorn or disdain. These were dictated, not as they professed to be, by a spirit of independence, but by that which, wheresoever it exists, comes in abatement of independence—by pride. A keen desire of aggrandisement in the eyes of others, a sensitive apprehension of humiliation in their eyes, are the constituents of pride, and though it may manifest itself in divers forms, leading a man, perhaps, to avoid a practical dependence upon others, and even leading him, as in the case which is the subject of Mr. Wordsworth's poem, to terminate, as far as possible, his intercourse with mankind—yet these very courses would be evidences of a weakness of nature; for one who was not unduly dependent upon the opinion of others for his peace of mind would not be driven to seek this shelter; on the contrary, he would go through the world, giving and taking, in the freedom of the feeling, that so long as he should satisfy his own conscience in his dealings with his fellow-creatures, he would always be sure to receive from them as much respect as he had occasion for. It is then this servility and cowardice of the inmost spirit, together with the artifices or the escapes naturally resorted to in such a state of slavery, that Mr. Wordsworth detects—when he bids us

know that pride,
Howe'er disguised in its own majesty, Is littleness.

So far, however, the sentiment expressed by Mr. Wordsworth, though largely contributing to his system of opinions, may not, perhaps, constitute a peculiarity of them; and in contrasting the sentiments of Burns with those of Wordsworth, we have not intended to represent the one poet any more than the other, as standing alone in his way of thinking; but only to contra-distinguish from the philosophic poet the mere man of genius who writes from the impulses of an ardent mind, and throws light upon human nature, less by the depth of his investigations, than by the liveliness of his sympathies; exhibiting, in truth, a subject for a philosopher to contemplate, rather than the spirit of philosophical contemplation. But proceeding with the passage, the next step takes us into Mr. Wordsworth's peculiar domain. We are told that He who feels contempt For any living thing, hath faculties That he has never used; that thought with him Is in its infancy.

It is here that, were we to understand the doctrine as delivered for acceptation by mankind at large, we should, as we have already intimated, take some exceptions. The moral government of the world appears to us to require, that in the every-day intercourse of ordinary man with man, room should be given to the operation of the harsher sentiments of our nature—anger, resentment, contempt. They were planted in us for a purpose, and are not essentially and necessarily wrong in themselves, although they may easily be wrong in their direction. What we have to do is not to subdue such feelings; and we are to control them, not with a view to their suppression, but only with a view to their just application. Let the sentiment of justice be paramount, and it will lead to such serious consideration of the grounds of our hostile feelings as will, in itself and of necessity, temper them; but neither need nor ought to suppress them, nor even to abate their vivacity further than is necessary to admit of clear perceptions and a just judgment of their objects. Anger, resentment, and contempt, are instruments of the penal law of nature and private society, which, as long as evil exists, must require to be administered; and the best interests of mankind demand that they should be tempered with justice much more than with mercy. The public laws of a community, and the penalties they denounce, have their chief importance by giving countenance and operation to the private penalties of society, the judgments of the street and the marketplace, searching and pervasive, by which alone evil inchoate can be contended with and destroyed. That Man, so far as he is liable to evil inclinations, should fear his neighbour, is as requisite for the good of society as that he should love his neighbour, and that which he will commonly stand most in fear of is his neighbour's just contempt.

Do we then, in so far as the doctrine in question is concerned, attribute to Mr. Wordsworth a false philosophy? We are by no means so presumptuous, nor (let us hope) so incapable of comprehending Mr. Wordsworth's views. In the first place, we conceive that Mr. Wordsworth adverted more especially to that species of contempt which is immediately connected with the pride denounced previously in the same passage, and the self-love denounced subsequently—the undue contempt which a man conjures up in himself through the workings of self-love, for the ends of self-aggrandisement, or perhaps more frequently to stave off a feeling of humiliation and self-reproach. But without insisting upon a qualification which the language employed may seem to some to refuse, we find in the proposition, taken even in all the absoluteness of its terms, no error, but, we should say, a peculiarity of sentiment, proceeding from a rare constitution of mind, adapted to that constitution, and when enjoined upon men whose minds are similarly constituted, not enjoined amiss.

—HENRY TAYLOR, "Wordsworth's *Poetical Works*,"
Quarterly Review, November 1834, pp. 325–329

GEORGE ELIOT (1839)

I have been so self-indulgent as to possess myself of Wordsworth at full length, and I thoroughly like much of the contents of the first three volumes which I fancy are only the low vestibule to the three remaining ones. What I could wish to have added to many of my favorite morceaux is an indication of less satisfaction in terrene objects, a more frequent upturning of the soul's eye. I never before met with so many of my own feelings, expressed just as I could like them.

—GEORGE ELIOT, letter to
Maria Lewis, November 22, 1839

ELIZABETH BARRETT BROWNING (1842)

In regard to Wordsworth's personality, Elizabeth Barrett Browning states that he is a thoughtful man, neither passionate nor cold, and compares him to a stock dove, a bird that coos but also broods. Browning observes

that Wordsworth is the opposite of Byron, who lacked sympathy but knew
passion. She sees Wordsworth as embodying and living the precepts of his
poetry, with each day bound to the next by natural piety. She describes
him as a Christian poet, his work revealing "the actual audible breathing of
his inward spirit's life."

He is scarcely, perhaps, of a passionate temperament, although still less
is he cold; rather quiet in his love, as the stockdove, and brooding over it
as constantly, and with as soft an inward song lapsing outwardly—serene
through deepness—saying himself of his thoughts, that they "do often lie too
deep for tears;" which does not mean that their painfulness will not suffer
them to be wept for, but that their closeness to the supreme Truth hallows
them, like the cheek of an archangel, from tears. Call him the very opposite of
Byron, who, with narrower sympathies for the crowd, yet stood nearer to the
crowd, because everybody understands passion. Byron was a poet through
pain. Wordsworth is a feeling man because he is a thoughtful man; he knows
grief itself by a reflex emotion; by sympathy rather than by suffering. He is
eminently and humanly expansive; and, spreading his infinite egotism over
all the objects of his contemplation, reiterates the love, life, and poetry of his
peculiar being in transcribing and chanting the material universe, and so sinks
a broad gulf between his descriptive poetry and that of the Darwinian painter-
poet school. Darwin was, as we have intimated, all optic nerve. Wordsworth's
eye is his soul. He does not see that which he does not intellectually discern,
and he beholds his own cloud-capped Helvellyn under the same conditions
with which he would contemplate a grand spiritual abstraction. In his view
of the exterior world,—as in a human Spinozism,—mountains and men's
hearts share in a sublime unity of humanity; yet his Spinozism does in nowise
affront God, for he is eminently a religious poet, if not, indeed, altogether
as generous and capacious in his Christianity as in his poetry; and, being
a true Christian poet, he is scarcely least so when he is not writing directly
upon the subject of religion; just as we learn sometimes without looking
up, and by the mere colour of the grass, that the sky is cloudless. But what
is most remarkable in this great writer is his poetical consistency. There is
a wonderful unity in these multiform poems of one man: they are "bound
each to each in natural piety," even as his days are: and why? because they
are his days—all his days, work days and Sabbath days—his life, in fact, and
not the unconnected works of his life, as vulgar men do opine of poetry and
do rightly opine of vulgar poems, but the sign, seal, and representation of his
life—nay, the actual audible breathing of his inward spirit's life. When Milton

said that a poet's life should be a poem, he spoke a high moral truth; if he had added a reversion of the saying, that a poet's poetry should be his life,—he would have spoken a critical truth, not low.

—ELIZABETH BARRETT BROWNING,
The Book of the Poets, 1842, *Life, Letters and Essays of Elizabeth Barrett Browning*, 1863

MARGARET FULLER
"MODERN BRITISH POETS" (1846)

Margaret Fuller was a journalist, critic, and women's rights activist associated with the American transcendental movement. Her essay is a strong defense of Wordsworth. She speaks of the poet in reverential terms, her intention to explain the emotional effect he has had on her and to respond to his critics. Fuller maintains that Wordsworth is easy to interpret because his great insight is expressed in sympathetic language that is lovingly rendered. Fuller is especially appreciative of Wordsworth as a guide for older people and maintains that the poet is indispensable for those who seek to live virtuously. In reply to his detractors, Fuller defends Wordsworth on the grounds that he is consistently being quoted and that this is clear evidence that he has indeed been accepted. In Fuller's estimation, Wordsworth is a philosophical poet who has found the true spirituality of life and is worthy of comparison to Shakespeare and a handful of unnamed poets. However, she makes a distinction in comparing him to other great poets, stating that Wordsworth's simplicity is his genius and his true originality, unlike those writers who are adept in matters of "melody, brilliance of fancy, dramatic power, or general versatility of talent."

Wordsworth! Beloved friend and venerated teacher; it is more easy and perhaps as profitable to speak of thee. It is less difficult to interpret thee, since no acquired nature but merely a theory severs thee from my mind. Classification on such a subject is rarely satisfactory, yet I will attempt to define in that way the impressions produced by Wordsworth on myself. I esteem his characteristics to be—of spirit,

Perfect simplicity,
Perfect truth,
Perfect love.

Of mind or talent,

Calmness,
Penetration,
Power of Analysis.

Of manner,

Energetic greatness,
Pathetic tenderness,
Mild, persuasive eloquence.

The time has gone by when groundlings could laugh with impunity at Peter Bell and the "Idiot Mother." Almost every line of Wordsworth has been quoted and requoted; every feeling echoed back, and every drop of that "cup of still and serious thought" drunk up by some "spirit profound"; enough to satisfy the giver.

Wordsworth is emphatically the friend and teacher of mature years. Youth, in whose bosom "the stately passions burn," is little disposed to drink with him from the

urn
Of lowly pleasure.

He has not an idealizing tendency, if by this be meant the desire of creating from materials supplied by our minds, and by the world in which they abide for a season, a new and more beautiful world. It is the aspiration of a noble nature animated by genius, it is allied with the resolve for self-perfection; and few without some of its influence can bring to blossom the bud of any virtue. It is fruitful in illusions, but those illusions have heavenly truth interwoven with their temporary errors. But the mind of Wordsworth, like that of the man of science, finds enough of beauty in the real present world. He delights in penetrating the designs of God rather than in sketching designs of his own. Generally speaking, minds in which the faculty of observation is so prominent have little enthusiasm, little dignity of sentiment. That is indeed an intellect of the first order which can see the great in the little, and dignify the petty operations of Nature by tracing through them her most sublime principles. Wordsworth scrutinizes man and nature with the exact and searching eye of a Cervantes, a Fielding, or a Richter, but without any love for that humorous wit which cannot obtain its needful food unaided by such scrutiny; while dissection merely for curiosity's sake is his horror. He has the delicacy of perception, the universality of feeling which distinguish Shakespeare and the three or four other poets of the first class, and might have taken rank with them had he been equally gifted with versatility of talent. Many might reply, "in wanting this last he wants the better half." To this I cannot agree. Talent, or facility in making use of thought, is dependent in a great measure on education and circumstance; while thought itself is immortal as the soul from which it radiates. Wherever we perceive a profound thought, however imperfectly expressed, we offer a higher homage than we can to commonplace thoughts, however beautiful, or if expressed with all that grace of art which it is often most easy for ordinary minds to acquire. There is a suggestive and stimulating power in original thought which cannot be gauged by the first sensation or temporary effect it produces. The circles grow wider and wider as the impulse is propagated through the deep waters of eternity. An exhibition of talent causes immediate delight; almost all of us can enjoy seeing a thing well done; not all of us can enjoy being roused to do and dare for ourselves. Yet when the mind is roused to penetrate the secret meaning of each human effort, a higher pleasure and a greater benefit may be derived from the rude but masterly sketch than from the elaborately finished miniature. In the former case our creative powers are taxed to supply what is wanting, while in the latter our tastes are refined by admiring what another has created. Now since I esteem Wordsworth as superior in originality and philosophic unity of thought to the other poets I have been discussing, I give him the highest place, though they may be superior to him either in melody, brilliancy of fancy, dramatic power, or general versatility of talent. Yet I do not place him on a par with those who combine those minor excellencies with originality and philosophic unity of thought. He is not a Shakespeare, but he is the greatest poet of the day; and this is more remarkable, as he is par excellence a didactic poet.

I have paid him the most flattering tribute in saying that there is not a line of his which has not been quoted and requoted. Men have found such a response in their lightest as well as their deepest feelings, such beautiful morality with such lucid philosophy, that every thinking mind has consciously or unconsciously appropriated something from Wordsworth. Those who have never read his poems have imbibed some part of their spirit from the public or private discourse of his happy pupils; and it is as yet impossible to estimate duly the effect which the balm of his meditations has had in allaying the fever of the public heart, as exhibited in the writings of Byron and Shelley.

—MARGARET FULLER, "Modern British Poets,"
Papers on Literature and Art, 1846

LEIGH HUNT (1848)

Leigh Hunt complains that Wordsworth's poetry lacks musicality, here understood as lyricism, and he finds the poet greatly diminished in his estimation, a poet who has become less the man Hunt took him to be when he defended Wordsworth against his critics.

⁂

Wordsworth, I am told, does not care for music! And it is very likely, for music (to judge from his verses) does not seem to care for him. I was astonished the other day, on looking in his works for the first time after a long interval, to find how deficient he was in all that may be called the musical side of a poet's nature,—the genial, the animal-spirited or bird-like,—the happily accordant. Indeed he does not appear to me, now, more than half the man I once took him for, when I was among those who came to the "rescue" for him, and exaggerated his works in the heat of "reaction."

—LEIGH HUNT, letter to "J. F.," July 8, 1848

MATTHEW ARNOLD "MEMORIAL VERSES" (1850)

In a tribute to Wordsworth, Matthew Arnold's poem "Memorial Verses" pays homage to Wordsworth's healing powers, declaring him a poet of consolation who was able to tug at the heartstrings. Though others counsel courage for this "iron age," Arnold wonders whether there will be another like Wordsworth.

⁂

Goethe in Weimar sleeps, and Greece,
Long since, saw Byron's struggle cease.
But one such death remained to come;
The last poetic voice is dumb—
We stand to-day by Wordsworth's tomb.
When Byron's eyes were shut in death,
We bowed our head and held our breath.
He taught us little; but our soul
Had felt him like the thunder's roll.
With shivering heart the strife we saw
Of passion with eternal law;
And yet with reverential awe
We watched the fount of fiery life
Which served for that Titanic strife.
    When Goethe's death was told, we said:
Sunk, then, is Europe's sagest head.
Physician of the iron age,
Goethe has done his pilgrimage.

He took the suffering human race,
He read each wound, each weakness clear;
And struck his finger on the place,
And said: Thou ailest here,
and here! He looked on Europe's dying hour
Of fitful dream and feverish power;
His eye plunged down the weltering strife,
The turmoil of expiring life—
He said: The end is everywhere,
Art still has truth, take refuge there!
And he was happy, if to know
Causes of things, and far below
His feet to see the lurid flow
Of terror, and insane distress,
And headlong fate, be happiness.
And Wordsworth!—Ah, pale ghosts, rejoice!
For never has such soothing voice
Been to your shadowy world conveyed,
Since erst, at morn, some wandering shade
Heard the clear song of Orpheus come
Through Hades, and the mournful gloom.
Wordsworth has gone from us—and ye,
Ah, may ye feel his voice as we!
He too upon a wintry clime
Had fallen—on this iron time
Of doubts, disputes, distractions, fears.
He found us when the age had bound
Our souls in its benumbing round;
He spoke, and loosed our heart in tears.
He laid us as we lay at birth
On the cool flowery lap of earth,
Smiles broke from us and we had ease;
The hills were round us, and the breeze
Went o'er the sun-lit fields again;
Our foreheads felt the wind and rain.
Our youth returned; for there was shed
On spirits that had long been dead,
Spirits dried up and closely furled,
The freshness of the early world.
Ah! since dark days still bring to light

Man's prudence and man's fiery might,
Time may restore us in his course
Goethe's sage mind and Byron's force;
But where will Europe's latter hour
Again find Wordsworth's healing power?
Others will teach us how to dare,
And against fear our breast to steel;
Others will strengthen us to bear—
But who, ah! who, will make us feel?
The cloud of mortal destiny,
Others will front it fearlessly—
But who, like him, will put it by?
Keep fresh the grass upon his grave,
O Rotha, with thy living wave!
Sing him thy best! for few or none
Hears thy voice right, now he is gone.

—MATTHEW ARNOLD, "Memorial Verses," 1850

GEORGE MEREDITH "THE POETRY OF WORDSWORTH" (1851)

Like Matthew Arnold before him, George Meredith hails Wordsworth as the sublime poet of the natural order.

A breath of the mountains, fresh born in the regions majestic,
That look with their eye-daring summits deep into the sky. The voice of
great Nature; sublime with her lofty conceptions,
Yet earnest and simple as any sweet child of the green lowly vale.

—GEORGE MEREDITH,
"The Poetry of Wordsworth," 1851

JOHN STUART MILL (1873)

John Stuart Mill speaks of Wordsworth's "miscellaneous poems" (in the two-volume 1815 edition) as poetry containing palliative properties that dispel or diminish his depression, citing the poems' soothing subject matter of natural and rural objects but especially their expression of feelings and thoughts induced by a landscape. Ultimately, Mill praises the poems' intrinsic humanity and commitment to renovating the social condition of man. With respect to the *Ode: Intimations of Immortality*, Mill identifies with Wordsworth's expression of his own youth but, most importantly, sees Wordsworth as having shown Mill the way to find consolation for his lost youth. "Compared with the greatest poets," Mill concedes, "he may be said to be the poet of unpoetical natures, possessed of quiet and contemplative tastes. But unpoetical natures are precisely those which require poetic cultivation." In this assessment, he is in agreement with Margaret Fuller.

—◦/\/\/◦— —◦/\/\/◦— —◦/\/\/◦—

I took up the collection of his poems from curiosity, with no expectation of mental relief from it, though I had before resorted to poetry with that hope. In the worst period of my depression, I had read through the whole of Byron (then new to me), to try whether a poet, whose peculiar department was supposed to be that of the intenser feelings, could rouse any feeling in me. As might be expected, I got no good from this reading, but the reverse. The poet's state of mind was too like my own. His was the lament of a man who had worn out all pleasures, and who seemed to think that life, to all who possess the good things of it, must necessarily be the vapid, uninteresting thing which I found it. His Harold and Manfred had the same burthen on them which I had; and I was not in a frame of mind to derive any comfort from the vehement sensual passion of his Giaours, or the sullenness of his Laras. But while Byron was exactly what did not suit my condition, Wordsworth was exactly what did. I had looked into the Excursion two or three years before, and found little in it; and I should probably have found as little, had I read it at this time. But the miscellaneous poems, in the two-volume edition of 1815 (to which little of value was added in the latter part of the author's life), proved to be the precise thing for my mental wants at that particular juncture.

In the first place, these poems addressed themselves powerfully to one of the strongest of my pleasurable susceptibilities, the love of rural objects and natural scenery; to which I had been indebted not only for much of the pleasure of my life, but quite recently for relief from one of my longest relapses into depression. In this power of rural beauty over me, there was a foundation laid for taking pleasure in Wordsworth's poetry; the more so, as his scenery lies mostly among mountains, which, owing to my early Pyrenean excursion, were my ideal of natural beauty. But Wordsworth would never have had any great effect on me, if he had merely placed before me beautiful pictures of natural scenery. Scott does this still better than Wordsworth, and a very second-rate landscape does it more effectually than any poet. What made Wordsworth's poems a medicine for my state of mind, was that they expressed, not mere outward beauty, but states of feeling, and of thought coloured by feeling, under the excitement of beauty. They seemed to be the very culture of the feelings, which I was in quest of. In them I seemed to draw from a source of inward joy, of sympathetic and imaginative pleasure, which could be shared in by all human beings; which had no connexion with struggle or imperfection, but would be made richer by every improvement in the physical or social condition of mankind. From them I seemed to learn what would be the perennial sources of happiness, when all the greater evils of life shall have been removed. And I felt myself at once better and happier as I came under their influence. There have certainly been, even in our own age, greater poets than Wordsworth; but poetry of deeper and loftier feeling could not have done for me at that time what his did. I needed to be made to feel that there was real, permanent happiness in tranquil contemplation. Wordsworth taught me this, not only without turning away from, but with a greatly increased interest in the common feelings and common destiny of human beings. And the delight which these poems gave me, proved that with culture of this sort, there was nothing to dread from the most confirmed habit of analysis. At the conclusion of the Poems came the famous Ode, falsely called Platonic, "Intimations of Immortality": in which, along with more than his usual sweetness of melody and rhythm, and along with the two passages of grand imagery but bad philosophy so often quoted, I found that he too had had similar experience to mine; that he also had felt that the first freshness of youthful enjoyment of life was not lasting; but that he had sought for compensation, and found it, in the way in which he now was teaching me to find it. The result was that I gradually, but completely, emerged from my habitual depression, and was never again subject to it. I long continued to value Wordsworth less according to his intrinsic merits, than by the measure of what he had done for me. Compared with the greatest poets, he may be said to be the poet of unpoetical natures, possessed of quiet and contemplative tastes. But unpoetical natures are precisely those which require poetic cultivation. This cultivation Wordsworth is much more fitted to give, than poets who are intrinsically far more poets than he.

—JOHN STUART MILL,
Autobiography, 1873, chapter 5

HARRIET MARTINEAU (1877)

In the following excerpt from her *Autobiography*, Harriet Martineau speaks of her youth, when she remembers holding Wordsworth in reverence, idolizing him as a poet important to her at that time of her life. However, Martineau maintains that Wordsworth's luster has since faded and that she is now disappointed and can no longer find his inspiration or hear the sounds of nature. She now questions why he is considered a philosophical poet when he is so self-absorbed. Admitting that some of his poems are eloquent and beautiful, at times examples of metaphysical meditations, and that they signal a break from the tradition of flamboyant rhetoric, Martineau declares that Wordsworth's brilliance pales in comparison to Shelley, Tennyson, and Keats, as well as the most shining representatives of classic English poetry. Martineau believes that the earlier praise heaped on Wordsworth for the benefits he bestowed have now settled to a lesser and more appropriate degree of appreciation.

There had been a period of a few years, in my youth, when I worshipped Wordsworth. I pinned up his likeness in my room; and I could repeat his poetry by the hour. He had been of great service to me at a very important time of my life. By degrees, and especially for ten or twelve years before I saw him, I found more disappointment than pleasure when I turned again to his works,—feeling at once the absence of sound, accurate, weighty thought, and of genuine poetic inspiration. It is still an increasing wonder with me that he should ever have been considered a philosophical poet,—so remarkably as the very basis of philosophy is absent in him, and so thoroughly self-derived, self-conscious and subjective is what he himself mistook for philosophy. As to his poetic genius, it needs but to open Shelley, Tennyson, or even poor Keats, and any of our best classic English poets, to feel at once that, with all their truth and all their charm, few of Wordsworth's pieces are poems. As eloquence, some of them are very beautiful; and others are didactic or metaphysical meditations or speculations poetically rendered: but, to my mind, this is not enough to constitute a man a poet. A benefactor, to poetry and to society, Wordsworth undoubtedly was. He brought us back out of a wrong track into a right one;—out of a fashion of pedantry, antithesis and bombast, in which thought was sacrificed to sound, and common sense was degraded, where it existed, by being made to pass for something else. He taught us to say what we had to say in a way,—not only the more rational but the more beautiful; and, as we have grown more simple in expression, we have become more unsophisticated and clear-seeing and far-seeing in our observation of the scene of life, if not of life itself. These are vast services to have rendered, if no more can be claimed for the poet. In proportion to our need was the early unpopularity of the reform proposed; and in proportion to our gratitude, when we recognized our benefactor, was the temporary exaggeration of his merits as a poet. His fame seems to have now settled in its proper level.

—HARRIET MARTINEAU, *Autobiography,*
ed. Maria Weston Chapman, 1877,
vol. 1, pp. 507–508

Matthew Arnold "Preface" (1879)

In his preface to *The Poems of Wordsworth*, Matthew Arnold declares that Wordsworth's longer works, *The Excursion* and *The Prelude*, do not measure up to the worth and value of his shorter poems. Furthermore, even among the seven volumes of his poems, Arnold notes that not all of them are deserving of praise, for a series of short poems, unlike longer works such as epics, requires consistency of inspiration; one bad poem has the potential of sullying or compromising the effect of the whole. However, Arnold assigns great virtue to Wordsworth's "ampler body of powerful work" in which the poet's superiority is made evident.

The Excursion and the Prelude, his poems of greatest bulk, are by no means Wordsworth's best work. His best work is in his shorter pieces, and many indeed are there of these which are of first-rate excellence. But in his seven volumes the pieces of high merit are mingled with a mass of pieces very inferior to them; so inferior to them that it seems wonderful how the same poet should have produced both. Shakespeare frequently has lines and passages in a strain quite false, and which are entirely unworthy of him. But one can imagine his smiling if one could meet him in the Elysian Fields and tell him so; smiling and replying that he knew it perfectly well himself, and what did it matter? But with Wordsworth the case is different. Work altogether inferior, work quite uninspired, flat and dull, is produced by him with evident unconsciousness of its defects, and he presents it to us with the same faith and seriousness as his best work. Now a drama or an epic fill the mind, and one does not look beyond them; but in a collection of short pieces the impression made by one piece requires to be continued and sustained by the piece following. In reading Wordsworth the impression made by one of his fine pieces is too often dulled and spoiled by a very inferior piece coming after it.

Wordsworth composed verses during a space of some sixty years; and it is no exaggeration to say that within one single decade of those years, between 1798 and 1808, almost all his really first-rate work was produced. A mass of inferior work remains, work done before and after this golden prime, imbedding the first-rate work and clogging it, obstructing our approach to it, chilling, not unfrequently, the high-wrought mood with which we leave it. To be recognised far and wide as a great poet, to be possible and receivable as a classic, Wordsworth needs to be relieved of a great deal of the poetical baggage which now encumbers him. To administer this relief is indispensable, unless he is to continue to be a poet for the few only,—a poet valued far below his real worth by the world.

There is another thing. Wordsworth classified his poems not according to any commonly received plan of arrangement, but according to a scheme of mental physiology. He has poems of the fancy, poems of the imagination, poems of sentiment and reflection, and so on. His categories are ingenious but farfetched, and the result of his employment of them is unsatisfactory. Poems are separated one from another which possess a kinship of subject or of treatment far more vital and deep than the supposed unity of mental origin which was Wordsworth's reason for joining them with others.

The tact of the Greeks in matters of this kind was infallible. We may rely upon it that we shall not improve upon the classification adopted by the Greeks for kinds of poetry; that their categories of epic, dramatic, lyric, and so forth, have a natural propriety, and should be adhered to. It may sometimes seem doubtful to which of two categories a poem belongs; whether this or that poem is to be called, for instance, narrative or lyric, lyric or elegiac. But there is to be found in every good poem a strain, a predominant note, which determines the poem as belonging to one of these kinds rather than the other; and here is the best proof of value of the classification, and of the advantage of adhering to it. Wordsworth's poems will never produce their due effect until they are freed from their present artificial arrangement, and grouped more naturally.

Disengaged from the quantity of inferior work which now obscures them, the best poems of Wordsworth, I hear many people say, would indeed stand out in great beauty, but they would prove to be very few in number, scarcely more than half a dozen. I maintain, on the other hand, that what strikes me with admiration, what establishes in my opinion Wordsworth's superiority, is the great and ample body of powerful work which remains to him, even after all his inferior work has been cleared away. He gives us so much to rest upon, so much which communicates his spirit and engages ours!

This is of very great importance. If it were a comparison of single pieces, or of three or four pieces, by each poet, I do not say that Wordsworth would stand decisively above Gray, or Burns, or Coleridge, or Keats, or Manzoni, or Heine. It is in his ampler body of powerful work that I find his superiority. His good work itself, his work which counts, is not all of it, of course, of equal value. Some kinds of poetry are in themselves lower kinds than others. The ballad kind is a lower kind; the didactic kind, still more, is a lower kind. Poetry of this latter sort counts, too, sometimes, by its biographical interest partly, not by its poetical interest pure and simple; but then this can only be when the poet producing it has the power and importance of Wordsworth, a power and importance which he assuredly did not establish by such didactic poetry alone. Altogether, it is, I say, by the great body of powerful and

significant work which remains to him, after every reduction and deduction
has been made, that Wordsworth's superiority is proved.

—MATTHEW ARNOLD, "Preface" to
The Poems of Wordsworth, 1879

EDMOND SCHERER "WORDSWORTH AND MODERN POETRY IN ENGLAND" (1882)

Edmond Scherer was a French theologian, critic, and politician who held
a great interest in English literature. Here, Scherer writes an unflattering
review, expounding on Wordsworth's faults and failings. Scherer finds that
Wordsworth, who embraced solitude, consequently lacks knowledge of
the real world, having chosen to remove himself from society. As a result,
he maintains that Wordsworth's poetry lacks "the sublime melancholy . . .
the audacious revolt in which the poetry of half a century ago delighted."
Scherer detects a decided lack of passion when comparing Wordsworth's
writing to the works of Byron, Heine, or Goethe.

I shall point out at once what is wanting and what is faulty in Wordsworth,
the qualities which he lacks, and the imperfections which disfigure his poetry.
Let us begin with the qualities lacking. No one acknowledges more fully than
I do the injustice, not to say the absurdity, of asking a man for something else
than he has chosen to give, or, worse still, reproaching him with not being
somebody else, and not what nature has made him. Therefore, it is not as a
reproach, nor even as a regret, that I examine what is wanting in Wordsworth;
it is merely to characterize his genius better, to set his poetical physiognomy
in stronger relief.

To great troubles of mind he was a stranger, and his nearest approaches
to tender sentiment are the pieces to the memory of that Lucy whom he
has himself described. As for political emotions, he had, like many others,
hailed in the French Revolution the dawn of a new era for humanity. His
sonnets bear witness to his wrath against the conqueror who dispelled his
dreams, who put an end to the Venetian Republic and the independence of
Switzerland, and who menaced England with invasion. There is nothing in all
this which goes beyond respectable Liberalism and patriotism.

Let us then make up our minds not to expect from Wordsworth either
that knowledge of the human heart which is given by life in the world, or that
inner and dramatic working of passion which no man describes well unless
he has been its victim, or those general views on history and society which are

formed partly by study, partly by experience in public affairs. Our poet was as much a stranger to the harassings of thought as to those of ambition, to the pangs of love and of hatred as to the resignation at which men arrive when they have seen how small are the great things of this world. He has nothing of the sublime melancholy, the ardent inquiry, the audacious revolt in which the poetry of half a century ago delighted. Still less has he the mocking scepticism, the raillery now gay now bitter, which followed the "songs of despair." He will never rank with those who like Byron, disturb the soul; who like Heine, arm it with irony; or who like Goethe, calm it with the virtues of knowledge. Wordsworth is simply a hermit who has studied nature much, and has constantly analyzed his own feelings. We could hardly call him a philosopher; his mind is too devoid of the element of reasoning and speculation. Even the name of thinker but half suits him: he is the contemplative man.

—EDMOND SCHERER, "Wordsworth and
Modern Poetry in England,"
1882, *Essays on English Literature,*
tr. George Saintsbury, 1891, pp. 199–201

AUBREY DE VERE "REMARKS ON THE PERSONAL CHARACTER OF WORDSWORTH'S POETRY" (1883)

Aubrey De Vere, an Irish poet and critic, writes in defense of Wordsworth, stating that in all but a few of his lesser poems both the "Affections" or "Fancy" are combined with the loftier faculty of the imagination. Thus, rather than the simplicity of vision that some critics have seen as a fault, De Vere maintains that for Wordsworth the heart and the intellect are successfully united in a spiritual alliance, indeed more so than in other contemporary poets.

It is easier to feel the strong personality of Wordsworth's poetry than to define critically in what it consists. I have suggested an approximate answer to this question, viz. that it consists—1st, in the unusually large number of qualities, intellectual and moral—qualities often not only remote from each other, but apparently opposed to each other—which are represented by his higher poetry; 2dly, in the absolute unity in which these various qualities are blended; and, 3dly, in the masterful moral strength which results from their united expression. This measureless strength was so deeply felt by Coleridge that in his Friend he describes Wordsworth's poetry as 'non verba sed tonitrua,' and elsewhere spoke of him as 'the Giant;' while admirers of a very different sort were but beginning to babble about the 'sweet simplicity' of his verse. Wordsworth did a signal injustice to his own poems when he classified them as poems of the 'Affections,' of the 'Fancy,' of the 'Imagination,' of 'Sentiment and Reflection.' There exist no poems which could less equitably be subjected to a classification so arbitrary. It but points to a partial truth, while it conceals one of primary importance. All of these faculties are doubtless found, though with diversities of proportion, in Wordsworth's poems; but they are commonly found in union, and they are found marshalled under the control of the highest poetic faculty, viz. the Imagination. *The Brothers,* 'A Farewell,' 'She dwelt among the untrodden ways,' 'Ruth,' nay, even 'Laodamia,' were classed among the 'Poems of the Affections;' but there was no reason why they should not have been equally classed among those of the 'Imagination,' to which, in his later editions, many poems were transferred. On the other hand, 'She was a phantom of delight,' 'Three years she grew in sun and shower,' 'A slumber did my spirit seal,' and 'Tintern Abbey,' were placed under the title, 'Poems of the Imagination:' but they might with equal justice have been referred to the category of the 'Affections;' while the 'Lines left upon a Seat in a Yew-Tree,' 'The Happy Warrior,' 'A Poet's Epitaph,' 'I heard a thousand blended notes,' and the 'Ode to Duty,' might as fitly have been classed with the poems of the 'Imagination' as with those of 'Sentiment and Reflection.' It is but in a few of Wordsworth's inferior poems, such as might have been written by his imitators, that the higher faculties and impulses are found in separation. In his best poetry the diverse elements of the human intellect and of the human heart are found, not only in a greater variety, but in a closer and more spiritual union, than in any other poetry of his time; and, from that union, rose the extraordinary largeness of character which belonged to it. That characteristic was felt by the discerning, even in his earlier day, when other poets were travelling over the world in search of sensational incidents or picturesque costume, while he seldom sought a theme except among the primary relations of humanity, and those influences of exterior nature by which human nature is moulded.

—Aubrey De Vere, "Remarks on the
Personal Character of Wordsworth's Poetry,"
1883, *Wordsworthiana,* ed. William Knight,
1889, pp. 148–150

William Watson
"Wordsworth's Grave" (1890)

William Watson's "Wordsworth's Grave" is an aptly titled tribute to Wordsworth's memory. Watson compares him to the other major romantic writers and hails him the poet of a rapturous peace that emanates from his love of nature.

———

Poet who sleepest by this wandering wave!

When thou wast born, what birth-gift hadst thou then? To thee what wealth
    was that the Immortals gave,

The wealth thou gavest in thy turn to men? Not Milton's keen, translunar
    music thine;

Not Shakespeare's cloudless, boundless human view; Not Shelley's flush of
    rose on peaks divine;

Nor yet the wizard twilight Coleridge knew. What hadst thou that could
    make so large amends

For all thou hadst not and thy peers possessed, Motion and fire, swift means
    to radiant ends?—

Thou hadst, for weary feet, the gift of rest. From Shelley's dazzling glow or
    thunderous haze,

From Byron's tempest-anger, tempest-mirth, Men turned to thee and
    found—not blast and blaze,

Tumult of tottering heavens, but peace on earth. Nor peace that grows by
    Lethe, scentless flower,

There in white languors to decline and cease; But peace whose names are
    also rapture, power,

Clear sight, and love: for these are parts of peace.

—WILLIAM WATSON, "Wordsworth's Grave," 1890

EDWARD DOWDEN (1897)

Citing some of the crucial facts of Wordsworth's earlier life, when he was a moody boy, and his early manhood, when he was an ardent supporter of the French Revolution, Edward Dowden wants to correct a serious misapprehension, namely that many readers assume Wordsworth was always a poet of tranquillity and perfect peace. As Dowden points out, Wordsworth was indeed involved in and very "near the vortex of the maelstrom," an experience that made a lasting impression on the poet. Dowden maintains that these intense passions remained resident in Wordsworth and ever present in his poetry, the poet finding a harmonious balance between the disparate faculties of the intellect and the emotions.

———

No one among his contemporaries was more deeply moved than was Wordsworth by the great events in France. The character of his mind fitted him in a peculiar degree for receiving the full influence of the French Revolution; the circumstances of his early life brought him near the vortex of the maelstrom; and that truth to his highest self, which it was a part of his very existence to retain,—that natural piety which bound his days each to each,—made it impossible that he should ever fling away from him as a worthless illusion the hopes and aspirations of his youth. Some readers of Wordsworth are misled in their judgment of the poet by the vulgar error that he was before all else tranquil, mild, gentle, an amiable pastoral spirit. He sang of the daisy and the celandine, the linnet and the lamb; and therefore he must have been always a serene, tender, benign contemplator of things that make for peace. There can be no greater mistake; at the heart of his peace was passion; his benignity was like the greensward upon a rocky hillside. As a boy, Wordsworth was violent and moody; in his early manhood he was stern, bold, worn by exhausting ardors. De Quincey observed that "the secret fire of a temperament too fervid" caused him to look older than his years. Above all, he was strong; and what disguises this fact from careless eyes is that Wordsworth's strength did not lie in a single part or province of his nature, that he brought his several powers into harmonious action, and that each power served to balance the others. Senses, intellect, emotions, imagination, conscience, will, were all of unusual vigor; but each helped the other, each controlled the other, each was to the other an impulse and a law. And thus an equilibrium was gained, resulting from a massive harmony of powers too commonly found among men of genius arrayed against one another in dangerous conflict. His senses were of unusual keenness; his eye lived on forms and colors, on light and shadow; his ear caught the finest differences of all homeless, wandering sounds; but the senses did not war against the spirit; they were auxiliar to higher powers, serving as scouts and intelligencers of the soul. His passions were of ample volume and of persistent force; indignation, wrath, stern joy, deep fears, boundless hopes, possessed him; but these were brought into the bondage of conscience, and became the ministers of love. His imaginative fervor again and again exhausted his physical strength; but the creative mood was balanced by a mood of wise passiveness; it was not the way with his imagination to start forth, as Shelley's imagination did, to create a world of its own upon some swift suggestion of beauty or delight; it rested on reality, brooded upon reality, coalesced with it, interpreted it. His visions and his desires were captured by his intellect, and were made substantial by a moral wisdom infused into them. His intellect did not operate singly and apart, but was vitalized by his passions. If he loved freedom with all the ardor of his soul, he loved order as well. If he hoped for the future with an indefatigable hope, he also reverenced the past. His will applied itself consciously and deliberately to the task of organizing his various faculties and supporting them in their allotted task during all the years of his self-dedication to the life poetic. Each power of his nature lived in and through every other power, and in the massive equilibrium which was the result, strength was masked by strength. And thus, having first effected an inward conciliation of the jarring elements of our humanity, he was enabled to become a reconciler for his age.

—EDWARD DOWDEN, *The French Revolution and English Literature*, 1897, pp. 197–200

DAVID WATSON RANNIE
"FELLOW-WORKERS IN ROMANTICISM" (1907)

David Watson Rannie discusses Wordsworth's relationship to and within the context of the second-generation romantic poets, all of whom celebrated the beauty of nature and championed the freedom of mankind. Rannie finds an affinity between Byron, the most antithetical of the group, and Wordsworth, as landscape poets whose invention of "a poetry of travel" is akin to Wordsworth's creation of a new pastoralism that broke with Renaissance and neoclassical conventions. Likewise, Rannie points out that Wordsworth and Shelley share deep affinities in regard to their individual conceptualizations of the spiritual and their belief in the essential unity of all things.

The question as to Wordsworth's affinities with contemporary poets who have become immortal, is not to be solved by collecting his opinions of them, or theirs of him. Wordsworth's own criticism was never enthusiastic, and often, when he was dealing with individuals, it was ill-informed, prejudiced, and conventional. Moreover, great as was his achievement in poetic reform, splendidly as he showed how imagination at its highest deals with poetic material, he was often imperfectly aware of the whereabouts of his own successes; and his theory of imagination, which he was eager to put in logical form, is, when one tries to grasp it, a mere vanishing cloud. There was a strong tendency, even among those who were hardly "Lakists," to accept the Lakist theory and to cut Wordsworth, or Wordsworth and Coleridge, off from the poetic movement of their age. (Compare C. Lamb's attitude to Byron, and the all but ignoring of Shelley and Keats.)

The other side of the account, no doubt, is more satisfactory. What Wordsworth said or wrote of the poetry of Coleridge, or Scott, or Keats, or Shelley, or Byron, might be blotted out with hardly a grain of appreciable loss. On the other hand, if we forget Byron's vulgar scorn, there is sufficient evidence that the poets we have named, although not Wordsworth's partisans, gave him the kind of consideration and veneration, the kind of admiring homage which the world now gives him without dissent. Yet, even so, their criticism was contemporary; and its historical interest is not equalled by its absolute value. Their consciousness, however, that Wordsworth, with whatever differences, was in poetry a fellow-worker, makes a better starting-point than Wordsworth's own self-consciousness, or the partisanship which flattered it. We can see what Wordsworth himself failed to see, that the other great poets of the Romantic Revival were in Wordsworth's circle: we only want to assure ourselves as to their claims and qualifications to stand there.

The Romantic Revival as a whole may be treated from many points of view. Perhaps one of the most practically useful approaches to it is made by considering its relation to Elizabethanism on the one hand, and to the dominant genius of the eighteenth century on the other. For, if we exclude Chaucer, as being outside our immediate question, and if we make the Elizabethan age and the eighteenth century large enough to include all the epoch-making English poetry between the *Shepheard's Calendar* and *Lyrical Ballads*, we shall prepare ourselves to realize what was done, and done in concert, for English poetry between 1798 and 1825. The change from where poetry stood under Dryden and Pope to where it stood under, say, Wordsworth and Shelley, is so startling that it cannot be ignored, and cannot easily be misunderstood. Had Dryden been what Chaucer has been called, the "father of English poetry," one might say with some plausibility that such poetry as he founded was hardly poetry at all, and that it was left for the poets of the Romantic Revival to distinguish the true from the nominal, the real from the official. With the poetry of Dryden and Pope, even with the poetry of Gray, the poetry of the first quarter of the nineteenth century has the slenderest affinities. Milton stands in a class by himself. Touching Dryden on the one hand, and easily reaching back into the Elizabethan age on the other, he has but slender relationship to either. Essentially, what the Elizabethans did for English poetry was to make it human, and to make it the vehicle of beauty. And they did it by inventing and perfecting the drama on the one hand, and the lyrical strain on the other. Spenser's great allegory is, like *Paradise Lost*, to some extent solitary: it is a poem of many aspects, partly didactic, partly Protestant, partly courtly, partly conventional-chivalric. It is the constant beauty and unfailingly sweet phraseology of the *Faerie Queene* which secure its immortality. Much more typical is the *Epithalamium*, with its whole-hearted exposition of love, its gorgeous imagery, its incomparable lyrical rapture. Here, and in Shakespeare, we have the best that Elizabeth's age could do for poetry.

It was much indeed; and yet it left much to be done, much towards which the eighteenth century accomplished nothing. Poetry was not yet "meditative"; it was not yet introspective; it was hardly yet ideal or universal. The glory of Elizabethanism was its actuality, its satisfaction with its own surroundings, its own successful, strong-pulsed life. England, the Queen, Protestantism, El Dorado—these were universals and ideals enough; and if at any point they failed, there was the past to supplement them, the past of Greece, the past of Rome. With such a world to be realized, to be held, by such intelligence, there was no room for philosophy, no temptation to sentimentalism: here was no place for bitter indignation; for eager longing, for scornful satire; no call to be over-stimulated by cosmopolitan ideals, or to reconstruct ultimate conceptions of God and man. Action and passion, the glory of the established order, so new and yet so strong; the romance of discovery, added to the immortal romance of love; were these things not the stuff of centuries of poetry?

But things move quickly; and the Elizabethan freshness died away. Puritanism came, suggesting a new synthesis of things; poetry, in spite of Milton, was forced into opposition; it became the minister of intelligence rather than of feeling, of criticism rather than of enjoyment; it lost its hold on beauty. Too much was sacrificed to form; too little play was allowed to individuality. Then, at last, individuality turned scornfully round on tradition. The world seemed cumbered with outworn tyrannies; and, except where there was revolution, the imagination took refuge in ideals, ideals of the past, ideals of the future. The sense of the beautiful reawoke, and insisted on expressing itself anew. Nature, which the Elizabethan had cared for after his fashion as a haunt of fairies or a background for human life, came to be loved for its own sake and for its infinite spiritual significance, as well as its infinite beauty and charm. Foreign landscape began to make appeal to the most insular of English patriots. Individual feeling, even the "pageant of bleeding hearts," was precious now as poetry. The relations of God and the world called out for poetic restatement.

In all these things we recognize the work of the Romantic Revival as a whole. How is the responsibility for it to be distributed?

Take the two most apparently antithetic of all the great poets of the age—Wordsworth and Byron. Nothing would have surprised and shocked Wordsworth more than to have been regarded as in any sense a co-operator with Byron. "Power," power prostituted for the most part to the basest uses, was all that that pure and stern mind would have allowed to the poet of *Childe Harold* and *Don Juan*. And we know that Byron, in his estimate of Wordsworth, never got much beyond contempt superinduced upon conventionalism. Yet how does the matter stand? Byron had Popian sympathies and did Popian work; yet Byron was as much an innovator on the poetic tradition as Wordsworth. His satire may be his best work; but *Childe Harold* lives and will live; the charm of the oriental tales will never wholly disappear; and Byron, after his fashion, was a lyrist, and not a wholly insincere one. His ways, indeed, lay far apart from Wordsworth's; yet, in one respect at least, he did Wordsworth's work. If Mrs. Radcliffe can be credited, as assuredly she can, with having rediscovered the beauty of Nature, so still more can Byron. If Wordsworth sang the praise of mountains and lakes in England, so, and with an equal enthusiasm, did Byron of mountains and lakes in Switzerland and Greece. Byron's sunset at Venice is as carefully observed, and treated with as much sense of the beautiful, as Wordsworth's green linnet or daisy. Moreover, no English poet before Byron would or could have written such a passage. It is as much a "romantic revival" as *The Ancient Mariner*; nay, it is not a revival, it is an origination.

Because Byron was a sentimentalist, a rhetorician, an egotist it is the shallowest criticism to deny him true and wonderful poetic inspiration. And though he was much of a *poseur*, a good deal of his poetry represented as genuine a return to Nature as Wordsworth's. His appropriation of European landscape for poetry, his invention of a poetry of travel, was an achievement closely akin to Wordsworth's invention of a new pastoralism. Both achievements were wholly free from imitativeness; in both there was a return to the *facts* of Nature from the ideal landscape of Spenser and Milton; both record impressions absolutely at first hand. Wordsworth maintained that Byron, when his poetry was nearest being good, plagiarized from him; and it is much the fashion to find Wordsworthian influence in the third and fourth cantos of *Childe Harold*. We may decline to take up the question of the plagiarism. As for influence, it is evident that the purest originality has parentage and ancestry; and that influence does not necessarily turn first-hand into second-hand work.

Another point of kinship between the two dissimilar poets is their common passion for liberty. Here there is essential unity with superficial diversity. Byron was nearly a generation younger than Wordsworth; and while the elderly senior poet was reposing in the Conservative atmosphere of Lord Liverpool's *régime*, the young Byron was plunging and kicking in the somewhat aimless energies of the new Radicalism. But these things do not count. In the politics of their poetry both men were pledged—so to put it—to tyrannicide, to the cause of nations against their oppressors. As Wordsworth's heart leaped for Switzerland and Venice and Spain, so did Byron's for Greece. And, long before the age at which Wordsworth became a timid Conservative, Byron, in a fantasy of self-devotion, had given his life for the kind of liberty which Wordsworth had most at heart.

Once more, if Byron is sometimes wearisome with his guidebook-like snippets of reminiscence, his sequences of appropriate poetical reflection, is not Wordsworth sometimes the same? What about *Ecclesiastical Sonnets*; what about those superabundant "Memorials" of tours in Scotland, tours on the Continent? To pause, with one's "foot upon a nation's dust," to "start a ghost at every corner," is of the essence of Romanticism.

Wordsworth and Byron, then, were not wholly antithetic; still less so were Wordsworth and Shelley. Wordsworth, for his part, mostly ignored Shelley, though he knew something of his poetry, and thought him a great *artist*, a master of style. Shelley thought of Wordsworth much as "the lost leader;" but he thought of him, at least early in his life, as an excellent poet. To Wordsworth, Shelley, like Byron, was a moral suspect, a teacher of dangerous doctrines, made all the more seductively dangerous by the fineness of the art by which they were conveyed. In Wordsworth's nature there were recurrent strata of commonplace; and these were often tapped in the course of his critical operations, especially upon contemporaries. One of the most characteristic of these strata was the conviction that poetry ought to be, and is, didactic in the sense in which teaching and preaching are; and the allied conviction, that a man's poetry is the mere transcript of his opinions. It is perhaps impossible to conceive Wordsworth reading through *Prometheus Unbound* with the care which he demanded from readers of *The Excursion*; but it is certain that, if he had done so, he would have regarded it as spreading atheism and rebellion clad in rainbows. If he had read *The Cenci*, he (who was capable of calling Coleridge's *Love* sensual and *Christabel* indelicate) would have said, "See what comes of loose notions about marriage!" As regarded his own poetry, Wordsworth of course transcended this view of things. There would have been a pretty to-do if anybody had called the *Tintern Abbey* lines pantheistic, or had tried to connect them with their author's infrequent church-going in those days. Wordsworth would have replied, and replied quite properly, that, however necessary dogma may be in religion, it is not required at all in poetry; and that, if a poet uses *quasi*-religious phraseology, he does so with at least a philosopher's or scientist's licence. And as to the church-going, he would have said to the critic qua critic, "What business is that of yours?"

The question as to the didactic motive and practical moral effect of any given poetry, and the question whether any supposed taint of life or opinion in a poet communicates itself to his writings, are among the most delicate problems in literary criticism. If Wordsworth failed to see that the problem is solved very differently in the cases of Byron and Shelley, we need not be very hard on him. Nor does it matter if he failed to recognize the essential kinship between his own work and Shelley's. For us who read both poets with inward as well as outward eyes, the kinship is plain enough.

The poets had very similar experiences in the education of feeling, that education which gives a permanent direction to poetic effort. Shelley has not left so much express autobiography as Wordsworth; but he has left enough, direct and indirect, to show how he was led to his view of the poetry of things. If we do not learn as much from *Alastor* and the *Hymn to Intellectual Beauty* as from *The Prelude* and the *Tintern Abbey* lines, we learn enough to convince us that both poets felt much the same need, and supplied it in much the same way. *Alastor*, for all its beauty and characteristic charm, is a dreary and morbid poem, and Wordsworth would doubtless have dismissed it as such, horrified at the suggestion that it had any affinity with himself. The hero of *Alastor* is not even Shelley as he was; he is Shelley as he might have been, as he was just saved from being. Yet Alastor is, *mutatis mutandis*, essentially what Wordsworth was at that stage in the "growth of a poet's mind" before "love of Nature" had begun to "lead to love of man"; before the "still, sad music of humanity" had entered to harmonize with the tones of early rapture. It is very likely that Shelley, who was much under Wordsworth's influence in those days, borrowed from Wordsworth the phrase "natural piety," which occurs in the third line of *Alastor*; and, at any rate, Shelley's hero, at the outset, is a recognizably Wordsworthian figure. Wordsworth, indeed, was never morbid: he never, so far as we know, made his bed "in charnels and on coffins," in the hope of inducing some communicative ghost to make known to him the secret of things. But, on the whole, the analysis of Alastor's early "natural piety" might be that of Wordsworth's—

> "If dewy morn, and odorous noon, and even,
> With sunset and its gorgeous ministers,
> And solemn midnight's tingling silentness;
> If autumn's hollow sighs in the sere wood,
> And winter robing with pure snow and crowns
> Of starry ice the gray grass and bare boughs;
>
> .   .   .   .
>
> If no bright bird, insect, or gentle beast
> I consciously have injured, but still loved
> And cherished these my kindred."

Alastor is a purely abstract figure; the mere shadow of a shade. The
feverish thirst of his egoism drives him into experiences of which there is no
counterpart in Wordsworth's biography or imagination. But, like Paracelsus,
like Aprile, or, for that matter, like Faust, Alastor is the victim of a false view
of the universe, a wilful taking of the part for the whole, the wilful rejection
of the divine obligations of fellowship. His ideal is never realized, because
he will have nothing to do with its appointed realization in the ministries of
social life. And the knowledge of this was a critical lesson of Wordsworth's
education as a poet. Shelley might have taken as the motto of his poem
Wordsworth's verses on Peel Castle—

> "Farewell, farewell the heart that lives alone,
> Housed in a dream, at distance from the Kind!
> Such happiness, wherever it be known,
> Is to be pitied; for 'tis surely blind.

> "But welcome fortitude, and patient cheer,
> And frequent sights of what is to be borne!
> Such sights, or worse, as are before me here,—
> Not without hope we suffer and we mourn."

In the *Hymn to Intellectual Beauty* Shelley speaks of himself without
mystification or disguise. But he first speaks of Beauty in the most universal
conception of it, and on its intellectual rather than its sensuous side,
in language which inevitably reminds us of Wordsworth. For what is
Wordsworth's most general and abstract conception of Beauty?

> "Beauty—a living Presence of the earth,
> Surpassing the most fair ideal Forms
> Which craft of delicate Spirits hath composed
> From earth's materials—waits upon my steps;
> Pitches her tents before me as I move,
> An hourly neighbour; Paradise, and groves
> Elysian, Fortunate Fields—like those of old
> Sought in the Atlantic Main—why should they be
> A history only of departed things,
> Or a mere fiction of what never was?
> For the discerning intellect of Man,
> When wedded to this goodly universe
> In love and holy passion, shall find these
> A simple produce of the common day."

In Shelley's *Hymn* Wordsworth's "cheerful faith is wanting." Beauty is a compensation for the blank and chill negation of things; it is not their efflorescence and fruition. And even Beauty, without which we could not live, has the fugitiveness of the rainbow, not the steadfastness of the day and night.

"Spirit of Beauty, that dost consecrate
With thine own tears all thou dost shine upon
Of human thought or form,—where art thou gone?
Why dost thou pass away and leave our state,
This dim vast vale of tears, vacant and desolate?
Ask why the sunlight not for ever
Weaves rainbows o'er yon mountain river,
Why aught should fail and fade that once is shown,
Why fear and dream and death and birth
Cast on the daylight of this earth
Such gloom—why man has such a scope
For love and hate, despondency and hope?

"No voice from some sublimer world hath ever
To sage or poet these responses given—
Therefore the names of Demon, Ghost, and Heaven
Remain the records of their vain endeavour,
Frail spells—whose uttered charm might not avail to sever,
From all we hear and all we see,
Doubt, chance, and mutability.
Thy light alone—like mist o'er mountains driven,
Or music by the night wind sent
Thro' strings of some still instrument,
Or moonlight on a midnight stream,
Gives grace and truth to life's unquiet dream."

The melancholy, the agnosticism of all this are, of course, quite foreign to Wordsworth; but not so, surely, is the idea which underlies the lines that follow—

"Man were immortal and omnipotent
Didst thou, unknown and awful as thou art,
Keep with thy glorious train, firm state within his heart.
Thou messenger of sympathies
That wax and wane in lovers' eyes—
Thou—that to human thought art nourishment,
Like darkness to a dying flame!"

Shelley's account of the development and purification of his sense of the unseen is very like Wordsworth's.

"While yet a boy," he tells us, "I sought for ghosts" but he neither heard nor saw them. Then suddenly there was revealed to him the more excellent way, and he saw Beauty—

"When musing deeply on the lot
Of life, at the sweet time when winds are wooing
All vital things that wake to bring
News of birds and blossoming—
Sudden, thy shadow fell on me;
I shrieked, and clasped my hands in ecstasy!"

And we remember Wordsworth at Hawkshead, first terrified by the spirituality of Nature, then, in later days—

"Only then
Contented, when with bliss ineffable
I felt the sentiment of Being spread
O'er all that moves and all that seemeth still;

.   .   .   .

O'er all that leaps and runs, and shouts and sings,
Or beats the gladsome air . . .
One song they sang, and it was audible."

The last stanza of Shelley's *Hymn* is closely Wordsworthian, with an echo even of the Wordsworthian phraseology—

"The day becomes more solemn and serene
    When noon is past—there is a harmony
    In autumn, and a lustre in its sky,
Which thro' the summer is not heard or seen,
As if it could not be, as if it had not been!
    Thus let thy power, which like the truth
    Of Nature on my passive youth
    Descended, to my onward life supply
    Its calm—to one who worships thee,
    Whom, Spirit fair, thy spells did bind
    To fear himself, and love all human kind."

We are reminded, not only of the conclusion of Wordsworth's *Immortality* Ode, but of the moral of those very early lines *Left on a Seat in a Yew Tree*, which haunted Charles Lamb after his visit to Nether Stowey—

"True dignity abides with him alone
Who, in the silent hour of inward thought,
Can still suspect, and still revere himself,
In lowliness of heart."

Shelley speaks of his "passive youth;" but that is not the impression left on us by his account of the attitude of young poets towards the secrets of things. Wordsworth might have more fittingly called his youth passive in this sense: he was the healthy, natural boy, whom Nature sought with her revelations,

"More like a man
Flying from something that he dreads, than one
Who sought the thing he loved."

Shelley, on the other hand, pursues Nature with shrill eager insistence; follows her over the world and into every region of thought and feeling; and will have her secret or die. That is the moral of Alastor's feverish quest and untimely end.

But there were deeper affinities between Wordsworth and Shelley than any similarities of poetic training and tendency. They were alike as poets, in realizing, conceiving, the Universe; and realizing it as spiritual and *quasi-personal*. This community brings them closely into line as fellow-workers in the Romanticism of the nineteenth century. They two, indeed, share, and share almost equally, the honour of giving to British literature a truly philosophical poetry, of conceiving for poetry the ideality and unity of the world, with the conviction of the theologian or the constructor of a philosophy. What is Wordsworth at his deepest and loveliest?

"I have felt
A presence that disturbs me with the joy
Of elevated thought; a sense sublime
Of something far more deeply interfused
Whose dwelling is the light of setting suns
And the round ocean and the living air,
And the blue sky, and in the mind of man;
A motion and a spirit that impels
All thinking things, all objects of all thought
And rolls through all things."

These lines may be said to be Wordsworth's text; they are the key to all his poetry. And an almost equal importance belongs to the lines from Shelley's

Adonais, in which the phrases march with something of the finality of the
clauses of a creed—

> "That Light whose smile kindles the Universe,
> That Beauty in which all things work and move.
> That Benediction which the eclipsing Curse
> Of birth can quench not, that sustaining Love
> Which through the web of being blindly wove
> By man and beast and earth and air and sea
> Burns bright or dim, as each are mirrors of
> The fire for which all thirst; now beams on me."

Every reader of both poets must recognize how representative both
those passages are; how the conviction of all things as combined in, and
informed by, a unity, to which it is not mere fancy to attribute thought and
love, explained, for Shelley and Wordsworth alike, both the beauty of Nature
and the destiny of Man. Wordsworth read the riddle as a realist, Shelley as
an idealist; but both were engaged on the same riddle, both found the same
solution. Wordsworth attained his universal through the humble folk and
temperate beauties among which he lived; Shelley through courageous and
boundless idealization, a new mythology, almost new heavens and a new
earth. But both (religion and theology apart) were, without knowing it,
worshippers in the same temple, heralds of the same hope.

Also they were alike in their essential devotion to human interests in
their poetry. It needs no exhaustive knowledge of Wordsworth to prove
that mountains and lakes, cuckoos and daisies, were not his real themes,
but Man, and his "unconquerable mind"; Man, Nature's child and spoiler;
whom Nature can punish or heal, but never rob of his lordship. Wordsworth
went to school to Socialism and Revolution; and what he learned in France
determined his bent towards the poetry of fellowship for ever, made certain
his farewell to "the heart that lives alone." Nature was but the second person
of the trinity on which he mused in his solitude; the other two persons were
Man and Human Life. Let us not be deceived as to Wordsworth's humanity
by his comparative indifference to the interest of sex, and by the hodden gray
and slow rustic movements of so many of his characters. No one needs to be
reminded of the *Sonnets Dedicated to National Independence and Liberty*, and
the passion with which they throb. But one might be tranced into ignoring
the depths of tragedy and pathos, and of every kind of human interest hidden
in so many homely-sounding little poems, in *Lucy Gray*, in the *Matthew*
group, in *Michael*, in *The Excursion*—indeed, where not?—unless one kept in
mind that the high argument was not scenery, not landscape, but—

"How exquisitely the individual mind
(And the progressive powers perhaps no less
Of the whole species) to the external world
Is fitted:—and how exquisitely too
(Theme this but little heard of among men)
The external world is fitted to the mind."

If the case was so with Wordsworth, it was equally so with Shelley. Matthew Arnold never made a stranger critical lapse than when he dismissed Shelley as a poet of clouds and sunsets, except when he proclaimed his failure as an interpreter of Nature. We need not ransack Shelley's biography in order to find evidence of his love of Man; it is the pulse and nerve of his poetry. We have just reminded ourselves of the moral of *Alastor*; we have just seen the poet's commerce with Beauty issue in a kind of summary of individual and social perfection—

"To fear himself, and love all human kind."

The essential, central Shelley is not in lovely bye-play like *The Cloud* and *The Sensitive Plant*, nor even in mystical invention like *The Witch of Atlas*. It is in *The Revolt of Islam, Prometheus Unbound, The Cenci, Hellas*—works instinct with sociality, with morality. Even poems primarily and ostensibly of Nature, even the *Skylark* and the *Ode to the West Wind*, take all their deepest meaning from the human problem and struggle, over against which Nature is set.

"We look before and after
And pine for what is not;
    Our sincerest laughter
    With some pain is fraught;
Our sweetest songs are those that tell of saddest thought."

"Drive my dead thoughts over the universe
Like withered leaves to quicken a new birth!
And, by the incantation of this verse,
Scatter, as from an unextinguished hearth
Ashes and sparks, my words among mankind!
Be through my lips to unawakened earth
The trumpet of a prophecy!"

Finally, if both Wordsworth and Shelley were poets of Man, and especially of social Man, and such serious philosophic poets of Man as British literature had hardly known before, they were conspicuously fellow-workers in the task of interpreting Nature, twin-priests of her mysteries, twin-prophets of her message. Wordsworth's work in this capacity needs no insisting on. Readers have dwelt, only too readily and exclusively, on his merits as a poet of landscape. They have recognized that he at least, after the long spell of blindness or crooked vision, wrote of natural phenomena with his eye on the object; at last spoke the "truth in love" of the common objects of the country. But Shelley's idealism has deceived many readers into the belief that his scenery was all *invented*: that his poetic world was fairyland, where realistic standards cannot be applied, and it is irrelevant to ask for truth of portraiture. And, so far as definite terrestrial effects are concerned, there is some justification for the belief. Shelley had the generalizing, not the particularizing habit in his Nature-work; and the habit prompts him, when he is dealing with the surface of the earth and its vegetation, to idealize his objects beyond reality. This is very conspicuous in *The Sensitive Plant*, in which Shelley might, if he would, have given us a real garden, and does not do so. But there was left for him one province—the world of the atmosphere, of the clouds, winds, and dews—where his genius hampered him with no stumbling-blocks, where his idealism was the handmaid of an unapproached and unapproachable fidelity to fact. Nothing, even in Wordsworth, is so true to Nature as Shelley's atmospheric and meteorological poetry. The atmosphere was his home, his element, and he could not report falsely of it. *The Cloud* is fantastic, if you will; but every statement may be verified every day. It is because the skylark is a bird of the air beyond all others—because it sings at heaven's gate—that Shelley so loved it; and it is because his poem is in the best sense realistic that it is so popular. The beauty of the *Ode to the West Wind* is in its truth; its imagination is in its exactitude. And when the poet, at the climax of his passion, calls for identification with the wind—*Be thou me, impetuous one!*—he does but proclaim himself as the very child and voice of the elements in the popular sense of the word. Such a poet of the weather, of water, air, and fire, so ethereal, so genuine, there had never been before.

Wordsworth's kinship with Keats was much more distant than his kinship with Shelley. To the one poet Wordsworth himself was as deaf and blind as to the other. The well-known story of his comment when Keats read him the Hymn to Pan, from *Endymion: A very pretty piece of paganism*, fairly represents, we may be sure, the kind of comment he would have made on the rest of Keats's poetry if he had known it. On the other hand, Keats was as much interested in Wordsworth as Shelley was; and something is to be learned from his recorded feelings and opinions about him as to the relations, if any, between Wordsworth's work and his own.

Wordsworth never saw Shelley; but Keats he met several times. They had a common friend in Haydon, the painter, who took pleasure in bringing them together. In December, 1817, Wordsworth, with his wife and Dora, was in London. He visited his brother, Dr. Christopher Wordsworth, at Lambeth, and saw many friends. The Lambs, of course, were much in his circle; Coleridge was at Highgate, and in sociable mood; the assiduous Crabb Robinson was everywhere to bear testimony. It was an important moment in British literature; Coleridge had just published *Biographia Literaria*, and was taking advice as to the wisdom of prosecuting *Blackwood*, of which the first number had appeared in October, for libel. Shelley's *Revolt of Islam* was just out, and so was Keats's first miscellaneous volume, which was to be followed by *Endymion* in the spring. *Lalla Rookh* was a poem of the year, and Coleridge was disgusted with it. Wordsworth did not please Crabb Robinson as much as usual on this occasion; he thought him sometimes contradictory and egotistical, and inclined to be hard on Coleridge. When Keats first saw Wordsworth, he too had an unpleasing impression. He thought him pompous and stiff; he kept him a long time waiting when he went to pay his respects, and came into the room dressed to dine with another Commissioner of Stamps, looking grand in knee-breeches, silk stockings, and stiff collar. To the Bohemian, open-necked Keats this was repellent. Yet he wanted to see more of Wordsworth, and Haydon arranged a dinner-party in his rooms for December 28th. Charles Lamb was there, and Wordsworth, and Keats's friend, Monkhouse. Everybody was at his best that day, though to Charles Lamb's best alcohol contributed considerably. There was much literary talk at dinner. Lamb's interventions in the midst of Wordsworth's solemn discourse reminded Haydon of the Fool's interruptions of Lear's passion. Lamb grew merrier and merrier. Wordsworth had been denouncing Voltaire. "Now," said Lamb, "you old lake poet, you rascally poet, why do you call Voltaire dull?" *À propos* of Newton's head in one of Haydon's pictures, they discussed poetry and science. "A fellow," Lamb said of Newton, "who believed nothing unless it was as clear as the three sides of a triangle!" Keats and he agreed that Newton's prism had destroyed the rainbow, as Keats afterwards sang in *Lamia*—

> "Do not all charms fly
> At the mere touch of cold philosophy?
> There was an awful rainbow once in heaven;
> We know her woof, her texture; she is given
> In the dull catalogue of common things.
> Philosophy will clip an angel's wings,
> Conquer all mysteries by rule and line,
> Empty the haunted air, and gnomed mine—
> Unweave a rainbow."

In all the fun and extravagance Wordsworth heartily joined after his manner. After dinner an inimitable intellectual toady—like Wordsworth, a Comptroller of Stamps—turned up, and his platitudes gave Lamb—now more than half-seas-over—a great opportunity. "Don't you think, sir," said the new guest to Wordsworth, "that Milton was a great genius?" The rest, though it has been told so often, must be told yet once more in Haydon's words. "Keats looked at me, Wordsworth at the Comptroller. Lamb, who was dozing by the fire, turned round and said, 'Pray, sir, did you say Milton was a great genius?' 'No, sir; I asked Mr. Wordsworth if he were not.' 'Oh,' said Lamb, 'then you are a silly fellow.' 'Charles! my dear Charles!' said Wordsworth; but Lamb, perfectly innocent of the confusion he had created, was off again by the fire. After an awful pause, the Comptroller said, 'Don't you think Newton a great genius?' I could not stand it any longer. Keats put his head into my books. . . . Wordsworth seemed asking himself, 'Who is this?' Lamb got up, and taking a candle, said, 'Sir, will you allow me to look at your phrenological development?' He then turned his back on the poor man, and at every question of the Comptroller he chaunted—

"'Diddle, diddle, dumpling, my son John
Went to bed with his breeches on.'

"The man in office, finding Wordsworth did not know who he was, said in a spasmodic and half-chuckling anticipation of assured victory, 'I have had the honour of some correspondence with you, Mr. Wordsworth.' 'With me, sir?' said Wordsworth, 'not that I remember.' 'Don't you, sir? I am a Comptroller of Stamps.' There was a dead silence; the Comptroller evidently thinking that was enough. While we were waiting for Wordsworth's reply, Lamb sung out—

"'Hey diddle, diddle,
The cat and the fiddle.'

"'My dear Charles!' said Wordsworth—

"'Diddle, diddle, dumpling, my son John,'"

chaunted Lamb, and then rising, exclaimed, 'Do let me have another look at that gentleman's organs.' Keats and I hurried Lamb into the painting-room, shut the door, and gave way to inextinguishable laughter. Monkhouse followed and tried to get Lamb away. We went back, but the Comptroller was irreconcilable. We soothed and smiled and asked him to supper. He stayed, though his dignity was sorely affected. However, being a good-natured man, we parted all in good humour, and no ill effects followed. All the while, until Monkhouse succeeded, we could hear Lamb struggling in the painting-room, and calling at intervals, 'Who is that fellow? Allow me to see his organs once more.'"

Keats's feeling about Wordsworth wavered, but was on the whole respectful and appreciative. In a sonnet of 1816 he dedicated to him four sonorous lines—

"Great spirits now on earth are sojourning
He of the cloud, the cataract, the lake,
Who on Helvellyn's summit, wide awake
Catches his freshness from Archangel's wing."

He probably agreed with Leigh Hunt, who, with many grumbles, recognized Wordsworth as the foremost of the reformers of poetry after the post-Restoration lapse, whose work was celebrated by Keats in his *Sleep and Poetry*. Haydon proposed to send the sonnet to Wordsworth; and Keats told him that the proposal put him "out of breath." "You know," he wrote, "with what reverence I would send my well-wishes to him." He was never weary of repeating the *Intimations of Immortality* Ode; and in January, 1818, when he was fresh from personal intercourse with Wordsworth, he spoke of *The Excursion* as one of the few satisfactory artistic products of the time. On the other hand, he was riled by much in both Wordsworth's personality and his poetry. He wrote to his brothers that Wordsworth had "left a bad impression wherever he visited in town by his egotism, vanity, and bigotry." Yet he maintained that he was "a great poet." He spoke of himself once as liking "half of Wordsworth." In a letter to John Hamilton Reynolds—who wrote the first skit on *Peter Bell*—he entered upon a subtle criticism of Wordsworth's achievement. He realized that the human heart was indeed, as Wordsworth claimed, the main region of his song. He wondered whether he had real "epic passion." He compared him with Milton. Both poets he felt to be partial, fragmentary; he wanted Wordsworth to produce something more, something different. With a truly critical instinct he took the *Tintern Abbey* lines as representing Wordsworth at his best, and he evidently felt in its fulness the power of those lines—how firmly they front the mystery of life; how clearly they see and show the light beyond it. Milton, he thought, had no such vision of the light. As for himself, he was but a child in knowledge of life, beginning to be conscious of its mystery and adversity, and of doors opening, but only into darkness.

In the summer of 1818 Keats was walking with a friend in the Lake country, and of course called at Rydal Mount. To his disappointment and displeasure Wordsworth was at Kendal taking part in the General Election of the year; so Keats could only leave a note on the mantelpiece. It was the election about which Wordsworth wrote his *Addresses to the Freeholders of Westmorland*; and Keats, though much more indifferent to politics than Shelley and Byron, was of course on the Liberal side, and antagonistic to Wordsworth accordingly.

Some months later, Keats was putting himself into a different poetic category from Wordsworth's, which he distinguished as the "egotistical sublime," and as containing Wordsworth alone. He ranked himself, on the other hand, as a normal poet, i.e. a non-moral one; an artist without preferences, having "as much delight in conceiving an Iago as an Imogen." Here he was deeply unjust to poetry; but he was not unjust to himself. Indeed, if we combine Keats's two self-estimates—this one, namely, and his consciousness of himself as hardly beyond the stage of childhood in his poetic experience of life, we shall understand his art, and the slenderness of the tie which binds it to Wordsworth's.

Keats did not live long enough to make the human heart or human life the main object—he hardly made it at all an object—of his song. He is perhaps the most non-moral poet in English, certainly the most non-moral English poet of modern times. And he was this not from any weakness, not from any error, but from a preoccupation with mere beauty which was entirely honourable and natural, and, as he himself recognized, belongs to the youth, the opening stage, of the poet's experience. He was not one to express at any time, like Shelley, his ecstasy in a "shriek"; but his thirst for the beautiful, his joy in it, was of the kind which Shelley felt when he made his quest "and clapped his hands" at his discovery. Only, as to Shelley, the intellectual and moral revealed themselves in such close contiguity with the beautiful, that he could hardly for a moment cease to be a moral poet; human error and human hope, as he conceived them, were interwoven with every show of Nature; and beauty was raised, by the presence of its opposites, into the unearthly and divine. Keats had his moral moments, his brief essays at a "criticism of life." In his *Ode to Melancholy* and in the great lyrical apostrophe to sorrow in *Endymion*, he touches the harp with all his might, and reveals a pessimism which would be unendurable if it were not fugitive. Here and there in *Hyperion*, he utters, without ceasing to be his best self, wisdom as deep and as mellow as ever was Shakespeare's or Wordsworth's.

> "Now comes the pain of truth to whom 'tis pain;
> O folly! for to bear all naked truths,
> And to envisage circumstance, all calm,
> That is the top of sovereignty."

The whole of Oceanus's speech in the second book, in which these lines occur, has exactly as much ethical as aesthetic value. It is very likely that if

Keats had lived, lived beyond his intoxication with beauty, his mere artist's satisfaction, he would have given us much poetry of a like strain. But, taking his fragmentary bequest as it stands, we feel that the central Keats is in *The Eve of S. Agnes*, *Lamia*, the *Ode to Autumn*, the *Ode to Psyche*; in poetry which shows him with a boundless appetite for the beautiful as the pleasurable, and not as an unearthly abstraction, but as actualized in beautiful things, taken indiscriminately from the earth and air, from Grecian mythology, or from mediaeval romance. The essential Keats is an artist, a painter of pictures for beauty's sake. And he is an artist, as we said, without preferences, "having as much delight in conceiving an Iago as an Imogen," except, we may add, that his moral sense is hardly as yet enough developed to make him take much interest in either of them.

Keats's non-morality, his love of "pretty pieces of Paganism," removes him very far from Wordsworth. But we are here comparing our poets, less with each other than with their predecessors; we are thinking of them as, among them, restoring to English poetry certain great things which it seemed to have lost; and the greater the unlikenesses within the band, the more interesting is the joint result. We have just quoted a passage from Keats which Wordsworth might have countersigned; and, as for Paganism, it has been pointed out that Wordsworth himself had a moment when he cried—

"Great God! I'd rather be
A Pagan suckled in a creed outworn;
So might I, standing on this pleasant lea,
Have glimpses that would make me less forlorn;
Have sight of Proteus rising from the sea;
Or hear old Triton blow his wreathed horn."

But it is not in such stray parallelisms that the fellowship of Keats and Wordsworth, or, indeed, the unity of all the great poets of the Romantic Revival, is to be found. Wordsworth and Keats were at least on the same plane in their sense, quick and novel and inspiring, of what Keats called the "poetry of earth"; they both possessed what is the innermost nerve of poetry, the power of finding the beautiful, and showing it in their words to others for all time. And, different as, in many respects, their ideas of it were, they were both wise enough to know that beauty is a unity in diversity; that it has its temperate and torrid zones; its simplicities as well as its complexities; its restraints as well as its licences; that it is here as well as yonder; in the spirit as well as in the body. Both poets meet in the shelter of Shelley's phrase—

"That Beauty in which all things work and move."

In this comprehensiveness of the beautiful is to be found the community of that poetry of the early nineteenth century to which Wordsworth was so great a contributor. Hardly one of his peers and younger contemporaries, certainly not Southey, not Byron, not Scott, but was alive with a quick sense of beauty such as generations had not felt. It is the quickness, the novelty, the pulsing throb of the sense, which makes it impossible for the poets of the Romantic Revival to disown one another. Poets with the classical ideal, poets like Milton and Gray, splendid as are their services to the beautiful, do not give the feeling of novelty, of young enthusiasm, which the Romanticists gave. They too cannot disown, be disowned; but they are in a separate province, the province held by tradition, by its majesty, its dignity, its repose.

Wordsworth has often been compared with Milton; but not, it seems, with any fruitful result. One may set the blank verse of the one beside that of the other to establish the inferiority of Wordsworth's. They were alike patriots, alike grave, moral, serious poets. But Wordsworth was an innovator and a restorer; and it was no tradition, Miltonic or other, that he restored, it was of his own underived, vigorous individuality that he gave. In spite of his sobriety, his narrowness, his cold welcome of novelty, the world in which he lived was a new world, and he saw and felt it anew, with an untaught and enthusiastic mind. His poetry was no product of culture; it was the immediate reaction of an original mind to the beautiful significance of things. And it was the same with his peers. They all felt the world afresh; and as they felt, they sang, a harmony of many voices.

—DAVID WATSON RANNIE, "Fellow-Workers in
Romanticism," from *Wordsworth and His Circle.*,
London: Methuen & Co., 1907, pp. 258–278

A.C. BRADLEY "WORDSWORTH" (1909)

A.C. Bradley praises Wordsworth for his ability to see things from a unique perspective. Bradley maintains that Wordsworth's way of looking at the world can be challenging to many readers because it is rooted in his experience of nature, an experience that can prove both strange and ironic to our own understanding of the world. According to Bradley, the best illustrations of the need to enter into Wordsworth's vision are those poems that received the most disparaging reviews, namely the ballads. "They arose almost always from some in incident which, for him," Bradley argues, "had a novel and arresting character and came on his mind with a certain shock; and if we do not get back to this through the poem, we remain outside it." Citing such responses as the negative commentary on

"Alice Fell," Bradley maintains that Wordsworth's unsuccessfully received poems were criticized by those who invalidated the subject of the pieces, a child crying inconsolably for the loss of a tattered cloak, rather than considering the profound tragedy that moved Wordsworth to relay the circumstances of an impoverished, orphaned girl. Those writers who heaped criticism on Wordsworth failed to understand and appreciate the sublimity inherent within this particular ballad. Furthermore, Bradley celebrates the poet's serene vision, which could only be cultivated in solitude, while he nevertheless remained a spokesman for humanity. "No poet is more emphatically the poet of community ... to that soul of joy and love which links together all Nature's children." Because of the poet's singular vision, Bradley concludes his essay by equating Wordsworth, above all other nineteenth-century poets, to Milton.

There have been greater poets than Wordsworth, but none more original. He saw new things, or he saw things in a new way. Naturally, this would have availed us little if his new things had been private fancies, or if his new perception had been superficial. But that was not so. If it had been, Wordsworth might have won acceptance more quickly, but he would not have gained his lasting hold on poetic minds. As it is, those in whom he creates the taste by which he is relished, those who learn to love him (and in each generation they are not a few), never let him go. Their love for him is of the kind that he himself celebrated, a settled passion, perhaps "slow to begin," but "never ending," and twined around the roots of their being. And the reason is that they find his way of seeing the world, his poetic experience, what Arnold meant by his "criticism of life," to be something deep, and therefore something that will hold. It continues to bring them joy, peace, strength, exaltation. It does not thin out or break beneath them as they grow older and wiser; nor does it fail them, much less repel them, in sadness or even in their sorest need. And yet—to return to our starting-point—it continues to strike them as original, and something more. It is not like Shakespeare's myriad-mindedness; it is, for good or evil or both, peculiar. They can remember, perhaps, the day when first they saw a cloud somewhat as Wordsworth saw it, or first really understood what made him write this poem or that; his unique way of seeing and feeling, though now familiar and beloved, still brings them not only peace, strength, exaltation, but a "shock of mild surprise"; and his paradoxes, long known by heart and found full of truth, still remain paradoxes.

If this is so, the road into Wordsworth's mind must be through his strangeness and his paradoxes, and not round them. I do not mean that they are everywhere in his poetry. Much of it, not to speak of occasional platitudes, is beautiful without being peculiar or difficult; and some of this may be as valuable as that which is audacious or strange. But unless we get hold of that, we remain outside Wordsworth's centre; and, if we have not a most unusual affinity to him, we cannot get hold of that unless we realise its strangeness, and refuse to blunt the sharpness of its edge. Consider, for example, two or three of his statements; the statements of a poet, no doubt, and not of a philosopher, but still evidently statements expressing, intimating, or symbolising, what for him was the most vital truth. He said that the meanest flower that blows could give him thoughts that often lie too deep for tears. He said, in a poem not less solemn, that Nature was the soul of all his moral being; and also that she can so influence us that nothing will be able to disturb our faith that all that we behold is full of blessings. After making his Wanderer tell the heart-rending tale of Margaret, he makes him say that the beauty and tranquillity of her ruined cottage had once so affected him

> That what we feel of sorrow and despair
> From ruin and from change, and all the grief
> The passing shows of Being leave behind,
> Appeared an idle dream, that could not live
> Where meditation was.
>   [*The Excursion*, I, 949–53]

He said that this same Wanderer could read in the silent faces of the clouds unutterable love, and that among the mountains all things for him breathed immortality. He said to "Almighty God,"

> But thy most dreaded instrument
> For working out a pure intent
> Is Man arrayed for mutual slaughter;
> Yea, Carnage is thy daughter.
>   [*Ode*, 1815, 106–9]

This last, it will be agreed, is a startling statement; but is it a whit more extraordinary than the others? It is so only if we assume that we are familiar with thoughts that lie too deep for tears, or if we translate "the soul of all my moral being" into "somehow concordant with my moral feelings," or convert "all that we behold" into "a good deal that we behold," or transform the Wanderer's reading of the silent faces of the clouds into an argument from "design." But this is the road round Wordsworth's mind, not into it.

Again, with all Wordsworth's best poems, it is essential not to miss the unique tone of his experience. This doubtless holds good of any true poet, but not in the same way. With many poems there is little risk of our failing either to feel what is distinctive of the writer, or to appropriate what he says. What is characteristic, for example, in Byron's lines, *On this day I complete my thirty-sixth year*, or in Shelley's *Stanzas written in dejection near Naples*, cannot escape discovery, nor is there any difficulty in understanding the mood expressed. But with Wordsworth, for most readers, this risk is constantly present in some degree. Take, for instance, one of the most popular of his lyrics, the poem about the daffodils by the lake. It is popular partly because it remains a pretty thing even to those who convert it into something quite undistinctive of Wordsworth. And it is comparatively easy, too, to perceive and to reproduce in imagination a good deal that is distinctive; for instance, the feeling of the sympathy of the waves and the flowers and the breeze in their glee, and the Wordsworthian "emotion recollected in tranquillity" expressed in the lines (written by his wife),

They flash upon that inward eye
Which is the bliss of solitude.

But there remains something still more intimately Wordsworthian:

I wandered lonely as a Cloud
That floats on high o'er vales and hills.

It is thrust into the reader's face, for these are the opening lines. But with many readers it passes unheeded, because it is strange and outside their own experience. And yet it is absolutely essential to the effect of the poem.

This poem, however, even when thoroughly conventionalised, would remain, as I said, a pretty thing; and it could scarcely excite derision. Our point is best illustrated from the pieces by which Wordsworth most earned ridicule, the ballad poems. They arose almost always from some incident which, for him, had a novel and arresting character and came on his mind with a certain shock; and if we do not get back to this through the poem, we remain outside it. We may, of course, get back to this and yet consider the poem to be more or less a failure. There is here therefore room for legitimate differences of opinion. Mr. Swinburne sees, no doubt, as clearly as Coleridge did, the intention of *The Idiot Boy* and *The Thorn*, yet he calls them "doleful examples of eccentricity in dullness," while Coleridge's judgment, though he criticised both poems, was very different. I believe (if I may venture into the company of such critics) that I see why Wordsworth wrote *Goody Blake and Harry Gill* and the *Anecdote for Fathers*, and yet I doubt if he has succeeded in either; but a great man, Charles James Fox, selected the former for special praise, and Matthew Arnold included the latter in a selection from which he excluded *The Sailor's Mother*. Indeed, of all the poems at first most ridiculed there is probably not one that has not been praised by some excellent judge. But they were ridiculed by men who judged them without attempting first to get inside them. And this is fatal.

I may bring out the point by referring more fully to one of them. *Alice Fell* was beloved by the best critic of the nineteenth century, Charles Lamb; but the general distaste for it was such that it was excluded "in policy" from edition after edition of Wordsworth's *Poems*; many still who admire *Lucy Gray* see nothing to admire in *Alice Fell*; and you may still hear the question asked, What could be made of a child crying for the loss of her cloak? And what, I answer, could be made of a man poking his stick into a pond to find leeches? What sense is there in asking questions about the subject of a poem, if you first deprive this subject of all the individuality it possesses in the poem? Let me illustrate this individuality methodically. A child crying for the loss of her cloak is one thing: quite another is a child who has an imagination, and who sees the tattered remnants of her cloak whirled round in the wheel-spokes of a carriage fiercely driven by strangers on lonesome ways through a night of storm in which the moon is drowned. And this child is making her way alone along this lonely road in this night, when her cloak is caught in the wheel. And she is fatherless and motherless, and her poverty (the poem is called *Alice Fell, or Poverty*) is so extreme that for the loss of her weather-beaten rag she does not "cry"; she weeps loud and bitterly; weeps as if her innocent heart would break; sits by the two strangers, who take her into their carriage and try to console her, insensible to all relief; sends forth sob after sob as if her grief could never, never have an end; checks herself for a moment to answer a question, and then weeps on as if she had lost her only friend, and the thought would choke her very heart. It was *this* poverty and *this* grief that Wordsworth described with his reiterated hammering blows. Is it not pathetic? And to Wordsworth it was more. To him grief like this is sublime. It is the agony of a soul from which something is torn away that was made one with its very being. What does it matter whether the thing is a woman, or a kingdom, or a tattered cloak? It is the passion that counts. Othello must not agonise for a cloak, but "the little orphan Alice Fell" has nothing else to agonise for. Is all this insignificant? And then—for this poem about a child is right to the last line—the storm and the tragedy clear clean away, and the new cloak is bought, of duffil grey, as warm a cloak as man can sell; and the child is as pleased as Punch. . . .

Wordsworth's morality is of one piece with his optimism and with his determination to seize and exhibit in everything the element of good. But this is a subject far too large for treatment here, and I can refer to it only in the most summary way. What Arnold precisely meant when he said that Wordsworth "put by" the cloud of human destiny I am not sure. That

Wordsworth saw this cloud and looked at it steadily is beyond all question. I am not building on such famous lines as

The still sad music of humanity,

or

       the fierce confederate storm
Of Sorrow, barricadoed evermore
Within the walls of cities;

or

Amid the groves, under the shadowy hills,
The generations are prepared; the pangs,
The internal pangs, are ready; the dread strife
Of poor humanity's afflicted will
Struggling in vain with ruthless destiny;[1]

for, although such quotations could be multiplied, isolated expressions, even when not dramatic, would prove little. But I repeat the remark already made, that if we review the subjects of many of Wordsworth's famous poems on human life,—the subjects, for example, of *The Thorn, The Sailor's Mother, Ruth, The Brothers, Michael, The Affliction of Margaret, The White Doe of Rylstone,* the story of Margaret in *Excursion,* i., half the stories told in *Excursion,* vi. and vii.—we find ourselves in the presence of poverty, crime, insanity, ruined innocence, torturing hopes doomed to extinction, solitary anguish, even despair. Ignore the manner in which Wordsworth treated his subjects, and you will have to say that his world, so far as humanity is concerned, is a dark world,—at least as dark as that of Byron. Unquestionably then he saw the cloud of human destiny, and he did not avert his eyes from it. Nor did he pretend to understand its darkness. The world was to him in the end "this unintelligible world," and the only "adequate support for the calamities of mortal life" was faith.[2] But he was profoundly impressed, through the experience of his own years of crisis, alike by the dangers of despondency, and by the superficiality of the views which it engenders. It was for him (and here, as in other points, he shows his natural affinity to Spinoza) a condition in which the soul, concentrated on its own suffering, for that very reason loses hold both of its own being and of the reality of which it forms a part. His experience also made it impossible for him to doubt that what he grasped

At times when most existence with herself
Is satisfied,

          [*The Excursion,* IX, 103–4]

—and these are the times when existence is most united in love with other existence—was, in a special sense or degree, the truth, and therefore that the evils which we suffer, deplore, or condemn, cannot really be what they seem to us when we merely suffer, deplore, or condemn them. He set himself to see this, as far as he could, and to show it. He sang of pleasure, joy, glee, blitheness, love, wherever in nature or humanity they assert their indisputable power; and turning to pain and wrong, and gazing at them steadfastly, and setting himself to present the facts with a quiet but unsparing truthfulness, he yet endeavoured to show what he had seen, that sometimes pain and wrong are the conditions of a happiness and good which without them could not have been, that no limit can be set to the power of the soul to transmute them into its own substance, and that, in suffering and even in misery, there may still be such a strength as fills us with awe or with glory. He did not pretend, I repeat, that what he saw sufficed to solve the riddle of the painful earth. "Our being rests" on "dark foundations," and "our haughty life is crowned with darkness."[3] But still what he showed was what he *saw*, and he saw it in the cloud of human destiny. We are not here concerned with his faith in the sun behind that cloud; my purpose is only to insist that he "fronted" it "fearlessly." . . .

Partly because he is the poet of mountains he is, even more pre-eminently, the poet of solitude. For there are tones in the mountain voice scarcely audible except in solitude, and the reader whom Wordsworth's greatest poetry baffles could have no better advice offered him than to do what he has probably never done in his life—to be on a mountain alone. But for Wordsworth not this solitude only, but all solitude and all things solitary had an extraordinary fascination.

> The outward shows of sky and earth,
> Of hill and valley, he has viewed;
> And impulses *of deeper birth*
> Have come to him in solitude.
>
>   ["A Poet's Epitaph"]

The sense of solitude, it will readily be found, is essential to nearly all the poems and passages we have been considering, and to some of quite a different character, such as the Daffodil stanzas. And it is not merely that the poet is alone; what he sees is so too. If the leech-gatherer and the soldier on the moon-lit road had not been solitary figures, they would not have awaked "the visionary power"; and it is scarcely fanciful to add that if the boy who was watching for his father's ponies had had beside him any more than

The *single* sheep and the one blasted tree,
> [*The Prelude* (1850), XII, 319]

the mist would not have advanced along the roads "in such indisputable shapes." With Wordsworth that power seems to have sprung into life at once on the perception of loneliness. What is lonely is a spirit. To call a thing lonely or solitary is, with him, to say that it opens a bright or solemn vista into infinity. He himself "wanders lonely as a cloud": he seeks the souls of lonely places: he listens in awe to

One voice, the solitary raven . . .
An iron knell, with echoes from afar:
> [*The Excursion*, IV, 1178–81]

against the distant sky he descries the shepherd,

A solitary object and sublime,
Above all height! like an aerial cross
Stationed alone upon a spiry rock
Of the Chartreuse, for worship.
> [*The Prelude* (1850), VIII, 272–75]

But this theme might be pursued for hours, and I will refer only to two poems more. The editor of the *Golden Treasury*, a book never to be thought of without gratitude, changed the title *The Solitary Reaper* into *The Highland Reaper*. He may have had his reasons. Perhaps he had met some one who thought that the Reaper belonged to Surrey. Still the change was a mistake: the "solitary" in Wordsworth's title gave the keynote. The other poem is *Lucy Gray*. "When I was little," a lover of Wordsworth once said, "I could hardly bear to read *Lucy Gray*, it made me feel so lonely." Wordsworth called it *Lucy Gray, or Solitude*, and this young reader understood him. But there is too much reason to fear that for half his readers his "solitary child" is generalised into a mere "little girl," and that they never receive the main impression he wished to produce. Yet his intention is announced in the opening lines, and as clearly shown in the lovely final stanzas, which give even to this ballad the visionary touch which distinguishes it from *Alice Fell*:

Yet some maintain that to this day
She is a living child;
That you may see sweet Lucy Gray
Upon the lonesome wild.

O'er rough and smooth she trips along,
And never looks behind;
And sings a solitary song
That whistles in the wind.

The solitariness which exerted so potent a spell on Wordsworth had in it nothing "Byronic." He preached in the *Excursion* against the solitude of "self-indulging spleen." He was even aware that he himself, though free from that weakness, had felt

perhaps too much
The self-sufficing power of Solitude.
[*The Prelude* (1850), II, 76–77]

No poet is more emphatically the poet of community. A great part of his verse—a part as characteristic and as precious as the part on which I have been dwelling—is dedicated to the affections of home and neighbourhood and country, and to that soul of joy and love which links together all Nature's children, and "steals from earth to man, from man to earth." And this soul is for him as truly the presence of "the Being that is in the clouds and air" and in the mind of man as are the power, the darkness, the silence, the strange gleams and mysterious visitations which startle and confuse with intimations of infinity. But solitude and solitariness were to him, in the main, one of these intimations. They had not for him merely the "eeriness" which they have at times for everyone, though that was essential to some of the poems we have reviewed. They were the symbol of power to stand alone, to be "self-sufficing," to dispense with custom and surroundings and aid and sympathy—a self-dependence at once the image and the communication of "the soul of all the worlds." Even when they were full of "sounds and sweet airs that give delight and hurt not," the solitude of the Reaper or of Lucy, they so appealed to him. But they appealed also to that austerer strain which led him to love "bare trees and mountains bare," and lonely places, and the bleak music of the old stone wall, and to dwell with awe, and yet with exultation, on the majesty of that "unconquerable mind" which through long years holds its solitary purpose, sustains its solitary passion, feeds upon its solitary anguish. For this mind, as for the blind beggar or the leech-gatherer, the "light of sense" and the sweetness of life have faded or "gone out"; but in it "greatness makes abode," and it "retains its station proud," "by form or image unprofaned." Thus, in whatever guise it might present itself, solitariness "carried far into his heart" the haunting sense of an "invisible world"; of some Life beyond this "transitory being" and "unapproachable by death";

Of Life continuous, Being unimpaired;
That hath been, is, and where it was and is
There shall endure,—existence unexposed
To the blind walk of mortal accident;
From diminution safe and weakening age;
While man grows old, and dwindles, and decays;
And countless generations of mankind
Depart; and leave no vestige where they trod.
                    [*The Excursion*, IV, 755–62]

For me, I confess, all this is far from being "mere poetry"—partly because I do not believe that any such thing as "mere poetry" exists. But whatever kind or degree of truth we may find in all this, everything in Wordsworth that is sublime or approaches sublimity has, directly or more remotely, to do with it. And without this part of his poetry Wordsworth would be "shorn of his strength," and would no longer stand, as he does stand, nearer than any other poet of the Nineteenth Century to Milton.

Notes

1. The quotations are from "Tintern Abbey"; the "Prospectus" to *The Recluse* (in *Poetical Works*, ed. De Selincourt and Darbishire, vol. 5); *The Excursion*, VI, 553 ff.—Ed.)

2. The second half of this sentence, true of the Wordsworth of the *Excursion*, is perhaps not quite true of his earlier mind.

3. [*The Excursion*, IV, 970; "Extempore Effusion upon the death of James Hogg"—Ed.]

—A.C. BRADLEY, "Wordsworth," from
Oxford Lectures on Poetry, London:
Macmillan & Co., Ltd., 1909

WORKS

DESCRIPTIVE SKETCHES

H.W. Garrod "Descriptive Sketches" (1923)

In his essay on *Descriptive Sketches*, Garrod maintains that this early work, which was completed in the autumn of 1792 and published in early 1793, was written during the time when Wordsworth was in France and experiencing the French Revolution firsthand. This immediacy of composition in itself underscores a striking difference from the theory Wordsworth set out in his preface to the *Lyrical Ballads*, namely that poetry is written in retrospect, with "emotion recollected in tranquility." Garrod speaks of a "Byronic gloom" that pervades *Descriptive Sketches* and that he likens to the pilgrimage of *Childe Harold*, a dreariness that he attributes to Wordsworth's dissatisfaction with himself and the personal and political events surrounding his life at that time, including the French Revolution and his affair with Annette Vallon. As a further effect of these self-recriminations, Garrod points out that his imaginative powers were likewise hampered, "like a wet mist, shrouding his faculties, in which he was halted and lost." Finally, Garrod finds an artificiality in the poem that he attributes to Wordsworth emulating Erasmus Darwin's poem *The Botanical Garden*.

The supreme period of Wordsworth's art is, as I have said, the great decade 1797–1807. The interesting, the intriguing, period, is the formative period lying behind this, the five years of storm and stress which were the crisis of the poet's moral and intellectual development. The poetry of these five years is neither considerable in amount nor great in quality. But as a part of literary history it is of first-rate interest; and an understanding of it is essential to a just appreciation of Wordsworth's later and greater work. Three poems only come into consideration. They are, firstly, *Descriptive Sketches*, completed in the autumn of 1792, when Wordsworth was at the height of his revolutionary ardour; secondly, *Guilt and Sorrow*, finished in 1794; and thirdly, the dramatic poem of the *Borderers*, finished in 1796. In what follows I shall attempt an examination of these three poems, and of the circumstances out of which they arose, using the relevant portions of the *Prelude* as a kind of line-for-line commentary upon them. But I will make here one or two prefatory remarks of a general character which may, I hope, serve as guiding lines for the subsequent detailed examination.

Descriptive Sketches was written when Wordsworth was actually in France, and among the moving scenes of the first act of the Revolution: when he had thoughts of throwing in his lot actively with the leaders of the Girondist party. It is in fact, as will appear presently, the only poem which he wrote in what I may call the full faith of the French Revolution. And yet it is, of all his poems, with the exception of *An Evening Walk*, the most artificial, the least like anything that he wrote subsequently, the most like everything that was worst in the conventional manner of the latter part of the eighteenth century. I say that it is the only poem which he wrote in the full faith of the French Revolution; and if, in doing so, I say something that needs explanation, it is something also which deserves emphasis. No doubt both *Guilt and Sorrow* and the *Borderers* reflect strongly the revolutionary temper. They breathe revolution. But not the French Revolution. The pure air of the French Revolution is in both poems infected through and through with the mists of English political theory. The book of the moment was the *Political Justice* of William Godwin—a work of immense influence in its generation, and of which I shall have a good deal to say later. Godwin is written across every page of both *Guilt and Sorrow* and the *Borderers*; and the paradox of Godwin is that he is a revolutionary who does not believe in revolution. The aim of the French Revolution was to replace the arbitrary will of despotism and aristocracy by what Rousseau had called the 'general will'. To Godwin the 'general will' is the source of all evil. In 1792 Wordsworth saw everything in the French Revolution: in 1795 he tended to see everything in Godwin. He was, in fact, in 1795 in revolt against the French Revolution, and was enrolling himself betimes as the disciple of an extreme individualism: an individualism to which any government was necessarily the antithesis of the good, any organized expression of the 'general will' merely an obstacle to the perfectibility of the individual.

I put all this now dogmatically and elliptically; and I shall endeavour to amplify it as we proceed. It is necessary to put it thus in the foreground, not only because Wordsworth himself (if we read the *Prelude* attentively) does so, but because it enables us to seize a distinction which is not unimportant, and which, as I have hinted already, seems sometimes to be missed by those who suppose Wordsworth, in his great period, to have drawn his strength and inspiration from the French Revolution. The strength of Wordsworth's supreme period is, in fact, not the Revolutionary Idea, but his own reaction, first upon the failure of that Idea, and then upon the failure of Godwinism. I may illustrate this here and now from a letter of Coleridge. Writing to Wordsworth in 1799, Coleridge urges him to 'write a poem in blank verse, addressed to those who, in consequence of the complete failure of the French Revolution, have thrown up all hope of the amelioration of mankind'. M. Legouis has rightly brought this letter into connexion with the concluding portion of the second book of the *Prelude* (written in 1800). If in these times, Wordsworth there says,

> If in these times of fear,
> This melancholy waste of hopes o'erthrown ... [1]
> ... if in this time
> Of dereliction and dismay, I yet
> Despair not of our nature, but retain
> A more than Roman confidence,[2] a faith
> That fails not, in all sorrow my support ...
> ... the gift is yours,
> Ye winds and sounding cataracts; 'tis yours,
> Ye mountains; thine, O Nature. Thou hast fed
> My lofty speculations, and in thee,
> For this uneasy heart of ours, I find
> A never-failing principle of joy
> And purest passion. (ii. 432 sqq.)

The whole effort, and the whole success, of Wordsworth's poetry during what I call his supreme decade is to bring to men disillusioned by the failure of the Revolutionary Idea the secret of a 'principle of joy' in the universe, 'a faith that fails not in all sorrow', a victory that lives in the very heart of defeat. The process by which he reached this success, by which he attained the discovery of this 'principle of joy', is obscurely related in the *Prelude*, with a good deal of deliberate, and admitted,[3] reserve, but on the whole with sufficient candour and clearness to enable us, with such external supplements as are available, to trace it in broad outline.

Descriptive Sketches, completed, as I have said, towards the close of 1792, was published in the early part of 1793. Its publication was synchronous with that of *An Evening Walk*. This synchronism, together with a similarity of style and versification between the two poems, has had the unfortunate effect of causing students of Wordsworth (or at any rate his casual readers) to regard them as proceeding from the same point of development. We know, however, from Wordsworth himself[4] that *An Evening Walk* was begun while he was still at school, and finished during his first two years at college. Wordsworth went to France in November 1791, after completing his three years at Cambridge, and remained there until certainly December of the following year. Nearly the whole of *Descriptive Sketches*, he himself expressly tells us,[5] was composed upon the banks of the Loire during those thirteen months.

The poem, however, purports to describe a walking tour through France and Switzerland, which Wordsworth made, in company with an undergraduate friend of the name of Jones, in the summer of 1790. This long gap between incident and narrative marks the first emergence of a peculiarity in Wordsworth's method of composition which continued with him so long as he wrote poetry. At the very beginning of the *Prelude* he calls our attention to the fact that its opening paragraphs were contemporary with the feelings which they express—he wrote what he felt on the very day upon which he felt it. But he is curiously careful, in that passage, to explain to us that this was contrary to his usual method of composition. He speaks of himself as being 'not used to make A present joy the matter of a song'. Similarly in the Epilogue to the *Waggoner* he tells us that it was his habit to keep a theme in his mind for years before putting it into verse. He speaks of

>   A shy spirit in my heart
> That comes and goes—will sometimes leap
> From hiding-places ten years deep,
> Or haunt me with familiar face,
> Returning like a ghost unlaid
> Until the debt I owe is paid.

We encounter here a doctrine which is part and parcel of Wordsworth's theory of poetic inspiration, and, as I hope to show later, of his theory of the relation between the mind and the senses. The theory has its formal expression in the preface to *Lyrical Ballads*. Poetry, we are there told, 'takes its origin from emotion recollected in tranquillity'.[6] Undoubtedly Wordsworth believed that this method reproduced with deeper truth the original impression. Aubrey de Vere reports a conversation with him in which he commends it, not as a method suitable merely to his own genius, but as of universal applicability. 'That which remained,' he said, 'the picture surviving in the mind, would have presented the ideal and essential truth of the scene, and done so in large part by discarding much which, though in itself striking, was not characteristic.'

The discerning reader will not fail to observe here congruences with the teaching of Aristotle; but he will perhaps—since it is but rarely that poets let us into their secrets of composition—be more interested in attending to Wordsworth's practice than to his theory. Wordsworth, as De Vere reports him, is speaking of the elimination of the unessential; and, save perhaps by implication, he does not touch the question how far it is possible for the poet, under the conditions proposed for him, to avoid obtruding on his original impression the mental environment of the time of composition. The question is interesting, not only in connexion with *Descriptive Sketches* but also as affecting the problem of the essential truthfulness of large parts of the *Prelude*. It so happens that Wordsworth has described this Swiss tour twice over; first in *Descriptive Sketches*, at a distance of two years, and subsequently, in a more partial fashion, in the sixth book of the *Prelude*. I have not space here (nor, perhaps, would it be relevant) to institute a detailed comparison of the two pieces. It will, however, be relevant (and will sufficiently hint wider theoretical implications) to show, as it can be shown, the essential untruthfulness of a great part of *Descriptive Sketches*. Wordsworth was two years distant from his object; but he did not yet understand, I would suppose, the conditions of his art. I will try and show how this was so; and when I have done so, I will point a contrast by calling attention to two passages in the sixth book of the *Prelude* which exhibit, as I think, a remarkable truth to impressions fourteen years old.

Readers of *Descriptive Sketches* have observed with some perplexity that, on the face of it, the poem depicts, not, as it should, a holiday tour, but the objectless wandering of a soul in despair. This is the record, not of an undergraduate tramp, but of the pilgrimage of some *Childe Harold* born out of due time—and very raw in his trade. The poet plainly sets out the cause of his travels at lines 45–6:

Me lured by hope her sorrows to remove
A heart that could not much itself approve.

These lines (of which the grammatical topsy-turveydom may be supposed to mirror a psychical condition) Mr. Harper explains by supposing that Wordsworth was uneasy at offending his relations by going abroad in a Long Vacation which should have been devoted to home study. Yet it is not very plausible that Wordsworth should say—for that is what Mr. Harper makes him say—that his reason for going abroad is that his conscience pricks him for not staying at home. Elsewhere (676) he speaks of his heart as being

Without one hope her written griefs to blot

save in the grave. It is to be feared that few of us look back with regret so tragically poignant upon a wasted vacation. Again, as he wanders through the villages, the 'maidens eye him with enquiring glance', and detect in his appearance 'crazing care' or 'desperate love'; while Nature, with a discernment drawn, perhaps, from a source not deeper than convention, showers

> Soft on his wounded heart her healing power.

This is indeed an undergraduate taking himself seriously!

It is fortunate (or unfortunate) that Wordsworth has himself left us a contemporary prose account of this Swiss tour, in the form of a letter to his sister. There this lost soul gives the following report of himself:

> 'I am in excellent health and spirits ... my spirits have been kept in a perpetual hurry of delight.... I feel a high enjoyment in reflecting that perhaps scarcely a day of my life[7] will pass in which I shall not derive ... happiness from these images ...'—

and a good deal more in the same buoyant strain.[8] With this letter may be compared *Prelude*, vi. 754:

> A glorious time, a happy time that was!

M. Legouis, more plausible, I think, than Mr. Harper, supposes that the gloomy strain which runs through the poem (and of which he supplies additional illustrations) is a mere modish affectation. Melancholy was a fashionable pose of the time; and in its weeds, M. Legouis thinks, Wordsworth dresses up 'the first vague unrest of his sense and feelings'. There are touches of wistful melancholy in the earlier *Evening Walk*. This explanation perhaps derives some countenance from Wordsworth himself, who, speaking of the tour in *Prelude*, vi, says that he found it sweet

> To feed a poet's tender melancholy
> And fond conceit of sadness. (vi. 366–7.)

But I think that neither M. Legouis nor Wordsworth himself quite avail to explain away the Byronic gloom of the poem. It is not a mere 'tender melancholy'; it is not in the same order as the fashionable Welt-Schmerz reflected in *An Evening Walk*. It has its source, not in any modish brooding over the pain of the world, but, admittedly, in a strong disapproval of self. Even M. Legouis is forced, before he has finished, to admit that it is no ordinary melancholy. 'Indeed, it is despair', he says, quite plainly.[9]

The simplest explanation, as it seems to me, is to suppose that Wordsworth has infused into the poem some element of the emotions of the period in which it was actually composed: that it reflects—in a confused and unreal fashion—both the first shock of the French Revolution and the episode of Annette; and that the unreality of it arises not from the fact that the poet is describing feelings two years old, but from the fact that he is struggling, in part at any rate, with recent, indeed present, emotions. In the last paragraphs of the poem the scene is actually placed on the banks of the Loire; Wordsworth, that is to say, takes himself and Jones to a region not in fact visited by them in 1790.[10] But it was here that the poem was written in 1792. The region is apostrophized thus, in lines 739 sqq.:

> And thou, fair favoured region which my soul
> Shall love till life has broke her golden bowl,
> Till death's cold hand her cistern-wheel assail,
> And vain regret and vain desire shall fail.

M. Legouis supposes the region addressed to be France in general, and the passion of the address to be the revolutionary passion. But the context does not justify this wider attribution, and Wordsworth has himself told us that in 1790 he cared very little for the issues of the Revolution. The lines, to my mind, have the note of a very personal sentiment; and once again I am inclined to think of Annette. I would call attention in this connexion to a number of passages in the poem which are marked by a purely sensuous quality, to which elsewhere in Wordsworth it would be hard to find analogues. We are carried repeatedly into an atmosphere which pervades no other part of Wordsworth: a world of 'dark-eyed maidens', of 'soft bosoms breathing round contagious sighs', of eyes that 'throw the sultry light of young desire', of 'the low-warbled breath of twilight lute'—and of much other rubbish of a like kind (14, 113, 148, 190, 748).

Another element of perplexity is created by occasional hints which the poem furnishes of religious scepticism. 'I think it has never been remarked', says Mr. Harper, 'that the poem contains a distinct confession of religious unbelief. Yet this is plainly the meaning of the four lines which conclude the passage describing the pilgrimage to the shrine of Einsiedeln' (676 sqq.). Addressing the credulous worshippers, he cries:

> Without one hope her written griefs to blot
> Save in the land where all things are forgot,
> My heart, alive to transports long unknown,
> Half wishes your delusion were her own.

Wordsworth suppressed this passage in later editions; and that this mood of religious unbelief did not belong to the Wordsworth of the actual Swiss tour, we may satisfy ourselves by a single passage from the letter to his sister from which I have already quoted. 'Among the awful scenes of the Alps', he writes, 'I had not a thought of man, or of a single created being: my whole soul was turned to him who produced the terrible majesty before me.' That was the Wordsworth of 1790; but not of 1792; and it is worth noticing that this conception of a God who makes, rather than is, Nature, hardly recurs in Wordsworth until the Excursion. Only there, after twenty years, does Wordsworth get back to what Coleridge called his 'I and my brother the Dean' manner. As to his religious beliefs in 1792–3 we have the testimony, not, I fancy, completely candid, of his nephew the bishop: 'His mind was whirled round in a vortex of doubt.' The reference is to the period immediately following the return from France. 'Not that he ever lapsed into scepticism', the bishop adds.[11] The thought in the *addendum* is, pretty obviously, born of the wish. The biographer is himself aware that, in poems not far removed in date from 1792–3, Wordsworth appears in some danger of 'divinizing the creation and dishonouring the creator', and that what he wrote might 'be perverted to a popular and pantheizing philosophy'.[12] After all, it was in 1796 that Coleridge spoke of Wordsworth as still 'at least a semi-atheist.'[13]

In this connexion it is interesting to compare that passage in *Descriptive Sketches* which deals with Wordsworth's visit to the Grande Chartreuse with the lines in the sixth book of the *Prelude* which describe the same incident. Wordsworth found the Chartreuse in possession of the revolutionary soldiery. In *Descriptive Sketches* the incident is viewed in a manner somewhat obviously detached and sceptical. Though he talks of 'Blasphemy within the shuddering fane', yet it is not difficult to see that, upon the whole, he derives some satisfaction from the fact that 'the power whose frown severe' used to 'tame reason till she crouched in fear' (i.e. the power of religious superstition) is now obliged to crouch before the revolutionary arms of 'Reason'. But the mood was not that of 1790. The mood of 1790 is more faithfully preserved in the *Prelude*. There Wordsworth describes the acute conflict set up in his mind between his ardour for revolutionary freedom and his sense of religion; and the passage ends in a prayer for 'these courts of mystery', this place of 'penitential fears and trembling hopes', which he treads 'in sympathetic reverence.'[14]

This is one of the two passages in the sixth book to which I promised to call attention, as illustrating the greater veracity and depth of the account of the Swiss tour given in the *Prelude*. The other, rather different in kind, is the well-known passage describing the crossing of the Alps.[15] It is the central episode of the whole tour, as depicted in the *Prelude*, the one great and deep memory. Crossing the Simplon Pass, Wordsworth and his friend became, for a space, parted from their guide. They proceeded to climb, in the belief that their way still led upward, nearer and nearer to the clouds. While they were expecting still to rise, they met a peasant, of whom they inquired the way, and who informed them that their proper route was in fact downward. Without knowing it they had crossed the Alps. The disillusionment was at the moment baffling; and here is Wordsworth's account of it. Imagination, he says, that 'awful power',

> rose from the mind's abyss
> Like an unfathered vapour that enwraps,
> At once, some lonely traveller. I was lost;
> Halted without an effort to break through;
> But to my conscious soul I *now* can say—
> 'I recognize thy glory'; in such strength
> Of usurpation, when the light of sense
> Goes out, but with a flush that has revealed
> The invisible world, doth greatness make abode,
> There harbours; whether we be young or old,
> Our destiny, our being's heart and home,
> Is with infinitude, and only there,
> With hope it is, hope that can never die,
> Effort and expectation and desire,
> And something evermore about to be.

Here it is to be noted, firstly that this central and supreme memory of the tour is lost wholly from *Descriptive Sketches*—not a word of it will you find there; and secondly, that what may be called the good faith of this memory is amply attested by the careful distinction which Wordsworth makes between his later, and his original, perception. At the actual time of the experience, the imaginative power was like a wet mist, shrouding his faculties, in which he was halted and lost. It was many years later that he 'recognized the glory'. While he held always to the doctrine that the truth of nature is given to us by the senses, he failed, in his early contacts with the external world, to 'recognize' the manner in which this in fact takes place; it was only later that he became aware of what is ultimately a fundamental truth for him, namely, that our highest perceptions come to us, through sense, indeed, but in and by the extinction of sense—when sense, in the act of being extinguished, throws a light upon the world beyond sense.[16]

The concluding portion of *Descriptive Sketches* contains political reflections which are obviously, and, I think, admittedly, coloured by the events of 1791–2.[17] These political reflections are in the main remarkable only for the fact that they are expressed in a manner the most artificial conceivable, the most unreal. I will notice only two matters of detail.

In line 706 Savoy is apostrophized as the 'slave of slaves'. A foot-note informs us that the passage was written before 'the emancipation of Savoy', though the poet regards it as 'scarce necessary' to point this out (to readers at once intelligent and sympathetic). Here we have the revolutionary with a vengeance. The annexation of Savoy by France is accepted as, on the face of it, her 'emancipation'. As good a comment upon the passage as any other is furnished by Burns. Burns 'commenced revolutionary' in as fine a spirit as Wordsworth. 'As for France', he says, 'I was her enthusiastic votary at the beginning of the business.' 'But when', he adds, 'she came to show her old avidity for conquest in annexing Savoy, &c., to her dominions, and invading the rights of Holland, I altered my sentiments.' Burns is thinking, as the reference to Holland shows, of a date somewhat later. But it is worth while, when the influence of the French Revolution upon British poetry is spoken of, to bring these two passages together.

Lines 780 sqq. show Wordsworth prepared for a new heaven and a new earth, which are perhaps to be won only by 'rousing hell's own aid'.[18] The effect of the struggle for freedom may be, he says, to set the world in flames. Yet from the 'innocuous flames'—they became a good deal less innocuous later—there will come a 'lovely birth':

Nature, as in her prime, her virgin reign
Begins, and Love and Truth compose her train.

The sense given here to the word 'Nature' is derived obviously from the system of Rousseau, the spiritual father of the Revolution. The French Revolution is as yet for Wordsworth the 'return to Nature' in its most naïve signification (not infrequently elsewhere the word 'Nature' is given the same meaning, e.g. *Prelude*, xi. 31[19]). Wordsworth suppressed the lines in the later edition of the poem; and a significant comment upon them (and upon their suppression) is furnished by the language of the disillusioned revolutionary in the third book of the *Excursion*:

Nature was my guide,
The nature of the dissolute. (*Exc.* iii. 807.)

The source of Wordsworth's artificial manner in *Descriptive Sketches* has been correctly indicated by M. Legouis. Wordsworth's poetic theory and practice in this period are derived from Erasmus Darwin, the grandfather of the great naturalist, and the author of a didactic poem, *The Botanical Garden*. Nobody now reads *The Botanical Garden*; yet at one time its author was thought by Coleridge to be 'the first literary figure in Europe'.[20] The different parts of the poem are interlarded with dialogues, in prose, upon the theory of poetry and art. 'The Muses are young ladies', says Darwin, 'and we expect to see them dressed.' And dressed they are, both in the *Botanical Garden* and in *Descriptive Sketches*; and their taste in dress is very bad indeed. But Darwin was not only a poet, with a theory of poetic diction; what is for our purpose, I fancy, much more important—and what M. Legouis omits to tell us—is that he was, in religion, a prominent free-thinker, and, in politics, an advanced radical. He was personally acquainted with, and carried on correspondence with, Rousseau. I know no evidence of any personal relations between Darwin and Wordsworth. But Darwin was an old member of Wordsworth's own college, St. John's; and from Bishop Wordsworth's *English Universities in the Eighteenth Century* we know that Darwin read, and admired, *Descriptive Sketches* on its first appearance. It is, I think, more than likely that, if only indirectly, he was in part responsible for the revolutionary and free-thinking turn given to Wordsworth's mind in 1791 and the following years.

Before I leave *Descriptive Sketches* I may mention a phenomenon in connexion with them which illustrates their unreality in a manner rather surprising—I owe the notice of it, once again, to M. Legouis. In notes to lines 372 and 475 Wordsworth mentions his indebtedness to the French poet and naturalist, Ramond de Carbonnières. M. Legouis has shown that his debt to this writer extends far beyond the two passages in which it is acknowledged. Wordsworth not only sees objects at second-hand, through the medium of Ramond's notes, but he sometimes puts this writer's ideas into his verses 'even where those ideas are at variance with his own impressions'. Examples of this are collected by M. Legouis, to whose book I may refer the reader.

Notes

1. i.e. the hopes of the French Revolution.
2. The phrase is not chosen at random; but has a specific reference to the rather showy Stoicism of the Godwinian philosophy.
3. See, especially, xi. 282 sqq.:

> Share with me, friend, the wish
> That some dramatic tale, endued with shapes
> Livelier, and flinging *out less guarded words*
> *Than suit the work we fashion*, might set forth
> What then I learned.

4. See above, p. 39.
5. Grosart, iii, p. 7.

6. Paragraph 23. In the essay upon the *Preface to Lyrical Ballads* I have attempted a detailed examination of this theory and its implications.

7. It may be noticed that, poorly as the results of the Swiss tour figure in *Descriptive Sketches*, Wordsworth did, none the less, long look back to it as a period of genuine spiritual illumination. In the eleventh book of the *Prelude*, among the chief calamities which oppress his mind when he thinks of Napoleon, he reckons the fact that the Alps must now lose for him their old beauty (xi, 409 sqq.).

8. Harper, i, pp. 93–4.

9. *Eng. Trans.*, p. 157.

10. Though Jones was not with Wordsworth on the Loire in 1790, Wordsworth was expecting him there in 1792, when the poem was being finished. The last four lines of the poem, therefore, will be less unreal than, prima facie, they appear.

11. *Memoirs*, i, p. 74.

12. *Ib.*, pp. 117–18.

13. *Letters*, i, p. 164. See also ib., p. 246.

14. *Descr. Sk.*, 53 sqq.; *Prelude*, vi, 414 sqq.

15. *Prelude*, vi. 562 sqq.

16. For this distinction between immediate perception and subsequent ideal recognition, cf. *Prelude*, vi, p. 739, where Wordsworth emphasizes the fact that many of the impressions of the tour were not instantaneous in their effects, but led only in a devious fashion to effects perceived long afterwards.

17. Lines 787–91 reflect, I would suggest, the episode (1792) related in *Prelude*, ix. 509–18.

18. 781: the crudity of the phrase (reminiscent, perhaps, of Virgil's *flectere si nequeo superos Acheronta movebo*) is noteworthy. See Coleridge: *Ode to the Departing Year*, 31–3.

19. In reading Wordsworth, it is always worth stopping to ask oneself, in any given passage, in what sense he is using the word *nature*. *Prelude*, xi. 31 illustrates this well. Even where he uses 'nature' as the equivalent of the external world, or our experience of it, it is his habit to colour that meaning with meanings derived from many of the other very vague uses of the word. 'Nature' stands often as the equivalent of the elementary principle of unintellectualized goodness in the world of both men and things: the antithesis of custom and formal reason. The different shades of meaning given to the word in the Revolutionary poets generally would furnish the theme of an interesting essay.

20. Hazlitt remarks that 'Coleridge always somehow contrived to prefer the unknown to the known' (*My First Acquaintance with Poets*). But the vogue of Darwin was undoubtedly considerable, especially in the ranks of the free-thinkers.

—H.W. GARROD, "Descriptive Sketches,"
from *Wordsworth: Lectures and Essays*,
Oxford: The Clarendon Press, 1st ed., 1923

LYRICAL BALLADS

The *Lyrical Ballads* was a cooperative enterprise of Wordsworth and Coleridge originating in the need to raise money for a trip to Germany. Perhaps no less motive of a force was the poets' ongoing desire to reveal in their work the joy and beauty of nature, while treating the themes and experiences common to all individuals.

WILLIAM WORDSWORTH "PREFACE" (1798)

In his preface to the *Lyrical Ballads*, Wordsworth states that it is his objective to study rustic life and people and then transform them imaginatively so as to highlight certain details and to make his subjects appealing and worthy of poetic scrutiny. Furthermore, Wordsworth affirms that his choice of subject matter is based on his belief that rural-based people live close to nature, an environment particularly suited to the cultivation of "the essential passions of the heart," a place far removed from the pretentiousness and diversions of city life. Thus, these individuals acquire a new dignity, and the language Wordsworth uses is likewise meant to reflect accurately their pure and straightforward manner of speaking, "because such men hourly communicate with the best objects from which the best part of language is originally derived; and because, from their rank in society . . . being less under the influence of social vanity, they convey their feelings and notions in simple and unelaborated expressions."

As to the vociferous objections to his revolutionary concept of poetry, Wordsworth responds to the harsh criticism from those who would decry his work as base in subject matter and diction. Wordsworth defends himself, labeling any invective lobbied at him as indicative of the critic and his or her biases rather than the actual quality of Wordsworth's poetry. Most importantly, the preface to the *Lyrical Ballads* is Wordsworth's manifesto of how and why he writes and contains the famous declaration of poetic belief: "For all good poetry is the spontaneous overflow of powerful feelings: and though this be true, Poems to which any value can be attached were never produced on any variety of subjects but by a man who, being possessed of more than usual organic sensibility, had also thought long and deeply." Above all else, Wordsworth wants to enlighten and guide his readers to confront and embrace those values he deems most important.

The principal object . . . proposed in these Poems was to choose incidents and situations from common life, and to relate or describe them, throughout, as far as was possible in a selection of language really used by men, and, at the same time, to throw over them a certain colouring of imagination, whereby ordinary things should be presented to the mind in an unusual aspect; and, further, and above all, to make these incidents and situations interesting by tracing in them, truly though not ostentatiously, the primary laws of our nature: chiefly, as far as regards the manner in which we associate ideas in a state of excitement. Humble and rustic life was generally chosen, because, in that condition, the essential passions of the heart find a better soil in which they can attain their maturity, are less under restraint, and speak a plainer and more emphatic language; because in that condition of life our elementary feelings coexist in a state of greater simplicity, and, consequently, may be more accurately contemplated, and more forcibly communicated; because the manners of rural life germinate from those elementary feelings, and, from the necessary character of rural occupations, are more easily comprehended, and are more durable; and, lastly, because in that condition the passions of men are incorporated with the beautiful and permanent forms of nature. The language, too, of these men has been adopted (purified indeed from what appear to be its real defects, from all lasting and rational causes of dislike or disgust) because such men hourly communicate with the best objects from which the best part of language is originally derived; and because, from their rank in society and the sameness and narrow circle of their intercourse, being less under the influence of social vanity, they convey their feelings and notions in simple and unelaborated expressions. Accordingly, such a language, arising out of repeated experience and regular feelings, is a more permanent, and a far more philosophical language, than that which is frequently substituted for it by Poets, who think that they are conferring honour upon themselves and their art, in proportion as they separate themselves from the sympathies of men, and indulge in arbitrary and capricious habits of expression, in order to furnish food for fickle tastes, and fickle appetites, of their own creation.

I cannot, however, be insensible to the present outcry against the triviality and meanness, both of thought and language, which some of my contemporaries have occasionally introduced into their metrical compositions; and I acknowledge that this defect, where it exists, is more dishonourable to the Writer's own character than false refinement or arbitrary innovation, though I should contend at the same time, that it is far less pernicious in the sum of its consequences. From such verses the Poems in these volumes will be found distinguished at least by one mark of difference, that each of them has a worthy *purpose*. Not that I always began to write with a distinct purpose formally conceived; but habits of meditation have, I trust, so prompted and regulated my feelings, that my descriptions of such objects as strongly excite those feelings, will be found to carry along with them a *purpose*. If this opinion be erroneous, I can have little right to the name of a Poet. For all good poetry is the spontaneous overflow of powerful feelings: and though this be true, Poems to which any value can be attached were never produced on any variety of subjects but by a man who, being possessed of more than usual organic sensibility, had also thought long and deeply. For our continued influxes of feeling are modified and directed by our thoughts, which are indeed the representatives of all our past feelings; and, as by contemplating the relation of these general representatives to each other, we discover what is really important to men, so, by the repetition and continuance of this act, our feelings will be connected with important subjects, till at length, if we be originally possessed of much sensibility, such habits of mind will be produced, that, by obeying blindly and mechanically the impulses of those habits, we shall describe objects, and utter sentiments, of such a nature, and in such connection with each other, that the understanding of the Reader must necessarily be in some degree enlightened, and his affections strengthened and purified.

—WILLIAM WORDSWORTH, "Preface" to
Lyrical Ballads, 1798, 1800

VIDA D. SCUDDER "WORDSWORTH AND NEW DEMOCRACY" (1895)

Vida Scudder was an educator and social activist who studied English literature at Oxford University and later taught English at Wellesley College. In the following excerpt discussing the *Lyrical Ballads*, Scudder extols their virtues as "exquisite" in rustic simplicity and intensely felt though austere in presentation. Scudder equates the historic and groundbreaking import of the *Lyrical Ballads* with the storming of the Bastille. For Scudder, the poems in the volume were a prophecy of the poetic innovation of the 1790s and reflect the promise of the French Revolution. Written when

Wordsworth was twenty-eight, the poems were composed from a retro-
spective viewing of youthful days and exhibit evidence of his depression
and disillusionment, revealing that he was "weighed down by the sorrows of life, drawn towards a diseased introspection and a study of psychological anomalies." In such poems as "The Female Vagrant," Scudder
sees Wordsworth as the precursor of Robert Browning. Nevertheless, she
maintains that these poems also manifest a peace of mind that was won
through great effort, a conquest over the loss of innocence, as exemplified
in "We Are Seven," and faith in a democratic future.

It is always worth while to linger over the starting-point of a poet's work. This
comes, with Wordsworth, just at the end of the eighteenth century. In 1798,
he and Coleridge published the tiny volume of *Lyrical Ballads.*

This little book was to the poetic revolution what the taking of the Bastille
was to the historic movement: shock, challenge, manifesto. It was far more
than this: it was the prophecy of the poetic achievement of an epoch. In
that sad and obscure decade, as in a dark night, shrouded by storm-cloud,
the poems shine like a pure, faint line of distant sky, holding the promise of
the coming day. All the phases of modern poetry are suggested by them,—
romanticism, alike external and spiritual, raised to the highest power in *The
Ancient Mariner;* unflinching studies of bare fact in "Animal Tranquillity and
Decay," and the little peasant-poems; poetry of mystical and philosophical
contemplation in "Tintern Abbey." Romantic verse, realistic verse, reflective
verse,—these were the three chief forms which our modern poetry was to
develop. Much of Wordsworth's most exquisite work is in this little volume,
work supreme in exalted simplicity, instinct with the buoyant, delicate vigor
of a youth intensely sensitive yet ascetically pure.

Lyrical Ballads distills youthfulness; yet its authors were not very young.
Keats at twenty-four had flung his passionate life away in song and love,
Shelley at twenty-eight had but two more years to live, and Shelley and Keats
alike take the world into their boyish confidence and grow up in public. Not
so their more reticent elder brother. Wordsworth was twenty-eight when he
published *Lyrical Ballads.* "Tintern Abbey" alone is enough to show us that
the book is no outcome of earliest youth.

Traces of a present struggle are indeed to be found in these pages. In
the poem, "The Female Vagrant," still more in that curious drama, *The
Borderers,* an attempt now read only from literary interest, we have a
glimpse of a strange Wordsworth morbid and depressed, weighed down by
the sorrows of life, drawn towards a diseased introspection and a study of
psychological anomalies. In place of simplicity and serenity we have subtlety

and unanswered questioning. The poems are still in the shadow of the agnosticism of disillusion. It is curious to read them, and to remember that many years later a Victorian poet was to resume the effort early abandoned by Wordsworth, to dwell with almost pathological interest upon the abnormal manifestations of character, and to adopt the dramatic rather than the contemplative method. But the century had a great deal to say before it was ready for a Browning. Wordsworth's false start was soon forgotten, even by himself, and he first gained the ear of the public and found his own soul in poetry simple as eternal childhood is simple, wise with the deep wisdom of utter peace.

But it is the peace of conquest, gravely pure. The light of spiritual victory, hardly won, rests upon it. All the early poems of Wordsworth shine with the radiance of a faith which has passed through death to victory and knows the glory of the Resurrection. It is impossible to describe the atmosphere of these brief, limpid, perfect poems—poems where a purely spiritual lustre seems to blend with the quiet light of common dawn. They are the expression of emotion recollected or better re-collected, in tranquillity. Their very simplicity, deeply sympathetic with the heart of childhood, is not of the natural child. It belongs to the new birth, the childhood of the Kingdom of Heaven. The contrast is evident, if we put beside Blake's "Infant Joy,"—the pure stammer of a natural baby,—Wordsworth's "We Are Seven,"—the tender bending of a soul that has suffered over the innocence of a child soul outside the ken of loss or pain. A chastened spirit; austere though youthful still, here speaks to us; and the buoyancy and living joy of the poetry are all the clearer because they shine through the limpid purity of lingering tears.

It is the faith in the new democracy that gives to the book its deepest pathos and fullest power. Symbolically rendered as a universal principle in *The Ancient Mariner,* this faith appears simple, earnest, and concrete in Wordsworth's studies of human life. Such brooding love of primal humanity is of an order never known before. The earlier dramatic method, the satiric method of the last century, are both as strange to the young Wordsworth as our own method of peering self-analysis. His attitude is all his own, a tender, reverent, direct contemplation of essential man. The old beggar and the child are his chosen subjects; creatures in whom not only interest of situation but interest of character have vanished or are reduced to lowest terms. Wordsworth watches from a distance which softens all that is distinctive into one common type, and blends the figure into unity with the wide world around. For it is man stripped more utterly than even Carlyle's Teufelsdrockh of all vesture of circumstance, who is dear to his spirit; man in whom the simple fact of absolute humanity shines forth in sacredness naked and supreme.

No boy could thus have written of human life. Wordsworth, when he wrote these poems, had known a great and definite experience. The passion, the tumult, the struggle of his life lay behind him and not before.

—VIDA D. SCUDDER, "Wordsworth and
New Democracy," *The Life of the Spirit in the
Modern English Poets*, 1895, pp. 60–64

ARTHUR SYMONS "WORDSWORTH" (1902)

Arthur Symons begins with a discussion of Wordsworth's sincerity, which he sees as the core of all his poetry. He goes on to describe the poet as in a persistent state of meditation, his mind not cluttered with preconceived ideas of others but, rather, occupied with the freshness of new discoveries. Nevertheless, and because of this fact, Symons believes that Wordsworth remains outside "that supreme intellectual energy of which we are a part." Stating that his thought processes were never commensurate with his depth of feeling, identifying a weakness in Wordsworth, Symons launches into a negative assessment of the poet, an attack that includes the notion that Wordsworth labored under the misapprehension that whatever emotions he felt and wrote down on impulse would automatically be transformed into poetry. Essentially, Symons presents the reader with an anemic Wordsworth, in contrast to the enormously energetic Coleridge. Symons observes that nature alone does not produce poetry, that artistry must be added and, because of this, Wordsworth's poetry is mechanical. He even faults Wordsworth with vanity for thinking otherwise. Added to these serious shortcomings, he suggests an even more significant one, namely that Wordsworth fails to understand the difference between poetry and prose. Symons looks primarily to *The Prelude* as an example of that flaw, for it is strung together by fragments and would have been more successful had it been rendered in prose.

Finally, according to Symons, Wordsworth is uncertain about the value of imagination and whether it can be relied on to reveal the truth. "Often he gives you the thing and his impressions of the thing, and then, with a childlike persistence of sincerity, his own doubt as to the precise truth of the thing." Symons concludes that the sonnet is a genre most suitable to Wordsworth's skills and temperament. "'The sonnet's scanty plot of ground' suited him so well because it forced him to be at once concise and dignified," Symons observes, "and yet allowed him to say straight out the particular message or emotion which was possessing him." Symons's evaluation concludes with an attack on Wordsworth's notion of tranquillity, a state of mind brought about by excluding all ideas alien to his own thinking, a process that Symons maintains requires a blocking out of all external sensations in the service of expressing one's own inward thoughts.

Sincerity was at the root of all Wordsworth's merits and defects; it gave him his unapproachable fidelity to nature, and also his intolerable fidelity to his own whims. Like Emerson, whom he so often resembled, he respected all intuitions, but, unlike Emerson, did not always distinguish between a whim and an intuition. His life was spent in a continual meditation, and his attitude towards external things was that of a reflective child, continually pondering over the surprise of his first impressions. I once heard Mr. Aubrey De Vere, who had been a friend of Wordsworth for many years, say that the frequent triviality of Wordsworth's reflections was due to the fact that he had begun life without any of the received opinions which save most men from so much of the trouble of thinking; but had found out for himself everything that he came to believe or to be conscious of. Thus what seems to most men an obvious truism not worth repeating, because they have never consciously thought it, but unconsciously taken it on trust, was to Wordsworth a discovery of his own, which he had had the happiness of taking into his mind as freshly as if he had been the first man and no one had thought about life before; or, as I have said, with the delighted wonder of the child. Realising early what value there might be to him in so direct an inheritance from nature, from his own mind at its first grapple with nature, he somewhat deliberately shut himself in with himself, rejecting all external criticism; and for this he had to pay the price which we must deduct from his ultimate gains. Wordsworth's power of thought was never on the level of his power of feeling, and he was wise, at least in his knowledge of himself, when he said:

> One impulse from a vernal wood
> May teach you more of man, Of moral evil and of good,
> Than all the sages can.

He felt instinctively, and his feeling was nature's. But thought, coming to him thus immediately as it did, and representing the thinking part of himself with unparalleled fidelity, spoke out of an intellect by no means so responsive to the finer promptings of that supreme intellectual energy of which we are a part. It is thus often when he is most solemnly satisfied with himself that he is really showing us his weakness most ingenuously: he would listen to no external criticism, and there was no inherent critical faculty to stand at his mind's elbow and remind him when he was prophesying in the divine language and when he was babbling like the village idiot.

Wordsworth desired to lead a continuously poetic life, and it seemed to him easy, inevitable, in one whose life was a continual meditation. It seemed to him that, if he wrote down in verse anything which came into his mind, however trivial, it would become poetry by the mere contact. His titles explain the conviction. Thus the beautiful poem beginning, "It is the first mild day of March," is headed, "To my Sister. Written at a small distance from my house, and sent by my little boy." In its bare outline it is really a note written down under the impulse of a particular moment, and it says: "Now that we have finished breakfast, let us go for a walk; put on a walking dress, and do not bring a book; it is a beautiful day, and we should enjoy it." Some kindly inspiration helping, the rhymed letter becomes a poem: it is an evocation of spring, an invocation to joy. Later on in the day Wordsworth will fancy that something else in his mind calls for expression, and he will sit down and write it in verse. There it will be; like the other, it will say exactly what he wanted to say, and he will put it in its place among his poems with the same confidence. But this time no kindly inspiration will have come to his aid; and the thing will have nothing of poetry but the rhymes.

What Wordsworth's poetic life lacked was energy, and he refused to recognise that no amount of energy will suffice for a continual production. The mind of Coleridge worked with extraordinary energy, seemed to be always at high thinking power, but Coleridge has left us less finished work than almost any great writer, so rare was it with him to be able faultlessly to unite, in his own words, "a more than usual state of emotion with more than usual order." Wordsworth was unconscious even of the necessity, or at least of the part played by skill and patience in waiting on opportunity as it comes, and seizing it as it goes. When one has said that he wrote instinctively, without which there could be no poetry, one must add that he wrote mechanically, and that he wrote always. Continual writing is really a bad form of dissipation; it drains away the very marrow of the brain. Nature is not to be treated as a handmaid of all work, and requires some coaxing before she will become one's mistress. There is a kind of unconscious personal vanity in the assumption that whatever interests or concerns me, however slightly, must be of interest to all the world. Only what is of intense interest to me, or concerns me vitally, will be of interest to all the world; and Wordsworth often wrote about matters which had not had time to sink into him, or the likelihood of taking root in any but the upper surface of his mind.

But there was another kind of forgetfulness which has had almost the most fatal consequences of any. Wordsworth never rightly apprehended what is essential in the difference between prose and poetry. Holding rightly that poetry can be a kind of religion, he admitted what Gautier has called "the heresy of instruction." He forgot that religion has its sacred ritual, in which no gesture is insignificant, and in which what is preached from the pulpit is by no means of higher importance than what is sung or prayed before the altar. He laboured to make his verse worthy, but he was not always conscious that a noble intention does not of itself make great art. In *The Prelude* he tells the story of his own mind, of his growth, not so much as a man, but as a poet; and he has left us a document of value, together with incidental fragments of fine poetry. But it is not a poem, because what Wordsworth tried to do was a thing which should have been done in prose. It is a talking about life, not a creation of life; it is a criticism of the imagination, not imagination at work on its own indefinable ends.

And yet, just here, out of this unconsciousness which leaves him so often at the mercy of all intrusions, clogged by fact, tied to scruple, a child in the mischief-working hands of his own childishness, we come upon precisely the quality which gives him his least questionable greatness. To Wordsworth nothing is what we call "poetry," that is, a fanciful thing, apart from reality; he is not sure whether even the imagination is so much as a transfiguring, or only an unveiling, of natural things. Often he gives you the thing and his impressions of the thing, and then, with a childlike persistence of sincerity, his own doubt as to the precise truth of the thing. Whether I am right or wrong, he says to us gravely, I indeed scarcely know; but certainly I saw or heard this, or fancied that I saw or heard it; thus what I am telling you is, to me at least, a reality. It is thus that, as Matthew Arnold has said finely, "it might seem that nature not only gave him the matter for his poem, but wrote his poem for him." He has none of the poet's pride in his own invention, only a confidence in the voices that he has heard speaking when others were aware of nothing but silence. Thus it is that in the interpretation of natural things he can be absolutely pellucid, like pure light, which renders to us every object in its own colours. He does not "make poetry" out of these things; he sets them down just as they came to him. It is the fault of "Laodamia," and of some pieces like it, that there Wordsworth breaks through his own wise rule, and sets himself to compose, not taking things as they come. "Laodamia" is an attempt to be classic, to have those classic qualities of calmness and balance and natural dignity which, in a poem like "The Leech-Gatherer," had come of themselves, through mere truth to nature, to the humbleness of fact and the grandeur of impassioned thought illuminating it. Here, on the contrary, Wordsworth would be Greek as the Greeks were, or rather as they seem to us, at our distance from them, to be; and it is only in single lines that he succeeds, all the rest of the poem showing an effort to be something not himself. Thus this profoundly natural poet becomes for once, as Matthew Arnold has noted, "artificial," in a poem which has been classed among his masterpieces.

In the sonnets, on the other hand, we find much of Wordsworth's finest work, alike in substance and in form. "The sonnet's scanty plot of ground" suited him so well because it forced him to be at once concise and dignified, and yet allowed him to say straight out the particular message or emotion which was possessing him. He felt that a form so circumscribed demanded not only something said in every line, but something said with a certain richness; that when so few words could be used, those words must be chosen with unusual care, and with an attention to their sound as well as to their meaning. The proportion, it is true, of his bad sonnets to his good sonnets is so great, that, even in Matthew Arnold's scrupulous selection, at least six out of the sixty would have been better omitted. Taking them at their best, you will find that nowhere in his work has he put so much of his finest self into so narrow a compass. Nowhere are there so many splendid single lines, lines of such weight, such imaginative ardour. And these lines have nothing to lose by their context, as almost all the fine lines which we find in the blank verse poems have to lose. Wordsworth's blank verse is so imperfect a form, so heavy, limp, drawling, unguided, that even in poems like "Tintern Abbey" we have to unravel the splendours, and, if we can, forget the rest. In *The Prelude* and *The Excursion* poetry comes and goes at its own will, and even then, for the most part,

Its exterior semblance doth belie Its soul's immensity.

What goes on is a kind of measured talk, which, if one is in the mood for it, becomes as pleasant as the gentle continuance of a good, thoughtful, easy-paced, prosy friend. Every now and then an ecstasy wakes out of it, and one hears singing, as if the voices of all the birds in the forest cried in a human chorus.

Wordsworth has told us in his famous prefaces exactly what was his own conception of poetry, and we need do no more than judge him by his own laws. "Poetry," he says, "is the breath and finer spirit of all knowledge; it is the impassioned expression which is in the countenance of all science." "The poet thinks and feels in the spirit of human passions." The poet is "a man pleased with his own passions and volitions, and who rejoices more than other men in the spirit of life that is in him." "I have said," he reiterates, "that poetry is the spontaneous overflow of powerful feelings; it takes its origin from emotion recollected in tranquillity; the emotion is contemplated till, by a species of reaction, the tranquillity gradually disappears, and an emotion kindred to that which was before the subject of contemplation is gradually produced, and does itself actually exist in the mind." The poet, then, deals with "truth, carried alive into the heart by passion." "I have at all times," he tells us, "endeavoured to look steadily at my subject," and, as for the subject, "I have wished to keep the reader in the company of flesh and blood, persuaded that by so doing I shall interest him." "Personifications of abstract ideas rarely occur in these volumes, and are utterly rejected as an ordinary device to elevate the style and raise it above prose." "Poetic diction," which is always insincere, inasmuch as it is not "the real language of men in *any situation*," is to be given up, and, "it may safely be affirmed that there neither is, nor can be, any essential difference between the language of prose and metrical composition." The language which alone is suitable for verse, and which requires no change in its transference from the lips of men to the printed page, is defined, not very happily, in the original preface of 1798, as "the language of conversation in the middle and lower classes of society," and, in the revised preface of 1800, with perfect exactitude, as "a selection of the real language of men in a state of vivid sensation."

When these true, but to us almost self-evident things were said, Wordsworth was daring, for the first time, to say what others, when they did it, had done without knowing; and he was supposed to be trying to revolutionise the whole art of poetry. In reality, he was bringing poetry back to its senses, which it had temporarily lost under the influence of that lucid madness which Pope imposed upon it. The style of Pope was still looked upon as the type of poetical style, though Blake and Burns had shown that the utmost rapture of personal passion and of imaginative vision could be expressed, even in the eighteenth century, in a style which was the direct utterance of nature in her two deepest moods. Pope is the most finished artist in prose who ever wrote in verse. It is impossible to read him without continuous admiration for his cleverness, or to forget, while reading him, that poetry cannot be clever. While Herrick or Crashaw, with two instinctively singing lines, lets us overhear that he is a poet, Pope brilliantly convinces us of everything that he chooses, except of that one fact. The only moments when he trespasses into beauty are the moments when he mocks its affectations; so that

> Die of a rose in aromatic

pain remains his homage, unintentional under its irony, to that "principle of beauty in all things" which he had never seen.

But it was not only against the directly anti-poetical principles of Pope that Wordsworth protested, but against much that was most opposed to it, against the hyperbolical exaggerations of the so-called "metaphysical poets" of the seventeenth century, and against the half-hearted and sometimes ill-directed attempts of those who, in a first movement of reaction against Pope, were trying to bring poetry back to nature, against Thomson, Cowper, and Crabbe. He saw that Thomson, trying to see the world with his own eyes, had only to some degree won back the forgotten "art of seeing," and that, even when he saw straight, he could not get rid of that "vicious style" which prevented him from putting down what he had seen, just as he saw it. Cowper's style is mean, rather than vicious; "some critics," says Wordsworth, after quoting some lines from a poem of Cowper, then and afterwards popular, "would call the language prosaic; the fact is, it would be bad prose, so bad that it is scarcely worse in metre." With Crabbe, who may have taught Wordsworth something, we have only to contrast, as the note to *Lucy Gray* asks us to do, "the imaginative influences which" Wordsworth "endeavoured to throw over common life with Crabbe's matter-of-fact style of handling subjects of the kind." For, seeming, as Wordsworth did to the critics of his time, to bring poetry so close to prose, to make of it something prosaic, he is really, if we will take him at his word, and will also judge him by his best, the advocate of a more than usually lofty view of poetry.

In saying that there is no essential difference between the language of prose and of verse, Wordsworth is pointing straight to what constitutes the essential difference between prose and poetry: metre. An old delusion reappeared the other day, when a learned writer on aesthetics quoted from Marlowe:

Was this the face that launched a thousand ships,
And burned the topless towers of Ilium?

and assured us that "it is certain that he could only have ventured on the sublime audacity of saying that a face launched ships and burned towers by escaping from the limits of ordinary language, and conveying his metaphor through the harmonious and ecstatic movements of rhythm and metre." Now, on the contrary, any writer of elevated prose, Milton or Ruskin, could have said in prose precisely what Marlowe said, and made fine prose of it; the imagination, the idea, a fine kind of form, would have been there; only one thing would have been lacking, the very finest kind of form, the form of verse. It would have been poetical substance, not poetry; the rhythm transforms it into poetry, and nothing but the rhythm.

When Wordsworth says "that the language of a large portion of every good poem, even of the most elevated character, must necessarily, except with reference to the metre, in no respect differ from that of good prose," he is admitting, on behalf of metre, all that any reasonable defender of "art for art's sake" ever claimed on its behalf. But he is not always, or not clearly, aware of the full meaning of his own argument, and not always consistent with it. He is apt to fall back on the conventional nicety of the worst writers whom he condemns, and can speak of

The fowl domestic and the household dog,

or can call a gun "the deadly tube," or can say of the organ,

While the tubed engine feels the inspiring blast.

He is frequently provincial in thought, and thus trivial in expression, as when he says with conviction:

Alas! that such perverted zeal
Should spread on Britain's favoured ground!

He can be trivial for so many reasons, one of which is a false theory of simplicity, not less than a lack of humour.

My little Edward, say why so;
My little Edward, tell me why,

is the language of a child, not of a grown man; and when Wordsworth uses it in his own person, even when he is supposed to be speaking to a child, he is not using "the real language of men" but the actual language of children. The reason why a fine poem like "The Beggars" falls so immeasurably below a poem like "The Leech-Gatherer" is because it has in it something of this infantile quality of speech. I have said that Wordsworth had a quality of mind which was akin to the child's fresh and wondering apprehension of things. But he was not content with using this faculty like a man; it dragged him into the depths of a second childhood hardly to be distinguished from literal imbecility. In a famous poem, "Simon Lee," he writes:

My gentle reader, I perceive
    How patiently you've waited;
And now I fear that you expect
    Some tale will be related.

There are more lines of the kind, and they occur, as you see, in what is considered one of Wordsworth's successes. If one quoted from one of the failures!

It was from Burns, partly, that Wordsworth learnt to be absolutely straightforward in saying what he had to say, and it is from Burns that he sometimes even takes his metres, as in the two fine poems written in his memory.

Well might I mourn that He was gone
Whose light I hailed when first it shone,

When, breaking forth as nature's own,
　　It showed my youth
How Verse may build a princely throne
　　On humble truth.

That has the very quality of Burns, in its admission of a debt which is more obvious than any other, except that general quickening of poetic sensibility, of what was sometimes sluggish in his intellect, which he owed to Coleridge, and that quickening of the gift of seeing with emotion, which he owed to his sister Dorothy. But, at his best and worst, hardly any poet seems so much himself, so untouched by the influence of other poets. When he speaks he is really speaking, and when speech passes into song, as in some of those happy lyrics which preserve a gravity in delight, the words seem to sing themselves unconsciously, to the tune of their own being. In what seems to me his greatest, as it is certainly his most characteristic poem, "The Leech-Gatherer," he has gathered up all his qualities, dignity, homeliness, meditation over man and nature, respectful pity for old age and poverty, detailed observation of natural things, together with an imaginative atmosphere which melts, harmonises, the forms of cloud and rock and pool and the voices of wind and man into a single composition. Such concentration, with him, is rare; but it is much less rare than is commonly supposed to find an almost perfect expression of a single mood or a single aspect of nature, as it has come to him in his search after everything that nature has to say to us or to show us. . . .

In one of his poems Wordsworth rebukes Byron because he

dares to take
Life's rule from passion craved for passion's sake;

and, in an utterance reported in Mr. Myers' Life, takes credit to himself for his moderation, in words which can hardly be read without a smile: "Had I been a writer of love-poetry, it would have been natural to me to write it with a degree of warmth which could hardly have been approved by my principles, and which might have been undesirable for the reader." Not unnaturally, Wordsworth was anxious for it to be supposed that he had not attained tranquillity without a struggle, and we hear much, from himself and others, of his restlessness, which sent him wandering about the mountains alone, of his nervous exhaustion after writing, of his violence of feeling, the feeling for his sister, for instance, which seems to have been the one strong and penetrating affection of his life. Were not these stirrings, after all, no more than breaths of passing wind ruffling the surface of a deep and calm lake? I think almost the most significant story told of Wordsworth is the one reported by Mr. Aubrey

De Vere about the death of his children. "Referring once," he tells us, "to two young children of his who had died about *forty years* previously, he described the details of their illnesses with an exactness and an impetuosity of troubled excitement, such as might have been expected if the bereavement had taken place but a few weeks before. The lapse of time seemed to have left the sorrow submerged indeed, but still in all its first freshness. Yet I afterwards heard that at the time of the illness, at least in the case of one of the two children, it was impossible to rouse his attention to the danger. He chanced to be then under the immediate spell of one of those fits of poetic inspiration which descended on him like a cloud. Till the cloud had drifted, he could see nothing beyond." The thing itself, that is to say, meant little to him: he could not realise it; what possessed him was the "emotion recollected in tranquillity," the thing as it found its way, imaginatively, into his own mind.

And it was this large, calm, impersonal power, this form of imagination, which, as he says,

> Is but another name for absolute power
> And clearest insight, amplitude of mind,
> And Reason in her most exalted mood,

which made him able to

> sit without emotion, hope, or aim,
> In the loved presence of his cottage fire,

and yet to look widely, dispassionately, into what in man is most akin to nature, seeing the passions almost at their origin, where they are still a scarcely conscious part of nature. Speaking of his feeling for nature, he tells us that,

> As if awakened, summoned, roused, constrained,
> I looked for universal things, perused
> The common countenance of earth and sky.

And so, in his reading of "the great book of the world," of what we call the human interest of it, he looked equally, and with the same sense of a constraining finger pointing along the lines, for universal things.

> Him who looks
> in steadiness, who hath among least things
> an under-sense of greatest; sees the parts
> as parts, but with a feeling of the whole,

is his definition of what he has aimed at doing: it defines exactly what he has done. The links of things as their roots begin to form in the soil, their close intertexture underground: that is what he shows us, completing his interpretation of nature. We must go to other poets for any vivid consciousness or representation of all that waves in the wind when sap and fibre become aware of themselves above ground. . . .

To Wordsworth there was an actual divine inhabitant of woods and rocks, a divinity implicit there, whom we had only to open our eyes to see, visible in every leaf and cranny. What with other men is a fancy, or at the most a difficult act of faith, is with him the mere statement of a fact. While other men search among the images of the mind for that poetry which they would impute to nature, Wordsworth finds it there, really in things, and awaiting only a quiet, loving glance. He conceives of things as loving back in return for man's love, grieving at his departure, never themselves again as they had been when he loved them. "We die, my friend," says the Wanderer, looking round on the cottage which had once been Margaret's;

> Nor we alone, but that which each man loved
> And prized in his particular nook of earth
> Dies with him, or is changed.

Even the spring in the garden seems conscious of a grief in things.

> Beside yon spring I stood,
> And eyed its waters till we seemed to feel
> One sadness, they and I. For them a bond
> Of brotherhood is broken: time has been
> When, every day, the touch of human hand
> Dislodged the natural sleep that binds them up
> In mortal stillness; and they ministered
> To human comfort.

What a responsiveness of the soul to the eye, "the most despotic of our senses," the sense of sight, as he calls it, truly! It is his chief reason for discontentment with cities, that in them the eye is starved, to the disabling or stunting of the growth of the heart:

> Among the close and overcrowded haunts
> Of cities, where the human heart is sick,
> And the eye feeds it not, and cannot feed.

The eye is realised by him as the chief influence for good in the world, an actual moral impulse, in its creation and radiation of delight. Sight, to him, is feeling; not, as it is with Keats, a voluptuous luxury, but with some of the astringent quality of mountain air. When he says that the valley "swarms with sensation," it is because, as he t ells us of one living among the Lakes, "he must have experienced, while looking on the unruffled waters, that the imagination by their aid is carried into recesses of feeling otherwise impenetrable." It is into these recesses of feeling that the mere physical delight of the eye carries him, and, the visible world so definitely apprehended, the feeling latent in it so vividly absorbed, he takes the further step, and begins to make and unmake the world about him.

> I had a world about me—'twas my own,
> I made it, for it only lived to me.

The Beatific Vision has come to him in this tangible, embodied form, through a kind of religion of the eye which seems to attain its final rapture, unlike most forms of mysticism, with open eyes. The tranquillity, which he reached in that consciousness of

> a motion and a spirit, that impels
> All thinking things, all objects of all thought,
> And rolls through all things,

is his own form of perfect spiritual happiness, or attainment. That "impassioned contemplation" of nature, which he prized above all things, was his way of closing the senses to all things external to his own contemplation. It came to him through sight, but through sight humanised into feeling, and illuminated by joy and peace. He saw nature purely, with no uneasy or unworthy emotions, which nature might need to purify. Nature may, indeed, do much to purify the soul of these emotions, but until these are at rest it cannot enter fully, it cannot possess the soul with itself. The ultimate joy, as Wordsworth knew, that comes to the soul from the beauty of the world, must enter as light enters a crystal, finding its own home there and its own flawless mirror.

Yet, as there is an ecstasy in which joy itself loses so much of separateness as to know that it is joy, so there is one further step which we may take in the companionship of nature; and this step Wordsworth took. In the note to that ode into which he has put his secret doctrine, the "Intimations of Immortality from Recollections of Early Childhood," he says, speaking of his early years: "I was often unable to think of external things as having external existence, and I communed with all that I saw as something not apart from, but inherent in, my own immaterial nature. Many times while going to school have I grasped at a wall or tree to recall myself from this abyss of idealism to the reality." To Wordsworth, external things existed so visibly, just because they had no existence apart from the one eternal and infinite being; it was for the principle of infinity in them that he loved them, and it was this principle of infinity which he seemed to recognise by a simple act of memory. It seemed to him, quite literally, that the child really remembers "that imperial palace whence we came"; less and less clearly as human life sets all its veils between the soul and that relapsing light. But, later on, when we seem to have forgotten, when the world is most real to us, it is by an actual recognition that we are reminded, now and again, as one of those inexplicable flashes carries some familiar, and certainly never seen, vision through the eyes to the soul, of that other, previous fragment of eternity which the soul has known before it accepted the comfortable bondage and limit of time. And so, finally, the soul, carried by nature through nature, transported by visible beauty into the presence of the source of invisible beauty, sees, in one annihilating flash of memory, its own separate identity vanish away, to resume the infinite existence which that identity had but interrupted.

—Arthur Symons, "Wordsworth,"
Fortnightly Review, January 1902, pp. 39–52

Charles Wharton Stork
"The Influence of the Popular Ballad on Wordsworth and Coleridge" (1914)

Charles Wharton Stork's essay focuses on the divergent ways that Wordsworth and Coleridge made use of the ballad tradition. Stork's discussion of the ballad influence goes beyond an examination of the poems in the *Lyrical Ballads* to include many of the pair's later works, although he begins his discussion with Wordsworth's famous preface to that work. As is well known based on their individual contributions to the *Lyrical Ballads*, Wordsworth was attracted to both the simplicity of the genre and its subject matter—which treated mainly the lives of the lower social classes—and the space it allowed for sentimentality and domestic concerns. Coleridge, on the other hand, was drawn to the ballad's supernatural trappings and its medieval origins with its focus on a remote time. However, despite Wordsworth's describing many of his poems as ballads, Stork maintains that few were actually in the tradition. He supports his argument by defining the ballad as a genre animated by action and suspense, treating its characters impersonally and objectively, characteristics that were antithetical to Wordsworth's poetic goals. Simply stated, the ballad aimed at telling a vivid and fast-paced story. Wordsworth, however, was interested in conveying the individual character's life and emotions in a slower-paced narrative that would cause the reader to reflect. At the same time, Wordsworth purposefully rejected any notion of the ballad being exclusively a melodramatic poem that could produce alarming effects. For Wordsworth, the characters' feelings were the heart of the matter, not the situation or settings of traditional ballads. While Stork identifies Wordsworth's genius in reworking the tradition by pointing out his original approach and departure from older conceptions as well as eighteenth-century conventions, Stork nevertheless finds inherent weaknesses in Wordsworth's reworking of the ballad, "insipidities in the poems which they inspired," works in which "a simple style more than any other demands an unusual inspiration in its matter to raise it above the commonplace." Stork also identifies a type of narcissism on Wordsworth's part to the extent that the poet's faithful portrayal of his characters' feelings are really just manifestations of how he saw them. Nevertheless, Stork finds a great deal of virtue in Wordsworth's reworking of the traditional ballad in that his efforts serve as a counterstatement to the Della Cruscans, a group of late-eigtheenth-century writers known for their sentimental poems, and other forms of eighteenth-century artificiality.

—◦◦◦— —◦◦◦— —◦◦◦—

Although both Wordsworth and Coleridge were strongly influenced by the popular ballad, they were attracted by this form for very different reasons and affected by it in very different ways. The one point in common is that this influence was in both cases mainly for good. Wordsworth was drawn to the ballad by its directness and simplicity of style, and by the fact that it often treats of the lower classes of men in what Rousseau would have called a natural state of society! Coleridge took up the ballad for a nearly opposite reason; *i.e.*, because of its remoteness from modern life, a remoteness that left him free play for his imagination. Thus, oddly, Wordsworth cultivated the ballad because it had *once* been close to common life; Coleridge because it was *now* remote from common life and gave him a form remarkably susceptible of that strangeness which the romantic genius habitually adds to beauty. Wordsworth preferred the domestic, or occasionally the sentimental-romantic, ballad; Coleridge markedly adhered to the supernatural ballad.

As the subject is rather complex for a brief survey, the following arrangement will be adopted: to examine in each author separately the influence of the ballad, first generally and in relation to his theory of poetry; secondly, in detail as to the subject, treatment, and form of the poetry itself.

At the outset we encounter Wordsworth's prefaces to the *Lyrical Ballads* and Coleridge's attempts to explain them in his *Biographia Literaria*. Wordsworth's theory of poetry has been such a mooted question that we are certain to overemphasize his statement of it unless we note what he himself thought of the *Prefaces*. In a side-note[1] on the manuscript of Barren Field's *Memoirs of the Life and Poetry of William Wordsworth* the poet asserts: "I never cared a straw about the 'theory,' and the 'preface' was written at the request of Mr. Coleridge, out of sheer good nature." And again: "I never was fond of writing prose." Coleridge, too,[2] claims the *Preface* as "half a child of my own brain." We may pause to note that it was rather unfair of the philosopher-critic to tempt his colleague into disadvantageous ground and then fall upon him.

What influence the *Reliques* had upon Wordsworth it may not be easy to determine; that he felt *such* an influence is proved by the following passage:[3] "I do not think that there is an able writer in verse of the present day who would not be proud to acknowledge his obligations to the '*Reliques*'; I know that it is so with my friends; and, for myself, I am happy on this occasion to make a public avowal of my own."

We may safely assert that the influence of ballad narrative treatment upon Wordsworth's conception of poetry was very slight and very indirect. He wrote but few real ballads, though he wrote a good many poems he called ballads. His theory of poetry clearly and repeatedly disavows the only purpose for which a true ballad can exist, *viz.*, the effective telling of a dramatic story for its own sake.

> The moving accident is not my trade;
> To freeze the blood I have no ready arts:
> 'Tis my delight, alone in summer shade,
> To pipe a simple song for thinking hearts.[4]

Again, speaking of the *White Doe*, he writes:[5] "I did not think the poem could ever be popular just because there was nothing in it to excite curiosity, and next because the main catastrophe was not a material but an intellectual one." All the action proceeding from the will of the chief agents is "fine-spun and unobtrusive"; Emily "is intended to be loved for what she *endures*." Let the dramatist "crowd his scene with gross and visible action"; but let the narrative poet "see if there are no victories in the world of spirit," let him bring out the interest in "the gentler movements and milder appearances of society and social intercourse, or the still more mild and gentle solicitations of irrational and inanimate nature." Wordsworth decries[6] the qualities of writing which "startle the world into attention by their audacity and extravagance" or by "a selection and arrangement of incidents by which the mind is kept upon the stretch of curiosity, and the fancy amused without the trouble of thought."

Other passages could be added, but the foregoing will suffice to show why Wordsworth's ballads as ballads are unsatisfying. His entire theory (which, at least in this case, underlay his practice) was opposed to the method of the popular ballad. The ballad depends upon action, Wordsworth upon description and reflection; the ballad is objective and impersonal, Wordsworth maintains[7] that the poet should treat of things not "as they *are*" but "as they *seem* to exist to the senses, and to the passions." Consequently the ballad proceeds, as Professor Gummere says,[8] by a "leaping and lingering" method, holding the attention by rapid movement, suspense, and adequate climax; whereas Wordsworth disbelieves[9] in "gross and violent stimulants" and says[10] that in his poems "the feeling therein developed gives importance to the action and situation, and not the action and situation to the feelings." The ballad is unconscious, existing in and for itself; but in Wordsworth's opinion[11] poetry should have a purpose and should be the product of a mind which has thought long and deeply.

In general we may say that no other of the great English poets was by temperament so incapable of writing a good ballad as Wordsworth. All that he got from the subject matter of the ballad was the idea of attaching his descriptions and reflections to a story, or, as it often proved, to an incident. What, then, were these "obligations" to the ballad which the poet was so careful to acknowledge?

The truth seems to be that Wordsworth's genius (which, as Coleridge says, was one of the most marked in English poetry) was scarcely at all imitative. The ballad first suggested to the philosopher that he should convey his teaching by means of narrative. Afterwards it suggested something else far more important; namely, that he should adopt a simple style, close to the usage of common people in real life. In any case, when Wordsworth wrote objectively, he would have written of the peasants who lived around him, but *Percy's Reliques* caused him to write in a more direct and intimate way than Crabbe had done. Yet though the style of *We are Seven* is simple, it is not with a ballad simplicity, but in a manner akin to Blake, whose every phrase must be pondered, even dreamt over, before we realize its full significance. As we read the *Lyrical Ballads* we get not so much the incident that is related, as the personality of the poet; we see things not as they are, but as they seemed to Wordsworth.

It was fortunate that such a profound poet should have early formed a style so lucid, but in other ways the choice of models was not advantageous. Wordsworth evidently thought[12] he was writing as primitive men had written, and justified his deviation from the prevalent fashion by declaring[13] that "poems are extant, written upon humble subjects, and in a more naked and simple style than I have aimed at, which have continued to give pleasure from generation to generation." The foregoing obviously refers to ballads. Wordsworth wrote of humble people as he thought they might have written of themselves, he strove to be a voice to those

> men endowed with highest gifts,
> The vision and the faculty divine,
> Yet wanting the accomplishment of verse.[14]

Whether or not he succeeded in this, he gave English literature some of its noblest poetry in the attempt, though his most successful narrative form was not the stanza but blank verse or octosyllabic couplets.

The reason why the narrative style of the *Lyrical Ballads* seems to us often so flat, even now that we know its elements of greatness, is easy to explain. The old ballads which the critics, from Sir Philip Sidney to Professor Child, have taught us to admire are elementally tragic and compelling; the ballads Wordsworth preferred tame and dilute Eighteenth-Century versions. He cultivated the spirit not of "the grand old ballad of Sir Patrick Spence," but of *The Babes in the Wood*;[15] and we may suppose he enjoyed less the stirring tales of Percy and Douglas, than[16] the "true simplicity and genuine pathos" of *Sir Cauline*, principally (as he knew) the product of the "Augustan" Thomas Percy. Without denying a certain merit to Wordsworth's favorites, we need not be surprised to find insipidities in the poems which they inspired. These faults are prominent from the fact that a simple style more than any other demands an unusual inspiration in its matter to raise it above the commonplace, and Wordsworth could never see when his subject fell from the significant to the trivial. The "gross and violent stimulants" of the old ballad narrative gave vitality to many a weak phrase and line; with the modern poet the interest of each passage started from a dead level and, being helped by no poetic convention of any sort, depended solely on the intrinsic power of the given poetic impulse.

Few writers have dared to depend upon pure poetry (re-inforced, however, by deep moral purpose) so entirely as did Wordsworth, who discarded story interest and all the adventitious helps of imagery associated with poetic stimuli. The result was that he earned all he won. It is of course true, as Coleridge says,[17] that in the *Lyrical Ballads* there is a certain "inconstancy of style" (we should call it a lack of integrity in tone) which intrudes because the poet will not choose suitable subjects, or, having chosen,[18] will not raise the weaker portions to the level of the best by the use of poetical conventions of any sort. But in the *Lyrical Ballads* Wordsworth has established the habit of absolute sincerity which has made his greatest passages and poems a model of what Bagehot justly calls "the pure style" in poetry. How large a share the ballad had in forming this habit every reader must judge for himself. The influence of Milton, while it tended to obviate baldness of style, was at the same time a re-inforcement to Wordsworth's native sincerity. Perhaps even Pope, with whom he rather unexpectedly asserts that he is familiar,[19] may have helped Wordsworth to clarity and memorable lines. But the ballad influence is always to be reckoned with, particularly in some of the greatest later poems.

Having considered the general influence of the ballad on Wordsworth's poetry and theory of poetry, we shall now take up the specific details of his practice. There are three distinct types of influence to be noted: first, imitations of the Eighteenth-Century domestic ballad, usually built around trifling incidents of the poet's own experience; secondly, ballads proper, impersonal poems with genuine story interest usually taken from tradition; and thirdly, poems founded on old ballad ideas but given a totally new significance.

In the first class the subjects are all modern and realistic. We think at once of *Lucy Gray, Peter Bell, Ruth, The Idiot Boy*, etc., etc. This is the class which illustrates Wordsworth's remark that the situations were only used to bring out the characters. Poetry of this class is very uneven, because the simplified style leaves each theme to stand or fall on its merits. In *Peter Bell* a great deal of incident is used rather unconvincingly to account for a change of heart in the hero. In *Ruth* the story brings out the chastened beauty of a soul ennobled by suffering. These two may stand as types of the poet's failure and success; as to the others, let every reader form his own opinion, remembering, however, that a trivial subject may be developed into a far from trivial poem.

A difficulty that besets us here is to distinguish between the ballad and the lyric in a given case. Where shall we class *The Reverie of Poor Susan*, or *The Childless Father*, or *The Fountain*? As all the poems are in a sense lyrical, *i.e.*, the vehicle of personal feeling, and none strictly a ballad, we shall give up any formal attempt to classify them. In the *Lyrical Ballads* Wordsworth sometimes uses subjects remote in place, but he introduces only two which are set in the traditional past. Of these *Hart-Leap Well* begins with a true narrative swing, but shirks the climax ("I will not stop to tell how far he fled Nor will I mention by what death he died"), runs into description and reflection, and ends with a moral. *Ellen Irwin* belongs to the second class of ballad influence.

Despite the praise given to the *Lyrical Ballads*, Wordsworth hardly ever returned to their method. He may have felt that the blank verse of *The Brothers* and *Michael* was a less dangerous and more dignified medium for the lessons he wished to impart by means of the life around him. At all events, his next attempts in the ballad are ballads proper, objective, set in the past and in story sufficient unto themselves. To this class belong *Ellen Irwin, The Seven Sisters, The Horn of Egremont Castle*, and *The Force of Prayer*. All of these subjects are medieval and all are on stock ballad themes; that is why they are so easy to classify. The point here to be noted is that, though all of these are respectable poems, never descending to bathos, they have contributed and will contribute very little to their author's reputation. When Wordsworth does with a ballad what a ballad should do, he achieves only mediocrity. Better are his earlier nondescript efforts, with their glaring faults and their characteristic virtues.

The third class is the most interesting of all, uniting as it does the attraction of the old ballad with some of the finest poetry in all of Wordsworth. To this we may perhaps relegate two poems from the Tour in Scotland, *Rob Roy's Grave* and *The Solitary Reaper*. The hero of the former appears in a dramatic monologue which anticipates the manner of Browning; it breathes healthy humor and a fine open-air spirit of liberty. In *The Solitary Reaper* we have a picture as immortal as any by Millet. So, Wordsworth believed, the two principal themes of the ballad were handed down; the "old, unhappy, far-off things" and the "familiar matter of to-day." It was the latter type which the poet had cultivated first; he was later to reflect the spirit of "battles long ago."

If there are any two poems of Wordsworth more strikingly noble than the rest, are they not the *Song at the Feast of Brougham Castle* and *The White Doe of Rylstone*? If we answer yes, the reason will be because in these two poems only is Wordsworth's philosophy of life brought into relief by contrast with its opposite. In Lord Clifford we have opposed glorious action and humble but soul-sufficing patience, and it is because the impulse to action is so splendidly connoted in the lines

Armor rusting in his halls
On the blood of Clifford calls

that the victory of forbearance is so memorable.

In the *White Doe* the case is similar, although the motives are less dramatically contrasted. This poem embodies perhaps the deepest expressions of Wordsworth's belief in the refining power of suffering, especially when it is endured amid "nature's old felicities."[20] The mystic symbolism of the doe is a new effect, slightly anticipated, perhaps, by such lyrics as *The Cuckoo* and by the fish in *Brougham Castle*. It was evidently Wordsworth's hope[21] that the story, taken bodily from the ballad *The Rising in the North*, might serve to present his convictions more clearly and forcibly than they could otherwise be stated, and although Hazlitt[22] thought the narrative part a "drag," the majority of critics have sustained the author's choice. The narrative is very spirited in itself and, as in the case of *Brougham Castle*, the virtues of action bring out most clearly the higher virtues of endurance. It would be out of place to praise further; we may only remark that in *The White Doe* Wordsworth makes his best use, both in style and in substance, of the popular ballad.

As we noted in treating the *Lyrical Ballads*, an accurate classification of ballad influence upon Wordsworth is impossible; but at least a few random cases of the first and third types should here be mentioned. After the *Lyrical Ballads* there are only two important stanzaic narrative poems dealing with the present, viz., *Fidelity* and *The Highland Boy*; a fact showing how far the poet had receded from his earlier practice. Both of these poems contain beauties far more noteworthy than any in the objective medieval ballads. A little-known piece, which is, however, remarkable from our point of view, is *George and Sarah Green*, perhaps the only poem composed as a balladist would have composed it. These lines were not the result of "emotion recollected in tranquillity"; for Wordsworth tells us[23] he "effused them" under the direct emotion caused by the event. They give that impression to the reader; the reflections attached are scarcely more complicated than those of a villager might have been, and the whole has the ballad quality of being more affecting than the sum of its parts—as if the poet had composed too fast to put in all he felt. Similar, but more extended and less poignant, is Wordsworth's last narrative effort, *The Westmoreland Girl*.

For the third class of influence, old ballad motives with modern treatment, we may perhaps claim the Yarrow series, with their haunting sense of ancient wrong and sorrow in the background of the scene. On the other hand, Wordsworth's early and very interesting play *The Borderers*, disappoints the promise of its title by giving us no hint of traditional matter save a passing allusion to the fairies. The classic *Laodamia* is out of our province; so are the medieval romances, *The Egyptian Maid* and *Artegal and Elidure*, both in the manner of Spenser. The faint traces noticeable in blank-verse poems such as *The Brothers* may also be passed by.

Nearly all the ballads of the first (contemporary) class (Part One of *Hart-Leap Well* belongs to the second) are told either by the poet or by some unnecessary third person, as opposed to the popular usage of never bringing in the pronoun "I." Again, Wordsworth's primary interest in character gives us individual figures instead of ballad types, people who merely do things. In his objective medieval ballads he has less chance for intimate analysis, a principal reason why these poems are nugatory. In the more subjective poems of our third class we have for the first time character contrast, that feature essential to all dramatic effects. Lord Clifford in *Brougham Castle* has two natures, the active spirit of the ballad hero and the passive fortitude developed in him by

The silence that is in the starry sky,
The sleep that is among the lonely hills.

In *The White Doe* Emily and Francis are represented minutely, the others almost with ballad brevity, but with the more effect in contrast for that very reason.

Wordsworth began with the regular four-line stanza, but soon branched out into variants; *e.g.*, an eight-line stave riming *a b a b c d c d*, in which the "*a*'s" have always a double ending. Then there are many original combinations of couplets and alternate rimes, such as those in the ten-line stanza of *Her Eyes are Wild* and the eleven-line stanza of *The Thorn*. It would be out of proportion here to enumerate others; suffice it to say that they are all built upon the two original ballad norms of the rimed couplet and the four-line stanza with alternate rimes. The poet seems to have been experimenting to find a slightly more complex arrangement that would make his lines appear somewhat less bare, in fact he tells us[24] that he thinks the stanza used in *Goody Blake* an improvement on the stereotyped method. In *Ellen Irwin* he imitates Bürger's *Lenore*. The foot is nearly always the iambus, notable exceptions being *The Reverie of Poor Susan* and *The Childless Father*, in anapests. In lyric flexibility *The White Doe* is reminiscent, not always happily, of *Christabel*.

The three most marked qualities of popular ballad style[25]—the refrain, repetition of conventional lines and phrases, and "incremental repetition"— are conspicuously rare, diminishing from a moderate importance in *We Are Seven* to negligibility in almost all poems after the *Lyrical Ballads*. We have refrains in *The Thorn* and *The Seven Sisters*, that of the latter, "the solitude of Bennorie," suggesting of course the ballad of *The Two Sisters*. *The Idiot Boy* abounds in repeated phrases, but as a rule Wordsworth followed the modern method of thinking out synonyms and finding original adjectives. Of incremental repetition used for dramatic suspense and climax, as in *Babylon*, *Edward*, and many more of the best popular ballads, there is not one example. There is no conscious alliteration in Wordsworth. His forced use of inversion, borrowed from the imitation ballads, decreases steadily.

As to the language of the *Lyrical Ballads* not being the language of real life, Coleridge[26] is of course right. In a broad sense Wordsworth never wrote of anybody but himself; he gives us[27] not people as they are but people as they appear to him. We cannot, therefore, expect him to make them talk as they really would talk. His creations have a very strong and definite actuality, but it is largely an actuality lent them by their creator. As a penetrating critic has said in another connection, fact plus imagination gives another fact—the final fact being, as Coleridge notes,[28] much more interesting and universal than the original. Had Wordsworth written as he proposed, his poems would have been a little better and a great deal worse. It was in imitation of the Eighteenth-Century ballad style, which Wordsworth supposed was an adaptation of the speech of real life, that Lucy Gray was made to answer, "That, father, will I gladly do," surely a cardinal specimen of the namby-pamby; it was from the poet's own heart that the lines came—

No mate, no comrade Lucy knew;
She dwelt on a wide moor,

—The sweetest thing that ever grew
Beside a human door.

This last is what we may call the Blake note, so much like the ballad—and so much more unlike! Of course the two blend in different proportions, the personal driving out the imitative as time goes on. But if the style of the ballad had done no more than help Wordsworth to find the language of common sense, it would have rendered an infinite service in those days of the Della Cruscans and other continuators of Eighteenth-Century artificiality. The extent of this influence, as already stated, can never be calculated in the case of a poet who so entirely assimilated and so strongly modified all that affected him from outside.

* * *

The question of ballad influence on Coleridge is comparatively simple, but extremely interesting none the less; for although but one poem of importance is directly involved, that happens to be *The Rime of the Ancient Mariner. The Three Graves*, the fragment of *The Dark Ladie* and *Alice du Clos* are the only other ballads, though suggestions of the tradition appear elsewhere. And not only is the field of ballad influence in Coleridge very limited, but the character of that influence is almost uniform. As noted at the beginning of this article, it consists of a medieval glamour and remoteness almost invariably tending toward the supernatural. Wordsworth had at first made use of the ballad process somewhat as he conceived a peasant might have done; its closeness to common life and its directness of style had impressed him; he may have liked to think he was keeping the convention alive. Coleridge, on the other hand, was in his best poetry primarily a stylist, or perhaps we should rather say an artist. As with De Quincey and Poe (both of whom, like himself, were a prey to stimulants) his soul was enamoured of a beauty exquisitely strange and terrible, a beauty not of time or place, but dwelling in the utmost regions of the imagination. Now to the generation of Coleridge (and largely to those following) the strange and the terrible seemed to belong of right to the Middle Ages. De Quincey's *Avenger* and Poe's *Fall of the House of Usher* show how these kindred geniuses sought a kindred atmosphere. It was almost inevitable that Coleridge should have anticipated them, and that he should have used the ballad, as Chatterton did, only because in many ways it connoted the medieval.

Coleridge's theory and practice of poetry were instinctively those of art for art's sake. Despite his admiration for Wordsworth's stronger and sounder genius, even despite his preference[29] of his friend's poetry to his own, he could not have written other than he did. Consequently, polemical critics must range themselves under the banner of Arnold or of Swinburne in the dispute as to the priority of the two poets. With this dispute we have here nothing to do. It is, however, important to notice Coleridge's emphasis on style. He maintains[30] that "poetry justifies as poetry new combinations of language, and commands the omission of many others allowable in other compositions. Wordsworth has not sufficiently admitted the former in his system and has in his practice too frequently sinned against the latter." Again,[31] "Every phrase, every metaphor, every personification should have its justifying clause in some passion" of the poet or his characters. He finds Wordsworth's *Preface*[32] "very grand, ... but in parts obscure and harsh in style." Coleridge was evidently a man who justified literature, especially poetry, pretty largely by its style. We need not, then, be surprised to find that the ballad for him was not a method of treating actual life as it appeared to him, but rather an assortment of poetic devices by which to give the effects he was planning.

But the ballad did far more for Coleridge than furnish him with a few pigments by which to obtain what we may call delocalized local color, a coloring which makes real to us the country of his imagination. It is not by a coincidence that his greatest finished poem, the one poem universally known and universally praised, happens to be a ballad. Coleridge's weaknesses were lack of substance, lack of purpose, and lack of virility. The popular ballad exists only by right of substance, because the composer has a story to tell; its purpose is clear and inevitable, to tell the story and be done with it; and its form—in stanza, line, and phrase—is terse and vigorous. Here, then, is the reason why, as Mr. Traill has observed,[33] "*The Ancient Mariner* abounds in qualities in which Coleridge's poetry is commonly deficient"; why here alone we have "an extraordinary[34] vividness of imagery and terse vigor of descriptive phrase"; why we find[35] "brevity and self-restraint" here and not in any other poem by the same author. It was surely the ballad convention that kept the poem going, and it was possibly the ballad tenacity of purpose that caused it to be finished; the incomplete *Dark Ladie* throws some doubt on the latter point.

As to the causes of Coleridge's failure with his other poems, much has been said that need not here be rehearsed. He himself asserted[36] that the alleged obscurity of his poetry came from the uncommon nature of his thought, not from any defect in expression. He said[37] that poetry nearly always consists of thought and feeling blended, and that with him philosophical opinions came in to such an extent as to form a peculiar style that was sometimes a fault and sometimes a virtue. But on this point Coleridge, the subtle specialist in criticism, contradicts himself; for in another place[38] he declares that Milton's definition of poetry as "simple, sensuous, and passionate" sums up the whole matter. The second statement is of course the sounder view. Doubtless Coleridge hoped to write of abstruse subjects in a style that would not be abstruse, but it was impossible to get any simple, sensuous, or passionate results out of such an involved mode of thought as his. One has only to look at his prose, with its continual discriminations, qualifications, and parentheses, to see what so often hindered him from being a poet. On the other hand, Wordsworth's philosophical ideas, though deep, were simple; and his conviction as to their truth was so strong as to become a passion, as witness particularly the *Ode on Intimations of Immortality*.

Why was it, we may ask, that in *The Ancient Mariner* Coleridge forgot his involutions and assumed the virtues he so seldom had?—how could he for this once adopt the methods of the ballad? The answer is to be found in a certain mysticism which the modern man feels in the finest passages of the old ballads, a mysticism far simpler than that of Coleridge, but sufficiently permeating to appeal strongly to his sympathies. This effect is hardly to be described, hardly even to be illustrated—one critic will find it where another will deny that it exists—but every true lover of the ballad will have felt it again and again in favorite passages. Perhaps as safe a selection as any is the stanza of *Sir Patrick Spence* which Coleridge himself prefixed to his *Dejection*:

Late, late yestreen I saw the new Moon,
With the old Moon in her arms;
And I fear, I fear, my Master dear!
We shall have a deadly storm.[39]

Anyone who has tried to teach the ballad knows how difficult it is to bring the latent beauty of such passages before an average mind; but once the beauty is perceived, it has a strangely pervasive and enduring power. This Coleridge felt as no other man has ever felt it. Launching into the story with typical ballad abruptness, he yielded himself to the narrative current and was borne by it safely through the labyrinthine reefs of metaphysics indicated by his own notes in the margin. Though *The Ancient Mariner* is true Coleridge, it is in this case a Coleridge that has given up his own intricate and nebulous mysticism for the more direct and concrete mysticism of the ballad.

Coming to the consideration of Coleridge's ballads in detail, we find the first of these to be *The Three Graves*. The first two parts of this poem seem[40] certainly to antedate *The Ancient Mariner*. In the first place the poet asserts[41] that the story was taken from facts, in the second the style very strongly suggests Wordsworth, especially in its imitation of faults which Coleridge later condemns. As in Wordsworth, the tale is put into the mouth of an unnecessary third person, and such a prosaic indirectness as the following indicates a most inartistic resemblance to its models:

> She started up—the servant maid
> Did see her when she rose;
> And she has oft declared to me
> The blood within her froze.

But the story itself was one that would have been abhorrent to Wordsworth; the idea of a mother's guilty love for the affianced husband of her daughter would have repelled him at once. Coleridge professes[42] to have chosen the subject not from "any partiality to tragic, much less to monstrous events," but for its imaginative and psychological interest. This defense, by the way, is exactly that which a modern decadent might use on a similar occasion. The treatment, too, is distinctly immoral, or, as some critics now prefer to call it, unmoral. That an innocent pair should suffer from the curse of the guilty mother is, at least to an average person, repugnant. Coleridge's *penchant* toward the supernatural appears in his dwelling on this point and even going so far as to imagine that

> the mother's soul to Hell
> By howling fiends was borne,—

an unsatisfactory bit of poetic justice, as her curse lives after her. But there is power in the poem, a power of just the sort that anticipates the success of later pieces. Throughout the stanzas we feel the uncanny genius of the poet struggling in a trammeling element, often rising head and shoulders above it. *The Three Graves* is far from being a good poem, but fragmentary and inchoate though it is, we can hardly understand *The Ancient Mariner* without it.

This brings us to the center of our subject. After the experiment of *The Three Graves* Coleridge selected just the theme that suited him, and in the treatment kept tolerably clear of the hampering influence of his colleague. To be sure, Wordsworth supplied the idea[43] that the suffering of the Mariner should be represented as an atonement for the death of the albatross, and no doubt the concluding moral "He prayeth best" was composed under his influence; but these can easily be detached from the body of the poem. We are all familiar with the agreement[44] in regard to the *Lyrical Ballads* by which Wordsworth was to bring out the supernatural side of natural scenes and Coleridge was to bring out the natural, the humanly comprehensible, side of his supernatural phantasies. It was only in *The Ancient Mariner* that Coleridge definitely carried out his share of the undertaking.

The Ancient Mariner, however, was not written to illustrate a theory or even to carry out a conscious purpose. Few phrases could better sum up the effect of the poem than that of an inspired undergraduate who called Coleridge "a literary Turner." There is in these two the same glorifying brilliance of color, the same triumph of beauty over mere subject, the same marvellous gift of style which raises their respective arts almost to the emotional level of music. Even the human soul living through the scenes of the poem, which Lamb thought the greatest achievement of all, is rendered in a light of unreality; for the Mariner's most passionate outcry awakens no real pain in us. Why, then, if they are so vague, do this poem and (say) Turner's *Ulysses Deriding Polyphemus* exercise such a powerful and enduring influence over us? In the case of Turner we know that it is largely from the firm command of draughtsmanship which he allows us to see more clearly in his water-colors. In Coleridge a similar firmness comes from the groundwork of the ballad, the most marked and dominating of all the conventional forms in poetic narrative. The conciseness of the ballad and its insistent progression demand a relation of the parts to the whole not unlike that required by the laws of perspective. (This, like most analogies, may be carried too far, but in general it seems to be not inaccurate.)

Taking his plot from a dream,[45] Coleridge began his long flight unhampered by the weight of actuality; course and destination indefinite, as it were. Though the Mariner tells the tale, the effect on the reader is almost that of an impersonal narrative. The speaker tells nothing of who he is and little of what he does, he is as a helpless soul passing through strange experiences. Consequently we feel the events of the poem very immediately; we do not watch the hero as we watch Lord Clifford or Emily Norton, we live his adventure with our inmost being. It would seem from this that *The White Doe* is nearer to the old ballad than is *The Ancient Mariner*, but in reality we feel that the Nortons are always illustrating a philosophical idea, whereas the Mariner neither reasons nor causes us to reason. The explanations of his voyage are as mystically simple as are those about death in *The Wife of Usher's Well* or about fairyland in *Thomas Rymer*; the modern poet exercises hardly more arbitrary control than does the nameless bard. In both cases we feel intensely but abstractly. We notice that Coleridge is often tempted to digress, but the ballad inspiration drives him on, just as it drove the author of *Sir Patrick Spence*.

The story exists for its own sake as a work of art; essentially it conveys, or should convey, no moral. Its one weakness in form is its promise of a moral suggested, as we have seen, by Wordsworth. For the shooting of the albatross is an absurdly small offense to bring about such a punishment, and the attempt to make the other sailors responsible by having them approve the deed is even worse; besides, the accomplices are punished with death, whereas the principal expiates his sin. Fortunately we feel these defects but slightly, for we must relinquish our judicial qualities to follow the magical flow of the lines.

We have been somewhat over-accenting the resemblance of *The Ancient Mariner* to the ballad; the differences must not be forgotten. As a poet of the highest imaginative power and the most exquisite technic, Coleridge raises every stanza, every phrase, to a miracle of design. The very absence of apparent effort in the process is the final proof of his perfect art. What we find in a happy stanza here and there among the old ballads is a regular rule with the modern poet. His similes are nearly always brief and his metaphors direct, but the best of ballads is dull and uninspired in comparison. His greater subtlety and sensitiveness make the old forms seem rough and childish; his control of sound and color is like a sixth sense. And yet the balance is not all on one side. If the ballad has no real description, Coleridge has no real narration. What we have called a story is but a succession of descriptions photographed on the receptive soul of the Mariner. No one does anything, least of all the hero. Tried in the heat of normal human interest (the test of the ballad), the story melts away to nothing, its appeal can be only to the few. To the peasant for whom *The Hunting of the Cheviot* was written, the whole would have seemed the "tale of a cock and a bull" that the early reviewers found it. The imagery and verbal music of Coleridge are opposed to the compact statement and strong beat of the ballad not wholly to the advantage of the former. After all, there is a difference between real and acquired simplicity.

The unfinished *Ballad of the Dark Ladie* is closely connected[46] with the more lyrical poem, *Love*. The latter piece, Coleridge tells us, was intended to be an introduction to the *Ballad*. But the incidental story told in *Love* is apparently not that of *The Dark Ladie*. In *Love* the knight wears on his shield a burning brand, whereas the *Dark Ladie* sends her page to find "the Knight that wears / The Griffin for his crest." We have little clue as to what the tale of the *Ballad* is to be, but this little seems to indicate another motive than that used in *Love*. When Lord Falkland speaks to his lady of stealing away to his castle "Beneath the twinkling stars" and she shrinks from the idea of darkness and wishes to be married at noon, we have a foreboding of the *Lenore* theme, the dead lover returned to claim a living bride. There is a *feel* of the German ballad of terror about the poem noticeable in the rather gushing sentiment and in the effort to arouse a shudder. Farther than this the evidence will not take us. In *Alice du Clos*, however, we have a distinctly German ballad with several passages reminiscent of Scott. The theme is violent and painful, the narrative style labored, the diction overwrought. The fragile strength of Coleridge is sadly strained in handling such material; crude acts, the staple of the ballad, belong to a world outside his knowledge. Nevertheless the poem has beautiful descriptive lines and one stirring passage in Scott's better style:

Scowl not at me; command my skill
To lure your hawk back, if you will,
But not a woman's heart.

Alice du Clos is at least a better excursion into the territory of the rough and
ready school of poetry than is Scott's ballad of *Glenfinlas* into the realm of
the fantastic.

Passing on to consider ballad influence in the poems which are not ballads,
we begin naturally with *Christabel*. If ever style without substance could make
a perfect poem, it would be in the case of this unrivalled piece of filigree work.
To Swinburne it seemed the acme of poetic art; but few even of the truest art-
lovers can be satisfied by melody without sequence, and color without shape.
The poem, if one must define it, is a sort of lyric romance-caprice, in which
the lights are always changing like those of moonlight on a waterfall. But there
are ballad elements in the misty atmosphere of *Christabel*. Terse and direct
phrasing often lends the same vividness to supernatural effects that we have
noted in *The Ancient Mariner* and *Sir Patrick Spence*. For instance,

And Christabel saw that lady's eye,
And nothing else saw she thereby.
Quoth Christabel, So let it be!
And as the lady bade, did she.
Her gentle limbs did she undress,
And lay down in her loveliness.

But the steady flow of the ballad narrative and the steady pulse of the ballad
stanza are not there to give purpose and consistency to the whole. Perhaps
it was because he had no traditional model to sustain him that Coleridge
confessed[47] he had "scarce poetical enthusiasm enough to finish Christabel."
This at least we know: the story in *Christabel* forgets itself in long descriptions,
loses itself in digressions, changes repeatedly, and never ends.

Kubla Khan in small corresponds to *Christabel* in large, except that in it
the element of mystery is oriental instead of medieval; a fact which reminds
us that at this period the oriental novel was rivaling the "Gothic" in tales of
terror. The only point of interest for us in the shorter poem is the "woman
wailing for her demon lover," a figure more indigenous to the medieval
ballad[48] than to the Arabian tale. *Dejection* in the line "The grand old ballad
of *Sir Patrick Spence*" gives us the only specific mention of a ballad or of *the*
ballad which has thus far appeared in Coleridge's published writings. His
quotation from *Sir Patrick* at the beginning of such a personal poem shows
how sensitive he was to the uncanny *feel* of ballad lines even when they

merely displayed a popular belief as to the weather. *The Knight's Tomb* also has a ballad touch. *Love* has been sufficiently treated in connection with *The Dark Ladie*. *The Water Ballad* is too feeble to deserve the second part of its title. *The Devil's Walk* is an excellent humorous ballad.

It remains only to examine the details of ballad influence on Coleridge. *The Three Graves* is in form an imitation of Wordsworth's early style with but a suggestion of independence. In *Parts One* and *Two* the four-line stanza is unvaried, in *Parts Three* and *Four* occur several of the five and six-line stanzas common in *The Ancient Mariner*. As the story is modern, no medievalism can be brought in.

The original form of the title, which was *The Rime of the Ancyent Marinere*, shows at once what effect the author intended to create, but later Coleridge covered his tracks. In the first version of the text two repetitions and the words "phere," "n'old" and "aventure" were excised, probably to diminish the appearance of borrowing from the ballad; the word "swound" was also changed, but later restored. The spelling was modernised as in the title; the cases were not numerous, "cauld," "Emerauld," "chuse" and "neres" being examples.[49] Coleridge's taste was well-nigh perfect in this point, for the vocabulary of the poem conveys the idea of remoteness and never of affectation. In contrast, the unfortunate phrase "bootless bene" in *The Force of Prayer* is almost the only archaism in Wordsworth.

Ballad repetition, similarly, though much more frequent than in Wordsworth, is used with great discrimination. The echoing of a single word gives a greater physical reality to the idea in

The ice was here, the ice was there
The ice was all around;

as in "Alone, alone, all, all alone" and "Water, water everywhere." Phrases are repeated and parallelism preserved with the same effect, *i.e.*, the reader's attention is kept on the sensuous object and not diverted to the style by any unnecessary change of the wording. The phenomena of sunrise and sunset are made particularly intimate by this means and by the added touch of personification. Incremental repetition is not carried beyond the progression

He holds him with his glittering eye.

followed at the opening of the next stanza by

He holds him with his glittering eye.

There is no refrain anywhere in Coleridge. Alliteration, rugged in the ballad, is toned down so as not to jar the delicate verbal music of the whole. "The furrow followed free" subtly relieves the insistence of the "f"s by the play of "r"s and "l." There is strong vowel alliteration[50] in "Alone, alone, all, all alone," but the change of shading and the fact that the "glottal catch" is so faint a sound serve again to show how perfect is the poet's ear. Inversion, which is often so awkward in Wordsworth, is handled with the same care that appears in the other details of *The Ancient Mariner*.

That Coleridge was working toward a more purely lyrical metre we see by his variants of the regular ballad stanza. Internal rime is frequent. The five-line stanza *a b c c b* is used sixteen times, so that the following form is nearly typical:

> With throats unslaked, with black lips baked
> We could nor laugh nor wail;
> Through utter drought all dumb we stood!
> I bit my arm, I sucked the blood,
> And cried, A sail, a sail!

Coleridge also cultivated the six-line stanza (occasionally found in the old ballad), often repeating with a slight variation in lines 5 and 6 the thought of lines 3 and 4, as in

> A spring of love gushed from my heart,
> And I blessed them unaware;
> Sure my kind saint took pity on me
> And I blest them unaware.

This device is used by Poe in *The Raven, Ulalume*, and *Annabel Lee*. One passage, lines 203–211, is very irregular, suggesting the movement of *Christabel*. Two similes, lines 446–451 and 433–438, are so extended as to divert the eye to the secondary picture, and the description of the hermit at the opening of Part Seven is an absolute digression. All these points show the tendency toward lyric freedom and diffuseness which were to prevail in *Christabel* and *Kubla Khan*.

It seems not worth while to examine the details of ballad influence on other poems more minutely than has already been done. *The Dark Ladie* is very regular, *Alice du Clos* very irregular.

In *The Three Graves* we have a failure in the unmodified ballad, in *Christabel* we have a failure, at least from the point of view of narrative, in the lyrical romance; *The Ancient Mariner* stands between them, combining the merits of tradition with the merits of the poet's individual genius. It is hardly a coincidence, we may repeat, that Coleridge's most famous poem is that in which he made the most well-considered use of the popular ballad.[51]

Notes

1. *Letters of the Wordsworth Family*, ed. Knight, Vol. III, p. 121.
2. *Coleridge's Letters* edited by Ernest Hartley Coleridge, p. 386.
3. *Essay Supplementary to the Preface*, 1815. *Prose Works of William Wordsworth*, ed. Knight, Vol. II, p. 247.
4. *Hart-Leap Well*, opening stanza of *Part Second*.
5. *Letters*, III, pp. 486, 407.
6. *Prose Works*, II, p. 253.
7. *Idem*, II, p. 226.
8. *The Popular Ballad*, p. 91.
9. *Prose Works*, I, p. 52
10. *Idem*, I, p. 51.
11. *Prose Works*, I, pp. 49, 50.
12. *Prose Works*, I, p. 77.
13. *Idem*, I, p. 66.
14. *The Excursion*, Book I, ll. 78–80.
15. *Prose Works*, I, p. 71.
16. *Prose Works*, II, p. 243.
17. *Biographia Literaria*, chap, XXII.
18. *Idem*, chap. XIV.
19. *Letters*, III, p. 122.
20. From the sonnet, *The Trosachs*.
21. *Letters*, I, p. 343.
22. *Letters*, II, p. 62. Coleridge also says in generalising, "Wordsworth should never have abandoned the contemplative position" (*Table Talk*, July 21, 1832).
23. *Letters*, III, p. 465.
24. *Prose Works*, I, p. 69.
25. Cf. Professor O. L. Kittredge's *Introduction* to the Cambridge edition of *English and Scottish Popular Ballads* and his references to Professor Gummere's works.
26. *Biog. Lit.*, chaps, XVII, XX.
27. Cf. p. 301, *supra*, and note. Wordsworth expressly says that some of his figures were composites (Dowden, *Studies in Literature*, p. 145 and note).
28. *Biog, Lit.*, chap. XVII.
29. Traill's *Life of Coleridge* (English Men of Letters Series), p. 41.
30. *Letters*, pp. 374–5.
31. *Idem*, p. 374.
32. *Idem*, p. 387.

33. *Life of Coleridge*, p. 47.

34. *Idem*, p. 51.

35. *Idem*, p. 53.

36. *Letters*, pp. 104–5.

37. *Idem*, p. 197.

38. *Idem*, p. 197.

39. The correct form of this line is: "That we will come to harm." Coleridge must have mixed stanzas 7 and 8 of Percy's version.

40. Quoted in Mr. J. D. Campbell's notes, Globe ed., p. 590.

41. *Ibid.*, p. 590.

42. *Ibid.*, p. 590, 589.

43. Quoted in Mr. Campbell's notes, Globe ed., p. 394.

44. *Biog. Lit.*, beginning of chap. XIV.

45. Quoted in Mr. Campbell's notes, Globe ed., p. 594.

46. Quoted in Mr. Campbell's notes to the Globe ed., p. 612–3.

47. *Letters*, p. 317.

48. Cf. the ballad *James Harris* or *The Demon Lover*, Cambridge ed. of *Ballads*.

49. One of Professor Archibald MacMechan's students has discovered that all Coleridge's borrowings came from the first volume of Percy.

50. Cf. the paper read by Professor F. N. Scott before The Modern Language Association, Dec. 30th, 1913.

51. In other chapters of a proposed book on ballad influence upon English poetry since 1705 the author hopes to show that the ballad has had in general a salutary effect in modifying the extreme individualism of the Romantic Poets.

—Charles Wharton Stork,
"The Influence of the Popular Ballad on
Wordsworth and Coleridge," *PMLA*,
vol. 29, no. 3, 1914, pp. 299–326

THE PRELUDE

Samuel Taylor Coleridge (1807)

Samuel Taylor Coleridge commemorates *The Prelude* as a prophetic poem and hails Wordsworth as a bold and transcendent poet who, beyond charting the history of his own mind, has made the spiritual realm accessible. Coleridge charts the chronological structure of the poem, referring first to

Wordsworth's early inspirational feelings in regard to the beauty in nature, "by vital breathings secret as the soul / Of vernal growth," through his boyhood awakening to the sublime and awesome power of the physical world, "of tides obedient to external force." In referring to the "Hyblean murmurs" that he imagines Wordsworth listening to in his younger days, Coleridge equates the poet's experience with the town of Hybla in Sicily, a place celebrated for its honey and, by extension, a poetic reference to melliflous sounds. Most important in Coleridge's poem is his treatment of the French Revolution. In paying homage to Wordsworth, Coleridge speaks of the genesis of Wordsworth's political and social consciousness in the poet's enthusiasm for the promises embodied by the French Revolution, "of the Social Sense / Distending wide, and man beloved as man, / Where France in all her towns lay vibrating." Later Coleridge pays tribute to Wordsworth's triumph over the disappointment felt at the outcome of events. Coleridge commends him on his powers of recuperation and the consolations he found in nature. Equally important in his admiration for Wordsworth's not succumbing to profound disillusionment is Coleridge's need for solace. Suffering from "a heart forlorn," Coleridge finds renewed hope in listening to his dear companion: "And when—O Friend! my comforter and guide! Strong in thyself, and powerful to give strength!—Thy long sustained Song finally closed, . . . / Scarce conscious, and yet conscious of its close I sate, . . . Absorbed, yet hanging still upon the sound—And when I rose, I found myself in prayer." Finally, the greatest accolade of all comes with Coleridge placing Wordsworth in the esteemed company of his great poetic forebears, thus characterizing him as a transcendent spirit beyond the reach of time: "I viewed thee in the choir / Of ever-enduring men. / The truly great / Have all one age, and from one visible space / Shed influence! They, both in power and act, / Are permanent, and Time is not with them."

Friend of the wise! and Teacher of the Good!
Into my heart have I received that Lay
More than historic, that prophetic Lay
Wherein (high theme by thee first sung aright)
Of the foundations and the building up
Of a Human Spirit thou hast dared to tell
What may be told, to the understanding mind
Revealable; and what within the mind
By vital breathings secret as the soul
Of vernal growth, oft quickens in the heart
Thoughts all too deep for words!—
                    Theme hard as high!

Of smiles spontaneous, and mysterious fears
(The first-born they of Reason and twin-birth),
Of tides obedient to external force,
And currents self-determined, as might seem,
Or by some inner Power; of moments awful,
Now in thy inner life, and now abroad,
When power streamed from thee, and thy soul received
The light reflected, as a light bestowed—
Of fancies fair, and milder hours of youth,
Hyblean murmurs of poetic thought
Industrious in its joy, in vales and glens
Native or outland, lakes and famous hills!
Or on the lonely high-road, when the stars
Were rising; or by secret mountain-streams,
The guides and the companions of thy way!
Of more than Fancy, of the Social Sense
Distending wide, and man beloved as man,
Where France in all her towns lay vibrating
Like some becalmed bark beneath the burst
Of Heaven's immediate thunder, when no cloud
Is visible, or shadow on the main.
For thou wert there, thine own brows garlanded,
Amid the tremor of a realm aglow,
Amid a mighty nation jubilant,
When from the general heart of human kind
Hope sprang forth like a full-born Deity!
—Of that dear Hope afflicted and struck down,
So summoned homeward, thenceforth calm and sure
From the dread watch-tower of man's absolute self,
With light unwaning on her eyes, to look
Far on—herself a glory to behold,
The Angel of the vision! Then (last strain)
Of Duty, chosen Laws controlling choice,
Action and joy!—An Orphic song indeed,
A song divine of high and passionate thoughts
To their own music chaunted!
                         O great Bard!
Ere yet that last strain dying awed the air,
With stedfast eye I viewed thee in the choir
Of ever-enduring men. The truly great

Have all one age, and from one visible space
Shed influence! They, both in power and act,
Are permanent, and Time is not with them,
Save as it worketh for them, they in it.
Nor less a sacred Roll, than those of old,
And to be placed, as they, with gradual fame
Among the archives of mankind, thy work
Makes audible, a linked lay of Truth,
Of Truth profound a sweet continuous lay,
Not learnt, but native, her own natural notes!
Ah! as I listened with a heart forlorn,
The pulses of my being beat anew:
And even as Life returns upon the drowned,
Life's joy rekindling roused a throng of pains—
Keen pangs of Love, awakening as a babe
Turbulent, with an outcry in the heart;
And fears self-willed, that shunned the eye of Hope;
And Hope that scarce would know itself from Fear;
Sense of past Youth, and Manhood come in vain,
And Genius given, and Knowledge won in vain;
And all which I had culled in wood-walks wild,
And all which patient toil had reared, and all,
Commune with thee had opened out—but flowers
Strewed on my corse, and borne upon my bier
In the same coffin, for the self-same grave!

That way no more! and ill beseems it me,
Who came a welcomer in herald's guise,
Singing of Glory, and Futurity,
To wander back on such unhealthful road,
Plucking the poisons of self-harm! And ill
Such intertwine beseems triumphal wreaths
Strew'd before thy advancing!
                              Nor do thou,
Sage Bard! impair the memory of that hour
Of thy communion with my nobler mind
By pity or grief, already felt too long!
Nor let my words import more blame than needs.
The tumult rose and ceased: for Peace is nigh
Where Wisdom's voice has found a listening heart.
Amid the howl of more than wintry storms,

The Halcyon hears the voice of vernal hours
Already on the wing.
            Eve following eve,
Dear tranquil time, when the sweet sense of Home
Is sweetest! moments for their own sake hailed
And more desired, more precious, for thy song,
In silence listening, like a devout child,
My soul lay passive, by thy various strain
Driven as in surges now beneath the stars,
With momentary stars of my own birth,
Fair constellated foam, still darting off
Into the darkness; now a tranquil sea,
Outspread and bright, yet swelling to the moon.
And when—O Friend! my comforter and guide!
Strong in thyself, and powerful to give strength!—
Thy long sustained Song finally closed,
And thy deep voice had ceased—yet thou thyself
Wert still before my eyes, and round us both
That happy vision of beloved faces—
Scarce conscious, and yet conscious of its close
I sate, my being blended in one thought
(Thought was it? or aspiration? or resolve?)
Absorbed, yet hanging still upon the sound—
And when I rose, I found myself in prayer.

—Samuel Taylor Coleridge,
"To William Wordsworth, Composed on the
Night after His Recitation of a Poem on the
Growth of an Individual Mind," 1807

Walter Pater "Wordsworth" (1874)

Walter Pater begins by addressing the distinction between "Fancy" and the more powerful faculty of the imagination, the difference between a lower and higher degree, respectively, of intensity within the poet's contemplation of his subject matter and the poetic work itself. Pater maintains that Wordsworth made the most of this distinction and, more importantly, exemplifies the higher or more complex metaphysical distinction given the power of his vision. Taking into account the shift in political thinking from the radical attachments associated with the French Revolution to his later conservatism in response to those excesses, Pater maintains that these biographical facts have caused Wordsworth's critics to see him as insincere and have prevented them from recognizing the virtue that exists in Wordsworth's poetry. Nevertheless, Pater admits to mediocrity in some of the poems, instances in which the poet is prosaic and boring or when his passive reflection fails him.

Pater utilizes the paradigm of higher and lower moods as a standard against which to measure Wordsworth's poetic achievement, an accomplishment Pater maintains requires an inherent trust, in those who read his early poetry, that they will ultimately be rewarded with an understanding of his unique vision. Pater looks to discover the specifics of Wordsworth's sensibility and what it is that the poet satisfies in us, namely the people and values he holds dear. In characterizing modern poetry, Pater finds that Wordsworth's "intimate consciousness" of natural things is an aspect of a new type of verse and that he, more so than his contemporaries, is more sensitive because of his own innate contentment and spiritual composure. Pater compares Wordsworth's life to some early Italian or Flemish painters whose celestial visions enabled them to live a long life marked by quiet and independent work.

Speaking of the earlier prototype, *The Recluse*, in which Wordsworth took leave of the world of men and social intercourse in order to be in close communion with nature, Pater links Wordsworth's belief in an animating spirit that inhabits all of nature to other historical epochs that held the same beliefs. He cites the moods of Greek gods, which in turn generated other "strange aftergrowths." Pater further likens Wordsworth's acute vision and awareness to earlier ages when poets held a similar belief in the spirituality to be found in nature. Accordingly, Pater points out that this elevation of nature led to Wordsworth's understanding of people in the context of a particular landscape, linking the two in an ennobling way. Nature is elevated to the level of human thought so that it, too, has expression: "The leech-gatherer on the moor, the woman 'stepping westward,' are for him natural objects, almost in the same sense as the aged thorn, or the lichened rock on the heath."

In regard to the English lake country where Wordsworth sowed his religious understanding, Pater maintains that the poet was able to connect its most minute details with the great "events of life," that nature was granted a human voice yoking the simple people of the dales to the earth and elevating them to objects of worship. As part of that motivation to foster respect for residents of rural areas, Wordsworth employs the real language of common parlance but, as Pater points out, he does not celebrate the rural way of life in order to achieve an atmosphere of calm. Rather, Wordsworth's objective was to set forth a sympathetic understanding of the daily lives of average humans, "all the pathetic episodes of their humble existence, their longing, their wonder at fortune, their poor pathetic pleasures . . . won so hardly in the struggle for bare existence." Pater further maintains that Wordsworth goes beyond a spiritual connection to offer a new vision, connecting chance incidents with a distant memory.

Pater maintains that Wordsworth is often at his best when he embraces speculative ideas and renders these ideas in a clear and bold expression of excitement. This process is best exemplified in those books of *The Prelude* that engage the way in which imagination and taste are rescued from decay. Pater concludes that Wordsworth's poetry, like all great poetry, is a continual protest against what one should truly aspire to and value, with contemplation as the goal rather than a means to an end, the ultimate goal being to witness life with the appropriate emotions.

Some English critics at the beginning of the present century had a great deal to say concerning a distinction, of much importance, as they thought, in the true estimate of poetry, between the *Fancy,* and another more powerful faculty—the *Imagination*. This metaphysical distinction, borrowed originally from the writings of German philosophers, and perhaps not always clearly apprehended by those who talked of it, involved a far deeper and more vital distinction, with which indeed all true criticism more or less directly has to do, the distinction, namely, between higher and lower degrees of intensity in the poet's perception of his subject, and in his concentration of himself upon his work. Of those who dwelt upon the metaphysical distinction between the Fancy and the Imagination, it was Wordsworth who made the most of it, assuming it as the basis for the final classification of his poetical writings; and it is in these writings that the deeper and more vital distinction, which, as I have said, underlies the metaphysical distinction, is most needed, and may best be illustrated.

For nowhere is there so perplexed a mixture as in Wordsworth's own poetry, of work touched with intense and individual power, with work of almost no character at all. He has much conventional sentiment, and some of that insincere poetic diction, against which his most serious critical efforts were directed: the reaction in his political ideas, consequent on the excesses of 1795, makes him, at times, a mere declaimer on moral and social topics; and he seems, sometimes, to force an unwilling pen, and write by rule. By making the most of these blemishes it is possible to obscure the true aesthetic value of his work, just as his life also, a life of much quiet delicacy and independence, might easily be placed in a false focus, and made to appear a somewhat tame theme in illustration of the more obvious parochial virtues. And those who wish to understand his influence, and experience his peculiar savour, must bear with patience the presence of an alien element in Wordsworth's work, which never coalesced with what is really delightful in it, nor underwent his special power. Who that values his writings most has not felt the intrusion there, from time to time, of something tedious and prosaic? Of all poets equally great, he would gain most by a skilfully made anthology. Such a selection would show, in truth, not so much what he was, or to himself or others seemed to be, as what, by the more energetic and fertile quality in his writings, he was ever tending to become. And the mixture in his work, as it actually stands, is so perplexed, that one fears to miss the least promising composition even, lest some precious morsel should be lying hidden within—the few perfect lines, the phrase, the single word perhaps, to which he often works up mechanically through a poem, almost the whole of which may be tame enough. He who thought that in all creative work the larger part was *given* passively, to the recipient mind, who waited so dutifully upon the gift, to whom so large a measure was sometimes given, had his times also of desertion and relapse; and he has permitted the impress of these too to remain in his work. And this duality there—the fitfulness with which the higher qualities manifest themselves in it, gives the effect in his poetry of a power not altogether his own, or under his control, which comes and goes when it will, lifting or lowering a matter, poor in itself; so that that old fancy which made the poet's art an enthusiasm, a form of divine possession, seems almost literally true of him.

This constant suggestion of an absolute duality between higher and lower moods, and the work done in them, stimulating one always to look below the surface, makes the reading of Wordsworth an excellent sort of training towards the things of art and poetry. It begets in those, who, coming across him in youth, can bear him at all, a habit of reading between the lines, a faith in the effect of concentration and collected-ness of mind in the right appreciation of poetry, an expectation of things, in this order, coming to one by means of a right discipline of the temper as well as of the intellect. He meets us with the promise that he has much, and something very peculiar, to give us, if we will follow a certain difficult way, and seems to have the secret of a special and privileged state of mind. And those who have undergone his influence, and followed this difficult way, are like people who have passed through some initiation, a *disciplina arcani,* by submitting to which they become able constantly to distinguish in art, speech, feeling, manners, that which is organic, animated, expressive, from that which is only conventional, derivative, inexpressive.

But although the necessity of selecting these precious morsels for oneself is an opportunity for the exercise of Wordsworth's peculiar influence, and induces a kind of just criticism and true estimate of it, yet the purely literary product would have been more excellent, had the writer himself purged away that alien element. How perfect would have been the little treasury, shut between the covers of how thin a book! Let us suppose the desired separation made, the electric thread untwined, the golden pieces, great and small, lying apart together.[1] What are the peculiarities of this residue? What special sense does Wordsworth exercise, and what instincts does he satisfy? What are the subjects and the motives which in him excite the imaginative faculty? What are the qualities in things and persons which he values, the impression and sense of which he can convey to others, in an extraordinary way?

An intimate consciousness of the expression of natural things, which weighs, listens, penetrates, where the earlier mind passed roughly by, is a large element in the complexion of modern poetry. It has been remarked as a fact in mental history again and again. It reveals itself in many forms; but is strongest and most attractive in what is strongest and most attractive in modern literature. It is exemplified, almost equally, by writers as unlike each other as Senancour and Theophile Gautier: as a singular chapter in the history of the human mind, its growth might be traced from Rousseau to Chateaubriand, from Chateaubriand to Victor Hugo: it has doubtless some latent connexion with those pantheistic theories which locate an intelligent soul in material things, and have largely exercised men's minds in some modern systems of philosophy: it is traceable even in the graver writings of historians: it makes as much difference between ancient and modern landscape art, as there is between the rough masks of an early mosaic and a portrait by Reynolds or Gainsborough. Of this new sense, the writings of Wordsworth are the central and elementary expression: he is more simply and entirely occupied with it than any other poet, though there are fine expressions of precisely the same thing in so different a poet as Shelley. There was in his own character a certain contentment, a sort of inborn religious placidity, seldom found united with a sensibility so mobile as his, which was favourable to the quiet, habitual observation of inanimate, or imperfectly animate, existence. His life of eighty years is divided by no very profoundly felt incidents: its changes are almost wholly inward, and it falls into broad, untroubled, perhaps somewhat monotonous spaces. What it most resembles is the life of one of those early Italian or Flemish painters, who, just because their minds were full of heavenly visions, passed, some of them, the better part of sixty years in quiet, systematic industry. This placid life matured a quite unusual sensibility, really innate in him, to the sights and sounds of the natural world—the flower and its shadow on the stone, the cuckoo and its echo. The poem of "Resolution and Independence" is a storehouse of such records: for its fulness of imagery it may be compared to Keats's *Saint Agnes' Eve*. To read one of his longer pastoral poems for the first time, is like a day spent in a new country: the memory is crowded for a while with its precise and vivid incidents—

> The pliant harebell swinging in the breeze
> On some grey rock;—
> The single sheep and the one blasted tree
> And the bleak music from that old stone wall;—
> In the meadows and the lower ground
> Was all the sweetness of a common dawn;—
> And that green corn all day is rustling in thine ears.

Clear and delicate at once, as he is in the outlining of visible imagery, he is more clear and delicate still, and finely scrupulous, in the noting of sounds; so that he conceives of noble sound as even moulding the human countenance to nobler types, and as something actually "profaned" by colour, by visible form, or image. He has a power likewise of realising, and conveying to the consciousness of the reader, abstract and elementary impressions—silence, darkness, absolute motion-lessness: or, again, the whole complex sentiment of a particular place, the abstract expression of desolation in the long white road, of peacefulness in a particular folding of the hills. In the airy building of the brain, a special day or hour even, comes to have for him a sort of personal identity, a spirit or angel given to it, by which, for its exceptional insight, or the happy light upon it, it has a presence in one's history, and acts there, as a separate power or accomplishment; and he has celebrated in many of his poems the "efficacious spirit," which, as he says, resides in these "particular spots" of time.

It is to such a world, and to a world of congruous meditation thereon, that we see him retiring in his but lately published poem of *The Recluse*—taking leave, without much count of costs, of the world of business, of action and ambition, as also of all that for the majority of mankind counts as sensuous enjoyment.[2]

And so it came about that this sense of a life in natural objects, which in most poetry is but a rhetorical artifice, is with Wordsworth the assertion of what for him is almost literal fact. To him every natural object seemed to possess more or less of a moral or spiritual life, to be capable of a companionship with man, full of expression, of inexplicable affinities and delicacies of intercourse. An emanation, a particular spirit, belonged, not to the moving leaves or water only, but to the distant peak of the hills arising suddenly, by some change of perspective, above the nearer horizon, to the passing space of light across the plain, to the lichened Druidic stone even, for a certain weird fellowship in it with the moods of men. It was like a "survival," in the peculiar intellectual temperament of a man of letters at the end of the eighteenth century, of that primitive condition, which some philosophers have traced in the general history of human culture, wherein all outward objects alike, including even the works of men's hands, were believed to be endowed with animation, and the world was "full of souls"—that mood in which the old Greek gods were first begotten, and which had many strange aftergrowths.

In the early ages, this belief, delightful as its effects on poetry often are, was but the result of a crude intelligence. But, in Wordsworth, such power of seeing life, such perception of a soul, in inanimate things, came of an exceptional susceptibility to the impressions of eye and ear, and was, in its essence, a kind of sensuousness. At least, it is only in a temperament exceptionally susceptible on the sensuous side, that this sense of the expressiveness of outward things comes to be so large a part of life. That he awakened "a sort of thought in sense," is Shelley's just estimate of this element in Wordsworth's poetry.

And it was through nature, thus ennobled by a semblance of passion and thought, that he approached the spectacle of human life. Human life, indeed, is for him, at first, only an additional, accidental grace on an expressive landscape. When he thought of man, it was of man as in the presence and under the influence of these effective natural objects, and linked to them by many associations. The close connexion of man with natural objects, the habitual association of his thoughts and feelings with a particular spot of earth, has sometimes seemed to degrade those who are subject to its influence, as if it did but reinforce that physical connexion of our nature with the actual lime and clay of the soil, which is always drawing us nearer to our end. But for Wordsworth, these influences tended to the dignity of human nature, because they tended to tranquillise it. By raising nature to the level of human thought he gives it power and expression: he subdues man to the level of nature, and gives him thereby a certain breadth and coolness and solemnity. The leech-gatherer on the moor, the woman "stepping westward," are for him natural objects, almost in the same sense as the aged thorn, or the lichened rock on the heath. In this sense the leader of the "Lake School," in spite of an earnest preoccupation with man, his thoughts, his destiny, is the poet of nature. And of nature, after all, in its modesty.

The English lake country has, of course, its grandeurs. But the peculiar function of Wordsworth's genius, as carrying in it a power to open out the soul of apparently little or familiar things, would have found its true test had he become the poet of Surrey, say! and the prophet of its life. The glories of Italy and Switzerland, though he did write a little about them, had too potent a material life of their own to serve greatly his poetic purpose.

Religious sentiment, consecrating the affections and natural regrets of the human heart, above all, that pitiful awe and care for the perishing human clay, of which relic-worship is but the corruption, has always had much to do with localities, with the thoughts which attach themselves to actual scenes and places. Now what is true of it everywhere, is truest of it in those secluded valleys where one generation after another maintains the same abiding-place; and it was on this side, that Wordsworth apprehended religion most strongly. Consisting, as it did so much, in the recognition of local sanctities, in the habit of connecting the stones and trees of a particular spot of earth with the great events of life, till the low walls, the green mounds, the half-obliterated epitaphs seemed full of voices, and a sort of natural oracles, the very religion of these people of the dales appeared but as another link between them and the earth, and was literally a religion of nature. It tranquillised them by bringing them under the placid rule of traditional and narrowly localised observances. "Grave livers," they seemed to him, under this aspect, with stately speech, and something of that natural dignity of manners, which underlies the highest courtesy.

And, seeing man thus as a part of nature, elevated and solemnised in proportion as his daily life and occupations brought him into companionship with permanent natural objects, his very religion forming new links for him with the narrow limits of the valley, the low vaults of his church, the rough stones of his home, made intense for him now with profound sentiment, Wordsworth was able to appreciate passion in the lowly. He chooses to depict people from humble life, because, being nearer to nature than others, they are on the whole more impassioned, certainly more direct in their expression of passion, than other men: it is for this direct expression of passion, that he values their humble words. In much that he said in exaltation of rural life, he was but pleading indirectly for that sincerity, that perfect fidelity to one's own inward presentations, to the precise features of the picture within, without which any profound poetry is impossible. It was not for their tameness, but for this passionate sincerity, that he chose incidents and situations from common life, "related in a selection of language really used by men." He constantly endeavours to bring his language near to the real language of men: to the real language of men, however, not on the dead level of their ordinary intercourse, but in select moments of vivid sensation, when this language is winnowed and ennobled by excitement. There are poets who have chosen rural life as their subject, for the sake of its passionless repose, and times when Wordsworth himself extols the mere calm and dispassionate survey of things as the highest aim of poetical culture. But it was not for such passionless calm that he preferred the scenes of pastoral life; and the meditative poet, sheltering himself, as it might seem, from the agitations of the outward world, is in reality only clearing the scene for the great exhibitions of emotion, and what he values most is the almost elementary expression of elementary feelings.

And so he has much for those who value highly the concentrated presentment of passion, who appraise men and women by their susceptibility to it, and art and poetry as they afford the spectacle of it. Breaking from time to time into the pensive spectacle of their daily toil, their occupations near to nature, come those great elementary feelings, lifting and solemnising their language and giving it a natural music. The great, distinguishing passion came to Michael by the sheep-fold, to Ruth by the wayside, adding these humble children of the furrow to the true aristocracy of passionate souls. In this respect, Wordsworth's work resembles most that of George Sand, in those of her novels which depict country life. With a penetrative pathos, which puts him in the same rank with the masters of the sentiment of pity in literature, with Meinhold and Victor Hugo, he collects all the traces of vivid excitement which were to be found in that pastoral world—the girl who rung her father's knell; the unborn infant feeling about its mother's heart; the instinctive touches of children; the sorrows of the wild creatures, even—their home-sickness, their strange yearnings; the tales of passionate regret that hang by a ruined farm-building, a heap of stones, a deserted sheepfold; that gay, false, adventurous, outer world, which breaks in from time to time to bewilder and deflower these quiet homes; not "passionate sorrow" only, for the overthrow of the soul's beauty, but the loss of, or carelessness for personal beauty even, in those whom men have wronged—their pathetic wanness; the sailor "who, in his heart, was half a shepherd on the stormy seas"; the wild woman teaching her child to pray for her betrayer; incidents like the making of the shepherd's staff, or that of the young boy laying the first stone of the sheepfold;—all the pathetic episodes of their humble existence, their longing, their wonder at fortune, their poor pathetic pleasures, like the pleasures of children, won so hardly in the struggle for bare existence; their yearning towards each other, in their darkened houses, or at their early toil. A sort of biblical depth and solemnity hangs over this strange, new, passionate, pastoral world, of which he first raised the image, and the reflection of which some of our best modern fiction has caught from him.

He pondered much over the philosophy of his poetry, and reading deeply in the history of his own mind, seems at times to have passed the borders of a world of strange speculations, inconsistent enough, had he cared to note such inconsistencies, with those traditional beliefs, which were otherwise the object of his devout acceptance. Thinking of the high value he set upon customariness, upon all that is habitual, local, rooted in the ground, in matters of religious sentiment, you might sometimes regard him as one tethered down to a world, refined and peaceful indeed, but with no broad outlook, a world protected, but somewhat narrowed, by the influence of received ideas. But he is at times also something very different from this, and something much bolder. A chance expression is overheard and placed in a new connexion, the sudden memory of a thing long past occurs to him, a distant object is relieved for a while by a random gleam of light—accidents turning up for a moment what lies below the surface of our immediate experience—and he passes from the humble graves and lowly arches of "the little rock-like pile" of a Westmoreland church, on bold trains of speculative thought, and comes, from point to point, into strange contact with thoughts which have visited, from time to time, far more venturesome, perhaps errant, spirits.

He had pondered deeply, for instance, on those strange reminiscences and forebodings, which seem to make our lives stretch before and behind us, beyond where we can see or touch anything, or trace the lines of connexion. Following the soul, backwards and forwards, on these endless ways, his sense of man's dim, potential powers became a pledge to him, indeed, of a future life, but carried him back also to that mysterious notion of an earlier state of existence—the fancy of the Platonists—the old heresy of Origen. It was in this mood that he conceived those oft-reiterated regrets for a half-ideal childhood, when the relics of Paradise still clung about the soul—a childhood, as it seemed, full of the fruits of old age, lost for all, in a degree, in the passing away of the youth of the world, lost for each one, over again, in the passing away of actual youth. It is this ideal childhood which he celebrates in his famous "Ode on the Recollections of Childhood," and some other poems which may be grouped around it, such as the lines on "Tintern Abbey," and something like what he describes was actually truer of himself than he seems to have understood; for his own most delightful poems were really the instinctive productions of earlier life, and most surely for him, "the first diviner influence of this world" passed away, more and more completely, in his contact with experience.

Sometimes as he dwelt upon those moments of profound, imaginative power, in which the outward object appears to take colour and expression, a new nature almost, from the prompting of the observant mind, the actual world would, as it were, dissolve and detach itself, flake by flake, and he himself seemed to be the creator, and when he would the destroyer, of the world in which he lived—that old isolating thought of many a brain-sick mystic of ancient and modern times.

At other times, again, in those periods of intense susceptibility, in which he appeared to himself as but the passive recipient of external influences, he was attracted by the thought of a spirit of life in outward things, a single, all-pervading mind in them, of which man, and even the poet's imaginative energy, are but moments—the old dream of the *anima mundi,* the mother of all things and their grave, in which some had desired to lose themselves, and others had become indifferent to the distinctions of good and evil. It would come, sometimes, like the sign of the *macrocosm* to Faust in his cell: the network of man and nature was seen to be pervaded by a common, universal life: a new, bold thought lifted him above the furrow, above the green turf of the Westmoreland churchyard, to a world altogether different in its vagueness and vastness, and the narrow glen was full of the brooding power of one universal spirit.

And so he has something, also, for those who feel the fascination of bold speculative ideas, who are really capable of rising upon them to conditions of poetical thought. He uses them, indeed, always with a very fine apprehension of the limits within which alone philosophical imaginings have any place in true poetry; and using them only for poetical purposes, is not too careful even to make them consistent with each other. To him, theories which for other men bring a world of technical diction, brought perfect form and expression, as in those two lofty books of *The Prelude,* which describe the decay and the restoration of Imagination and Taste. Skirting the borders of this world of bewildering heights and depths, he got but the first exciting influence of it, that joyful enthusiasm which great imaginative theories prompt, when the mind first comes to have an understanding of them; and it is not under the influence of these thoughts that his poetry becomes tedious or loses its blitheness. He keeps them, too, always within certain ethical bounds, so that no word of his could offend the simplest of those simple souls which are always the largest portion of mankind. But it is, nevertheless, the contact of these thoughts, the speculative boldness in them, which constitutes, at least for some minds, the secret attraction of much of his best poetry—the sudden passage from lowly thoughts and places to the majestic forms of philosophical imagination, the play of these forms over a world so different, enlarging so strangely the bounds of its humble churchyards, and breaking such a wild light on the graves of christened children.

And these moods always brought with them faultless expression. In regard to expression, as with feeling and thought, the duality of the higher and lower moods was absolute. It belonged to the higher, the imaginative mood, and was the pledge of its reality, to bring the appropriate language with it. In him, when the really poetical motive worked at all, it united, with absolute justice, the word and the idea; each, in the imaginative flame, becoming inseparably one with the other, by that fusion of matter and form, which is the characteristic of the highest poetical expression. His words are themselves thought and feeling; not eloquent, or musical words merely, but that sort of creative language which carries the reality of what it depicts, directly, to the consciousness.

The music of mere metre performs but a limited, yet a very peculiar and subtly ascertained function, in Wordsworth's poetry. With him, metre is but an additional grace, accessory to that deeper music of words and sounds, that moving power, which they exercise in the nobler prose no less than in formal poetry. It is a sedative to that excitement, an excitement sometimes almost painful, under which the language, alike of poetry and prose, attains a rhythmical power, independent of metrical combination, and dependent rather on some subtle adjustment of the elementary sounds of words themselves to the image or feeling they convey. Yet some of his pieces, pieces prompted by a sort of half-playful mysticism, like the "Daffodils" and "The Two April Mornings," are distinguished by a certain quaint gaiety of metre, and rival by their perfect execution, in this respect, similar pieces among our own Elizabethan, or contemporary French poetry. And those who take up these poems after an interval of months, or years perhaps, may be surprised at finding how well old favourites wear, how their strange, inventive turns of diction or thought still send through them the old feeling of surprise. Those who lived about Wordsworth were all great lovers of the older English literature, and oftentimes there came out in him a noticeable likeness to our earlier poets. He quotes unconsciously, but with new power of meaning, a clause from one of Shakespeare's sonnets; and, as with some other men's most famous work, the "Ode on the Recollections of Childhood" had its anticipator.[3] He drew something too from the unconscious mysticism of the old English language itself, drawing out the inward significance of its racy idiom, and the not wholly unconscious poetry of the language used by the simplest people under strong excitement—language, therefore, at its origin.

The office of the poet is not that of the moralist, and the first aim of Wordsworth's poetry is to give the reader a peculiar kind of pleasure. But through his poetry, and through this pleasure in it, he does actually convey to the reader an extraordinary wisdom in the things of practice. One lesson, if men must have lessons, he conveys more clearly than all, the supreme importance of contemplation in the conduct of life.

Contemplation—impassioned contemplation—that, is with Wordsworth the end-in-itself, the perfect end. We see the majority of mankind going most often to definite ends, lower or higher ends, as their own instincts may determine; but the end may never be attained, and the means not be quite the right means, great ends and little ones alike being, for the most part, distant, and the ways to them, in this dim world, somewhat vague. Meantime, to higher or lower ends, they move too often with something of a sad countenance, with hurried and ignoble gait, becoming, unconsciously, something like thorns, in their anxiety to bear grapes; it being possible for people, in the pursuit of even great ends, to become themselves thin and impoverished in spirit and temper, thus diminishing the sum of perfection in the world, at its very sources. We understand this when it is a question of mean, or of intensely selfish ends—of Grandet, or Javert. We think it bad morality to say that the end justifies the means, and we know how false to all higher conceptions of the religious life is the type of one who is ready to do evil that good may come. We contrast with such dark, mistaken eagerness, a type like that of Saint Catherine of Siena, who made the means to her ends so attractive, that she has won for herself an undying place in the *House Beautiful,* not by her rectitude of soul only, but by its "fairness"—by those quite different qualities which commend themselves to the poet and the artist.

Yet, for most of us, the conception of means and ends covers the whole of life, and is the exclusive type or figure under which we represent our lives to ourselves. Such a figure, reducing all things to machinery, though it has on its side the authority of that old Greek moralist who has fixed for succeeding generations the outline of the theory of right living, is too like a mere picture or description of men's lives as we actually find them, to be the basis of the higher ethics. It covers the meanness of men's daily lives, and much of the dexterity and the vigour with which they pursue what may seem to them the good of themselves or of others; but not the intangible perfection of those whose ideal is rather in *being* than in *doing*—not those *manners* which are, in the deepest as in the simplest sense, *morals,* and without which one cannot so much as offer a cup of water to a poor man without offence—not the part of "antique Rachel," sitting in the company of Beatrice; and even the moralist might well endeavour rather to withdraw men from the too exclusive consideration of means and ends, in life.

Against this predominance of machinery in our existence, Wordsworth's poetry, like all great art and poetry, is a continual protest. Justify rather the end by the means, it seems to say: whatever may become of the fruit, make sure of the flowers and the leaves. It was justly said, therefore, by one who had meditated very profoundly on the true relation of means to ends in life, and on the distinction between what is desirable in itself and what is desirable only as machinery, that when the battle which he and his friends were waging had been won, the world would need more than ever those qualities which Wordsworth was keeping alive and nourishing.[4]

That the end of life is not action but contemplation—*being* as distinct from *doing*—a certain disposition of the mind: is, in some shape or other, the principle of all the higher morality. In poetry, in art, if you enter into their true spirit at all, you touch this principle, in a measure: these, by their very sterility, are a type of beholding for the mere joy of beholding. To treat life in the spirit of art, is to make life a thing in which means and ends are identified: to encourage such treatment, the true moral significance of art and poetry. Wordsworth, and other poets who have been like him in ancient or more recent times, are the masters, the experts, in this art of impassioned contemplation. Their work is, not to teach lessons, or enforce rules, or even to stimulate us to noble ends; but to withdraw the thoughts for a little while from the mere machinery of life, to fix them, with appropriate emotions, on the spectacle of those great facts in man's existence which no machinery affects, "on the great and universal passions of men, the most general and interesting of their occupations, and the entire world of nature,"—on "the operations of the elements and the appearances of the visible universe, on storm and sunshine, on the revolutions of the seasons, on cold and heat, on loss of friends and kindred, on injuries and resentments, on gratitude and hope, on fear and sorrow." To witness this spectacle with appropriate emotions is the aim of all culture; and of these emotions poetry like Wordsworth's is a great nourisher and stimulant. He sees nature full of sentiment and excitement; he sees men and women as parts of nature, passionate, excited, in strange grouping and connexion with the grandeur and beauty of the natural world:—images, in his own words, "of man suffering, amid awful forms and powers."

Such is the figure of the more powerful and original poet, hidden away, in part, under those weaker elements in Wordsworth's poetry, which for some minds determine their entire character; a poet somewhat bolder and more passionate than might at first sight be supposed, but not too bold for true poetical taste; an unimpassioned writer, you might sometimes fancy, yet thinking the chief aim, in life and art alike, to be a certain deep emotion; seeking most often the great elementary passions in lowly places; having at least this condition of all impassioned work, that he aims always at an absolute sincerity of feeling and diction, so that he is the true forerunner of the deepest and most passionate poetry of our own day; yet going back also, with something of a protest against the conventional fervour of much of the poetry popular in his own time, to those older English poets, whose unconscious likeness often comes out in him.

Notes

1. Since this essay was written, such selections have been made, with excellent taste, by Matthew Arnold and Professor Knight.

2. In Wordsworth's prefatory advertisement to the first edition *of The Prelude,* published in 1850, it is stated that that work was intended to be introductory to *The Recluse;* and that *The Recluse,* if completed, would have consisted of three parts. The second part is *The Excursion.* The third part was only planned; but the first book of the first part was left in manuscript by Wordsworth—though in manuscript, it is said, in no great condition of forwardness for the printers. This book, now for the first time printed in *extenso* (a very noble passage from it found place in that prose advertisement to *The Excursion),* is included in the latest edition of Wordsworth by Mr. John Morley. It was well worth adding to the poet's great bequest to English literature. A true student of his work, who has formulated for himself what he supposes to be the leading characteristics of Wordsworth's genius, will feel, we think, lively interest in testing them by the various fine passages in what is here presented for the first time. Let the following serve for a sample:—

> Thickets full of songsters, and the voice Of lordly birds, an unexpected sound Heard now and then from morn to latest eve, Admonishing the man who walks below Of solitude and silence in the sky:—These have we, and a thousand nooks of earth Have also these, but nowhere else is found, Nowhere (or is it fancy?) can be found The one sensation that is here; 'tis here, Here as it found its way into my heart In childhood, here as it abides by day, By night, here only; or in chosen minds That take it with them hence, where'er they go.—'Tis, but I cannot name it, 'tis the sense Of majesty, and beauty, and repose, A blended holiness of earth and sky, Something that makes this individual spot, This small abiding-place of many men, A termination, and a last retreat, A centre, come from wheresoe'er you will, A whole without dependence or

defect, Made for itself, and happy in itself, Perfect contentment, Unity entire.

3. Henry Vaughan, in "The Retreat."
4. See an interesting paper, by Mr. John Morley, on "The Death of Mr. Mill," *Fortnightly Review,* June 1873.

—WALTER PATER, "Wordsworth,"
1874, from *Appreciations,* 1889

THOMAS BABINGTON MACAULAY (1850)

Thomas Babington Macaulay finds that, in comparison to *The Excursion,* *The Prelude* is an inferior poem, a work of diminished beauty that suffers from the repetition of worn-out phrases describing the landscape and its salutary effect on the mind. Though *The Prelude* is marked by an occasional fine description or inspired passage, the story of the French Revolution and its importance to Wordsworth's youthful impressions is rendered far less interesting than the account given in *The Excursion.*

I brought home, and read, the *Prelude.* It is a poorer *Excursion;* the same sort of faults and beauties; but the faults greater and the beauties fainter, both in themselves and because faults are always made more offensive, and beauties less pleasing, by repetition. The story is the old story. There are the old raptures about mountains and cataracts; the old flimsy philosophy about the effect of scenery on the mind; the old crazy, mystical metaphysics; the endless wildernesses of dull, flat, prosaic twaddle; and here and there fine descriptions and energetic declamations interspersed. The story of the French Revolution, and of its influence on the character of a young enthusiast, is told again at greater length, and with less force and pathos, than in the *Excursion.* The poem is to the last degree Jacobinical, indeed Socialist. I understand perfectly why Wordsworth did not choose to publish it in his lifetime.

—THOMAS BABINGTON MACAULAY, *Journal,*
July 28, 1850, cited in G. Otto Trevelyan,
The Life and Letters of Lord Macaulay,
1876, vol. 2, pp. 238–239

F.W.H. MYERS (1881)

F.W.H. Myers finds *The Prelude,* an epic of Wordsworth's education, to be boring, self-centered, "egotistic," and rendered with little skill at subtlety.

Nevertheless, Myers finds the poem honest in what it sets out to do, believing it delivers dignity in its attempt to teach a moral lesson. He also finds it uplifting as it relates the progress of the poet's soul. All in all, Myers commends Wordsworth for creating a unity between his inner being and the lake country that was his home.

Already Wordsworth's minor poems had dealt almost entirely with his own feelings, and with the objects actually before his eyes; and it was at Goslar that he planned, and on the day of his quitting Goslar that he began, a much longer poem, whose subject was to be still more intimately personal, being the development of his own mind. This poem, dedicated to Coleridge, and written in the form of a confidence bestowed on an intimate friend, was finished in 1805, but was not published till after the poet's death. Mrs. Wordsworth then named it *The Prelude,* indicating thus the relation which it bears to the *Excursion*—or, rather, to the projected poem of the *Recluse,* of which the *Excursion* was to form only the Second out of three Divisions. One Book of the First Division of the *Recluse* was written, but is yet unpublished; the Third Division was never even begun, and "the materials," we are told, "of which it would have been formed have been incorporated, for the most part, in the author's other publications." Nor need this change of plan be regretted: didactic poems admit easily of mutilation; and all that can be called plot in this series of works is contained in the *Prelude,* in which we see Wordsworth arriving at those convictions which in the *Excursion* he pauses to expound.

It would be too much to say that Wordsworth has been wholly successful in the attempt—for such the *Prelude* virtually is—to write an epic poem on his own education. Such a poem must almost necessarily appear tedious and egoistic, and Wordsworth's manner has not tact enough to prevent these defects from being felt to the full. On the contrary, in his constant desire frugally to extract, as it were, its full teaching from the minutest event which has befallen him, he supplements the self-complacency of the autobiographer with the conscientious exactness of the moralist, and is apt to insist on trifles such as lodge in the corners of every man's memory, as if they were unique lessons vouchsafed to himself alone.

Yet it follows from this very temper of mind that there is scarcely any autobiography which we can read with such implicit confidence as the *Prelude.* In the case of this, as of so many of Wordsworth's productions, our first dissatisfaction at the form which the poem assumes yields to a recognition of its fitness to express precisely what the poet intends. Nor are there many men who, in recounting the story of their own lives, could combine a candour so absolute with so much dignity; who could treat their personal history so impartially as a means of conveying lessons of general truth; or who, while chronicling such small things, could remain so great. The *Prelude* is a book of good augury for human nature. We feel in reading it as if the stock of mankind were sound. The soul seems going on from strength to strength by the mere development of her inborn power. And the scene with which the poem at once opens and concludes—the return to the Lake country as to a permanent and satisfying home—places the poet at last amid his true surroundings, and leaves us to contemplate him as completed by a harmony without him, which he of all men most needed to evoke the harmony within.

—F.W.H. Myers, Wordsworth, 1881, pp. 36–37

ODE: INTIMATIONS OF IMMORTALITY

Wordsworth's *Ode: Intimations of Immortality* is a profoundly philosophical poem. Written in the most formal of lyric genres, the ode (the word derives from a Greek word meaning to "sing" or "chant"), it was originally intended for formal occasions and state functions. Here, Wordsworth addresses Plato's belief in the immortal soul that exists before and after death and replaces it with his own conviction that children have a divine wisdom that adults no longer possess. Wordsworth differs fundamentally from Plato in that the ancient Greek philosopher believed that when the soul begins its earthly journey, all knowledge of eternal ideas are forgotten and must be recollected through philosophical discipline, while Wordsworth believed that the newborn child enters the world "trailing clouds of glory," with a vision of its celestial origins that gradually "fade into the light of common day" as the child grows. For Wordsworth, the loss of celestial vision is compensated for in later years when man achieves transcendental faith.

George McLean Harper
"The 'Intimations Ode'" (1916)

Harper's commentary concerns the journey of the soul from the joy of childhood, a consecrated time when the young possess an innate goodness completely unencumbered by the "blunted and decaying faculties" of adult life, to the consolation of later years when a person finds reward and comfort in the exercise of reason and "the philosophic mind." Equally important to Harper is his clarification on the meaning of immortality in the ode, which here is a "surmise" that the privileged state of childhood emanates from some prior existence. Harper maintains that this notion was unique to Wordsworth.

The great "Intimations" ode is a stumbling block to prosaic and a temptation to over-speculative minds. To the former it seems a mass of disconnected though splendid beauties, and when they try to find its indwelling idea they either despise what they think they have discovered, as too thin and vague to be of much consequence, or condemn it as a profanely audacious attempt to meddle with things divinely hidden from human sight. To minds that love "those wingy mysteries in divinity, and airy subtleties in religion, which have unhinged the brains of better heads," the poem offers congenial employment. Wordsworth himself, in a most regrettable Fenwick note, made an unnecessary and almost humiliating concession to pragmatical and timid readers. "I think it right," he says, "to protest against a conclusion, which has given pain to some good and pious persons, that I meant to inculcate such a belief"—*i.e.*, belief in a prior state of existence. "It is," he continues, "far too shadowy a notion to be recommended to faith, as more than an element in our instincts of immortality. But let us bear in mind that, though the idea is not advanced in revelation, there is nothing there to contradict it, and the fall of man presents an analogy in its favour." This deprecation of popular judgment is unfortunate in several ways. Historically it misrepresents the author as he was when he wrote the ode, for there is no evidence that he then believed in a written "revelation," and every evidence that he did not believe in "the fall of man." And, furthermore, it has diverted attention from the central idea of the poem, an idea supported by his own experience and that of thousands, and has brought into undue prominence, even by denying his intention to do so, a subsidiary and purely speculative notion.

The ode was probably conceived in the spring of 1802, immediately after he had written the nine lines which are its germ, and of which he used the last three as its motto:

My heart leaps up when I behold
A rainbow in the sky:
So was it when my life began;
So is it now I am a man;
So be it when I shall grow old,
Or let me die!
The Child is father of the Man;

And I could wish my days to be
Bound each to each by natural piety.

On March 26, 1802, Dorothy records in her Journal: "William wrote to Annette, then worked at 'The Cuckoo,'" and, listening to the cuckoo's song, we remember, he could beget again the golden time of childhood. In the evening of the same day, she adds, "he wrote 'The Rainbow,'" and next day "William wrote part of an ode." On June 17, she says, "William added a little to the Ode he is writing." The poem was continued at intervals during the next four years, and appeared in the edition of 1807, after which it was never much altered. There is no reason to doubt the accuracy of Wordsworth's statement in the Fenwick note that "two years at least passed between the writing of the first four stanzas and the remaining part."

In these stanzas, with an exquisitely light touch, the poet describes an experience which perhaps is rare—I have known many persons to disclaim it for themselves—but which has startled many sensitively organized youths, observant of their mental states. It is an experience that vindicates for childhood a superior delicacy of perception, a superior impressibility as compared with later years. So vivid are these sensations, so deep these emotions, that long afterwards, in favourable moments, they flash into consciousness. Science would probably say that some hidden coil of the brain unrolls. The person to whom these forgotten memories recur connects them rather with some object or incident which appears to have occasioned them, and they are called "recognitions." We seem to perceive again something perceived long ago, and never since. It is like the repetition of a dream. To certain minds these flashes come not seldom, but chiefly before middle life. They illumine and measure the distance the soul has travelled, for they recall and place side by side with blunted and decaying faculties the fresh and glorious powers of unworn childhood. The momentary joy is succeeded by a sense of depression, as we realize that the years, our busy servants, have robbed us of life itself. This is the theme of those first four stanzas.

A natural deduction, and one, as we have seen, which Wordsworth would regard as highly significant, is that the perceptions and feelings of childhood have peculiar value. Compared with them, the testimony of later years is dull and confused. The moral instincts of childhood have a similar directness and vigour, and should be obeyed. The child, by his acute perceptions, his tense grasp of reality, and his unsophisticated habits of mind, is closer to truth than the man, and finds in nature an all-sufficient teacher. But here the poet checks himself, and he puts this inference to a test in the tenth and eleventh stanzas. The result marks a great change in his philosophy. Though acknowledging almost all that he had claimed for childhood, he remembers that there have been gains as well as losses, and sings:

We will grieve not, rather find
Strength in what remains behind;
In the primal sympathy
Which having been must ever be;
In the soothing thoughts that spring
Out of human suffering;
In the faith that looks through death,
In years that bring the philosophic mind.

Mankind claims him, and the sway of reason. But while thus extending his allegiance, he repeats his vows to nature:

And O, ye Fountains, Meadows, Hills, and Groves,
Forebode not any severing of our loves!
Yet in my heart of hearts I feel your might;
I only have relinquished one delight
To live beneath your more habitual sway.

The whole of "The Prelude" does not say more, as to the central principle that had governed Wordsworth's early life, and had lately been broadened, but not abandoned. A favoured childhood close to nature, the acceptance of Rousseau's doctrine of original goodness, a tempering due to rich experience of human love and reverent admission of painful duty—this is the history of Wordsworth's soul hitherto. The golden record runs through six great poems: "Wisdom and Spirit of the universe," "Lines Composed a Few Miles above Tintern Abbey," the "Ode to Duty," the "Happy Warrior," "The Prelude," and the "Intimations." A final great document in support of Wordsworth's creed is his "Answer to the Letter of Mathetes," published in *The Friend*, in 1809. Though I shall have more to say of it in its place, I cannot forbear quoting a glorious passage which restates the main theme of the "Intimations" ode. Speaking of the Generous Young Man, he says: "Granted that the sacred light of childhood is and must be for him no more than a remembrance. He may, notwithstanding, be remanded to nature, and with trustworthy hopes, founded less upon his sentient than upon his intellectual being; to nature, as leading on insensibly to the society of reason, but to reason and will, as leading back to the wisdom of nature. A reunion, in this order accomplished, will bring reformation and timely support; and the two powers of reason and nature, thus reciprocally teacher and taught, may advance together in a track to which there is no limit." And, again, he speaks of nature as "a teacher of truth through joy and through gladness, and as a creatress of the faculties by a process of smoothness and delight." Diffidence and veneration, he says, "are the sacred attributes of youth; its appropriate calling is not to distinguish in the fear of being deceived or degraded, not to analyze with scrupulous minuteness, but to accumulate in genial confidence; its instinct, its safety, its benefit, its glory, is to love, to admire, to feel, and to labour." As there are two types of mind, the synthetic and the analytic, the one that is impressed by resemblances and the one that feels differences, so in the individual are there creative as distinguished from critical faculties, and the former are most alert in childhood.

That the central theme of the ode is the magisterial sanctity of childhood is further indicated by the three lines from "The Rainbow" which the poet prefixed to it:

> The Child is Father of the Man.
> And I could wish my days to be
> Bound each to each by natural piety.

"Piety" is here used in its original sense, of reverence for filial obligation. The Man is to respect the Child surviving in him, to obey its monitions, to work upon its plan. What, then, is the subsidiary idea, which the Fenwick note unduly emphasizes, upon which commentators have spent themselves, and which, to be sure, is elaborately indicated in the title of the ode? It is a surmise, nothing more, that the excellence of childhood may be an inheritance from a previous and presumably superior state of existence. This is not, like the other idea, original with Wordsworth, in the only senses in which any such thought can be original—that is to say, either inborn or something conquered and assimilated. It was altogether derivative, extrinsic, and novel to him. It is connected with no other of his writings. It is alien to his mind. He habitually poetizes the facts of nature and human experience, shunning equally the cloudland of metaphysics and the light mists of fancy. But he had, as his soul's companion, the greatest speculative genius our race ever produced; and a dream of a prenatal state of the soul, superior in happiness and wisdom, had been embodied by Coleridge in a poem several years before. It is the "Sonnet composed on a journey homeward, the author having received intelligence of the birth of a son, Sept. 20, 1796":

> Oft o'er my brain does that strange fancy roll
> Which makes the present (while the flash doth last)
> Seem a mere semblance of some unknown past.
> Mixed with such feelings, as perplex the soul

Self-questioned in her sleep; and some have said
We lived, ere yet this robe of flesh we wore.
O my sweet baby, when I reach my door
If heavy looks should tell me thou art dead,
(As, sometimes, through excess of hope, I fear)
I think that I should struggle to believe
Thou wert a spirit, to this nether sphere
Sentenced for some more venial crime to grieve;
Did'st scream, then spring to meet Heaven's quick reprieve.
While we wept idly o'er thy little bier.

In his note to this sonnet, in the edition of 1797, Coleridge acknowledged his indebtedness to Plato's "Phaedo." Plato's argument, or perhaps we should call it his poetical suggestion, is that "if there is an absolute beauty, and goodness, and an absolute essence of all things; and if to this, which is now discovered to have existed in our former state, we refer all our sensations, and with this compare them, finding these ideas to be pre-existent and our inborn possession—then our souls must have had a prior existence."[1]

In Wordsworth this conception seems to have been merely derivative,—how different, therefore, from most of his ideas, to which the praise in Coleridge's "Biographia Literaria" so justly belongs, when he says (Chapter XXII.) that a characteristic excellence of Wordsworth's is "a weight and sanity of the thoughts and sentiments, won, not from books, but from the poet's own meditative observation." "They are *fresh*," he adds, "and have the dew upon them."

As one who habitually rises late can hardly believe his senses when he sees yesterday's commonplace world transformed by dawn into an enchanted garden of trembling roseate mysteries, so we wonder and so we doubt in reading the "Intimations" ode. Its radiance comes and goes through a shimmering veil. Yet, when we look close, we find nothing unreal or unfinished. This beauty, though supernal, is not evanescent. It bides our return, and whoever comes to seek it as a little child will find it. The imagery, though changing at every turn, is fresh and simple. The language, though connected with thoughts so serious that they impart to it a classic dignity, is natural and for the most part plain. The metrical changes are swift, and follow the sense as a melody by Schubert or Brahms is moulded to the text. Nevertheless, a peculiar glamour surrounds the poem. It is the supreme example of what I may venture to term the romance of philosophic thought.

If we bear in mind what is the important and profoundly Wordsworthian idea of the ode, and what the secondary and less characteristic notion appended to this, we shall find few difficulties of detail.[2]

Notes

1. Jowett's translation.

2. Dowden's interpretation of line 199.

> Another race hath been, and other palms are won

—namely, that "the sun, like a strong man going forth to his race," has now reached the goal and won the palm; and so with the life of man when death comes "—appears to me at fault. The palms for which the child strove were instinctive joys; the man has aimed at love and duty. The human heart has been disciplined by tenderness and fear, as well as by gladness, till now

> The meanest flower that blows can give
> Thoughts that do often lie too deep for tears.

I must confess that for many years I could not understand the fourth and fifth lines of the eleventh stanza. Several Wordsworthians whom I have consulted, among them Miss Arnold of Fox How, Mr. Gordon Wordsworth, and Mr. Ernest Hartley Coleridge, agree in the following interpretation, as expressed by the last-named gentleman: "I have relinquished *one* delight—*i.e.*, the glory and the dream—with the result that I am living under Nature's more habitual sway, exchanging the spontaneous, intuitive response to Nature for a conscious and voluntary submission." Mr. Gordon Wordsworth says: "Perhaps the choice of the word 'relinquish' is unfortunate; we generally use it of a wholly voluntary act, and in this case it seems rather the inevitable result of the passing of time."

—GEORGE MCLEAN HARPER,
"The 'Intimations Ode,'" from *William
Wordsworth: His Life, Works, and Influence*, vol.
II, London: John Murray, 1916, pp. 121–127

H.W. GARROD "THE 'IMMORTAL ODE'" (1923)

H.W. Garrod discusses the evolution of the ode, begun in the spring of 1802, and emphasizes the significance of the fact that in that year the poem ended at the fourth stanza with an epigram he believes is the key to understanding the work: "days . . . bound each to each by natural piety." For Garrod, the fact that the poem was not completed until 1806 is evidence that Wordsworth underwent a crisis wherein the "glory and the freshness" of sensation had faded in his later years, signaling a significant shift in the poem from sensibility to the poet's adoption of "the philosophic mind." When Wordsworth returned to the poem four years later, stanzas v-viii, according to Garrod, supply the answer to the poem in the form of the doctrine of anamnesis or reminiscence, the ultimate source derived from Plato and the neo-Platonists. However, the immediate source is linked to Coleridge and a sonnet he wrote in 1796 on learning of the birth of his son Hartley. The "four years' darling" in the Ode refers to the young boy.

Garrod's essay is preoccupied with correcting the notion that Wordsworth is not espousing the Platonic idea of pre-existence but, rather, is expressing an innermost feeling to which time and place are not applicable. In other words, Garrod is pointing to the transcendental element. Furthermore, he points out that in Wordsworth's later years, the poet would have been concerned that the doctrine of pre-existence ran counter to the teachings of the church and could possibly be misconstrued. Contrary to Plato, Garrod points out that Wordsworth's notion of pre-existence "is, in fact, not a theory of knowledge, but a romance of sensation" and that ultimately this extraordinary vision is used up, the result being that Wordsworth is trying to console both himself and the reader that the vision has been replaced with "the philosophic mind."

⎯⎯ ⎯⎯ ⎯⎯

It is worth while first to reconstruct the circumstances in which the *Ode* was written. It was begun in the spring of 1802. Wordsworth was at Dove Cottage, with his sister. Coleridge had just returned to the Lake Country and had paid them a visit at Grasmere. That was on 18–20th March. The importance of Coleridge's presence will appear shortly. On 22nd March Dorothy Wordsworth records in her journal that, on a mild morning, William 'worked at the Cuckoo poem'; and again on 25th March 'A beautiful morning. W. worked at the Cuckoo'. Then on the next day: 'William wrote to Annette, then worked at the Cuckoo . . . ' in the evening 'he wrote the *Rainbow*'. I will try and indicate in a moment the significance of these poems in relation to the *Ode*. On the day following, 27th March, 'Wm. wrote part of an Ode'—this was *the* Ode. Later, 17th June, 'Wm. added a little to the Ode he is writing'.

First the *Cuckoo*. This is the poem placed second among the *Poems of the Imagination*.[1] The voice of the cuckoo brings to Wordsworth 'a tale Of *visionary* hours'—a tale of days of childhood when the cuckoo was 'an invisible thing, a voice, a mystery'. As he hears him now again, once more suddenly the earth 'appears to be An unsubstantial faery place That is meet home for thee'. He is back in the world of those visionary experiences of childhood which he regarded as the source of the deepest illumination.

He had no sooner finished the *Cuckoo* than he began upon the *Rainbow*. The sight of the rainbow still brings to him the old 'leaping up of the heart' which he had as a boy. He prays that it may always continue to be so:

> The child is father of the man
> And I could wish my days to be
> Bound each to each by natural piety.

In the edition of 1815 these lines are prefixed as a motto to the *Ode*. There is the external link, that they were composed contemporaneously with it. But there is an inner connexion, the significance of which has, I think, not been fully apprehended. In the first place it has, I fancy, not been pointed out that, when in lines 22–3 of the *Ode* Wordsworth says

> To me alone there came a thought of grief:
> A timely utterance gave that thought relief,

the timely utterance may very well be the Rainbow poem itself. Secondly, the conception of human days bound together by natural piety is the clue to the interpretation of the *Ode* in its entirety. I shall try to make this clear as we proceed.

The *Ode*, so far as it was carried at this time, ended with the fourth stanza; and was not completed in its entirety until 1806. This we know from Wordsworth's own statement in the Fenwick Notes—though we must not necessarily suppose, I think, that fragments and scraps of the later stanzas had not taken at least inchoate form at the earlier date. But so far as it was a complete piece in 1802, it ended with lines 56–7:

> Whither is fled the visionary gleam?
> Where is it now, the glory and the dream?

It is not, I think, accident that the poem broke off thus at this unanswered question: that between the question and the answer there intervenes a period of no less than four years. We are here, I am inclined to suppose, brought up against a crisis, a turning-point, in Wordsworth's intellectual development. Until now he has lived in 'the glory and the freshness' of the senses, in the immediate report given by the senses of a 'principle of joy' in the world. But with advancing years this report comes to be fitful and dim. 'The things that I have seen I now can see no more.'

What does that mean? How does that happen? And, if it happens, as it does, what is the meaning and value, as against the early gift of vision, of the 'years which bring the philosophic mind'?

Wordsworth, as I have said, undoubtedly had these visionary experiences in great intensity both of number and quality. Undoubtedly they were to him the most real and valuable thing in life. We may shrug our shoulders, but so it was; and we must start out from that. We shall not understand him unless we attune ourselves to his mood, which is, for him, one of philosophy and not fancy. Examples of a fanciful expression of the same mood occur of course in many places in literature.

Sing me a song of a lad that is gone,
Say, could that lad be I?
Merry of soul he sailed on a day,
Over the sea to Skye.
Give me again all that was there,
Give me the sun that shone!
Give me the eyes, give me the soul,
Give me the lad that's gone!

But Stevenson's pretty poem takes us to, and keeps us in, a wholly different world. Wordsworth is propounding to us with all the seriousness of which he is capable a question which has not merely crossed his fancy but which is for him the central question of the imaginative life.

The first four stanzas of the *Ode* put the fact: 'There hath passed a glory from the earth'; and in the last two lines of them, ask the explanation of it. Stanzas vi–viii give the explanation in the form of the doctrine of *anamnesis* or Reminiscence. Stanzas ix–xi are an attempt to vindicate the value of a life from which 'vision' has fled.

The ultimate source of the doctrine of reminiscence is, of course, Plato and the Neo-Platonists. The immediate source, however, upon which Wordsworth drew can hardly be in doubt. It was not Plato, but Coleridge. Here are the opening lines of a sonnet written by Coleridge, in 1796, on receiving intelligence of the birth of a son (the son was Hartley Coleridge):

Oft o'er my brain does that strong fancy roll
Which makes the present (while the flash doth last)
Seem a mere semblance of some unknown past,
Mixed with such feelings as perplex the soul
Self-questioned in her sleep; and some have said
We lived ere yet this robe of flesh we wore.

In a note appended to this sonnet Coleridge refers merely to Plato. In a letter, however, to his friend Poole, he seems to indicate Fénelon as his nearest source. 'Almost all the followers', he says, 'of Fénelon believe that men are

degraded intelligences, who had all once lived together in a paradisiacal, or
perhaps heavenly, state. The first four lines express a feeling which I have often
had—the present has appeared like a vivid dream or exact similitude of some
past circumstances.' That Wordsworth drew upon Coleridge is indicated,
not only by the general consideration of his philosophic indebtedness to
Coleridge, but also by the fact that the first hint in him of the reminiscence
doctrine occurs (as it occurs in Coleridge) in connexion with Hartley
Coleridge—in the opening line of the verses *To H. C., Six Years Old*:

O thou whose fancies from afar are brought.

These verses are usually said to have been composed in 1802. But they
are quoted by Coleridge in *Anima Poetae* (p. 15) under the date 1801, at a
time when Hartley was only four years old. Look now at lines 85–6 of the
Immortality Ode:

Behold the child among his new-born blisses,
A six years' darling of a pigmy size.

The first edition has 'a four years' darling'. I cannot help thinking that the
child depicted in the *Ode* is actually Hartley Coleridge; that there is a close
connexion between the two poems, and that in both Wordsworth, at a
later date, altered 'four' to 'six', as more suited to the habits and disposition
ascribed to the child. In any case we may, I think, without improbability
regard Coleridge as the source from which the reminiscence doctrine took
rise in Wordsworth's imagination. That being so, it is interesting to find
Coleridge, in that part of the *Biographia Literaria* where he speaks of the *Ode
on Immortality*, warning the reader against taking Wordsworth's doctrine of
preexistence in the literal and 'ordinary interpretation'. 'The Ode', he says,

'was intended for such readers only as had been accustomed to
watch the flux and reflux of their inmost nature, to venture at times
into the twilight realms of consciousness, and to feel a deep interest
in modes of inmost being, to which they know that the attributes
of time and space are inapplicable and alien, but which can yet not
be conveyed, save in symbols of time and space. For such readers
the sense is sufficiently plain, and they will be as little disposed to
charge Mr. Wordsworth with believing the Platonic pre-existence
in the ordinary interpretation of the words, as I am to believe that
Plato himself ever meant or taught it!'

Wordsworth himself in later life was somewhat concerned as to the use
to which he had put the doctrine. Yet what he is concerned about is, not that

the doctrine may not be true, but that it may be intrusive; that it is not a part of the teaching of the Church, and may be misconceived as qualifying, or superseding, that teaching.[2] Nothing that he says anywhere suggests that he entertained the doctrine otherwise than seriously; and this is only another of the cases where, as I have said, we shall not understand him unless we believe what he tells us. I am no more in doubt that Wordsworth believed the doctrine than I doubt that Plato did—Coleridge's scepticism, it will be noticed, extends even to Plato.[3]

But for Wordsworth, it should be made clear, the doctrine has both a different foundation and a different significance from that which it has in Plato. Wordsworth, as I have said, is a pure sensationalist. Plato, on the other hand, is a pure intellectualist. To Plato the doctrine of reminiscence is a theory of knowledge: an explanation of how we get to know and think. The senses are the source of all error. The world of 'Ideas' alone has truth. It is only by escape from the contamination of the senses, only by getting away from eyes and ears, that we are able truly to see and hear, and to come to the truth of things. The process is a long and painful labour of abstraction. But to Wordsworth the truth of things comes in flashes, in gleams of sense-perception; and in abstraction the truth dies. Wordsworth's doctrine is, in fact, not a theory of knowledge, but a romance of sensation. The absorbing interest of Plato is in the logical meanings of things; to Wordsworth logical meanings are precisely that part of things which has no value. There is some degree of delusion, therefore, in speaking of the Platonism of Wordsworth; and if we are to read the *Ode* rightly we shall do well to begin by putting Plato out of our minds.

Our pre-natal existence is guaranteed for Plato by the fact that we can reason at all; by the power in us to form class-conceptions. It is guaranteed to Wordsworth by a passivity of response to sense-impressions; and in this connexion I feel obliged to reiterate what I have already said in another connexion. In considering the character of the impressions made upon Wordsworth by Nature, we must conceive ourselves always, I believe, to be dealing with impressions made upon a consciousness highly abnormal. The flashes thrown by sense on the invisible world came to him with a frequency and fullness of illumination not given to ordinary men. And just as his experience here is not ordinary, so I conceive it to be not ordinary in respect of that phenomenon which is the main theme of the *Ode*—in respect of the manner in which, as we pass from childhood to youth, and from youth to manhood, the flashes of vision become ever more and more faint and intermittent.

That this is what happened in Wordsworth's own case it is not possible to doubt. He tells us so; he reiterates it; we may even say that it is a chief trouble of his soul—for the things that are thus passing from him are precisely the things which he regards as more precious than anything else in life. Yet so far as we can judge, so far as general report can be trusted, Wordsworth's experience in this particular is not that of ordinary men. One is tempted to the conjecture that the extraordinary force and frequency of the visionary experiences of his earlier years exhausted prematurely—actually wore out by over-use—the faculty of vision itself. In the *Ode*, and elsewhere, Wordsworth endeavours to persuade himself—and us—that he has replaced this visionary gift by some other gift or gifts; that he still draws upon sources of experience not inferior in depth and clearness. But *does* he? In all that matters to us, that is to say in his poetry, does he? The great *Ode* closes the two volumes of 1807. Why is it that thereafter we pass into the dark, or, at any rate, out of the fullness of light, that we are conscious that, 'where e'er we go', 'there hath passed a glory' from his poetry, and that the things which we have seen with his eyes, we 'now can see no more'? In this early decay of a faculty abnormally developed and abnormally employed I am inclined (leaving the faculty itself unexplained in its origin and nature) to seek at least a partial explanation of the extraordinary decline in poetic power which begins with the ending of the *Ode*. Wordsworth did cease to see things.

This is not, of course, an explanation which will satisfy any one who supposes that Wordsworth was like other people; that 'inspiration' is a metaphor, and the epithet 'seer' a courtesy title. For myself, when poets tell me that they are inspired, I am disposed to believe them—I have found it always the shortest way, not only of placating them, but of understanding them. It may even be that it is the only way.

There are two passages of Wordsworth which should always be read in connexion with the *Ode*; and in both of which we have a somewhat pathetic expression of his sense of lost vision. Of these the first is to be found in the concluding portion of the twelfth book of the *Prelude*—I have already quoted the opening lines of it:

> O mystery of man, from what a depth
> Proceed thy honours. I am lost, but see
> In simple childhood something of the base
> On which thy greatness stands; but this I feel
> That from thyself it comes, that thou must give,
> Else never canst receive. The days gone by
> Return upon me almost from the dawn
> Of life: the hiding-places of man's power
> Open: *I would approach them, but they close.*
> *I see by glimpses now; when age comes on,*

May scarcely see at all; and I would give,
While yet we may, as far as words can give,
Substance and life to what I feel, enshrining,
Such is my hope, the spirit of the past
For future restoration. (xii. 272–86.)

The words which I have put into italics are sufficiently significant to stand without comment. The passage was composed about the time at which the *Ode* was brought to completion. By the side of it may be set a stanza of the *Ode composed upon an Evening of extraordinary Splendour and Beauty*: a poem written in 1818:[4]

Such hues from their celestial urn
Were wont to stream before mine eye,
Where'er it wandered in the morn
Of blissful infancy.
This glimpse of glory, why renewed?
Nay, rather speak with gratitude;
For if a vestige of those gleams
Survived, 'twas only in my dreams.
Dread Power, whom peace and calmness serve
No less than Nature's threatening voice,
From THEE if I would swerve;
O, let thy grace remind me of the light
Full early lost, and fruitlessly deplored;
Which at this moment on my waking sight
Appears to shine, by miracle restored;
My soul, though yet confined to earth,
Rejoices in a second birth!
'Tis past, the visionary splendour fades;
And night approaches with her shades. (61–80.)

When Wordsworth speaks here of

the light
Full early lost, and fruitlessly deplored,

it is the same light as that of which he speaks in the *Ode on Immortality* as 'the fountain-light of all our day' and 'the master-light of all our seeing'. And when he speaks of this light as 'fruitlessly deplored', it can hardly be but that the reference in those words is to the great *Ode* itself; and we must suppose Wordsworth to have had the sense that the *Ode*, great as it is, was great in a somewhat 'fruitless' fashion; that, philosophically, it failed; that it did not answer adequately the questions which it set out to solve. When I say 'adequately', I mean adequately from the point of view which Wordsworth had reached in 1818. By that date he had reached a theistic position which the *Evening Voluntaries*, as a whole, reflect. Nature is no longer identified with God or the divine; but God is conceived in an external relation, as the creator of Nature; and our perception of Nature and its glory we owe, no longer to the free senses, but to 'Grace'. Grace 'reminds us of the light'. Similarly in the fourth of the *Evening Voluntaries*, By grace divine, he says,

> By grace divine,
> Not otherwise, O Nature, we are thine,
> Through good and evil, thine. (16–18.)

To such a mood the great *Ode* must necessarily appear a 'fruitless' achievement.

But if we get away from the Wordsworth of 1818, and look at the *Ode* from the point of view of the Wordsworth of 1797–1807, we have still to ask, Whether it achieves its end, whether it is, in fact, successful in vindicating a life no longer, or only rarely, visited by these 'visionary gleams' which belong to the fullness and purity of the free senses. The vindication of such a life is attempted in the last three stanzas of the poem. The ninth stanza begins, or purports to begin, on a note of gladness:

> O joy, that in our embers
> Is something that doth live!

Even so, it is not a very auspicious beginning. The fire of joy seems, after all, to be nor more than a spark among the smouldering embers of a dying life. It is just 'something that doth live', a something better than nothing in a decolorated and frigescent world. Nor is this living *something*, in the dying embers of Wordsworth's imagination, readily or easily apprehensible. At first sight, he would appear to tell us no more than that the loss of light is adequately compensated by the recollection of it. That is certainly something not consistent with ordinary human experience—we were happy indeed were it possible for us in the lean years of life to fill the empty granaries of the heart by thinking upon more kindly summers. But neither is it possible, nor is it likely that it appeared so to Wordsworth.

What, then, is he really trying to say to us in the last three stanzas of the *Ode*?

In order to answer this question satisfactorily, it is necessary that, in conjunction with Wordsworth's speculations upon nature and the goodness of Nature, we should consider to some extent also his view of certain aspects of the moral life. I have said that the lines from the Rainbow poem, prefixed to the *Ode*, were intended to serve, as I thought, as a clue to the poem. The child is father of the man, Wordsworth there says,

> And I could wish my days to be
> Bound each to each by natural piety.

The idea here put to us is illustrated, rather unexpectedly, in a poem of a quite different character—the *Happy Warrior*. The Happy Warrior is described as one who,

> when brought
> Among the tasks of real life, hath wrought
> Upon the plan that pleased his childish thought.

The Happy Warrior is, in fact, one who has bound his days together. He has so bound up his life that the pure and free impressions of childhood, its visionary experiences, are the inspiration of his mature age. The poem takes us from the natural to the moral world; but the principle at issue is the same, nor does Wordsworth part these two worlds so sharply, as we do. The principle is further illustrated, in its purely moral aspect, in the *Ode to Duty*:

> There are who ask not if thine eye
> Be on them; who in love and truth,
> Where no misgiving is, rely
> Upon the genial strength of youth:
> Glad hearts without reproach or blot,
> Who do thy work and know it not.
> Long may the kindly influence last;
> But thou, if they should totter, teach them to stand fast!

I doubt whether Wordsworth, in his best period, ever abandoned the doctrine that the highest moral achievement is that which presents itself as an inspiration, that which is part of our natural life, that which is bound up with childhood and its unthinking 'vision'. Duty is a second-best; we seek support from that power when higher and freer powers fail us. The purer moral life is that which so binds together our days that the vision of childhood suffices to later years.[5]

Notes
1. I mention that because the poem is in form somewhat slight and fanciful. Wordsworth placed it where it is because to him it was neither.

2. Grosart, iii, pp. 194–5.

3. Coleridge, in a late piece, *Phantom or Fact*, draws again on the doctrine.

4. No. ix of the *Evening Voluntaries*; but not an original part of that series (which dates as a whole from 1833: Grosart. iii. 145).

5. We may profitably conceive the *Prelude*, accordingly, as a self-examination directed towards binding together the poet's own days, his different periods, and moments, of inspired consciousness.

—H.W. GARROD, "The 'Immortal Ode,'"
from *Wordsworth: Lectures and Essays*,
Oxford: The Clarendon Press, 1st ed.,
1923, pp. 112–124

THE WHITE DOE OF RHYLSTONE

The White Doe of Rhylstone, or The Fate of the Nortons is based on the ballad "The Rising of the North," which had appeared in Thomas Percy's *Reliques*. The story concerns a brief rebellion in 1569–70 by members of the conservative Roman Catholic Church in northern England, who were protesting against the Protestant Elizabeth I. Wordsworth's poem is an imaginative reworking of that legend, displaying the influence of Sir Walter Scott's romantic vision of medieval England. The historical figure the legend appropriates is Richard Norton, the master of Rylstone Hall, and his eight sons, who joined the Percys and Nevilles, two esteemed, long-standing northern families, in the revolt. Norton's other children, Francis and Emily, remained neutral. Francis is killed in an effort to save the Banner of the Five Wounds, which was carried by his father and bore an image of the cross along with the five wounds of Christ. Thus, Emily is left as the lone survivor and finds consolation in the company of a white doe. Though *The White Doe of Rhylstone* is meant to be an account of historical events, Wordsworth wrote himself into it, for he, too, was mourning the death of his brother John and was attempting to convey his own deep sense that suffering must be accepted and that it can enhance the imagination. In *The White Doe*, salvation comes from enduring the hardships of being the lone survivor. Though Wordsworth wrote the poem in 1808, he did not publish it until 1815.

JOHN WILSON (1815)

The *White Doe* is not in season; venison is not liked in Edinburgh. It wants flavor; a good Ettrick wether is preferable. Wordsworth has more of the poetical character than any living writer, but he is not a man of first-rate intellect; his genius oversets him.

—JOHN WILSON, letter to James Hogg, 1815,
cited in Mary Gordon, *"Christopher North":
A Memoir of John Wilson,* 1863, p. 130

FRANCIS JEFFREY, LORD JEFFREY
"WORDSWORTH'S *WHITE DOE*" (1815)

Once again, Francis Jeffrey shows himself to be Wordsworth's severest critic in declaring *The White Doe* to be "the very worst poem we ever saw imprinted in a quarto volume," a work utterly devoid of redeeming characteristics, wholly pathetic in its simplicity. Of its excesses, Francis states that the poem suffers from the poet's narcissism—an intoxication with his own poetic powers, which in turn produces a sappy sentimentality. Jeffrey finds Wordsworth's efforts in general too dependent on the ancient ballads of the north country, his own works that result merely pale and feeble imitations of these old poems.

This, we think, has the merit of being the very worst poem we ever saw imprinted in a quarto volume; and though it was scarcely to be expected, we confess, that Mr Wordsworth, with all his ambition, should so soon have attained to that distinction, the wonder may perhaps be diminished, when we state, that it seems to us to consist of a happy union of all the faults, without any of the beauties, which belong to his school of poetry. It is just such a work, in short, as some wicked enemy of that school might be supposed to have devised, on purpose to make it ridiculous; and when we first took it up, we could not help fancying that some ill-natured critic had taken this harsh method of instructing Mr Wordsworth, by example, in the nature of those errors, against which our precepts had been so often directed in vain. We had not gone far, however, till we felt intimately, that nothing in the nature of a joke could be so insupportably dull;—and that this must be the work of one who honestly believed it to be a pattern of pathetic simplicity, and gave it out as such to the admiration of all intelligent readers.

In this point of view, the work may be regarded as curious at least, if not in some degree interesting; and, at all events, it must be instructive to be made aware of the excesses into which superior understandings may be betrayed, by long self-indulgence, and the strange extravagances into which they may run, when under the influence of that intoxication which is produced by unrestrained admiration of themselves. This poetical intoxication, indeed, to pursue the figure a little farther, seems capable of assuming as many forms as the vulgar one which arises from wine; and it appears to require as delicate a management to make a man a good poet by the help of the one, as to make him a good companion by means of the other. In both cases, a little mistake as to the dose or the quality of the inspiring fluid may make him absolutely outrageous, or lull him over into the most profound stupidity, instead of brightening up the hidden stores of his genius: And truly we are concerned to say, that Mr. Wordsworth seems hitherto to have been unlucky in the choice of his liquor—or of his bottle holder. In some of his odes and ethic exhortations, he was exposed to the public in a state of incoherent rapture and glorious delirium, to which we think we have seen a parallel among the humbler lovers of jollity. In the *Lyrical Ballads,* he was exhibited, on the whole, in a vein of very pretty deliration; but in the poem before us, he appears in a state of low and maudlin imbecility, which would not have misbecome Master Silence himself, in the close of a social day. Whether this unhappy result is to be ascribed to any adulteration of his Castalian cups, or to the unlucky choice of his company over them, we cannot presume to say. It may be, that he has dashed his Hippocrene with too large an infusion of lake water, or assisted its operation too exclusively by the study of the ancient historical ballads of 'the north countrie.' That there are palpable imitations of the style and manner of those venerable compositions in the work before us, is indeed undeniable; but it unfortunately happens, that while the hobbling versification, the mean diction, and flat stupidity of these models are very exactly copied, and even improved upon, in this imitation, their rude energy, manly simplicity, and occasional felicity of expression, have totally disappeared; and, instead of them, a large allowance of the author's own metaphysical sensibility, and mystical wordiness, is forced into an unnatural combination with the borrowed beauties which have just been mentioned.

—Francis Jeffrey, Lord Jeffrey,
"Wordsworth's *White Doe,*" *Edinburgh
Review,* October 1815, pp. 355–356

John Campbell Shairp
"The White Doe of Rylstone" (1881)

John Campbell Shairp was a Scottish critic who taught at Oxford University and was the author of *The Poetic Interpretation of Nature.* Shairp praises the beauty with which Wordsworth imbued *The White Doe* and the skill he demonstrated in weaving a poem out of a seemingly minor incident. Shairp describes the narrative as the story of the end of feudal chivalry as embodied in the tale of the sufferings of the lone survivor who finds the healing balm of nature and time. The pastoral world of Wharfdale and of the fells around Bolton lend their beauty to the work. Shairp asserts that no one could visit the actual locales and not be stirred by the impressive landscape. He has high praise for the skill Wordsworth demonstrates in raising the heroine to sainthood and for how various elements were melded by his imagination into a romantic narrative. Yet, Shairp maintains that in Wordsworth's analysis of character there is a strong autobiographical element; the feelings attributed to his heroine are actually those of the poet.

What is it that gives to it its chief power and charm? Is it not the imaginative use which the poet has made of the White Doe? With her appearance the poem opens, with her reappearance it closes. And the passages in which she is introduced are radiant with the purest light of poetry. A mere floating tradition she was, which the historian of Craven had preserved. How much does the poet bring out of how little! It was a high stroke of genius to seize on this slight traditionary incident, and make it the organ of so much. What were the objects which he had to describe and blend into one harmonious whole? They were these:

> The last expiring gleam of feudal chivalry, ending in the ruin of an ancient race, and the desolation of an ancestral home.
> The sole survivor, purified and exalted by the sufferings she had to undergo.
> The pathos of the decaying sanctities of Bolton, after wrong and outrage, abandoned to the healing of nature and time.
> Lastly, the beautiful scenery of pastoral Wharfdale, and of the fells around Bolton, which blends so well with these affecting memories.

All these were before him—they had melted into his imagination, and waited to be woven into one harmonious creation. He takes the White Doe, and makes her the exponent, the symbol, the embodiment of them all. The one central aim—to represent the beatification of the heroine—how was this to be attained? Had it been a drama, the poet would have made the heroine give forth in speeches her hidden mind and character. But this was a romantic narrative. Was the poet to make her soliloquize, analyze her own feelings, lay bare her heart in metaphysical monologue? This might have been done by some modern poets, but it was not Wordsworth's way of exhibiting character, reflective though he was. When he analyzes feelings they are generally his own, not those of his characters. To shadow forth that which is invisible, the sanctity of Emily's chastened soul, he lays hold of this sensible image—a creature, the purest, most innocent, most beautiful in the whole realm of nature—and makes her the vehicle in which he embodies the saintliness, which is a thing invisible. It is the hardest of all tasks to make spiritual things sensuous, without degrading them. I know not where this difficulty has been more happily met; for we are made to feel that, before the poem closes, the doe has ceased to be a mere animal, or a physical creature at all, but in the light of the poet's imagination has been transfigured into a heavenly apparition—a type of all that is pure, and affecting, and saintly. And not only the chastened soul of her mistress, but the beautiful Priory of Bolton, the whole vale of Wharf, and all the surrounding scenery, are illumined by the glory which she makes; her presence irradiates them all with a beauty and an interest more than the eye discovers. Seen through her as an imaginative transparency, they become spiritualized; in fact, she and they alike become the symbols and expression of the sentiment which pervades the poem—a sentiment broad and deep as the world. And yet, any one who visits these scenes in a mellow autumnal day, will feel that she is no alien or adventitious image, imported by the caprice of the poet, but one altogether native to the place, one which gathers up and concentrates all the undefined spirit and sentiment which lie spread around it. She both glorifies the scenery by her presence, and herself seems to be a natural growth of the scenery, so that it finds in her its most appropriate utterance. This power of imagination to divine and project the very corporeal image, which suits and expresses the spirit of a scene, Wordsworth has many times shown. Notably, for instance, do those ghostly shapes, which might meet at noontide under the dark dome of the fraternal yews of Borrowdale, embody the feeling awakened when one stands there. But never perhaps has he shown this embodying power of imagination more felicitously than when he made the White Doe the ideal exponent of the scenery, the memories, and the sympathies which cluster around Bolton Priory.

—JOHN CAMPBELL SHAIRP, "The White Doe of Rylstone," *Aspects of Poetry*, 1881, pp. 319–321

THE EXCURSION

Wordsworth's longest poem, *The Excursion*, was published in 1814, and it was his original intention that it would become the second part of an earlier philosophical poem, *The Recluse*, which was never completed. *The*

Excursion is a dramatic poem presented in the form of a debate among four speakers—the Poet, the Wanderer, the Solitary, and the Pastor—and takes place over the course of a few days. While contemporary reviews were mostly quite harsh, *The Excursion* received a far more favorable reception later on. Many Victorian readers found it to be a source of comfort, its spirituality offering solace in their own uncertain times.

WILLIAM HAZLITT "OBSERVATIONS ON MR. WORDSWORTH'S POEM THE *EXCURSION*" (1814)

Hazlitt does not present a favorable review, rather he sees *The Excursion* as a long narcissistic poem. He discusses how the poem is an exact rendition of the actual landscape it depicts and wonders if, in fact, Wordsworth would have allowed the existence of a "druidical temple" to encroach on the utter wildness and primordial nature of the world he wants to convey and the sensations he seeks to evoke.

Hazlitt then proceeds to categorize the work, stating that it is "a philosophical pastoral poem" and "a scholastic romance" and above all occasions the outpouring of Wordsworth's emotions, "the outgoings of his own heart, the shapings of his own fancy." Here, *The Excursion* is characterized as a type of poem in which the poet's imagination is all. Likewise, the human beings presented are also basic and elemental, generalized individuals who lack differentiation, as the recluse, pastor, and pedlar, or peddler are all versions of the poet himself. Hazlitt suggests that Wordsworth is afraid of any poetic competition and thus closed off from the real world in what is a circumscribed poem. "The power of his mind preys upon itself," Hazlitt notes. "It is as if there were nothing but himself and the universe. He lives in the busy solitude of his own heart; in the deep silence of thought."

———

The poem of *The Excursion* resembles that part of the country in which the scene is laid. It has the same vastness and magnificence, with the same nakedness and confusion. It has the same overwhelming, oppressive power. It excites or recalls the same sensations which those who have traversed that wonderful scenery must have felt. We are surrounded with the constant sense and superstitious awe of the collective power of matter, of the gigantic and eternal forms of nature, on which, from the beginning of time, the hand of man has made no impression. Here are no dotted lines, no hedge-row beauties, no box-tree borders, no gravel walks, no square mechanic inclosures; all is left loose and irregular in the rude chaos of aboriginal nature. The boundaries of hill and valley are the poet's only geography, where we wander with him incessantly over deep beds of moss and waving fern, amidst the troops of red-deer and wild animals. Such is the severe simplicity of Mr. Wordsworth's taste, that we doubt whether he would not reject a druidical temple, or time-hallowed ruin as too modern and artificial for his purpose. He only familiarises himself or his readers with a stone, covered with lichens, which has slept in the same spot of ground from the creation of the world, or with the rocky fissure between two mountains caused by thunder, or with a cavern scooped out by the sea. His mind is, as it were, coeval with the primary forms of things; his imagination holds immediately from nature, and 'owes no allegiance' but 'to the elements.'

The *Excursion* may be considered as a philosophical pastoral poem,—as a scholastic romance. It is less a poem on the country, than on the love of the country. It is not so much a description of natural objects, as of the feelings associated with them; not an account of the manners of rural life, but the result of the poet's reflections on it. He does not present the reader with a lively succession of images or incidents, but paints the outgoings of his own heart, the shapings of his own fancy. He may be said to create his own materials; his thoughts are his real subject. His understanding broods over that which is 'without form and void,' and 'makes it pregnant.' He sees all things in himself. He hardly ever avails himself of remarkable objects or situations, but, in general, rejects them as interfering with the workings of his own mind, as disturbing the smooth, deep, majestic current of his own feelings. Thus his descriptions of natural scenery are not brought home distinctly to the naked eye by forms and circumstances, but every object is seen through the medium of innumerable recollections, is clothed with the haze of imagination like a glittering vapour, is obscured with the excess of glory, has the shadowy brightness of a waking dream. The image is lost in the sentiment, as sound in the multiplication of echoes.

> And visions, as prophetic eyes avow,
> Hang on each leaf, and cling to every bough.

In describing human nature, Mr. Wordsworth equally shuns the common 'vantage-grounds of popular story, of striking incident, or fatal catastrophe, as cheap and vulgar modes of producing an effect. He scans the human race as the naturalist measures the earth's zone, without attending to the picturesque points of view, the abrupt inequalities of surface. He contemplates the passions and habits of men, not in their extremes, but in their first elements; their follies and vices, not at their height, with all their embossed evils upon their heads, but as lurking in embryo,—the seeds of the disorder inwoven with our very constitution. He only sympathises with those simple forms of feeling, which mingle at once with his own identity, or with the stream of general humanity. To him the great and the small are the same; the near and the remote; what appears, and what only is. The general and the permanent, like the Platonic ideas, are his only realities. All accidental varieties and individual contrasts are lost in an endless continuity of feeling, like drops of water in the ocean-stream! An intense intellectual egotism swallows up every thing. Even the dialogues introduced in the present volume are soliloquies of the same character, taking different views of the subject. The recluse, the pastor, and the pedlar, are three persons in one poet. We ourselves disapprove of these 'interlocutions between Lucius and Caius' as impertinent babbling, where there is no dramatic distinction of character. But the evident scope and tendency of Mr. Wordsworth's mind is the reverse of dramatic. It resists all change of character, all variety of scenery, all the bustle, machinery, and pantomime of the stage, or of real life,—whatever might relieve, or relax, or change the direction of its own activity, jealous of all competition. The power of his mind preys upon itself. It is as if there were nothing but himself and the universe. He lives in the busy solitude of his own heart; in the deep silence of thought. His imagination lends life and feeling only to 'the bare trees and mountains bare'; peoples the viewless tracts of air, and converses with the silent clouds!

—WILLIAM HAZLITT, "Observations on
Mr. Wordsworth's Poem the *Excursion*,"
1814, *The Round Table*, 1817

FRANCIS JEFFREY, LORD JEFFREY
"WORDSWORTH'S *EXCURSION*" (1814)

Francis Jeffrey was a Scottish critic who continually denigrated Wordsworth's work and eventually became the poet's nemesis. In his well-known critique of *The Excursion* and its peculiar system, Jeffrey declares it an abysmal failure, finding it far weaker and less authentic than Wordsworth's previous writings. The critic finds the poem burdened by unrestrained wordiness and too derivative or imitative of the poetry of William Cowper and John Milton. Turning to the short biography contained within the poem, Jeffrey maintains that Wordsworth is hopeless and tries to dissuade him from his prior "wanton and capricious" experiments in an attempt to salvage whatever brief moments of beauty and sympathy are to be found.

Jeffrey attacks Wordsworth personally and poetically by assaulting his chosen subject matter of children and rural inhabitants who cannot read. Jeffrey also attributes this failure to Wordsworth's predilection for seclusion, his lake retreat is likened to the worship of "paltry idols." The attack continues with Jeffrey stating that Wordsworth has actually deluded himself in regard to his genius, as he has no basis of comparison or means to measure it, living as he does outside society. This chosen way of life, Jeffrey argues, renders the poet's output clumsy for he works without thought to how he will be perceived and without the sophisticated arbiters of taste found in polished circles. Jeffrey sees solitude as deleterious to Wordsworth both personally and professionally, as indicative of a supreme narcissism in Wordsworth's view of himself. Thus, *The Excursion* not only provides evidence of mental illness or instability in the poet, it is unreadable with its "unwieldy phrases" and preposterous pretensions to profound feelings that Wordsworth foolishly believes are equivalent to poetic inspiration.

Jeffrey finds traces of the Methodist rhetoric as well in *The Excursion*, phrasing he considers "mystical verbiage" that seems to sweep Wordsworth off his feet and cause him to believe that he espouses a divine truth. This supposed didactic work comprised of a series of lectures between three interlocutors is devoid of interest for the reader for it simply relates each character's opinion. For Jeffrey, *The Excursion* seems to point only to an old theme, namely the need to have faith in a higher and beneficent power. In choosing the obsolete pedlar, a humiliated moral teacher, Wordsworth demonstrates a misguided notion of taste. "A man who went about selling flannel and pocket-handkerchiefs in this lofty diction," Jeffrey writes, "would soon frighten away all his customers; and would infallibly pass either for a madman, or for some learned and affected gentleman." In sum, Jeffrey's scathing review finds Wordsworth to be highly immature and *The Excursion* exhibiting the poet's "affected passion for simplicity and humble life, most awkwardly combined with a taste for mystical refinements, and all the gorgeousness of obscure phraseology."

This will never do. (*The Excursion*) bears no doubt the stamp of the author's heart and fancy; but unfortunately not half so visibly as that of his peculiar system. His former poems were intended to recommend that system, and to bespeak favour for it by their individual merit;—but this, we suspect, must be recommended by the system—and can only expect to succeed where it has been previously established. It is longer, weaker, and tamer, than any of Mr Wordsworth's other productions; with less boldness of originality, and less even of that extreme simplicity and lowliness of tone which wavered so prettily, in the *Lyrical Ballads,* between silliness and pathos. We have imitations of Cowper, and even of Milton here, engrafted on the natural drawl of the Lakers—and all diluted into harmony by that profuse and irrepressible wordiness which deluges all the blank verse of this school of poetry, and lubricates and weakens the whole structure of their style.

Though it fairly fills four hundred and twenty good quarto pages, without note, vignette, or any sort of extraneous assistance, it is stated in the title—with something of an imprudent candour—to be but 'a portion' of a larger work; and in the preface, where an attempt is rather unsuccessfully made to explain the whole design, it is still more rashly disclosed, that it is but 'a part of the second part of a *long* and laborious work'—which is to consist of three parts.

What Mr Wordsworth's ideas of length are, we have no means of accurately judging; but we cannot help suspecting that they are liberal, to a degree that will alarm the weakness of most modern readers. As far as we can gather from the preface, the entire poem—or one of them, for we really are not sure whether there is to be one or two—is of a biographical nature; and is to contain the history of the author's mind, and of the origin and progress of his poetical powers, up to the period when they were sufficiently matured to qualify him for the great work on which he has been so long employed. Now, the quarto before us contains an account of one of his youthful rambles in the vales of Cumberland, and occupies precisely the period of three days; so that, by the use of a very powerful *calculus,* some estimate may be formed of the probable extent of the entire biography.

This small specimen, however, and the statements with which it is prefaced, have been sufficient to set our minds at rest in one particular. The case of Mr Wordsworth, we perceive, is now manifestly hopeless; and we give him up as altogether incurable, and beyond the power of criticism. We cannot indeed altogether omit taking precautions now and then against the spreading of the malady;—but for himself, though we shall watch the progress of his symptoms as a matter of professional curiosity and instruction, we really think it right not to harass him any longer with nauseous remedies,—but rather to throw in cordials and lenitives, and wait in patience for the natural termination of the disorder. In order to justify this desertion of our patient, however, it is proper to state why we despair of the success of a more active practice.

A man who has been for twenty years at work on such matter as is now before us, and who comes complacently forward with a whole quarto of it after all the admonitions he has received, cannot reasonably be expected to 'change his hand, or check his pride,' upon the suggestion of far weightier monitors than we can pretend to be. Inveterate habit must now have given a kind of sanctity to the errors of early taste; and the very powers of which we lament the perversion, have probably become incapable of any other application. The very quantity, too, that he has written, and is at this moment working up for publication upon the old pattern, makes it almost hopeless to look for any change of it. All this is so much capital already sunk in the concern; which must be sacrificed if it be abandoned: and no man likes to give up for lost the time and talent and labour which he has embodied in any permanent production. We were not previously aware of these obstacles to Mr Wordsworth's conversion; and, considering the peculiarities of his former writings merely as the result of certain wanton and capricious experiments on public taste and indulgence, conceived it to be our duty to discourage their repetition by all the means in our power. We now see clearly, however, how the case stands;—and, making up our minds, though with the most sincere pain and reluctance, to consider him as finally lost to the good cause of poetry, shall endeavour to be thankful for the occasional gleams of tenderness and beauty which the natural force of his imagination and affections must still shed over all his productions,—and to which we shall ever turn with delight, in spite of the affectation and mysticism and prolixity, with which they are so abundantly contrasted.

Long habits of seclusion, and an excessive ambition of originality, can alone account for the disproportion which seems to exist between this author's taste and his genius; or for the devotion with which he has sacrificed so many precious gifts at the shrine of those paltry idols which he has set up for himself among his lakes and his mountains. Solitary musings, amidst such scenes, might no doubt be expected to nurse up the mind to the majesty of poetical conception,—(though it is remarkable, that all the greater poets lived, or had lived, in the full current of society):—But the collision of equal minds,—the admonition of prevailing impressions—seems necessary to reduce its redundancies, and repress that tendency to extravagance or puerility, into which the self-indulgence and self-admiration of genius is so apt to be betrayed, when it is allowed to wanton, without awe or restraint, in the triumph and delight of its own intoxication. That its flights should be graceful and glorious in the eyes of men, it seems almost to be necessary that they should be made in the consciousness that men's eyes are to behold them,—and that the inward transport and vigour by which they are inspired, should be tempered by an occasional reference to what will be thought of them by those ultimate dispensers of glory. An habitual and general knowledge of the few settled and permanent maxims, which form the canon of general taste in all large and polished societies—a certain tact, which informs us at once that many things, which we still love and are moved by in secret, must necessarily be despised as childish, or derided as absurd, in all such societies—though it will not stand in the place of genius, seems necessary to the success of its exertions; and though it will never enable any one to produce the higher beauties of art, can alone secure the talent which does produce them, from errors that must render it useless. Those who have most of the talent, however, commonly acquire this knowledge with the greatest facility;—and if Mr Wordsworth, instead of confining himself almost entirely to the society of the dalesmen and cottagers, and little children, who form the subjects of his book, had condescended to mingle a little more with the people that were to read and judge of it, we cannot help thinking, that its texture would have been considerably improved: At least it appears to us to be absolutely impossible, that any one who had lived or mixed familiarly with men of literature and ordinary judgment in poetry, (of course we exclude the coadjutors and disciples of his own school), could ever have fallen into such gross faults, or so long mistaken them for beauties. His first essays we looked upon in a good degree as poetical paradoxes,—maintained experimentally, in order to display talent, and court notoriety;—and so maintained, with no more serious belief in their truth, than is usually generated by an ingenious and animated defence of other paradoxes. But when we find, that he has been for twenty years exclusively employed upon articles of this very fabric, and that he has still enough of raw material on hand to keep him so employed for twenty years to come, we cannot refuse him the justice of believing that he is a sincere convert to his own system, and must ascribe the peculiarities of his composition, not to any transient affectation, or accidental caprice of imagination, but to a settled perversity of taste or understanding, which has been fostered, if not altogether created, by the circumstances to which we have already alluded.

The volume before us, if we were to describe it very shortly, we should characterize as a tissue of moral and devotional ravings, in which innumerable changes are rung upon a few very simple and familiar ideas:—but with such an accompaniment of long words, long sentences, and unwieldy phrases— and such a hubbub of strained raptures and fantastical sublimities, that it is often extremely difficult for the most skilful and attentive student to obtain a glimpse of the author's meaning—and altogether impossible for an ordinary reader to conjecture what he is about. Moral and religious enthusiasm, though undoubtedly poetical emotions, are at the same time but dangerous inspirers of poetry; nothing being so apt to run into interminable dulness or mellifluous extravagance, without giving the unfortunate author the slightest intimation of his danger. His laudable zeal for the efficacy of his preachments, he very naturally mistakes for the ardour of poetical inspiration;—and, while dealing out the high words and glowing phrases which are so readily supplied by themes of this description, can scarcely avoid believing that he is eminently original and impressive:—All sorts of commonplace notions and expressions are sanctified in his eyes, by the sublime ends for which they are employed; and the mystical verbiage of the methodist pulpit is repeated, till the speaker entertains no doubt that he is the elected organ of divine truth and persuasion. But if such be the common hazards of seeking inspiration from those potent fountains, it may easily be conceived what chance Mr Wordsworth had of escaping their enchantment,—with his natural propensities to wordiness, and his unlucky habit of debasing pathos with vulgarity. The fact accordingly is, that in this production he is more obscure than a Pindaric poet of the seventeenth century; and more verbose 'than even himself of yore;' while the wilfulness with which he persists in choosing his examples of intellectual dignity and tenderness exclusively from the lowest ranks of society, will be sufficiently apparent, from the circumstance of his having thought fit to make his chief prolocutor in this poetical dialogue, and chief advocate of Providence and Virtue, *an old Scotch Pedlar*—retired indeed from business—but still rambling about in his former haunts, and gossiping among his old customers, without his pack on his shoulders. The other persons of the drama are, a retired military chaplain, who has grown half an atheist and half a misanthrope—the wife of an unprosperous weaver—a servant girl with her infant—a parish pauper, and one or two other personages of equal rank and dignity.

The character of the work is decidedly didactic; and more than nine tenths of it are occupied with a species of dialogue, or rather a series of long sermons or harangues which pass between the pedlar, the author, the old chaplain, and a worthy vicar, who entertains the whole party at dinner on the last day of their excursion. The incidents which occur in the course of it are as few and trifling as can be imagined;—and those which the different speakers narrate in the course of their discourses, are introduced rather to illustrate their arguments or opinions, than for any interest they are supposed to possess of their own.—The doctrine which the work is intended to enforce, we are by no means certain that we have discovered. In so far as we can collect, however, it seems to be neither more nor less than the old familiar one, that a firm belief in the providence of a wise and beneficent Being must be our great stay and support under all afflictions and perplexities upon earth—and that there are indications of his power and goodness in all the aspects of the visible universe, whether living or inanimate—every part of which should therefore be regarded with love and reverence, as exponents of those great attributes. We can testify, at least, that these salutary and important truths are inculcated at far greater length, and with more repetitions, than in any ten volumes of sermons that we ever perused. It is also maintained, with equal conciseness and originality, that there is frequently much good sense, as well as much enjoyment, in the humbler conditions of life; and that, in spite of great vices and abuses, there is a reasonable allowance both of happiness and goodness in society at large. If there be any deeper or more recondite doctrines in Mr Wordsworth's book, we must confess that they have escaped us;—and, convinced as we are of the truth and soundness of those to which we have alluded, we cannot help thinking that they might have been better enforced with less parade and prolixity. His effusions on what may be called the physiognomy of external nature, or its moral and theological expression, are eminently fantastic, obscure, and affected. . . .

Nobody can be more disposed to do justice to the great powers of Mr Wordsworth than we are; and, from the first time that he came before us, down to the present moment, we have uniformly testified in their favour, and assigned indeed our high sense of their value as the chief ground of the bitterness with which we resented their perversion. That perversion, however, is now far more visible than their original dignity; and while we collect the fragments, it is impossible not to lament the ruins from which we are condemned to pick them. If any one should doubt of the existence of such a perversion, or be disposed to dispute about the instances we have hastily brought forward, we would just beg leave to refer him to the general plan and the characters of the poem now before us.—Why should Mr Wordsworth have made his hero a superannuated Pedlar? What but the most wretched and provoking perversity of taste and judgment, could induce any one to place his chosen advocate of wisdom and virtue in so absurd and fantastic a condition? Did Mr Wordsworth really imagine, that his favourite doctrines were likely to gain any thing in point of effect or authority by being put into the mouth of a person accustomed to higgle about tape, or brass sleeve-buttons? Or is it not plain that, independent of the ridicule and disgust which such a personification must give to many of his readers, its adoption exposes his work throughout to the charge of revolting incongruity, and utter disregard of probability or nature? For, after he has thus wilfully debased his moral teacher by a low occupation, is there one word that he puts into his mouth, or one sentiment of which he makes him the organ, that has the most remote reference to that occupation? Is there any thing in his learned, abstracted, and logical harangues, that savours of the calling that is ascribed to him? Are any of their materials such as a pedlar could possibly have dealt in? Are the manners, the diction, the sentiments, in any, the very smallest degree, accommodated to a person in that condition? or are they not eminently and conspicuously such as could not by possibility belong to it? A man who went about selling flannel and pocket-handkerchiefs in this lofty diction, would soon frighten away all his customers; and would infallibly pass either for a madman, or for some learned and affected gentleman, who, in a frolic, had taken up a character which he was peculiarly ill qualified for supporting.

The absurdity in this case, we think, is palpable and glaring; but it is exactly of the same nature with that which infects the whole substance of the work—a puerile ambition of singularity engrafted on an unlucky predilection for truisms; and an affected passion for simplicity and humble life, most awkwardly combined with a taste for mystical refinements, and all the gorgeousness of obscure phraseology. His taste for simplicity is evinced, by sprinkling up and down his interminable declamations, a few descriptions of baby-houses, and of old hats with wet brims; and his amiable partiality for humble life, by assuring us, that a wordy rhetorician, who talks about Thebes, and allegorizes all the heathen mythology, was once a pedlar—and making him break in upon his magnificent orations with two or three awkward notices of something that he had seen when selling winter raiment about the country—or of the changes in the state of society, which had almost annihilated his former calling.

—Francis Jeffrey, Lord Jeffrey, from
"Wordsworth's *Excursion*," *Edinburgh Review*,
November 1814, pp. 1–6, 29–30

Henry Crabb Robinson (1814)

In the following excerpt from Robinson's *Diary*, the critic states that he has enjoyed *The Excursion* for its wisdom and its representation of the parson's unconquerable vigor of mind despite the loss of his wife. Still, Robinson notes, there are passages that are protracted and long winded.

⁓⁓ ⁓⁓ ⁓⁓

November 2lst.—In the evening I stepped over to Lamb, and sat with him from ten to eleven. He was very chatty and pleasant. Pictures and poetry were the subjects of our talk. He thinks no description in *The Excursion* so good as the history of the country parson who had been a courtier. In this I agree with him. But he dislikes *The Magdalen*, which he says would be as good in prose; in which I do *not* agree with him.

November 23rd.—This week I finished Wordsworth's poem. It has afforded me less intense pleasure on the whole, perhaps, than I had expected, but it will be a source of frequent gratification. The wisdom and high moral character of the work are beyond anything of the same kind with which I am acquainted, and the spirit of the poetry flags much less frequently than might be expected. There are passages which run heavily, tales which are prolix, and reasonings which are spun out, but in general the narratives are exquisitely tender. That of the courtier parson, who retains in solitude the feelings of high society, whose vigour of mind is unconquerable, and who, even after the death of his wife, appears able for a short time to bear up against desolation and wretchedness, by the powers of his native temperament, is most delightful. Among the discussions, that on Manufactories, in the eighth book, is admirably managed, and forms, in due subordination to the incomparable fourth book, one of the chief excellences of the poem. Wordsworth has succeeded better in light and elegant painting in this poem than in any other. His Hanoverian and Jacobite are very sweet pictures.

—HENRY CRABB ROBINSON, *Diary*,
November 21 and 23, 1814

ROBERT SOUTHEY (1814)

In his letter to Sir Walter Scott, Robert Southey responds to Francis Jeffrey's scathing review, stating that the self-important Jeffrey might also perch on Skiddaw Mountain and delude himself into thinking that he flattened it, an aim similar to that of his withering critiques.

Jeffrey I hear has written what his admirers call a *crushing* review of the *Excursion*. He might as well seat himself upon Skiddaw and fancy that he crushed the mountain. I heartily wish Wordsworth may one day meet with him, and lay him alongside, yard-arm and yard-arm in argument.

—ROBERT SOUTHEY, letter to
Sir Walter Scott, December 24, 1814

SAMUEL TAYLOR COLERIDGE (1817)

In his brilliant analysis of *The Excursion*, Samuel Taylor Coleridge defends Wordsworth from those antagonists who complain that he does not develop his arguments enough to persuade his readers. Coleridge is interested in demonstrating how far-reaching Wordsworth's poetic theories are and argues the writer's influence is proof of the poem's worth: "But let it likewise be shown how far the influence has acted; whether diffusively, or only by starts; whether the number and importance of the poems and passages thus infected be great or trifling compared with the sound portion; and lastly, whether they are inwoven into the texture of his works, or are loose and separable." Coleridge argues that Wordsworth's true worth is to be found in his genius, stating that *The Excursion* exhibits an important unity that is proof of such superior ability. Moreover, Coleridge maintains that Wordsworth exhibits his genius because, in writing of humble people or his close observation of nature, he adapted his style and expression in order to reflect the subject matter. Nevertheless, Coleridge responds to various faults he has found in *The Excursion*, including Wordsworth's irregular and fluctuating style, "the sudden and unprepared transitions from lines or sentences of peculiar felicity (at all events striking and original) to a style not only unimpassioned but undistinguished." Coleridge also identifies three modes of language that Wordsworth employs: (1) that which is peculiar to poetry, (2) that which is only proper in prose, and (3) that which is neutral or common to both. Furthermore, Coleridge astutely points out the issue of expectation in reading poetry, specifically that the reader anticipates and looks forward to an elaborate use of words that will evoke beautiful images and, conversely, its absence in a poem leaves the reader dissatisfied.

Another defect that Coleridge identifies is a mundane quality in *The Excursion*. He feels Wordsworth gives too much detail about how objects and characters appear to him, a wordiness that can be distracting from what is essential to creating a poetic effect. Coleridge maintains that, since the reader wants to indulge his or her senses and delight in imaginative imagery, a poem not fulfilling those expectations results in disappointment. Coleridge sees a surfeit of detail as creating a labored and self-conscious quality that reveals an "anxiety of explanation." This, in turn, leads to Wordsworth's projection of his own feelings onto his human subjects.

In response to the charge that Wordsworth brought only lower-class characters to his work, Coleridge's essay formulates a brilliant response in which he imagines Wordsworth putting the critic on the defensive by asking why he reads meanness of character when Wordsworth intended to praise such individuals through the vehicle of a "prideless impartiality in poetry," whether the subject matter was an "armed baron, a laurel'd bard, etc., or . . . an old pedlar." Wordsworth maintained that all people deserved to be treated with the same respect. Nevertheless, Coleridge contends that the premise of *The Excursion* is aligned more with the provenance of the moral philosopher and, thus, is more appropriately the subject matter for sermons or moral essays, for *The Excursion* conflates the boundaries between poetry and prose, philosophy and fiction. Coleridge maintains that the poet needs to proceed on the premise of affording delight, and he expresses doubt whether these humble people, who "are unschooled and illiterate," can really be called poets. To grant poetic genius to a simple character renders that character false and creates a credibility gap between the poet's skillful use of language and the forced effect of seeming lesser than or falsely modest in the face of his true talents. Coleridge also faults *The Excursion* for being pompous in thought, particularly the parts in which the imagery is not appropriate to the simple subject matter. However, Coleridge asserts that only a man of Wordsworth's stature could conceive of this type of incommensurability. In sum, Coleridge believes the defects of *The Excursion* are minor in comparison to Wordsworth's profound depth of feeling and imagination.

If Mr. Wordsworth has set forth principles of poetry which his arguments are insufficient to support, let him and those who have adopted his sentiments be set right by the confutation of those arguments and by the substitution of more philosophical principles. And still let the due credit be given to the portion and importance of the truths which are blended with his theory: truths, the too exclusive attention to which had occasioned its errors by tempting him to carry those truths beyond their proper limits. If his mistaken theory has at all influenced his poetic compositions, let the effects be pointed out and the instances given. But let it likewise be shown how far the influence has acted; whether diffusively, or only by starts; whether the number and importance of the poems and passages thus infected be great or trifling compared with the sound portion; and lastly, whether they are inwoven into the texture of his works, or are loose and separable. The result of such a trial would evince beyond a doubt what it is high time to announce decisively and aloud, that the supposed characteristics of Mr Wordsworth's poetry, whether admired or reprobated; whether they are simplicity or simpleness; faithful adherence to essential nature or wilful selections from human nature of its meanest forms and under the least attractive associations: are as little the real characteristics of his poetry at large as of his genius and the constitution of his mind.

In a comparatively small number of poems he chose to try an experiment; and this experiment we will suppose to have failed. Yet even in these poems it is impossible not to perceive that the natural tendency of the poet's mind is to great objects and elevated conceptions. The poem entitled 'Fidelity' is for the greater part written in language as unraised and naked as any perhaps in the two volumes. Yet take the following stanza and compare it with the preceding stanzas of the same poem:

> There sometimes does a leaping fish
> Send through the tarn a lonely cheer;
> The crags repeat the raven's croak
> In symphony austere;
> Thither the rainbow comes—the cloud,
> And mists that spread the flying shroud;
> And sunbeams; and the sounding blast,
> That if it could would hurry past,
> But that enormous barrier holds it fast.

Or compare the four last lines of the concluding stanza with the former half:

> Yes, proof was plain that since the day
> On which the traveller thus had died,
> The dog had watched about the spot,
> Or by his master's side:
> *How nourished here for such long time*
> *He knows who gave that love sublime,*
> *And gave that strength of feeling, great*
> *Above all human estimate.*

Can any candid and intelligent mind hesitate in determining which of these best represents the tendency and native character of the poet's genius? Will he not decide that the one was written because the poet *would* so write, and the other because he could not so entirely repress the force and grandeur of his mind, but that he must in some part or other of every composition write otherwise? In short, that his only disease is the being out of his element; like the swan, that having amused himself for a while with crushing the weeds on the river's bank soon returns to his own majestic movements on its reflecting and sustaining surface. Let it be observed that I am here supposing the imagined judge to whom I appeal to have already decided against the poet's theory, as far as it is different from the principles of the art generally acknowledged.

I cannot here enter into a detailed examination of Mr Wordsworth's works; but I will attempt to give the main results of my own judgement after an acquaintance of many years and repeated perusals. And though to appreciate the defects of a great mind it is necessary to understand previously its characteristic excellences, yet I have already expressed myself with sufficient fulness to preclude most of the ill effects that might arise from my pursuing a contrary arrangement. I will therefore commence with what I deem the prominent defects of his poems hitherto published.

The first characteristic, though only occasional defect, which I appear to myself to find in these poems is the inconstancy of the style. Under this name I refer to the sudden and unprepared transitions from lines or sentences of peculiar felicity (at all events striking and original) to a style not only unimpassioned but undistinguished. He sinks too often and too abruptly to that style which I should place in the second division of language, dividing it into the three species: first, that which is peculiar to poetry; second, that which is only proper in prose; and third, the neutral or common to both. There have been works, such as Cowley's essay on Cromwell, in which prose and verse are intermixed (not as in the Consolation of Boetius, or the Argenis of Barclay, by the insertion of poems supposed to have been spoken or composed on occasions previously related in prose, but) the poet passing from one to the other as the nature of the thoughts or his own feelings dictated. Yet this mode of composition does not satisfy a cultivated taste. There is something unpleasant in the being thus obliged to alternate states of feeling so dissimilar, and this too in a species of writing the pleasure from which is in part derived from the preparation and previous expectation of the reader. A portion of that awkwardness is felt which hangs upon the introduction of songs in our modern comic operas; and to prevent which the judicious Metastasio (as to whose exquisite taste there can be no hesitation, whatever doubts may be entertained as to his poetic genius) uniformly placed the aria at the end of the scene, at the same time that he almost always raises and impassions the style of the recitative immediately preceding. Even in real life the difference is great and evident between words used as the arbitrary marks of thought, our smooth market-coin of intercourse with the image and superscription worn out by currency, and those which convey pictures either borrowed from one outward object to enliven and particularize some other; or used allegorically to body forth the inward state of the person speaking; or such as are at least the exponents of his peculiar turn and unusual extent of faculty. So much so indeed, that in the social circles of private life we often find a striking use of the latter put a stop to the general flow of conversation, and by the excitement arising from concentered attention produce a sort of damp and interruption for some minutes after. But in the perusal of works of literary art we *prepare* ourselves for such language; and the business of the writer, like that of a painter whose subject requires unusual splendor and prominence, is so to raise the lower and neutral tints, that what in a different style would be the commanding colors are here used as the means of that gentle degradation requisite in order to produce the effect of a whole. Where this is not achieved in a poem, the metre merely reminds the reader of his claims in order to disappoint them; and where this defect occurs frequently, his feelings are alternately started by anticlimax and hyperclimax. . . .

The second defect I could generalize with tolerable accuracy if the reader will pardon an uncouth and new coined word. There is, I should say, not seldom a *matter-of-factness* in certain poems. This may be divided into, first, a laborious minuteness and fidelity in the representation of objects and their positions as they appeared to the poet himself; secondly, the insertion of accidental circumstances, in order to the full explanation of his living characters, their dispositions and actions: which circumstances might be necessary to establish the probability of a statement in real life, where nothing is taken for granted by the hearer, but appear superfluous in poetry, where the reader is willing to believe for his own sake. To this accidentality I object, as contravening the essence of poetry, which Aristotle pronounces to be σπουδαιότατον καὶ φιλοσοφώτον γένος, the most intense, weighty and philosophical product of human art; adding, as the reason, that it is the most catholic and abstract. The following passage from Davenant's prefatory letter to Hobbes well expresses this truth: 'When I considered the actions which I meant to describe (those inferring the persons) I was again persuaded rather to choose those of a former age than the present; and in a century so far removed as might preserve me from their improper examinations who know not the requisites of a poem, nor how much pleasure they lose (and even the pleasures of heroic poesy are not unprofitable) who take away the liberty of a poet, and fetter his feet in the shackles of an historian. For why should a poet doubt in story to mend the intrigues of fortune by more delightful conveyances of probable fictions, because austere historians have entered into bond to truth; an obligation which were in poets as foolish and unnecessary as is the bondage of false martyrs, who lie in chains for a mistaken opinion. *But by this I would imply, that truth, narrative and past is the idol of historians (who worship a dead thing), and truth operative, and by effects continually alive, is the mistress of poets, who hath not her existence in matter, but in reason.*' For this minute accuracy in the painting of local imagery, the lines in the *Excursion*, pp. 96, 97 and 98 may be taken, if not as a striking instance, yet as an illustration of my meaning. It must be some strong motive (as, for instance, that the description was necessary to the intelligibility of the tale) which could induce me to describe in a number of verses what a draftsman could present to the eye with incomparably greater satisfaction by half a dozen strokes of his pencil, or the painter with as many touches of his brush. Such descriptions too often occasion in the mind of a reader who is determined to understand his author a feeling of labour, not very dissimilar to that with which he would construct a diagram, line by line, for a long geometrical proposition. It seems to be like taking the pieces of a dissected map out of its box. We first look at one part, and then at another, then join and dove-tail them; and when the successive acts of attention have been completed, there is a retrogressive effort of mind to behold it as a whole. The poet should paint to the imagination, not to the fancy; and I know no happier case to exemplify the distinction between these two faculties. Masterpieces of the former mode of poetic painting abound in the writings of Milton, ex. gr.

> The fig-tree, not that kind for fruit renown'd,
> But such as at this day to Indians known
> In Malabar or Decan spreads her arms
> Branching so broad and long, that in the ground
> The bended twigs take root, *and daughters grow*
> *About the mother-tree, a pillar'd shade*
> *High over-arched, and* ECHOING WALKS BETWEEN:
> *There oft the Indian Herdsman shunning heat*
> *Shelters in cool, and tends his pasturing herds*
> *At loopholes cut through thickest shade.*
> (Milton, P.L. 9, 1100.)

This is creation rather than painting, or if painting, yet such, and with such co-presence of the whole picture flash'd at once upon the eye, as the sun paints in a camera obscura. But the poet must likewise understand and command what Bacon calls the *vestigia communia* of the senses, the latency of all in each, and more especially as by a magical *penna duplex,* the excitement of vision by sound and the exponents of sound. Thus, 'the echoing walks between' may be almost said to reverse the fable in tradition of the head of Memnon in the Egyptian statue. Such may be deservedly entitled the *creative words* in the world of imagination.

The second division respects an apparent minute adherence to matter-of-fact in character and incidents; a biographical attention to probability, and an anxiety of explanation and retrospect. Under this head I shall deliver, with no feigned diffidence, the results of my best reflection on the great point of controversy between Mr Wordsworth and his objectors; namely, on the choice of his characters. I have already declared, and I trust justified, my utter dissent from the mode of argument which his critics have hitherto employed. To their question, why did you chuse such a character, or a character from such a rank of life? the poet might, in my opinion, fairly retort: why with the conception of my character did you make wilful choice of mean or ludicrous associations not furnished by me but supplied from your own sickly and fastidious feelings? How was it indeed probable that such arguments could have any weight with an author whose plan, whose guiding principle and main object it was to attack and subdue that state of association which leads us to place the chief value on those things on which man differs from man, and to forget or disregard the high dignities which belong to human nature, the sense and the feeling which may be, and ought to be, found in all ranks? The feelings with which, as Christians, we contemplate a mixed congregation rising or kneeling before their common maker, Mr Wordsworth would have us entertain at all times, as men and as readers; and by the excitement of this lofty yet prideless impartiality in poetry, he might hope to have encouraged its continuance in real life. The praise of good men be his! In real life and, I trust, even in my imagination, I honor a virtuous and wise man, without reference to the presence or absence of artificial advantages. Whether in the person of an armed baron, a laurel'd bard, etc., or of an old pedlar, or still older leach-gatherer, the same qualities of head and heart must claim the same reverence. And even in poetry I am not conscious that I have ever suffered my feelings to be disturbed or offended by any thoughts or images which the poet himself has not presented.

But yet I object nevertheless, and for the following reasons. First, because the object in view, as an immediate object, belongs to the moral philosopher, and would be pursued not only more appropriately, but in my opinion with far greater probability of success, in sermons or moral essays than in an elevated poem. It seems, indeed, to destroy the main fundamental distinction, not only between a poem and prose, but even between philosophy and works of fiction, inasmuch as it proposes truth for its immediate object instead of pleasure. Now till the blessed time shall come when truth itself shall be pleasure, and both shall be so united as to be distinguishable in words only, not in feeling, it will remain the poet's office to proceed upon that state of association which actually exists as general; instead of attempting first to make it what it ought to be, and then to let the pleasure follow. But here is unfortunately a small *hysteron-proteron*. For the communication of pleasure is the introductory means by which alone the poet must expect to moralize his readers. Secondly: though I were to admit, for a moment, this argument to be groundless; yet how is the moral effect to be produced by merely attaching the name of some low profession to powers which are least likely, and to qualities which are assuredly not more likely, to be found in it? The poet, speaking in his own person, may at once delight and improve us by sentiments which teach us the independence of goodness, of wisdom, and even of genius, on the favors of fortune. And having made a due reverence before the throne of Antonine, he may bow with equal awe before Epictetus among his fellow-slaves—

and rejoice
In the plain presence of his dignity.

Who is not at once delighted and improved, when the *poet* Wordsworth
himself exclaims,

O many are the poets that are sown
By Nature; men endowed with highest gifts,
The vision and the faculty divine,
Yet wanting the accomplishment of verse,
Nor having e'er, as life advanced, been led
By circumstance to take unto the height
The measure of themselves, these favoured beings,
All but a scattered few, live out their time,
Husbanding that which they possess within,
And go to the grave unthought of. Strongest minds
Are often those of whom the noisy world
Hears least.

(Excursion, B.I.)

To use a colloquial phrase, such sentiments, in such language, do one's
heart good; though I for my part have not the fullest faith in the *truth* of
the observation. On the contrary I believe the instances to be exceedingly
rare; and should feel almost as strong an objection to introduce such a
character in a poetic fiction as a pair of black swans on a lake, in a fancy-
landscape. When I think how many and how much better books than
Homer, or even than Herodotus, Pindar or Eschylus, could have read, are
in the power of almost every man, in a country where almost every man is
instructed to read and write; and how restless, how difficulty hidden, the
powers of genius are, and yet find even in situations the most favorable,
according to Mr Wordsworth, for the formation of a pure and poetic
language, in situations which ensure familiarity with the grandest objects
of the imagination, but one Burns among the shepherds of Scotland,
and not a single poet of humble life among those of *English* lakes and
mountains; I conclude that Poetic Genius is not only a very delicate but a
very rare plant.

But be this as it may, the feelings with which

I think of Chatterton, the marvellous boy,
The sleepless soul that perish'd in his pride:
Of Burns, that walk'd in glory and in joy
Behind his plough upon the mountain-side,

are widely different from those with which I should read a poem where the
author, having occasion for the character of a poet and a philosopher in the
fable of his narration, had chosen to make him a chimney-sweeper; and
then, in order to remove all doubts on the subject, had invented an account
of his birth, parentage and education, with all the strange and fortunate
accidents which had concurred in making him at once poet, philosopher
and sweep! Nothing but biography can justify this. If it be admissible even
in a novel, it must be one in the manner of De Foe's, that were meant to pass
for histories, not in the manner of Fielding's: in the life of Moll Flanders, or
Colonel Jack, not in a Tom Jones or even a Joseph Andrews. Much less then
can it be legitimately introduced in a poem, the characters of which, amid
the strongest individualization, must still remain representative. The precepts
of Horace, on this point, are grounded on the nature both of poetry and of
the human mind. They are not more peremptory than wise and prudent. For
in the first place a deviation from them perplexes the reader's feelings, and
all the circumstances which are feigned in order to make such accidents less
improbable divide and disquiet his faith, rather than aid and support it. Spite
of all attempts, the fiction will appear, and unfortunately not as fictitious but
as false. The reader not only knows that the sentiments and the language are
the poet's own, and his own too in his artificial character, as poet; but by the
fruitless endeavours to make him think the contrary he is not even suffered
to forget it. The effect is similar to that produced by an epic poet when the
fable and characters are derived from Scripture history, as in the *Messiah* of
Klopstock, or in Cumberland's *Calvary:* and not merely suggested by it as in
the *Paradise Lost* of Milton. That illusion, contradistinguished from delusion,
that *negative* faith which simply permits the images presented to work by
their own force, without either denial or affirmation of their real existence by
the judgement, is rendered impossible by their immediate neighbourhood to
words and facts of known and absolute truth. A faith which transcends even
historic belief must absolutely put out this mere poetic analogon of faith, as
the summer sun is said to extinguish our household fires when it shines full
upon them. What would otherwise have been yielded to as pleasing fiction is
repelled as revolting falsehood. The effect produced in this latter case by the
solemn belief of the reader is in a less degree brought about in the instances
to which I have been objecting, by the baffled attempts of the author to *make*
him believe.

Add to all the foregoing the seeming uselessness both of the project and
of the anecdotes from which it is to derive support. Is there one word, for
instance, attributed to the pedlar in the Excursion characteristic of a pedlar?
One sentiment that might not more plausibly, even without the aid of any

previous explanation, have proceeded from any wise and beneficent old man of a rank or profession in which the language of learning and refinement are natural and to be expected? Need the rank have been at all particularized, where nothing follows which the knowledge of that rank is to explain or illustrate? When on the contrary this information renders the man's language, feelings, sentiments and information a riddle which must itself be solved by episodes of anecdote? Finally when this, and this alone, could have induced a genuine poet to inweave in a poem of the loftiest style, and on subjects the loftiest and of the most universal interest such minute matters of fact, not unlike those furnished for the obituary of a magazine by the friends of some obscure *ornament of society lately deceased* in some obscure town, as

> Among the hills of Athol he was born.
> There on a small hereditary farm,
> An unproductive slip of rugged ground,
> His father dwelt; and died in poverty:
> While he, whose lowly fortune I retrace,
> The youngest of three sons, was yet a babe,
> A little one—unconscious of their loss.
> But ere he had outgrown his infant days
> His widowed mother, for a second mate,
> Espoused the teacher of the village school;
> Who on her offspring zealously bestowed
> Needful instruction.
> From his sixth year, the boy of whom I speak,
> In summer tended cattle on the hills;
> But through the inclement and the perilous days
> Of long-continuing winter, he repaired
> To his step-father's school, etc.

For all the admirable passages interposed in this narration might, with trifling alterations, have been far more appropriately and with far greater verisimilitude told of a poet in the character of a poet; and without incurring another defect which I shall now mention, and a sufficient illustration of which will have been here anticipated.

Third: an undue predilection for the dramatic form in certain poems, from which one or other of two evils result. Either the thoughts and diction are different from that of the poet, and then there arises an incongruity of style; or they are the same and indistinguishable, and then it presents a species of ventriloquism, where two are represented as talking while in truth one man only speaks.

The fourth class of defects is closely connected with the former; but yet are such as arise likewise from an intensity of feeling disproportionate to such knowledge and value of the objects described as can be fairly anticipated of men in general, even of the most cultivated classes; and with which therefore few only, and those few particularly circumstanced, can be supposed to sympathize: in this class I comprize occasional prolixity, repetition and an eddying instead of progression of thought. As instances, see pages 27, 28 and 62 of the *Poems*, vol. i, and the first eighty lines of the Sixth Book of the *Excursion*.

Fifth and last: thoughts and images too great for the subject. This is an approximation to what might be called *mental* bombast, as distinguished from verbal; for as in the latter there is a disproportion of the expressions to the thoughts, so in this there is a disproportion of thought to the circumstance and occasion. This, by the bye, is a fault of which none but a man of genius is capable. It is the awkwardness and strength of Hercules with the distaff of Omphale.

It is a well-known fact that bright colours in motion both make and leave the strongest impressions on the eye. Nothing is more likely too than that a vivid image or visual spectrum thus originated may become the link of association in recalling the feelings and images that had accompanied the original impression. But if we describe this in such lines, as

They flash upon that inward eye,
Which is the bliss of solitude!

in what words shall we describe the joy of retrospection when the images and virtuous actions of a whole well-spent life pass before that conscience which is indeed the inward eye: which is indeed 'the bliss of solitude'? Assuredly we seem to sink most abruptly, not to say burlesquely and almost as in a medley, from this couplet to

And then my heart with pleasure fills,
And dances with the *daffodils*.
                              (Vol. i. p. 320)

The second instance is from vol. ii., page 12, where the poet having gone out for a day's tour of pleasure meets early in the morning with a knot of gipsies, who had pitched their blanket-tents and straw beds, together with their children and asses, in some field by the road-side. At the close of the day on his return our tourist found them in the same place. 'Twelve hours,' says he,

Twelve hours, twelve bounteous hours are gone,
while I

Have been a traveller under open sky,
Much witnessing of change and cheer,
Yet as I left I find them here!

Whereat the poet, without seeming to reflect that the poor tawny wanderers might probably have been tramping for weeks together through road and lane, over moor and mountain, and consequently must have been right glad to rest themselves, their children and cattle for one whole day; and overlooking the obvious truth that such repose might be quite as necessary for them as a walk of the same continuance was pleasing or healthful for the more fortunate poet; expresses his indignation in a series of lines, the diction and imagery of which would have been rather above than below the mark, had they been applied to the immense empire of China improgressive for thirty centuries:

The weary Sun betook himself to rest,—
Then issued Vesper from the fulgent west,
Outshining like a visible God,
The glorious path in which he trod!
And now ascending, after one dark hour,
And one night's diminution of her power,
Behold the mighty Moon! this way
She looks as if at them—but they
Regard not her:—oh, better wrong and strife,
Better vain deed or evil than such life!
The silent Heavens have goings-on:
The stars have tasks!—but these have none!

The last instance of this defect (for I know no other than these already cited), is from the 'Ode,' page 351, vol. ii, where, speaking of a child, 'a six years' darling of a pigmy size,' he thus addresses him:

Thou best philosopher, who yet dost keep
Thy heritage! Thou eye among the blind,
That, deaf and silent, read'st the eternal deep—
Haunted for ever by the eternal mind—
Mighty Prophet! Seer blest!
On whom those truths do rest,
Which we are toiling all our lives to find!
Thou, over whom thy immortality
Broods like the day, a master o'er the slave,
A presence which is not to be put by!

Now here, not to stop at the daring spirit of metaphor which connects the epithets 'deaf and silent' with the apostrophized eye: or (if we are to refer it to the preceding word *philosopher*) the faulty and equivocal syntax of the passage; and without examining the propriety of making a 'master *brood* o'er a slave,' or the day brood at all; we will merely ask, what does all this mean? In what sense is a child of that age a philosopher? In what sense does he read 'the eternal deep'? In what sense is he declared to be 'for ever haunted' by the Supreme Being? or so inspired as to deserve the splendid titles of a mighty prophet, a blessed seer? By reflection? by knowledge? by conscious intuition? or by any form or modification of consciousness? These would be tidings indeed; but such as would pre-suppose an immediate revelation to the inspired communicator and require miracles to authenticate his inspiration. Children at this age give us no such information of themselves; and at what time were we dipt in the Lethe, which has produced such utter oblivion of a state so godlike? There are many of us that still possess some remembrances, more or less distinct, respecting themselves at six years old; pity that the worthless straws only should float while treasures, compared with which all the mines of Golconda and Mexico were but straws, should be absorbed by some unknown gulf into some unknown abyss.

But if this be too wild and exorbitant to be suspected as having been the poet's meaning; if these mysterious gifts, faculties and operations are not accompanied with consciousness; who else is conscious of them? or how can it be called the child, if it be no part of the child's conscious being? For aught I know, the thinking spirit within me may be substantially one with the principle of life and of vital operation. For aught I know, it may be employed as a secondary agent in the marvellous organization and organic movements of my body. But surely it would be strange language to say that I construct my heart! or that I propel the finer influences through my nerves! or that I compress my brain, and draw the curtains of sleep round my own eyes! Spinoza and Behmen were on different systems both Pantheists; and among the ancients there were philosophers, teachers of the EN KAI ΠΑΝ, who not only taught that God was All, but that this All constituted God. Yet not even these would confound the part, as a part, with the Whole, as the whole. Nay, in no system is the distinction between the individual and God, between the modification and the one only substance, more sharply drawn than in that of Spinoza. Jacobi indeed relates of Lessing that after a conversation with him at the house of the poet Gleim (the Tyrtaeus and Anacreon of the German Parnassus) in which conversation L. had avowed privately to Jacobi his reluctance to admit any personal existence of the Supreme Being, or the possibility of personality except in a finite Intellect, and while they were sitting at table a shower of rain came on unexpectedly.

Gleim expressed his regret at the circumstance, because they had meant to drink their wine in the garden: upon which Lessing, in one of his half-earnest, half-joking moods, nodded to Jacobi and said, 'It is I, perhaps, that am doing that,' i.e. raining! and J. answered, 'Or perhaps I'; Gleim contented himself with staring at them both, without asking for any explanation.

So with regard to this passage. In what sense can the magnificent attributes above quoted be appropriated to a child, which would not make them equally suitable to a bee, or a dog, or a field of corn; or even to a ship, or to the wind and waves that propel it? The omnipresent Spirit works equally in them as in the child; and the child is equally unconscious of it as they. It cannot surely be that the four lines immediately following are to contain the explanation?

> To whom the grave
> Is but a lonely bed without the sense or sight
> Of day or the warm light,
> A place of thought where we in waiting lie.

Surely, it cannot be that this wonder-rousing apostrophe is but a comment on the little poem of 'We Are Seven'? that the whole meaning of the passage is reducible to the assertion that a child, who by the bye at six years old would have been better instructed in most Christian families, has no other notion of death than that of lying in a dark, cold place? And still, I hope, not as in a place of thought! not the frightful notion of lying awake in his grave! The analogy between death and sleep is too simple, too natural, to render so horrible a belief possible for children; even had they not been in the habit, as all Christian children are, of hearing the latter term used to express the former. But if the child's belief be only that 'he is not dead, but sleepeth,' wherein does it differ from that of his father and mother, or any other adult and instructed person? To form an idea of a thing's becoming nothing, or of nothing becoming a thing, is impossible to all finite beings alike, of whatever age and however educated or uneducated. Thus it is with splendid paradoxes in general. If the words are taken in the common sense, they convey an absurdity; and if, in contempt of dictionaries and custom, they are so interpreted as to avoid the absurdity, the meaning dwindles into some bald truism. Thus you must at once understand the words contrary to their common import, in order to arrive at any sense; and according to their common import, if you are to receive from them any feeling of sublimity or admiration.

Though the instances of this defect in Mr Wordsworth's poems are so few that for themselves it would have been scarcely just to attract the reader's attention toward them, yet I have dwelt on it, and perhaps the more for this very reason. For being so very few, they cannot sensibly detract from the reputation of an author who is even characterized by the number of profound truths in his writings which will stand the severest analysis; and yet few as they are, they are exactly those passages which his blind admirers would be most likely, and best able, to imitate. But Wordsworth, where he is indeed Wordsworth, may be mimicked by copyists, he may be plundered by plagiarists; but he cannot be imitated except by those who are not born to be imitators. For without his depth of feeling and his imaginative power his sense would want its vital warmth and peculiarity; and without his strong sense, his mysticism would become sickly—mere fog and dimness!

—SAMUEL TAYLOR COLERIDGE,
from chapter 22, *Biographia Literaria*, 1817

GEORGE GORDON, LORD BYRON "DEDICATION" (1819)

And Wordsworth, in a rather long 'Excursion'
(I think the quarto holds five hundred pages),
Has given a sample from the vasty version
Of his new system to perplex the sages;
Tis poetry—at least by his assertion,
And may appear so when the dog-star rages—
And he who understands it would be able
To add a story to the Tower of Babel.

—GEORGE GORDON, LORD BYRON,
"Dedication" to *Don Juan*, 1819

WILLIAM HAZLITT "MR. WORDSWORTH" (1825)

In this excerpt from *The Spirit of the Age*, William Hazlitt discusses the way in which Wordsworth's concern with and method of expression are reflective of the times in which he lived. Hazlitt maintains that Wordsworth is illustrative of a certain dullness and lackluster quality that infected his era, possessing a "hebetude" intellect that, at another time, would not have been noticed. Not a passionate poet given to extravagant or fantastic rhetoric, Wordsworth is portrayed by Hazlitt as writing in the vernacular in order to convey homely truths, that he is keenly attuned to the human heart, viewing it from multiple perspectives, while at the same time taming his passionate nature as well. Hazlitt maintains that Wordsworth, a poet of great sympathy who aspires to infuse his verse with a palliative power, set it as his goal to create a new system of poetry in which he could demonstrate truth by exposing the artificial and by juxtaposing "the spirit of humanity, [with] ... the spirit of fashion and of the world!" Instead of passionate rhetoric, Hazlitt sees Wordsworth as conveying his own intense emotional response to nature: "The purple pall, the nodding plume of tragedy are exploded as mere pantomime and trick, to return to the simplicity of truth and nature."

Hazlitt traces the origin of Wordsworth's new kind of poetry to the revolutionary fervor of an age that encouraged experimentation in poetry as well as in politics. In line with the reformation of society, Hazlitt regards Wordsworth's poetry as based on a spirit of equality that is demonstrated in his chosen subject matter, the representation of real individuals and everyday occurrences, a poetry that necessarily eschews ornamentation. He states that Wordsworth had a fundamental disdain for human vanity and pride, similar to that found in Sir Henry Taylor's 1834 critique in the *Quarterly Review*. In addition, Hazlitt sees the *Lyrical Ballads* as a natural emanation of these poetic goals. "The incidents are trifling," he notes, "in proportion to his contempt for imposing appearances; the reflections are profound, according to the gravity and the aspiring pretensions of his mind." Hazlitt goes on to suggest that it is possible that such an adamant focus on nature is due to Wordsworth's own disappointed hopes and thwarted ambition.

***

Mr. Wordsworth's genius is a pure emanation of the Spirit of the Age. Had he lived in any other period of the world, he would never have been heard of. As it is, he has some difficulty to contend with the hebetude of his intellect, and the meanness of his subject. With him 'lowliness is young ambition's ladder': but he finds it a toil to climb in this way the steep of Fame. His homely Muse can hardly raise her wing from the ground, nor spread her hidden glories to the sun. He has 'no figures nor no fantasies, which busy *passion* draws in the brains of men': neither the gorgeous machinery of mythologic lore, nor the splendid colours of poetic diction. His style is vernacular: he delivers household truths. He sees nothing loftier than human hopes; nothing deeper than the human heart. This he probes, this he tampers with, this he poises, with all its incalculable weight of thought and feeling, in his hands; and at the same time calms the throbbing pulses of his own heart, by keeping his eye ever fixed on the face of nature. If he can make the lifeblood flow from the wounded breast, this is the living colouring with which he paints his verse: if he can assuage the pain or close up the wound with the balm of solitary musing, or the healing power of plants and herbs and 'skyey influences,' this is the sole triumph of his art. He takes the simplest elements of nature and of the human mind, the mere abstract conditions inseparable from our being, and tries to compound a new system of poetry from them; and has perhaps succeeded as well as any one could. *'Nihil humani a me alienum puto'*—is the motto of his works. He thinks nothing low or indifferent of which this can be affirmed: every thing that professes to be more than this, that is not an absolute essence of truth and feeling, he holds to be vitiated, false, and spurious. In a word, his poetry is founded on setting up an opposition (and pushing it to the utmost length) between the natural and the artificial; between the spirit of humanity, and the spirit of fashion and of the world!

It is one of the innovations of the time. It partakes of, and is carried along with, the revolutionary movement of our age: the political changes of the day were the model on which he formed and conducted his poetical experiments. His Muse (it cannot be denied, and without this we cannot explain its character at all) is a levelling one. It proceeds on a principle of equality, and strives to reduce all things to the same standard. It is distinguished by a proud humility. It relies upon its own resources, and disdains external show and relief. It takes the commonest events and objects, as a test to prove that nature is always interesting from its inherent truth and beauty, without any of the ornaments of dress or pomp of circumstances to set it off. Hence the unaccountable mixture of seeming simplicity and real abstruseness in the *Lyrical Ballads*. Fools have laughed at, wise men scarcely understand them. He takes a subject or a story merely as pegs or loops to hang thought and feeling on; the incidents are trifling, in proportion to his contempt for imposing appearances; the reflections are profound, according to the gravity and the aspiring pretensions of his mind.

His popular, inartificial style gets rid (at a blow) of all the trappings of verse, of all the high places of poetry: 'the cloud-capt towers, the solemn temples, the gorgeous palaces,' are swept to the ground, and 'like the baseless fabric of a vision, leave not a wreck behind.' All the traditions of learning, all the superstitions of age, are obliterated and effaced. We begin *de novo*, on a *tabula rasa* of poetry. The purple pall, the nodding plume of tragedy are exploded as mere pantomime and trick, to return to the simplicity of truth and nature. Kings, queens, priests, nobles, the altar and the throne, the distinctions of rank, birth, wealth, power, the judge's robe, the marshal's truncheon, the ceremony that to great ones 'longs,' are not to be found here. The author tramples on the pride of art with greater pride. The Ode and Epode, the Strophe and the Antistrophe, he laughs to scorn. The harp of Homer, the trump of Pindar and of Alcaeus are still. The decencies of costume, the decorations of vanity are stripped off without mercy as barbarous, idle, and Gothic. The jewels in the crisped hair, the diadem on the polished brow are thought meretricious, theatrical, vulgar; and nothing contents his fastidious taste beyond a simple garland of flowers. Neither does he avail himself of the advantages which nature or accident holds out to him. He chooses to have his subject a foil to his invention, to owe nothing but to himself. He gathers manna in the wilderness, he strikes the barren rock for the gushing moisture. He elevates the mean by the strength of his own aspirations; he clothes the naked with beauty and grandeur from the stores of his own recollections. No cypress grove loads his verse with funeral pomp: but his imagination lends 'a sense of joy

> To the bare trees and mountains bare,
> And grass in the green field.'

No storm, no shipwreck startles us by its horrors: but the rainbow lifts its head in the cloud, and the breeze sighs through the withered fern. No sad vicissitude of fate, no overwhelming catastrophe in nature deforms his page: but the dew-drop glitters on the bending flower, the tear collects in the glistening eye.

> Beneath the hills, along the flowery vales,
> The generations are prepared; the pangs,
> The internal pangs are ready; the dread strife
> Of poor humanity's afflicted will,
> Struggling in vain with ruthless destiny.

As the lark ascends from its low bed on fluttering wing, and salutes the morning skies; so Mr. Wordsworth's unpretending Muse, in russet guise, scales the summits of reflection, while it makes the round earth its footstool, and its home! Possibly a good deal of this may be regarded as the effect of disappointed views and an inverted ambition. Prevented by native pride and indolence from climbing the ascent of learning or greatness, taught by political opinions to say to the vain pomp and glory of the world, 'I hate ye,' seeing the path of classical and artificial poetry blocked up by the cumbrous ornaments of style and turgid *commonplaces,* so that nothing more could be achieved in that direction but by the most ridiculous bombast or the tamest servility; he has turned back partly from the bias of his mind, partly perhaps from a judicious policy—has struck into the sequestered vale of humble life, sought out the Muse among sheep-cotes and hamlets and the peasant's mountain-haunts, has discarded all the tinsel pageantry of verse, and endeavoured (not in vain) to aggrandise the trivial and add the charm of novelty to the familiar. No one has shown the same imagination in raising trifles into importance: no one has displayed the same pathos in treating of the simplest feelings of the heart. Reserved, yet haughty, having no unruly or violent passions, (or those passions having been early suppressed,) Mr. Wordsworth has passed his life in solitary musing, or in daily converse with the face of nature. He exemplifies in an eminent degree the power of *association;* for his poetry has no other source or character. He has dwelt among pastoral scenes, till each object has become connected with a thousand feelings, a link in the chain of thought, a fibre of his own heart. Every one is by habit and familiarity strongly attached to the place of his birth, or to objects that recall the most pleasing and eventful circumstances of his life. But to the author of the *Lyrical Ballads,* nature is a kind of home; and he may be said to take a personal interest in the universe. There is no image so insignificant that it has not in some mood or other found the way into his heart: no sound that does not awaken the memory of other years.—

To him the meanest flower that blows can give
Thoughts that do often lie too deep for tears.

The daisy looks up to him with sparkling eye as an old acquaintance: the cuckoo haunts him with sounds of early youth not to be expressed: a linnet's nest startles him with boyish delight: an old withered thorn is weighed down with a heap of recollections: a grey cloak, seen on some wild moor, torn by the wind, or drenched in the rain, afterwards becomes an object of imagination to him: even the lichens on the rock have a life and being in his thoughts. He has described all these objects in a way and with an intensity of feeling that no one else had done before him, and has given a new view or aspect of nature. He is in this sense the most original poet now living, and the one whose writings could the least be spared: for they have no substitute elsewhere. The vulgar do not read them, the learned, who see all things through books, do not understand them, the great despise, the fashionable may ridicule them: but the author has created himself an interest in the heart of the retired and lonely student of nature, which can never die. Persons of this class will still continue to feel what he has felt: he has expressed what they might in vain wish to express, except with glistening eye and faultering tongue! There is a lofty philosophic tone, a thoughtful humanity, infused into his pastoral vein. Remote from the passions and events of the great world, he has communicated interest and dignity to the primal movements of the heart of man, and ingrafted his own conscious reflections on the casual thoughts of hinds and shepherds. Nursed amidst the grandeur of mountain scenery, he has stooped to have a nearer view of the daisy under his feet, or plucked a branch of white-thorn from the spray: but in describing it, his mind seems imbued with the majesty and solemnity of the objects around him—the tall rock lifts its head in the erectness of his spirit; the cataract roars in the sound of his verse; and in its dim and mysterious meaning, the mists seem to gather in the hollows of Helvellyn, and the forked Skiddaw hovers in the distance. There is little mention of mountainous scenery in Mr. Wordsworth's poetry; but by internal evidence one might be almost sure that it was written in a mountainous country, from its bareness, its simplicity, its loftiness and its depth!

His later philosophic productions have a somewhat different character. They are a departure from, a dereliction of his first principles. They are classical and courtly. They are polished in style, without being gaudy; dignified in subject, without affectation. They seem to have been composed not in a cottage at Grasmere, but among the half-inspired groves and stately recollections of Cole-Orton. We might allude in particular, for examples of what we mean, to the lines on a Picture by Claude Lorraine, and to the exquisite poem, entitled 'Laodamia.' The last of these breathes the pure spirit of the finest fragments of antiquity—the sweetness, the gravity, the strength, the beauty and the languor of death—

Calm contemplation and majestic pains.

Its glossy brilliancy arises from the perfection of the finishing, like that of careful sculpture, not from gaudy colouring—the texture of the thoughts has the smoothness and solidity of marble. It is a poem that might be read aloud in Elysium, and the spirits of departed heroes and sages would gather round to listen to it! Mr. Wordsworth's philosophic poetry, with a less glowing aspect and less tumult in the veins than Lord Byron's on similar occasions, bends a calmer and keener eye on mortality; the impression, if less vivid, is more pleasing and permanent; and we confess it (perhaps it is a want of taste and proper feeling) that there are lines and poems of our author's, that we think of ten times for once that we recur to any of Lord Byron's. Or if there are any of the latter's writings, that we can dwell upon in the same way, that is, as lasting and heart-felt sentiments, it is when laying aside his usual pomp and pretension, he descends with Mr. Wordsworth to the common ground of a disinterested humanity. It may be considered as characteristic of our poet's writings, that they either make no impression on the mind at all, seem mere *nonsense-verses,* or that they leave a mark behind them that never wears out. They either

Fall blunted from the indurated breast—

without any perceptible result, or they absorb it like a passion. To one class of readers he appears sublime, to another (and we fear the largest) ridiculous. He has probably realised Milton's wish,—'and fit audience found, though few'; but we suspect he is not reconciled to the alternative. There are delightful passages in the *Excursion,* both of natural description and of inspired reflection (passages of the latter kind that in the sound of the thoughts and of the swelling language resemble heavenly symphonies, mournful *requiems* over the grave of human hopes); but we must add, in justice and in sincerity, that we think it impossible that this work should ever become popular, even in the same degree as the *Lyrical Ballads.* It affects a system without having any intelligible clue to one; and instead of unfolding a principle in various and striking lights, repeats the same conclusions till they become flat and insipid. Mr. Wordsworth's mind is obtuse, except as it is the organ and the receptacle of accumulated feelings: it is not analytic, but synthetic; it is reflecting, rather than theoretical. The *Excursion,* we believe, fell still-born from the press. There was something abortive, and clumsy, and ill-judged in the attempt. It was long and laboured. The personages, for the most part, were low, the fare rustic: the plan raised expectations which were not fulfilled, and the effect was like being ushered into a stately hall and invited to sit down to a splendid banquet in the company of clowns, and with nothing but successive courses of apple-dumplings served up. It was not even *toujours perdrix!* Mr. Wordsworth, in his person, is above the middle size, with marked features, and an air somewhat stately and Quixotic. He reminds one of some of Holbein's heads, grave, saturnine, with a slight indication of sly humour, kept under by the manners of the age or by the pretensions of the person. He has a peculiar sweetness in his smile, and great depth and manliness and a rugged harmony, in the tones of his voice. His manner of reading his own poetry is particularly imposing; and in his favourite passages his eye beams with preternatural lustre, and the meaning labours slowly up from his swelling breast. No one who has seen him at these moments could go away with an impression that he was a 'man of no mark or likelihood.' Perhaps the comment of his face and voice is necessary to convey a full idea of his poetry. His language may not be intelligible, but his manner is not to be mistaken. It is clear that he is either mad or inspired. In company, even in a *tete-a-tete,* Mr. Wordsworth is often silent, indolent, and reserved. If he is become verbose and oracular of late years, he was not so in his better days. He threw out a bold or an indifferent remark without either effort or pretension, and relapsed into musing again. He shone most (because he seemed most roused and animated) in reciting his own poetry, or in talking about it. He sometimes gave striking views of his feelings and trains of association in composing certain passages; or if one did not always understand his distinctions, still there was no want of interest—there was a latent meaning worth inquiring into, like a vein of ore that one cannot exactly hit upon at the moment, but of which there are sure indications. His standard of poetry is high and severe, almost to exclusiveness. He admits of nothing below, scarcely of any thing above himself. It is fine to hear him talk of the way in which certain subjects should have been treated by eminent poets, according to his notions of the art. Thus he finds fault with Dryden's description of Bacchus in the 'Alexander's Feast,' as if he were a mere good-looking youth, or boon companion—

Flushed with a purple grace,
He shows his honest face—

instead of representing the God returning from the conquest of India, crowned with vine-leaves, and drawn by panthers, and followed by troops of satyrs, of wild men and animals that he had tamed. You would think, in hearing him speak on this subject, that you saw Titian's picture of the meeting of *Bacchus and Ariadne*—so classic were his conceptions, so glowing his style. Milton is his great idol, and he sometimes dares to compare himself with him. His Sonnets, indeed, have something of the same high-raised tone and prophetic spirit. Chaucer is another prime favourite of his, and he has been at the pains to modernize some of the *Canterbury Tales*. Those persons who look upon Mr. Wordsworth as a merely puerile writer, must be rather at a loss to account for his strong predilection for such geniuses as Dante and Michael Angelo. We do not think our author has any very cordial sympathy with Shakespear. How should he? Shakespear was the least of an egotist of any body in the world. He does not much relish the variety and scope of dramatic composition. 'He hates those interlocutions between Lucius and Caius.' Yet Mr. Wordsworth himself wrote a tragedy when he was young; and we have heard the following energetic lines quoted from it, as put into the mouth of a person smit with remorse for some rash crime:

Action is momentary, The motion of a muscle this way or that;
Suffering is long, obscure, and infinite!

Perhaps for want of light and shade, and the unshackled spirit of the drama, this performance was never brought forward. Our critic has a great dislike to Gray, and a fondness for Thomson and Collins. It is mortifying to hear him speak of Pope and Dryden, whom, because they have been supposed to have all the possible excellences of poetry, he will allow to have none. Nothing, however, can be fairer, or more amusing, than the way in which he sometimes exposes the unmeaning verbiage of modern poetry. Thus, in the beginning of Dr. Johnson's *Vanity of Human Wishes*—

Let observation with extensive view
Survey mankind from China to Peru—

he says there is a total want of imagination accompanying the words, the same idea is repeated three times under the disguise of a different phraseology: it comes to this—'let *observation,* with extensive *observation, observe* mankind'; or take away the first line, and the second, Survey mankind from China to Peru, literally conveys the whole. Mr. Wordsworth is, we must say, a perfect Drawcansir as to prose writers. He complains of the dry reasoners and matter-of-fact people for their want of *passion;* and he is jealous of the rhetorical declaimers and rhapsodists as trenching on the province of poetry. He condemns all French writers (as well of poetry as prose) in the lump. His list in this way is indeed small. He approves of Walton's *Angler,* Paley, and some other writers of an inoffensive modesty of pretension. He also likes books of voyages and travels, and *Robinson Crusoe.* In art, he greatly esteems Bewick's woodcuts, and Waterloo's sylvan etchings. But he sometimes takes a higher tone, and gives his mind fair play. We have known him enlarge with a noble intelligence and enthusiasm on Nicolas Poussin's fine landscape-compositions, pointing out the unity of design that pervades them, the superintending mind, the imaginative principle that brings all to bear on the same end; and declaring he would not give a rush for any landscape that did not express the time of day, the climate, the period of the world it was meant to illustrate, or had not this character of *wholeness* in it. His eye also does justice to Rembrandt's fine and masterly effects. In the way in which that artist works something out of nothing, and transforms the stump of a tree, a common figure into an *ideal* object, by the gorgeous light and shade thrown upon it, he perceives an analogy to his own mode of investing the minute details of nature with an atmosphere of sentiment; and in pronouncing Rembrandt to be a man of genius, feels that he strengthens his own claim to the title. It has been said of Mr. Wordsworth, that 'he hates conchology, that he hates the Venus of Medicis.' But these, we hope, are mere epigrams and *jeux-d'esprit,* as far from truth as they are free from malice; a sort of running satire or critical clenches—

Where one for sense and one for rhyme
Is quite sufficient at one time.

We think, however, that if Mr. Wordsworth had been a more liberal and candid critic, he would have been a more sterling writer. If a greater number of sources of pleasure had been open to him, he would have communicated pleasure to the world more frequently. Had he been less fastidious in pronouncing sentence on the works of others, his own would have been received more favourably, and treated more leniently. The current of his feelings is deep, but narrow; the range of his understanding is lofty and aspiring rather than discursive. The force, the originality, the absolute truth and identity with which he feels some things, makes him indifferent to so many others. The simplicity and enthusiasm of his feelings, with respect to nature, renders him bigotted and intolerant in his judgments of men and things. But it happens to him, as to others, that his strength lies in his weakness; and perhaps we have no right to complain. We might get rid of the cynic and the egotist, and find in his stead a commonplace man. We should 'take the good the Gods provide us': a fine and original vein of poetry is not one of their most contemptible gifts, and the rest is scarcely worth thinking of, except as it may be a mortification to those who expect perfection from human nature; or who have been idle enough at some period of their lives, to deify men of genius as possessing claims above it. But this is a chord that jars, and we shall not dwell upon it.

Lord Byron we have called, according to the old proverb, 'the spoiled child of fortune': Mr. Wordsworth might plead, in mitigation of some peculiarities, that he is 'the spoiled child of disappointment.' We are convinced, if he had been early a popular poet, he would have borne his honours meekly, and would have been a person of great *bonhommie* and frankness of disposition. But the sense of injustice and of undeserved ridicule sours the temper and narrows the views. To have produced works of genius, and to find them neglected or treated with scorn, is one of the heaviest trials of human patience. We exaggerate our own merits when they are denied by others, and are apt to grudge and cavil at every particle of praise bestowed on those to whom we feel a conscious superiority. In mere self-defence we turn against the world, when it turns against us; brood over the undeserved slights we receive; and thus the genial current of the soul is stopped, or vents itself in effusions of petulance and self-conceit. Mr. Wordsworth has thought too much of contemporary critics and criticism; and less than he ought of the award of posterity, and of the opinion, we do not say of private friends, but of those who were made so by their admiration of his genius. He did not court popularity by a conformity to established models, and he ought not to have been surprised that his originality was not understood as a matter of course. He has *gnawed too much on the bridle*; and has often thrown out crusts to the critics, in mere defiance or as a point of honour when he was challenged, which otherwise his own good sense would have withheld. We suspect that Mr. Wordsworth's feelings are a little morbid in this respect, or that he resents censure more than he is gratified by praise. Otherwise, the tide has turned much in his favour of late years—he has a large body of determined partisans—and is at present sufficiently in request with the public to save or relieve him from the last necessity to which a man of genius can be reduced—that of becoming the God of his own idolatry!

—WILLIAM HAZLITT, from "Mr. Wordsworth,"
The Spirit of the Age, 1825

JOHN WILSON "AN HOUR'S TALK ABOUT POETRY" (1831)

John Wilson does not like *The Excursion*, describing it as a collection of beautiful and sublime poems rather than one large unified work. He finds that it lacks a beginning, a coherent middle, and most significantly does not have an identifiable end. "[I]n its present shape it comprehends but a Three Days' Walk," he argues, "we have but to think of an Excursion of three weeks, three months, or three years, to feel the difference between a Great and a Long Poem."

He is the High Priest of Nature—or, to use his own words, or nearly so, he is the High Priest "in the metropolitan temple built by Nature in the heart of mighty poets." But has he—even he—ever written a Great Poem? If he has—it is not the *Excursion*. Nay—the *Excursion* is not a Poem. It is a series of Poems, all swimming in the light of poetry, some of them sweet and simple, some elegant and graceful, some beautiful and most lovely, some of "strength and state," some majestic, some magnificent, some sublime. But though it has an opening, it has no beginning; you can discover the middle only by the numerals on the page; and the most serious apprehensions have been very generally entertained that it has no end. While Pedlar, Poet, and Solitary breathe the vital air, may the *Excursion,* stop where it will, be renewed; and as in its present shape it comprehends but a Three Days' Walk, we have but to think of an Excursion of three weeks, three months, or three years, to feel the difference between a Great and a Long Poem. Then the life of man is not always limited to the term of threescore and ten years! What a Journal might it prove at last! Poetry in profusion till the land overflowed; but whether in one volume, as now, or in fifty, in future, not a Great Poem—nay, not a Poem at all—nor ever to be so esteemed, till the principles on which Great Poets build the lofty rhyme are exploded, and the very names of Art and Science smothered and lost in the bosom of Nature, from which they arose.

—JOHN WILSON, "An Hour's Talk about Poetry,"
Blackwood's Edinburgh Magazine,
September 1831, pp. 477–478

LESLIE STEPHEN "WORDSWORTH'S ETHICS" (1876)

Sir Leslie Stephen praises Wordsworth for having found the poetic formula to unite reason and experience into a moral philosophy. His essay shows the influence of Darwinian theories of human evolution as based on primitive instincts. Stephen's essay is preoccupied with explaining the ways in which Wordsworth is a moral philosopher and, in so doing, interprets his major precepts, corrects certain misapprehensions, and identifies specific ambiguities. The *Ode: Intimations of Immortality* is held to be the pinnacle of this ideal. Stephen defends the notion of childhood as proof of a preexistent soul as a concept that Wordsworth himself said he did not take seriously, instead believing that the glory and freshness of childhood is nonetheless important on the instinctive level despite what scientific explanations might theorize as to its origins. Stephen dismisses modern psychologists who attribute the instincts of a child to the "accumulated and inherited experience of past generations," stating that Wordsworth's own predilection for wild scenery bears evidence of the influence of a more "primitive" state of the world. Wordsworth would have rejected such outlandish reasoning that the child is an amalgamation of inherited tendencies from past generations, in favor of his own understanding that the child remembers its former communion with the divine. Wordsworth's *Ode: Intimations of Immortality* thus gives poetic expression to a fundamental truth of childhood—its inherent spirituality.

Though other poets have pondered the meaning of childhood—whether as short-lived portion of a rapidly fleeting youth to be exploited for all it holds or a melancholy reflection that the ravages of time too quickly encroach on the promise of youth—they have failed to see what Wordsworth so eloquently expressed, namely that youth instructs and thereby creates the adult the child will eventually become. Thus, while Shelley and Byron, in their individual capacities, could not find a solution to the predicament of loss, Wordsworth teaches us consolation and a new way to accept the inevitability of mortality. This, according to Stephen, is Wordsworth's supreme aspiration, to lead us from childish instincts to reasoned convictions. His most distinct virtue is that he does not dogmatically insist on any formula for "distinguishing between that which nature teaches us and the interpretations which we impose upon nature." Nevertheless, Stephen locates an inherent uncertainty in Wordsworth's belief that contemplation of nature will transport the individual to a blessed state in which the fullness of life will be revealed, as Wordsworth does not account for human evil, whether through scientific explanation of a biological competition to survive or spiritual interpretation of the corruption of the soul. Stephen sees the Wordsworthian belief that the love of nature will lead to a greater moral understanding as too vague and simplistic, and, as proof of this problem, he discusses *The Excursion* as presenting three detectably different Wordsworths—the wanderer and the pastor, who are essentially two reflections of the same poet, and the solitary, who derives antithetical, misanthropic lessons from his experience of nature. Furthermore, Stephen points out that in order to accept Wordsworth's view of the harmony found in nature, one must be in the proper frame of mind, "rightly prepared" to appreciate divine unity in the face of "apparent disorder." That mind requires training, and we must be shown how to see clearly.

According to Stephen, Wordsworth is attempting to explain how we develop our moral being. During a boy's childhood, nature speaks in primitive joy with the accompanying sounds of animals and mountain streams, the beauty of the woods and the stars. The young girl, on the other hand, is unconsciously taken with the grace of clouds and the bending willow tree. Our earliest passions are associated with the sublime and the beautiful, and Wordsworth's love of the natural realm is for a place for harmonious human interaction, not the savage wildness found in Byron. In regard to Wordsworth's love of the contemplative life, Stephen indicates that the poet is not advocating a life of inaction but rather the need to experience intervals of time when the individual, while still attendant to the needs of others, turns from the world of people and learning in order to foster a tranquil and focused communion with nature, a practice advocated by all teachers of morality. Moreover, Stephen points out that Wordsworth's desire to "cultivate the primitive emotions" so that one sees and understands every incident and object as a symbol of the spiritual sets him in opposition to science, which compartmentalizes nature and focuses on the particular as a basis of proof. In essence, Stephen is outlining the difference between Wordsworth's organic conception of natural and human harmony as opposed to science's mechanical approach to humanity and nature, in which minute and fragmentary aspects can be incorporated into some generalized system.

With respect to *The White Doe of Rylstone*, Stephen says that it demonstrates that death can have a unifying influence for the survivors, while such poems as "Michael," "The Leech-Gatherer" and "Laodamia" show the futility of grief. Stephen assuredly believes that sorrow has its place as a teacher and that Wordsworth tells his readers that they must first acquire a nobility of character and then turn outward toward a sympathy for others. Stephen sees that this thinking reaches its height in "The Character of the Happy Warrior," a poem that shows how the impulses of youth are transformed into adult concerns. Ultimately, Stephen maintains that the core of Wordsworth's ethical philosophy is the conversion of instinct into a reason that understands the divine order of the universe and the necessity for people to live in accordance with that organization. Ultimately, despite objections that others will apply a different scheme for understanding human emotion, Wordsworth has succeeded in healing humanity and teaching men how to live more virtuously.

The great aim of moral philosophy is to unite the disjoined elements, to end the divorce between reason and experience, and to escape from the alternative of dealing with empty but symmetrical formulas or concrete and chaotic facts. No hint can be given here as to the direction in which a final solution must be sought. Whatever the true method, Wordsworth's mode of conceiving the problem shows how powerfully he grasped the questions at issue. If his doctrines are not symmetrically expounded, they all have a direct bearing upon the real difficulties involved. They are stated so forcibly in his noblest poems that we might almost express a complete theory in his own language. But, without seeking to make a collection of aphorisms from his poetry, we may indicate the cardinal points of his teaching.

The most characteristic of all his doctrines is that which is embodied in the great ode upon the "Intimations of Immortality." The doctrine itself—the theory that the instincts of childhood testify to the pre-existence of the soul—sounds fanciful enough; and Wordsworth took rather unnecessary pains to say that he did not hold it as a serious dogma. We certainly need not ask whether it is reasonable or orthodox to believe that "our birth is but a sleep and a forgetting." The fact symbolised by the poetic fancy—the glory and freshness of our childish instincts—is equally noteworthy, whatever its cause. Some modern reasoners would explain its significance by reference to a very different kind of pre-existence. The instincts, they would say, are valuable, because they register the accumulated and inherited experience of past generations. Wordsworth's delight in wild scenery is regarded by them as due to the "combination of states that were organised in the race during barbarous times, when its pleasurable activities were amongst the mountains, woods, and waters." In childhood we are most completely under the dominion of these inherited impulses. The correlation between the organism and its medium is then most perfect, and hence the peculiar theme of childish communion with nature.

Wordsworth would have repudiated the doctrine with disgust. He would have been "on the side of the angels." No memories of the savage and the monkey, but the reminiscences of the once-glorious soul could explain his emotions. Yet there is this much in common between him and the men of science whom he denounced with too little discrimination. The fact of the value of these primitive instincts is admitted, and admitted for the same purpose. Man, it is agreed, is furnished with sentiments which cannot be explained as the result of his individual experience. They may be intelligible, according to the evolutionist, when regarded as embodying the past experience of the race; or, according to Wordsworth, as implying a certain mysterious faculty imprinted upon the soul. The scientific doctrine, whether sound or not, has modified the whole mode of approaching ethical problems; and Wordsworth, though with a very different purpose, gives a new emphasis to the facts, upon a recognition of which, according to some theorists, must be based the reconciliation of the great rival schools—the intuitionists and the utilitarians. The parallel may at first sight seem fanciful; and it would be too daring to claim for Wordsworth the discovery of the most remarkable phenomenon which modern psychology must take into account. There is, however, a real connection between the two doctrines, though in one sense they are almost antithetical. Meanwhile we observe that the same sensibility which gives poetical power is necessary to the scientific observer. The magic of the Ode, and of many other passages in Wordsworth's poetry, is due to his recognition of this mysterious efficacy of our childish instincts. He gives emphasis to one of the most striking facts of our spiritual experience, which had passed with little notice from professed psychologists. He feels what they afterwards tried to explain.

The full meaning of the doctrine comes out as we study Wordsworth more thoroughly. Other poets—almost all poets—have dwelt fondly upon recollections of childhood. But not feeling so strongly, and therefore not expressing so forcibly, the peculiar character of the emotion, they have not derived the same lessons from their observation. The Epicurean poets are content with Herrick's simple moral—

Gather ye rosebuds while ye may

—and with this simple explanation—

That age is best which is the first,
When youth and blood are warmer.

Others more thoughtful look back upon the early days with the passionate regret of Byron's verses:

There's not a joy the world can give like that it takes
        away,
When the glow of early thought declines in feeling's
        dull decay;

'Tis not on youth's smooth cheek the blush alone
    which fades so fast,
But the tender bloom of heart is gone, ere youth itself
    be past.

Such painful longings for the "tender grace of a day that is dead" are spontaneous and natural. Every healthy mind feels the pang in proportion to the strength of its affections. But it is also true that the regret resembles too often the maudlin meditation of a fast young man over his morning's soda-water. It implies, that is, a non-recognition of the higher uses to which the fading memories may still be put. A different tone breathes in Shelley's pathetic but rather hectic moralisings, and his lamentations over the departure of the "spirit of delight." Nowhere has it found more exquisite expression than in the marvellous "Ode to the West Wind." These magical verses—his best, as it seems to me—describe the reflection of the poet's own mind in the strange stir and commotion of a dying winter's day. They represent, we may say, the fitful melancholy which oppresses a noble spirit when it has recognised the difficulty of forcing facts into conformity with the ideal. He still clings to the hope that his "dead thoughts" may be driven over the universe,

Like withered leaves to quicken a new birth.

But he bows before the inexorable fate which has cramped his energies:

A heavy weight of years has chained and bowed
One too like thee; tameless and swift and proud.

Neither Byron nor Shelley can see any satisfactory solution, and therefore neither can reach a perfect harmony of feeling. The world seems to them to be out of joint, because they have not known how to accept the inevitable, nor to conform to the discipline of facts. And, therefore, however intense the emotion, and however exquisite its expression, we are left in a state of intellectual and emotional discontent. Such utterances may suit us in youth, when we can afford to play with sorrow. As we grow older we feel a certain emptiness in them. A true man ought not to sit down and weep with an exhausted debauchee. He cannot afford to confess himself beaten with the idealist who has discovered that Rome was not built in a day, nor revolutions made with rose-water. He has to work as long as he has strength; to work in spite of, even by strength of, sorrow, disappointment, wounded vanity, and blunted sensibilities; and therefore he must search for some profounder solution for the dark riddle of life.

This solution it is Wordsworth's chief aim to supply. In the familiar verses which stand as a motto to his poems—

The child is father to the man,
And I could wish my days to be
Bound each to each by natural piety—

the great problem of life, that is, as he conceives it, is to secure a continuity between the period at which we are guided by half-conscious instincts, and that in which a man is able to supply the place of these primitive impulses by reasoned convictions. This is the thought which comes over and over again in his deepest poems, and round which all his teaching centred. It supplies the great moral, for example, of "The Leech-Gatherer":

My whole life I have lived in pleasant thought,
　　As if life's business were a summer mood:
As if all needful things would come unsought
　　To genial faith still rich in genial good.

When his faith is tried by harsh experience, the leech-gatherer comes,

Like a man from some far region sent
To give me human strength by apt admonishment;

for he shows how the "genial faith" may be converted into permanent strength by resolution and independence. The verses most commonly quoted, such as—

We poets in our youth begin in gladness,
But thereof come in the end despondency and sadness,

give the ordinary view of the sickly school. Wordsworth's aim is to supply an answer worthy not only of a poet, but a man. The same sentiment again is expressed in the grand "Ode to Duty," where the

Stern daughter of the voice of God

is invoked to supply that 'genial sense of youth" which has hitherto been a sufficient guidance; or in the majestic morality of "The Happy Warrior"; or in the noble verses of "Tintern Abbey"; or, finally, in the great ode which gives most completely the whole theory of that process by which our early intuitions are to be transformed into settled principles of feeling and action.

Wordsworth's philosophical theory, in short, depends upon the asserted identity between our childish instincts and our enlightened reason. The doctrine of a state of pre-existence as it appears in other writers—as, for example, in the Cambridge Platonists—was connected with an obsolete metaphysical system, and the doctrine—exploded in its old form—of innate ideas. Wordsworth does not attribute any such preternatural character to the "blank misgivings" and "shadowy recollections" of which he speaks. They are invaluable data of our spiritual experience; but they do not entitle us to lay down dogmatic propositions independently of experience. They are spontaneous products of a nature in harmony with the universe in which it is placed, and inestimable as a clear indication that such a harmony exists. To interpret and regulate them belongs to the reasoning faculty and the higher imagination of later years. If he does not quite distinguish between the province of reason and emotion—the most difficult of philosophical problems—he keeps clear of the cruder mysticism, because he does not seek to elicit any definite formulas from those admittedly vague forebodings which lie on the border-land between the two sides of our nature. With his invariable sanity of mind, he more than once notices the difficulty of distinguishing between that which nature teaches us and the interpretations which we impose upon nature. He carefully refrains from pressing the inference too far.

The teaching, indeed, assumes that view of the universe which is implied in his pantheistic language. The Divinity really reveals Himself in the lonely mountains and the starry heavens. By contemplating them we are able to rise into that "blessed mood" in which for a time the burden of the mystery is rolled off our souls, and we can "see into the life of things." And here we must admit that Wordsworth is not entirely free from the weakness which generally besets thinkers of this tendency. Like Shaftesbury in the previous century, who speaks of the universal harmony as emphatically though not as poetically as Wordsworth, he is tempted to adopt a too facile optimism. He seems at times to have overlooked that dark side of nature which is recognised in theological doctrines of corruption, or in the scientific theories about the fierce struggle for existence. Can we in fact say that these early instincts prove more than the happy constitution of the individual who feels them? Is there not a teaching of nature very apt to suggest horror and despair rather than a complacent brooding over soothing thoughts? Do not the mountains which Wordsworth loved so well, speak of decay and catastrophe in every line of their slopes? Do they not suggest the helplessness and narrow limitations of man, as forcibly as his possible exaltation? The awe which they strike into our souls has its terrible as well as its amiable side; and in moods of depression the darker aspect becomes more conspicious than the brighter. Nay, if we admit that we have instincts which are the very substance of all that afterwards becomes ennobling, have we not also instincts which suggest a close alliance with the brutes? If the child amidst his newborn blisses suggests a heavenly origin, does he not also show sensual and cruel instincts which imply at least an admixture of baser elements? If man is responsive to all natural influences, how is he to distinguish between the good and the bad, and, in short, to frame a conscience out of the vague instincts which contain the germs of all the possible developments of the future?

To say that Wordsworth has not given a complete answer to such difficulties, is to say that he has not explained the origin of evil. It may be admitted, however, that he does to a certain extent show a narrowness of conception. The voice of nature, as he says, resembles an echo; but we "unthinking creatures" listen to "voices of two different natures." We do not always distinguish between the echo of our lower passions and the "echoes from beyond the grave." Wordsworth sometimes fails to recognise the ambiguity of the oracle to which he appeals. The "blessed mood" in which we get rid of the burden of the world, is too easily confused with the mood in which we simply refuse to attend to it. He finds lonely meditation so inspiring that he is too indifferent to the troubles of less self-sufficing or clear-sighted human beings. The ambiguity makes itself felt in the sphere of morality. The ethical doctrine that virtue consists in conformity to nature becomes ambiguous with him, as with all its advocates, when we ask for a precise definition of nature. How are we to know which natural forces make for us and which fight against us?

The doctrine of the love of nature, generally regarded as Wordsworth's great lesson to mankind, means, as interpreted by himself and others, a love of the wilder and grander objects of natural scenery; a passion for the "sounding cataract," the rock, the mountain, and the forest; a preference, therefore, of the country to the town, and of the simpler to the more complex forms of social life. But what is the true value of this sentiment? The unfortunate Solitary in the Excursion is beset by three Wordsworths; for the Wanderer and the Pastor are little more (as Wordsworth indeed intimates) than reflections of himself, seen in different mirrors. The Solitary represents the anti-social lessons to be derived from communion with nature. He has become a misanthrope, and has learnt from *Candide* the lesson that we clearly do not live in the best of all possible worlds. Instead of learning the true lesson from nature by penetrating its deeper meanings, he manages to feed

Pity and scorn and melancholy pride

by accidental and fanciful analogies, and sees in rock pyramids or obelisks a rude mockery of human toils. To confute this sentiment, to upset *Candide*,

This dull product of a scoffer's pen,

is the purpose of the lofty poetry and versified prose of the long dialogues which ensue. That Wordsworth should call Voltaire dull is a curious example of the proverbial blindness of controversalists; but the moral may be equally good. It is given most pithily in the lines—

We live by admiration, hope, and love;
And even as these are well and wisely fused,
The dignity of being we ascend.

"But what is Error?" continues the preacher; and the Solitary replies by saying, "somewhat haughtily," that love, admiration, and hope are "mad fancy's favourite vassals." The distinction between fancy and imagination is, in brief, that fancy deals with the superficial resemblances, and imagination with the deeper truths which underlie them. The purpose, then, of *The Excursion*, and of Wordsworth's poetry in general, is to show how the higher faculty reveals a harmony which we overlook when, with the Solitary, we

Skim along the surfaces of things.

The rightly prepared mind can recognise the divine harmony which underlies all apparent disorder. The universe is to its perceptions like the shell whose murmur in a child's ear seems to express a mysterious union with the sea. But the mind must be rightly prepared. Everything depends upon the point of view. One man, as he says in an elaborate figure, looking upon a series of ridges in spring from their northern side, sees a waste of snow, and from the south a continuous expanse of green. That view, we must take it, is the right one which is illuminated by the "ray divine." But we must train our eyes to recognise its splendour; and the final answer to the Solitary is therefore embodied in a series of narratives, showing by example how our spiritual vision may be purified or obscured. Our philosophy must be finally based, not upon abstract speculation and metaphysical arguments, but on the diffused consciousness of the healthy mind. As Butler sees the universe by the light of conscience, Wordsworth sees it through the wider emotions of awe, reverence, and love, produced in a sound nature.

The pantheistic conception, in short, leads to an unsatisfactory optimism in the general view of nature, and to an equal tolerance of all passions as equally "natural." To escape from this difficulty we must establish some more discriminative mode of interpreting nature. Man is the instrument played upon by all impulses, good or bad. The music which results may be harmonious or discordant. When the instrument is in tune, the music will be perfect; but when is it in tune, and how are we to know that it is in tune?

That problem once solved, we can tell which are the authentic utterances and which are the accidental discords. And by solving it, or by saying what is the right constitution of human beings, we shall discover which is the true philosophy of the universe, and what are the dictates of a sound moral sense. Wordsworth implicitly answers the question by explaining, in his favourite phrase, how we are to build up our moral being.

The voice of nature speaks at first in vague emotions, scarcely distinguishable from mere animal bouyancy. The boy, hooting in mimicry of the owls, receives in his heart the voice of mountain torrents and the solemn imagery of rocks, and woods, and stars. The sportive girl is unconsciously moulded into stateliness and grace by the floating clouds, the bending willow, and even by silent sympathy with the motions of the storm. Nobody has ever shown, with such exquisite power as Wordsworth, how much of the charm of natural objects in later life is due to early associations, thus formed in a mind not yet capable of contemplating its own processes. As old Matthew says in the lines which, however familiar, can never be read without emotion—

My eyes are dim with childish tears,
    My heart is idly stirred;
For the same sound is in my ears
    Which in those days I heard.

And the strangely beautiful address to the cuckoo might be made into a text for a prolonged commentary by an aesthetic philosopher upon the power of early association. It curiously illustrates, for example, the reason for Wordsworth's delight in recalling sounds. The croak of the distant raven, the bleat of the mountain lamb, the splash of the leaping fish in the lonely tarn, are specially delightful to him, because the hearing is the most spiritual of our senses; and these sounds, like the cuckoo's cry, seem to convert the earth into an "unsubstantial fairy place." The phrase "association" indeed implies a certain arbitrariness in the images suggested, which is not quite in accordance with Wordsworth's feeling. Though the echo depends partly upon the hearer, the mountain voices are specially adapted for certain moods. They have, we may say, a spontaneous affinity for the nobler affections. If some early passage in our childhood is associated with a particular spot, a house or a street will bring back the petty and accidental details: a mountain or a lake will revive the deeper and more permanent elements of feeling. If you have made love in a palace, according to Mr. Disraeli's prescription, the sight of it will recall the splendour of the object's dress or jewellery; if, as Wordsworth would prefer, with a background of mountains, it will appear in later days as if they had absorbed, and were always ready again to radiate forth, the tender and hallowing influences which then for the first time entered your life. The elementary and deepest passions are most easily associated with the sublime and beautiful in nature.

> The primal duties shine aloft like stars;
> The charities that soothe, and heal, and bless,
> Are scattered at the feet of man like flowers.

And therefore if you have been happy enough to take delight in these natural and universal objects in the early days, when the most permanent associations are formed, the sight of them in later days will bring back by preordained and divine symbolism whatever was most ennobling in your early feelings. The vulgarising associations will drop off of themselves, and what was pure and lofty will remain.

From this natural law follows another of Wordsworth's favourite precepts. The mountains are not with him a symbol of anti-social feelings. On the contrary, they are in their proper place as the background of the simple domestic affections. He loves his native hills, not in the Byronic fashion, as a savage wilderness, but as the appropriate framework in which a healthy social order can permanently maintain itself. That, for example, is, as he tells us, the thought which inspired *The Brothers,* a poem which excels all modern idylls in weight of meaning and depth of feeling, by virtue of the idea thus embodied. The retired valley of Ennerdale, with its grand background of hills, precipitous enough to be fairly called mountains, forces the two lads into closer affection. Shut in by these "enormous barriers," and undistracted by the ebb and flow of the outside world, the mutual love becomes concentrated. A tie like that of family blood is involuntarily imposed upon the little community of dalesmen. The image of sheep-tracks and shepherds clad in country grey is stamped upon the elder brother's mind, and comes back to him in tropical calms; he hears the tones of his waterfalls in the piping shrouds; and when he returns, recognises every fresh scar made by winter storms on the mountain sides, and knows by sight every unmarked grave in the little churchyard. The fraternal affection sanctifies the scenery, and the sight of the scenery brings back the affection with overpowering force upon his return. This is everywhere the sentiment inspired in Wordsworth by his beloved hills. It is not so much the love of nature pure and simple, as of nature seen through the deepest human feelings. The light glimmering in a lonely cottage, the one rude house in the deep valley, with its "small lot of life-supporting fields and guardian rocks," are necessary to point the moral and to draw to a definite focus the various forces of sentiment. The two veins of feeling are inseparably blended. The

peasant noble, in the "Song at the Feast of Brougham Castle," learns equally
from men and nature:—

> Love had he found in huts where poor men lie;
>   His daily teachers had been woods and hills,
> The silence that is in the starry skies,
>   The sleep that is among the lonely hills.

Without the love, the silence and the sleep would have had no spiritual
meaning. They are valuable as giving intensity and solemnity to the positive
emotion.

The same remark is to be made upon Wordsworth's favourite teaching of
the advantages of the contemplative life. He is fond of enforcing the doctrine of
the familiar lines, that we can feed our minds "in a wise passiveness," and that

> One impulse from the vernal wood
>   Can teach you more of man,
> Of moral evil and of good,
>   Than all the sages can.

And, according to some commentators, this would seem to express the
doctrine that the ultimate end of life is the cultivation of tender emotions
without reference to action. The doctrine, thus absolutely stated, would be
immoral and illogical. To recommend contemplation in preference to action
is like preferring sleeping to waking; or saying, as a full expression of the
truth, that silence is golden and speech silvern. Like that familiar phrase,
Wordsworth's teaching is not to be interpreted literally. The essence of such
maxims is to be one-sided. They are paradoxical in order to be emphatic. To
have seasons of contemplation, of withdrawal from the world and from books,
of calm surrendering of ourselves to the influences of nature, is a practice
commended in one form or other by all moral teachers. It is a sanitary rule,
resting upon obvious principles. The mind which is always occupied in a
multiplicity of small observations, or the regulation of practical details, loses
the power of seeing general principles and of associating all objects with the
central emotions of "admiration, hope, and love." The philosophic mind is
that which habitually sees the general in the particular, and finds food for the
deepest thought in the simplest objects. It requires, therefore, periods of repose,
in which the fragmentary and complex atoms of distracted feeling which
make up the incessant whirl of daily life may have time to crystallise round
the central thoughts. But it must feed in order to assimilate; and each process
implies the other as its correlative. A constant interest, therefore, in the joys
and sorrows of our neighbours is as essential as quiet, self-centred rumination.

It is when the eye "has kept watch o'er man's mortality," and by virtue of the tender sympathies of "the human heart by which we live," that to us

The meanest flower which blows can give
Thoughts that do often lie too deep for tears.

The solitude which implies severance from natural sympathies and affections is poisonous. The happiness of the heart which lives alone,

Housed in a dream, an outcast from the kind,
. . .
Is to be pitied, for 'tis surely blind.

Wordsworth's meditations upon flowers or animal life are impressive because they have been touched by this constant sympathy. The sermon is always in his mind, and therefore every stone may serve for a text. His contemplation enables him to see the pathetic side of the small pains and pleasures which we are generally in too great a hurry to notice. There are times, of course, when this moralising tendency leads him to the regions of the namby-pamby or sheer prosaic platitude. On the other hand, no one approaches him in the power of touching some rich chord of feeling by help of the pettiest incident. The old man going to the fox-hunt with a tear on his cheek, and saying to himself,

The key I must take, for my Helen is dead;

or the mother carrying home her dead sailor's bird; the village schoolmaster, in whom a rift in the clouds revives the memory of his little daughter; the old huntsman unable to cut through the stump of rotten wood—touch our hearts at once and for ever. The secret is given in the rather prosaic apology for not relating a tale about poor Simon Lee:

O reader! had you in your mind
    Such stores as silent thought can bring,
O gentle reader! you would find
    A tale in everything.

The value of silent thought is so to cultivate the primitive emotions that they may flow spontaneously upon every common incident, and that every familiar object becomes symbolic of them. It is a familiar remark that a philosopher or man of science who has devoted himself to meditation upon some principle or law of nature, is always finding new illustrations in the most unexpected quarters. He cannot take up a novel or walk across the street without hitting upon appropriate instances. Wordsworth would apply the principle to the building up of our "moral being." Admiration, hope, and love should be so constantly in our thoughts, that innumerable sights and sounds which are meaningless to the world should become to us a language incessantly suggestive of the deepest topics of thought.

This explains his dislike to science, as he understood the word, and his denunciations of the "world." The man of science is one who cuts up nature into fragments, and not only neglects their possible significance for our higher feelings, but refrains on principle from taking it into account. The primrose suggests to him some new device in classification, and he would be worried by the suggestion of any spiritual significance as an annoying distraction. Viewing all objects "in disconnection, dead and spiritless," we are thus really waging

> An impious warfare with the very life
> Of our own souls.

We are putting the letter in place of the spirit, and dealing with nature as a mere grammarian deals with a poem. When we have learnt to associate every object with some lesson

> Of human suffering or of human joy;

when we have thus obtained the "glorious habit,"

> By which sense is made
> Subservient still to moral purposes,
> Auxiliar to divine;

the "dull eye" of science will light up; for, in observing natural processes, it will carry with it an incessant reference to the spiritual processes to which they are allied. Science, in short, requires to be brought into intimate connection with morality and religion. If we are forced for our immediate purpose to pursue truth for itself, regardless of consequences, we must remember all the more carefully that truth is a whole, and that fragmentary bits of knowledge become valuable as they are incorporated into a general system. The tendency of modern times to specialism brings with it a characteristic danger. It requires to be supplemented by a correlative process of integration. We must study details to increase our knowledge; we must accustom ourselves to look at the detail in the light of the general principles in order to make it fruitful.

The influence of that world which "is too much with us late and soon" is of the same kind. The man of science loves barren facts for their own sake. The man of the world becomes devoted to some petty pursuit without reference to ultimate ends. He becomes a slave to money, or power, or praise, without caring for their effect upon his moral character. As social organisation becomes more complete, the social unit becomes a mere fragment instead of being a complete whole in himself. Man becomes

> The senseless member of a vast machine,
> Serving as doth a spindle or a wheel.

The division of labour, celebrated with such enthusiasm by Adam Smith,[4] tends to crush all real life out of its victims. The soul of the political economist may rejoice when he sees a human being devoting his whole faculties to the performance of one subsidiary operation in the manufacture of a pin. The poet and the moralist must notice with anxiety the contrast between the old-fashioned peasant who, if he discharged each particular function clumsily, discharged at least many functions, and found exercise for all the intellectual and moral faculties of his nature, and the modern artisan doomed to the incessant repetition of one petty set of muscular expansions and contractions, and whose soul, if he has one, is therefore rather an encumbrance than otherwise. This is the evil which is constantly before Wordsworth's eyes, as it has certainly not become less prominent since his time. The danger of crushing the individual is a serious one according to his view; not because it implies the neglect of some abstract political rights, but from the impoverishment of character which is implied in the process. Give every man a vote, and abolish all interference with each man's private tastes, and the danger may still be as great as ever. The tendency to "differentiation"—as we call it in modern phraseology—the social pulverisation, the lowering and narrowing of the individual's sphere of action and feeling to the pettiest details, depends upon processes underlying all political changes. It cannot therefore, be cured by any nostrum of constitution-mongers, or by the negative remedy of removing old barriers. It requires to be met by profounder moral and religious teaching. Men must be taught what is the really valuable part of their natures, and what is the purest happiness to be extracted from life, as well as allowed to gratify fully their own tastes; for who can say that men encouraged by all their surroundings and appeals to the most obvious motives to turn themselves into machines, will not deliberately choose to be machines? Many powerful thinkers have illustrated Wordsworth's doctrine more elaborately, but nobody has gone more decisively to the root of the matter.

One other side of Wordsworth's teaching is still more significant and original. Our vague instincts are consolidated into reason by meditation, sympathy with our fellows, communion with nature, and a constant devotion to "high endeavours." If life run smoothly, the transformation may be easy, and our primitive optimism turn imperceptibly into general complacency. The trial comes when we make personal acquaintance with sorrow, and our

early bouyancy begins to fail. We are tempted to become querulous or to lap
ourselves in indifference. Most poets are content to bewail our lot melodiously,
and admit that there is no remedy unless a remedy be found in "the luxury of
grief." Prosaic people become selfish though not sentimental. They laugh at
their old illusions, and turn to the solid consolations of comfort. Nothing is
more melancholy than to study many biographies, and note—not the failure
of early promise which may mean merely an aiming above the mark—but
the progressive deterioration of character which so often follows grief and
disappointment. If it be not true that most men grow worse as they grow old,
it is surely true that few men pass through the world without being corrupted
as much as purified.

Now Wordsworth's favourite lesson is the possibility of turning grief and
disappointment into account. He teaches in many forms the necessity of
"transmuting" sorrow into strength. One of the great evils is a lack of power

An agonising sorrow to transmute.

The Happy Warrior is, above all, the man who in face of all human miseries
can

Exercise a power
Which is our human nature's highest dower;
Controls them, and subdues, transmutes, bereaves
Of their bad influence, and their good receives;

who is made more compassionate by familiarity with sorrow, more placable
by contest, purer by temptation, and more enduring by distress.[5] It is owing
to the constant presence of this thought, to his sensibility to the refining
influence of sorrow, that Wordsworth is the only poet who will bear reading
in times of distress. Other poets mock us by an impossible optimism, or
merely reflect the feelings which, however we may play with them in times of
cheerfulness, have now become an intolerable burden. Wordsworth suggests
the single topic which, so far at least as this world is concerned, can really be
called consolatory. None of the ordinary commonplaces will serve, or serve at
most as indications of human sympathy. But there is some consolation in the
thought that even death may bind the survivors closer, and leave as a legacy
enduring motives to noble action. It is easy to say this; but Wordsworth has
the merit of feeling the truth in all its force, and expressing it by the most
forcible images. In one shape or another the sentiment is embodied in most
of his really powerful poetry. It is intended, for example, to be the moral of
The White Doe of Rylstone. There, as Wordsworth says, everything fails so far
as its object is external and unsubstantial; everything succeeds so far as it is

moral and spiritual. Success grows out of failure; and the mode in which it grows is indicated by the lines which give the keynote of the poem. Emily, the heroine, is to become a soul

> By force of sorrows high
> Uplifted to the purest sky
> Of undisturbed serenity.

The White Doe is one of those poems which make many readers inclined to feel a certain tenderness for Jeffrey's dogged insensibility; and I confess that I am not one of its warm admirers. The sentiment seems to be unduly relaxed throughout; there is a want of sympathy with heroism of the rough and active type, which is, after all, at least as worthy of admiration as the more passive variety of the virtue; and the defect is made more palpable by the position of the chief actors. These rough borderers, who recall William of Deloraine and Dandie Dinmont, are somehow out of their element when preaching the doctrines of quietism and submission to circumstances. But, whatever our judgment of this particular embodiment of Wordsworth's moral philosophy, the inculcation of the same lesson gives force to many of his finest poems. It is enough to mention "The Leech-Gatherer," the "Stanzas on Peele Castle," *Michael,* and, as expressing the inverse view of the futility of idle grief, "Laodamia," where he has succeeded in combining his morality with more than his ordinary beauty of poetical form. The teaching of all these poems falls in with the doctrine already set forth. All moral teaching, I have sometimes fancied, might be summed up in the one formula, "Waste not." Every element of which our nature is composed may be said to be good in its proper place; and therefore every vicious habit springs out of the misapplication of forces which might be turned to account by judicious training. The waste of sorrow is one of the most lamentable forms of waste. Sorrow too often tends to produce bitterness or effeminacy of character. But it may, if rightly used, serve only to detach us from the lower motives, and give sanctity to the higher. That is what Wordsworth sees with unequalled clearness, and he therefore sees also the condition of profiting. The mind in which the most valuable elements have been systematically strengthened by meditation, by association of deep thought with the most universal presences, by constant sympathy with the joys and sorrows of its fellows, will be prepared to convert sorrow into a medicine instead of a poison. Sorrow is deteriorating so far as it is selfish. The man who is occupied with his own interests makes grief an excuse for effeminate indulgence in self-pity. He becomes weaker and more fretful. The man who has learnt habitually to think of himself as part of a greater whole, whose conduct has been habitually directed to noble ends, is purified and strengthened by the spiritual convulsion. His disappointment, or his loss of some beloved object, makes him more anxious to fix the bases of his happiness widely and deeply, and to be content with the consciousness of honest work, instead of looking for what is called success.

But I must not take to preaching in the place of Wordsworth. The whole theory is most nobly summed up in the grand lines already noticed on "The Character of the Happy Warrior." There Wordsworth has explained in the most forcible and direct language the mode in which a grand character can be formed; how youthful impulses may change into manly purpose; how pain and sorrow may be transmuted into new forces; how the mind may be fixed upon lofty purposes; how the domestic affections—which give the truest happiness—may also be the greatest source of strength to the man who is

More brave for this, that he has much to lose;

and how, finally, he becomes indifferent to all petty ambition—

Finds comfort in himself and in his cause;
And, while the mortal mist is gathering, draws
His breath in confidence of Heaven's applause.
    This is the Happy Warrior, this is he
    Whom every man in arms should wish to be.

We may now see what ethical theory underlies Wordsworth's teaching of the transformation of instinct into reason. We must start from the postulate that there is in fact a Divine order in the universe; and that conformity to this order produces beauty as embodied in the external world, and is the condition of virtue as regulating our character. It is by obedience to the "stern lawgiver," Duty, that flowers gain their fragrance, and that "the most ancient heavens" preserve their freshness and strength. But this postulate does not seek for justification in abstract metaphysical reasoning. The "Intimations of Immortality" are precisely intimations, not intellectual intuitions. They are vague and emotional, not distinct and logical. They are a feeling of harmony, not a perception of innate ideas. And, on the other hand, our instincts are not a mere chaotic mass of passions, to be gratified without considering their place and function in a certain definite scheme. They have been implanted by the Divine hand, and the harmony which we feel corresponds to a real order. To justify them we must appeal to experience, but to experience interrogated by a certain definite procedure. Acting upon the assumption that the Divine order exists, we shall come to recognise it, though we could not deduce it by an *a priori* method.

The instrument, in fact, finds itself originally tuned by its Maker, and may preserve its original condition by careful obedience to the stern teaching of life. The bouyancy common to all youthful and healthy natures then changes into a deeper and more solemn mood. The great primary emotions retain the original impulse, but increase their volume. Grief and disappointment are transmuted into tenderness, sympathy, and endurance. The reason, as it develops, regulates, without weakening, the primitive instincts. All the greatest, and therefore most common, sights of nature are indelibly associated with "admiration, hope, and love;" and all increase of knowledge and power is regarded as a means for furthering the gratification of our nobler emotions. Under the opposite treatment, the character loses its freshness, and we regard the early happiness as an illusion. The old emotions dry up at their source. Grief produces fretfulness, misanthropy, or effeminacy. Power is wasted on petty ends and frivolous excitement, and knowledge becomes barren and pedantic. In this way the postulate justifies itself by producing the noblest type of character. When the "moral being" is thus built up, its instincts become its convictions, we recognise the true voice of nature, and distinguish it from the echo of our passions. Thus we come to know how the Divine order and the laws by which the character is harmonised are the laws of morality.

To possible objections it might be answered by Wordsworth that this mode of assuming in order to prove is the normal method of philosophy. "You must love him," as he says of the poet,

> Ere to you
> He will seem worthy of your love.

The doctrine corresponds to the *crede ut intelligas* of the divine; or to the philosophic theory that we must start from the knowledge already constructed within us by instincts which have not yet learnt to reason. And, finally, if a persistent reasoner should ask why—even admitting the facts—the higher type should be preferred to the lower, Wordsworth may ask, Why is bodily health preferable to disease? If a man likes weak lungs and a bad digestion, reason cannot convince him of his error. The physician has done enough when he has pointed out the sanitary laws obedience to which generates strength, long life, and power of enjoyment. The moralist is in the same position when he has shown how certain habits conduce to the development of a type superior to its rivals in all the faculties which imply permanent peace of mind and power of resisting the shocks of the world without disintegration. Much undoubtedly remains to be said. Wordsworth's teaching, profound and admirable as it may be, has not the potency to silence the scepticism which has gathered strength since his day, and assailed fundamental—or what to him seemed fundamental—tenets of his system. No one can yet say what transformation may pass upon the thoughts and emotions for which he found utterance in speaking of the divinity and sanctity of nature. Some people vehemently maintain that the words will be emptied of all meaning if the old theological conceptions to which he was so firmly attached should disappear with the development of new modes of thought. Nature, as regarded by the light of modern science, will be the name of a cruel and wasteful, or at least of a purely neutral and indifferent power, or perhaps as merely an equivalent for the Unknowable, to which the conditions of our intellect prevent us from ever attaching any intelligible predicate. Others would say that in whatever terms we choose to speak of the mysterious darkness which surrounds our little island of comparative light, the emotion generated in a thoughtful mind by the contemplation of the universe will remain unaltered or strengthen with clearer knowledge; and that we shall express ourselves in a new dialect without altering the essence of our thought. The emotions to which Wordsworth has given utterance will remain, though the system in which he believed should sink into oblivion; as, indeed, all human systems have found different modes of symbolising the same fundamental feelings. But it is enough vaguely to indicate considerations not here to be developed.

It only remains to be added once more that Wordsworth's poetry derives its power from the same source as his philosophy. It speaks to our strongest feelings because his speculation rests upon our deepest thoughts. His singular capacity for investing all objects with a glow derived from early associations; his keen sympathy with natural and simple emotions; his sense of the sanctifying influences which can be extracted from sorrow, are of equal value to his power over our intellects and our imaginations. His psychology, stated systematically, is rational; and, when expressed passionately, turns into poetry. To be sensitive to the most important phenomena is the first step equally towards a poetical or a scientific exposition. To see these truly is the condition of making the poetry harmonious and the philosophy logical. And it is often difficult to say which power is most remarkable in Wordsworth. It would be easy to illustrate the truth by other than moral topics. His sonnet, noticed by De Quincey, in which he speaks of the abstracting power of darkness, and observes that as the hills pass into twilight we see the same sight as the ancient Britons, is impressive as it stands, but would be equally good as an illustration in a metaphysical treatise. Again, the sonnet beginning

With ships the sea was sprinkled far and wide,

is at once, as he has shown in a commentary of his own, an illustration of a curious psychological law—of our tendency, that is, to introduce an arbitrary principle of order into a random collection of objects—and, for the same reason, a striking embodiment of the corresponding mood of feeling. The little poem called "Stepping Westward" is in the same way at once a delicate expression of a specific sentiment and an acute critical analysis of the subtle associations suggested by a single phrase. But such illustrations might be multiplied indefinitely. As he has himself said, there is scarcely one of his poems which does not call attention to some moral sentiment, or to a general principle or law of thought, of our intellectual constitution.

Finally, we might look at the reverse side of the picture, and endeavour to show how the narrow limits of Wordsworth's power are connected with certain moral defects; with the want of quick sympathy which shows itself in his dramatic feebleness, and the austerity of character which caused him to lose his special gifts too early and become a rather commonplace defender of conservatism; and that curious diffidence (he assures us that it was "diffidence") which induced him to write many thousand lines of blank verse entirely about himself. But the task would be superfluous as well as ungrateful. It was his aim, he tells us, "to console the afflicted; to add sunshine to daylight by making the happy happier; to teach the young and the gracious of every age to see, to think, and therefore to become more actively and securely virtuous;" and, high as was the aim he did much towards its accomplishment.

Notes

1. J. S. Mill and Whewell were, for their generation, the ablest exponents of two opposite systems of thought upon such matters. Mill has expressed his obligations to Wordsworth in his *Autobiography,* and Whewell dedicated to Wordsworth his *Elements of Morality* in acknowledgment of his influence as a moralist.
2. The poem of Henry Vaughan, to which reference is often made in this connection, scarcely contains more than a pregnant hint.
3. As, for example, in the "Lines on Tintern Abbey": "If this be but a vain belief."
4. See Wordsworth's reference to the *Wealth of Nations,* in *The Prelude,* Book xiii.
5. So, too, in *The Prelude:*—

> Then was the truth received into my heart,
> That, under heaviest sorrow earth can bring,
> If from the affliction somewhere do not grow
> Honour which could not else have been a faith,
> An elevation, and a sanctity;

If new strength be not given, nor old restored,
The fault is ours, not Nature's.

—LESLIE STEPHEN, from "Wordsworth's Ethics,"
1876, *Hours in a Library,* 1874–79,
1904, vol. 3, pp. 139–178

T.E. BROWN (1894)

I have just read *The Excursion.* In book viii, I think, occurs the celebrated
line—

Goes sounding on his dim and perilous way.

Surely I have read somewhere that that line was Coleridge's. Puzzled, I had
recourse to Milton, but it was not there, however worthy of him. In *The
Excursion* it is quite *in situ,* and there are no marks of quotation. Isn't this
all terribly sciolistic? I ought to know these things, but I don't. By-the-bye,
in reading *The Excursion* after a long interval, I feel so much how good it
would have been for Wordsworth to have gone to Oxford. He is a thorough
Cantab, has no philosophical vocabulary, and really rather bores one with
his constant philosophizing, which is under difficulties and often only half
intelligible. Some periods, all involved and crude of phrase, I can't construe.

—T.E. BROWN, letter to S.T. Irwin,
December 11, 1894

THE PATRIOTIC AND POLITICAL SONNETS

WILLIAM WORDSWORTH (1807)

In Wordsworth's letter to Lady Beaumont, he thanks her for taking an
interest in his work and wants to respond to any disappointment she may
be feeling. He speaks of the need for people to love human nature and
God before they can truly understand and take delight in poetry. Among
the individuals consumed with the vanity of worldly concerns and their
own self-importance in the scheme of things are "those persons who
live, or wish to live, in the broad light of the world—among those who
either are, or are striving to make themselves, people of consideration
in society."

Wordsworth wants Lady Beaumont to know how best to appreciate
his sonnets, despite their current negative reception, by stating that

his poem is meant to instruct those who are suffering and to teach all mankind how to experience the world and become more virtuous.

He is not afraid of London society and its malign passions, as his poems are addressed to kindly people. He states that his desire is to awaken the imagination of this second class of people. Referring most likely to Samuel Rogers, his literary patron and a poet adhering to the neoclassical belief in poetic decorum, Wordsworth defends the unity of his poems to liberty on the basis that, taken as a whole, they convey a comprehensiveness of spirit. Wordsworth appears quite confident in his poetic powers and the precept on which they are based:

> I would boldly say at once, that these Sonnets, while they each fix the attention upon some important sentiment separately considered, do at the same time collectively make a Poem on the subject of Civil Liberty and national independence, which, either for simplicity of style or grandeur of moral sentiment, is, alas! likely to have few parallels in the Poetry of the present day.

Wordsworth's letter to Lady Beaumont concludes with the same strong sense of belief in himself, despite the false pretenses of London high society. The poet asserts that the efficacy of his poems lies in their ability to inculcate benevolent and compassionate feelings in the audience to whom the works are directed.

———————————————————

Though I am to see you so soon I cannot but write a word or two, to thank you for the interest you take in my Poems as evinced by your solicitude about their immediate reception. I write partly to thank you for this and to express the pleasure it has given me, and partly to remove any uneasiness from your mind which the disappointments you sometimes meet with in this labour of love may occasion. I see that you have many battles to fight for me; more than in the ardour and confidence of your pure and elevated mind you had ever thought of being summoned to; but be assured that this opposition is nothing more than what I distinctly foresaw that you and my other Friends would have to encounter. I say this, not to give myself credit for an eye of prophecy, but to allay any vexatious thoughts on my account which this opposition may have produced in you. It is impossible that any expectations can be lower than mine concerning the immediate effect of this little work upon what is called the Public. I do not here take into consideration the envy and malevolence, and all the bad passions which always stand in the way of a work of any merit from a living Poet; but merely think of the pure absolute honest ignorance, in which all worldlings of every rank and situation must be enveloped, with respect to the thoughts, feelings, and images, on which the life of my Poems depends. The things which I have taken, whether from within or without,—what have they to do with routs, dinners, morning calls, hurry from door to door, from street to street, on foot or in Carriage; with Mr. Pitt or Mr. Fox, Mr. Paul or Sir Francis Burdett, the Westminster Election or the Borough of Honiton; in a word, for I cannot stop to make my way through the hurry of images that present themselves to me, what have they to do with endless talking about things nobody cares anything for except as far as their own vanity is concerned, and this with persons they care nothing for but as their vanity or selfishness is concerned; what have they to do (to say all at once) with a life without love? in such a life there can be no thought; for we have no thought (save thoughts of pain) but as far as we have love and admiration. It is an awful truth, that there neither is, nor can be, any genuine enjoyment of Poetry among nineteen out of twenty of those persons who live, or wish to live, in the broad light of the world—among those who either are, or are striving to make themselves, people of consideration in society. This is a truth, and an awful one, because to be incapable of a feeling of Poetry in my sense of the word is to be without love of human nature and reverence for God.

Upon this I shall insist elsewhere; at present let me confine myself to my object, which is to make you, my dear Friend, as easy-hearted as myself with respect to these Poems. Trouble not yourself upon their present reception; of what moment is that compared with what I trust is their destiny, to console the afflicted, to add sunshine to daylight by making the happy happier, to teach the young and the gracious of every age, to see, to think and feel, and therefore to become more actively and securely virtuous; this is their office, which I trust they will faithfully perform long after we (that is, all that is mortal of us) are mouldered in our graves. I am well aware how far it would seem to many I overrate my own exertions when I speak in this way, in direct connection with the Volumes I have just made public.

I am not, however, afraid of such censure, insignificant as probably the majority of those poems would appear to very respectable persons; I do not mean London wits and witlings, for these have too many bad passions about them to be respectable even if they had more intellect than the benign laws of providence will allow to such a heartless existence as theirs is; but grave, kindly-natured, worthy persons, who would be pleased if they could. I hope that these Volumes are not without some recommendations, even for Readers of this class, but their imagination has slept; and the voice which is the voice of my Poetry without Imagination cannot be heard.

Leaving these, I was going to say a word to such Readers as Mr. Rogers. Such!—how would he be offended if he knew I considered him only as a representative of a class, and not as unique! 'Pity,' says Mr. R., 'that so many trifling things should be admitted to obstruct the view of those that have merit;' now, let this candid judge take, by way of example, the sonnets, which, probably, with the exception of two or three other Poems for which I will not contend appear to him the most trifling, as they are the shortest, I would say to him, omitting things of higher consideration, there is one thing which must strike you at once if you will only read these poems,—that those to Liberty, at least, have a connection with, or a bearing upon, each other, and therefore, if individually they want weight, perhaps, as a Body, they may not be so deficient, at least this ought to induce you to suspend your judgement, and qualify it so far as to allow that the writer aims at least at comprehensiveness. But dropping this, I would boldly say at once, that these Sonnets, while they each fix the attention upon some important sentiment separately considered, do at the same time collectively make a Poem on the subject of Civil Liberty and national independence, which, either for simplicity of style or grandeur of moral sentiment, is, alas! likely to have few parallels in the Poetry of the present day. Again, turn to the 'Moods of my own Mind'. There is scarcely a Poem here of above thirty Lines, and very trifling these poems will appear to many; but, omitting to speak of them individually, do they not, taken collectively, fix the attention upon a subject eminently poetical, viz., the interest which objects in nature derive from the predominance of certain affections more or less permanent, more or less capable of salutary renewal in the mind of the being contemplating these objects? This is poetic, and essentially poetic, and why? because it is creative.

But I am wasting words, for it is nothing more than you know, and if said to those for whom it is intended, it would not be understood.

I see by your last Letter that Mrs. Fermor has entered into the spirit of these 'Moods of my own Mind.' Your transcript from her Letter gave me the greatest pleasure; but I must say that even she has something yet to receive from me. I say this with confidence, from her thinking that I have fallen below myself in the Sonnet beginning—'With ships the sea was sprinkled far and nigh.' As to the other which she objects to, I will only observe that there is a misprint in the last line but two, 'And *though* this wilderness' for 'And *through* this wilderness'—that makes it unintelligible. This latter Sonnet for many reasons, though I do not abandon it, I will not now speak of; but upon the other, I could say something important in conversation, and will attempt now to illustrate it by a comment which I feel will be very inadequate to convey my meaning. There is scarcely one of my Poems which does not aim to direct the attention to some moral sentiment, or to some general principle, or law of thought, or of our intellectual constitution. For instance in the present case, who is there that has not felt that the mind can have no rest among a multitude of objects, of which it either cannot make one whole, or from which it cannot single out one individual, whereupon may be concentrated the attention divided among or distracted by a multitude? After a certain time we must either select one image or object, which must put out of view the rest wholly, or must subordinate them to itself while it stands forth as a Head:

> Now glowed the firmament
> With living sapphires! Hesperus, that *led*
> The starry host, rode brightest; till the Moon,
> Rising in clouded majesty, at length,
> Apparent *Queen,* unveiled *her peerless* light,
> And o'er the dark her silver mantle threw.

Having laid this down as a general principle, take the case before us. I am represented in the Sonnet as casting my eyes over the sea, sprinkled with a multitude of Ships, like the heavens with stars, my mind may be supposed to float up and down among them in a kind of dreamy indifference with respect either to this or that one, only in a pleasurable state of feeling with respect to the whole prospect. 'Joyously it showed,' this continued till that feeling may be supposed to have passed away, and a kind of comparative listlessness or apathy to have succeeded, as at this line, 'Some veering up and down, one knew not why.' All at once, while I am in this state, comes forth an object, an individual, and my mind, sleepy and unfixed, is awakened and fastened in a moment. 'Hesperus, that *led* The starry host,' is a poetical object, because the glory of his own Nature gives him the pre-eminence the moment he appears; he calls forth the poetic faculty, receiving its exertions as a tribute; but this Ship in the Sonnet may, in a manner still more appropriate, be said to come upon a mission of the poetic Spirit, because in its own appearance and attributes it is barely sufficiently distinguished to rouse the creative faculty of the human mind; to exertions at all times welcome, but doubly so when they come upon us when in a state of remissness. The mind being once fixed and rouzed, all the rest comes from itself; it is merely a lordly Ship, nothing more:

> This ship was nought to me, nor I to her,
> Yet I pursued her with a lover's look.

My mind wantons with grateful joy in the exercise of its own powers, and, loving its own creation,

> This ship to all the rest I did prefer,

making her a sovereign or a regent, and thus giving body and life to all the rest; mingling up this idea with fondness and praise—

where she comes the winds must stir;

and concluding the whole with

On went She, and due north her journey took.

Thus taking up again the Reader with whom I began, letting him know how long I must have watched this favorite Vessel, and inviting him to rest his mind as mine is resting.

Having said so much upon a mere 14 lines, which Mrs. Fermor did not approve, I cannot but add a word or two upon my satisfaction in finding that my mind has so much in common with hers, and that we participate so many of each other's pleasures. I collect this from her having singled out the two little Poems, the Daffodils, and the Rock crowned with snowdrops. I am sure that whoever is much pleased with either of these quiet and tender delineations must be fitted to walk through the recesses of my poetry with delight, and will there recognise, at every turn, something or other in which, and over which, it has that property and right which knowledge and love confer. The line, 'Come, blessed barrier, etc.,' in the sonnet upon Sleep, which Mrs. F. points out, had before been mentioned to me by Coleridge, and indeed by almost everybody who had heard it, as eminently beautiful. My letter (as this 2nd sheet, which I am obliged to take, admonishes me) is growing to an enormous length; and yet, saving that I have expressed my calm confidence that these Poems will live, I have said nothing which has a particular application to the object of it, which was to remove all disquiet from your mind on account of the condemnation they may at present incur from that portion of my contemporaries who are called the Public. I am sure, my dear Lady Beaumont, if you attach any importance it can only be from an apprehension that it may affect me, upon which I have already set you at ease, or from a fear that this present blame is ominous of their future or final destiny. If this be the case, your tenderness for me betrays you; be assured that the decision of these persons has nothing to do with the Question; they are altogether incompetent judges. These people in the senseless hurry of their idle lives do not *read* books, they merely snatch a glance at them that they may talk about them. And even if this were not so, never forget what I believe was observed to you by Coleridge, that every great and original writer, in proportion as he is great or original, must himself create the taste by which he is to be relished; he must teach the art by which he is to be seen; this, in a certain degree, even to all persons, however wise and pure may be their lives, and however unvitiated their taste; but for those who dip into books in order to give an opinion of them, or talk about them to take up an opinion—for this multitude of unhappy, and misguided, and misguiding beings, an entire regeneration must be produced; and if this be possible, it must be a work *of time*. To conclude, my ears are stone-dead to this idle buzz, and my flesh as insensible as iron to these petty stings; and after what I have said I am sure yours will be the same. I doubt not that you will share with me an invincible confidence that my writings (and among them these little Poems) will cooperate with the benign tendencies in human nature and society, wherever found; and that they will, in their degree, be efficacious in making men wiser, better, and happier. Farewell; I will not apologise for this Letter, though its length demands an apology. Believe me, eagerly wishing for the happy day when I shall see you and Sir George here, most affectionately yours,

Wm Wordsworth.

—WILLIAM WORDSWORTH, letter to
Lady Beaumont, May 21, 1807

W.J. DAWSON "PATRIOTIC AND POLITICAL POEMS" (1908)

W.J. Dawson begins his essay with a defense of Wordsworth in the face of accusations that his later poetry lacked the ardor and concern for social issues that were so important to the poet in his early, radical years. Citing the sonnets written between 1803 to 1816 as the strongest statement that the poet held fast to an abiding interest in politics and the need to champion the cause of all people, especially the poor and humble, Dawson states unequivocally that the poet remained steadfast in his passionate devotion to political and humanitarian causes in his patriotic poems. In Dawson's estimation, Wordsworth's ability to convey issues of national concern within his poems is an achievement that surpasses all his poetic predecessors, except for John Milton: "His prose does not indeed glow with so intense a passion, nor is it so gorgeous as Milton's, but it is animated and inspired by the same spirit." For Dawson, this identification of spirituality in the political poems is absolutely critical to appreciating Wordsworth's commitment to his youthful ideals, for he sought to express his patriotism with restraint, relying on "diviner" convictions of truth, rather than vehement emotions. In a word, Dawson sees Wordsworth's restraint in his political poems as evidence of his heroism quietly moderated to a "lofty spirit."

An excellent and eloquent critic, Professor Dowden, has spoken of Wordsworth's "uncourageous elder years," and has founded the phrase upon this sentence of Wordsworth's: "Years have deprived me of courage, in the sense which the word bears when applied by Chaucer to the animation of birds in spring-time." A little reflection will, I think, show that this confession of the poet hardly justifies the phrase of the critic. Nevertheless, it is a general impression that Wordsworth began life an ardent Radical, and ended it as a staunch Conservative. If this were all, the phrase might be allowed to pass, but the impression such a phrase creates is that Wordsworth not merely renounced his early hopes and creed, but grew apathetic towards the great human causes which stirred his blood in youth. Browning's fine poem of the *Lost Leader* has often been applied to Wordsworth, and it has been assumed in many quarters, with what degree of truth we do not know, that Browning had Wordsworth in his mind when he wrote that powerful and pathetic indictment. However this may be, nothing is commoner than the assumption that one result of Wordsworth's remote seclusion from the stress of life was that he lost interest in public affairs, and cared little for the great movements of his day. Than this assumption nothing can be false. To say nothing of the prose writings of Wordsworth, few poets have given us a larger body of patriotic poetry, and poetry impregnated with politics, than Wordsworth. Perhaps it is because the finest poems of Wordsworth are those that deal with the emotions of man in the presence of Nature, that comparatively little interest attaches to his patriotic poetry. Such poetry, however, Wordsworth wrote throughout his life, and if he was not altogether a political force, it is quite certain that he never ceased to take a keen interest in politics. He had national aims, and was full of the most ardent love of country. It may be well to recall to the minds of my readers this aspect of Wordsworth's life and influence.

As regards the earlier part of his life, Wordsworth has left an abundant record of his thoughts in his prose writings. No poet, save Milton, has written with so large a touch upon national affairs, and has displayed so lofty a spirit. His prose does not indeed glow with so intense a passion, nor is it so gorgeous as Milton's, but it is animated and inspired by the same spirit. And in its more passionate passages something of Milton's pomp of style is discernible—something of his overwhelming force of language and cogency of thought. Wordsworth's tract on the *Convention of Cintra* belongs to the same class of writings as Milton's *Areopagitica*, and while not its equal in sustained splendour of diction, it is distinguished by the same breadth of view and eager patriotism. Wordsworth has himself defined excellence of writing as the conjunction of reason and passion, and, judged by this test, Wordsworth's occasional utterances on politics attain a rare excellence. It would have been singular in such an age if any man who possessed emotion enough to be a poet had nothing to say upon the great events which were altering the map of Europe. Wordsworth from the first never concealed his opinions on these subjects. He went as far as he could in apologizing for the errors of the French Revolution, when he said truly that "Revolution is not the season of true liberty." The austerity which characterized his whole life characterizes the very temper of his apology for the excesses of the Revolution. He shed no tears over the execution of Louis. He laments a larger public calamity, "that any combination of circumstances should have rendered it necessary or advisable to veil for a moment the statutes of the laws, and that by such emergency the cause of twenty-five millions of people, I may say of the whole human race, should have been so materially injured. Any other sorrow for the death of Louis is irrational and weak." He is even ardent Republican enough to argue for equality, and to say that in the perfect state "no distinctions are to be admitted but such as have evidently for their object the general good." This last sentence strikes the key-note in much of the philosophy of Wordsworth. "Simplification was," as John Morley has observed, "the key-note of the revolutionary time." That lesson Wordsworth thoroughly learned, and never forgot. It is the very essence of the democratic spirit to pierce beneath the artificial distinctions of a time, and grasp the essential; to take man for what he is, not for what he seems to be; to reverence man wherever he is found, and to reverence not least the man who toils in the lowliest walks of life. If this be the spirit of democracy then Wordsworth kept the democratic faith whole and undefiled. So far from repudiating the political creed of his life, he spiritualized it, and lived in obedience to its essential elements all his life. That in later life he manifested an incapacity for the rapid assimilation of new ideas; that his notions stiffened, and his perceptions failed; that he opposed Catholic Emancipation and the Reform Bill, is merely to say, in other words, that Wordsworth grew old. It is a rare spectacle, perhaps the rarest, to see a great mind resist the stiffening of age, and retain its versatility and freshness of outlook in the last decades of life. Wordsworth was never a versatile man, and never had any marked capacity for the assimilation of new ideas. But how very far Wordsworth was from ever being a fossilized Tory we may judge by his own saying in later life: "I have no respect whatever for Whigs, but I have a good deal of the Chartist in me." However his political insight may have failed him in his apprehension of the party measures of his later life, it cannot be seriously questioned that Wordsworth always remained true at heart to the cause of the people, and never swerved in his real reverence for man as man.

The urgency of the political passion in Wordsworth can be felt all through the days of the great war, and perhaps the noblest record of that period is in the long series of sonnets which Wordsworth wrote between the years 1803 and 1816. In the year 1809 he wrote scarcely anything that was not related to the life of nations. It was then that he apostrophized Saragossa, and lamented over the submission of the Tyrolese. And if few poets have written so largely on the current events of their day, it may certainly be added that no poet has showed a more cosmopolitan spirit. It was indeed a time when England was in closer touch with the struggling nationalities of the Continent than ever before. A common calamity had drawn together all the peoples of Europe who still loved liberty. England had never breathed the spirit of so large a life as in those troublous days. She had never known a period of such intense suspense and united enthusiasm. The beacon-fire was built on every hill; every village-green resounded to the clang of martial drill; every port had its eager watchers, who swept the waste fields of sea with restless scrutiny. Children were sent to bed with all their clothes neatly packed beside them, in case the alarm of war should break the midnight silence; and invasion was for months an hourly fear. It was one of those moments of supreme peril and passion which come rarely in the life of nations: one of those great regenerating moments when factions perish, and a nation rises into nobler life; and the stress of that great period is felt in every line that Wordsworth wrote. His patriotism was of that diviner kind which founds itself on principles of universal truth and righteousness. It was no splendid prejudice, no insularity of thought, no mere sentimental love of country: it gathered in its embrace the passions of Europe, and pleaded in its strenuous eloquence the cause of the oppressed throughout the world. This breadth of view which characterized Wordsworth's patriotism is its noblest characteristic. It is a catholic love of liberty which gives him spiritual comradeship with every man who has toiled or suffered for his country. And this spirit can find no fuller exemplification than in his noble sonnet, written in 1802,

TO TOUSSAINT L'OUVERTURE

Toussaint, the most unhappy man of men!
Whether the whistling Rustic tend his plow
Within thy hearing, or thy head be now
Pillowed in some dark dungeon's earless den;
O miserable Chieftain! where and when
Wilt thou find patience? Yet die not! do thou
Wear rather in thy bonds a cheerful brow;
Though fallen thyself, never to rise again,

Live, and take comfort! Thou hast left behind
Powers that will work for thee; air, earth, and skies;
There's not a breathing of the common wind
That will forget thee. Thou hast great allies;
Thy friends are exaltations, agonies,
And love, and man's unconquerable mind.

But catholic as Wordsworth's patriotic sympathies were, the noblest expressions of his patriotism are his addresses and appeals to his own countrymen. If in later life he did not discern the true spirit of his times, and unconsciously resisted the august spirit of progress, it was in part because his honest pride of country grew with his growth and strengthened with his age. He was loath to admit faults and flaws in a form of government which seemed to meet every just demand of liberty and order. Besides, the great hindrance to democratic development was to Wordsworth not discoverable in any error or defect of government, but in the defective method of life which his countrymen adopted. When he is called upon to judge the political measures of his day, his touch is not sure, nor his discrimination wise; but when he estimates the tendencies of the social life of England he is always clear, cogent, and convincing. His social grasp is always surer than his political, and his finest sonnets are those in which he combines his social insight with patriotic passion. Such a sonnet is this:

When I have borne in memory what has tamed
    Great nations, how ennobling thoughts depart
    When men change swords for ledgers, and desert
The student's bower for gold, some fear, unnamed
I had, my country!—am I to be blamed?
    Now when I think of thee, and what thou art,
    Verily in the bottom of my heart
Of those unfilial fears I am ashamed.
    For dearly must we prize thee; we who find
In thee a bulwark for the cause of men;
    And I by my affection was beguiled.
What wonder if a poet now and then.
    Among the many movements of his mind,
    Felt for thee as a lover or a child?

And this is a note which is struck again and again. In the hour of peril his countrymen rose to the supreme daring of the occasion. What he fears is that the relaxation of that intense moral strain may mean that national life may lose its saving salt of lofty purpose, and sink into carnal contentment and repose. "Getting and spending we lay waste our powers" is the thought that frequently recurs in his later poems. He fears the enervation of prosperity more than the buffeting of adversity. When nations are surfeited with victory and peace, they are too apt to lose the Spartan temper of austere devotion to their country which made them great in warlike days. And why Wordsworth so often recurs to this thought, is that his pride in his country has no bounds. For the nation which has saved the liberties of Europe to fall into inglorious self-indulgence would be the last calamity in the possible tragedy of nations. It is in the hour when such fears beset him, that he appeals to "Sidney, Marvel, Harrington," who

> Knew how genuine glory is put on,
> Taught us how rightfully a nation shone
> In splendour, what strength was that would not bend
> But in magnanimous meekness.

It is then also he thinks of Milton, whose "soul was as a star and dwelt apart," and invokes that mighty shade which haunts the Puritan past of England—

> We are selfish men;
> O raise us up, return to us again.
> And give us manners, virtue, freedom, power.

And it is when the memory of that heroic past of England is most vivid to his mind that he touches his highest note of dignified and haughty pride, and scorns the thought

> That this most famous stream in bogs and sands
> Should perish! and to evil and to good
> Be lost forever. In our halls is hung
>   Armoury of the invincible knights of old;
> We must be free or die, who speak the tongue
>   That Shakespeare spake: the faith and morals hold
> Which Milton held. In everything we are sprung
>   Of earth's first blood; have titles manifold.

The patriotism of Wordsworth is not violent or frenzied; it is comparatively restrained; but, for that very reason, in the moments of its highest utterance there is a depth and force in it such as few writers display. When habitually calm men break the barriers of reserve, there is something strangely impressive in their passion. There is nothing more impressive in Wordsworth, as indicative of the strength of his emotions, than these occasional bursts of exalted patriotism, and their force is heightened by the contrast they furnish to his habitual serenity of temper.

There is one poem of Wordsworth's which stands out in particular prominence as the greatest of all his poems which express the spirit of patriotism: that is the *Happy Warrior*. This poem was written in the year 1806, and was inspired by the death of Nelson. It was in the autumn of the previous year that Nelson had fallen on the deck of the *Victory*, and the shock of sorrow and consternation which passed over England has never been equalled by any similar public calamity. Certainly the death of no individual has ever called forth so spontaneous and general a lamentation. Nelson was to the England of his day the very incarnation of manly courage and heroic virtue. The fascination of his name affected every class of society. He seemed to sum up in himself that reverence for duty which is so characteristic a feature of the English race. Between Nelson and Wordsworth there could be little in common, save this bond of ardent patriotism, but that was sufficient to call forth from Wordsworth one of his finest poems. Just as we can specify certain poems which constitute the high-water mark of Wordsworth's genius in philosophic or lyric poetry, so we can confidently take this poem as his maturest word in patriotic poetry. It breathes the very spirit of consecrated heroism. Some points of the poem were suggested by a more private sorrow—the loss at sea of his brother John; but it was out of the larger emotion occasioned by the death of Nelson that the poem originated. It is the idealized Nelson who stands before us in these verses:

> But who, if he be called upon to face
> Some awful moment, to which Heaven has joined
> Great issues, good or bad for human kind,
> Is happy as a Lover, and attired
> With sudden brightness, like a Man inspired:
> And, through the heat of conflict, keeps the law
> In calmness made, and sees what he foresaw;
> Or if an unexpected call succeed.
> Come when it will, is equal to the need.
> He who, though thus endued as with a sense
> And faculty for storm and turbulence,
> Is yet a Soul whose master-bias leans
> To homefelt pleasures, and to gentler scenes.
> This is the Happy Warrior, this is He
> That every man in arms should wish to be.

When we read these words we are reminded of a passage in the *Recluse*, in which Wordsworth tells us he could never read of two great war-ships grappling without a thrill of emulation, more ardent than wise men should know. It is a passage which throws a new light upon the nature of Wordsworth. If he was serene, it was not because he was lethargic; if he urged the blessedness of regulated passions, it was not because his own heart was cold: he, too, had a passionate nature and heroic fibre in him, and that courageous and soldierly temper is fitly vindicated and expressed in the lofty spirit of his patriotic poems.

—W.J. Dawson, "Patriotic and Political Poems,"
from *The Makers of English Poetry*, H. Revell
Company, 1908, pp. 136–145

THE RIVER DUDDON SONNETS

Unsigned (1820)

Writing shortly after the publication of Wordsworth's sonnets on the Duddon River, the author of the following excerpt provides a generally favorable review, commending the series for celebrating the "picturesque beauty" of the Duddon in a lofty and noble manner. The issue of seriousness is essential to this critic, for much of his praise of the Duddon sonnets is based on a comparison to two previously completed works, *Peter Bell* and "The Waggoner," both of which he finds ridiculous in subject matter and highly objectionable. Wordsworth is here praised for his outstanding portrait of Reverend Robert Walker, the curate of Seathwaite, a devoted and self-sacrificing parish priest much loved by his parishioners. Most importantly for this critic, however, is the fact that Wordsworth's sonnets are written in blank verse, a style that he believes the poet excels in, for it removes all possibilities of the ludicrous versification that mars his lyrical poetry. "It is remarkable," the anonymous reviewer asserts, "that both his prose and his blank verse are in general quite free from the puerilities and vulgarities which disfigure many of his lyrical pieces."

This publication is designed to form, together with "The Thanksgiving Ode," "The Tale of Peter Bell," and "The Waggoner," the third and last volume of the Author's *Miscellaneous Poems*. Mr. Wordsworth appears to be satisfied that he has written enough; quite enough, at least, for the illustration of his theory, which if the Public do not by this time understand or appreciate, it is not his fault: with this volume, therefore, the indignant Author closes his metrical labours. But a poet has lived too long, who has written quite enough. Measured by this rule, Mr. Wordsworth's literary existence has long touched

upon superannuation: the Author of the *Excursion* is almost forgotten in
the Author of Peter Bell, and the Poet's warmest admirers are beginning to
he ashamed of standing out for the genius of a man who, whether in the
wantonness of self-conceit, or from infirmity of judgement, could, in an age
of brilliant competition like the present, deem such productions as those
worthy of the Press. It is evident that Mr. Wordsworth has felt the universal
ridicule which they brought upon him, from the manner in which he calls
upon his friend Peter, in the following sonnet, not to mind the naughty critics.
It is entitled, a 'Sonnet on the detraction which followed the publication of a
certain poem.' 'See *Milton's Sonnet*,' it is added, 'beginning "A Book was writ
of late called Tetrachordon."' We shall see into that matter presently.

'A Book came forth of late called, "Peter Bell;"
Not negligent the style;—the matter? good
As aught that song records of Robin Hood,
Or Roy, renowned through many a Scottish dell;
But some (who brook these hacknied themes full well,
Nor heat, at Tam o' Shanter's name, their blood)
Wax'd wroth, and with foul claws, a harpy brood—
On Bard and Hero clamorously fell.
Heed not, wild Rover once through heath and glen
Who mad'st at length the better life thy choice,
Heed not such onset! nay, if praise of men
To thee appear not an unmeaning voice,
Lift up that grey-haired forehead, and rejoice
In the just tribute of thy Poet's pen!'

Mr. Wordsworth has very frequently puzzled us before now by the
equivocal character of his lighter productions: his gravity is often so
facetious, and his humour is often so grave, that we have been at a loss to
know whether to take him as in jest or in earnest. This is the case with the
above lines. We should certainly have supposed from the reference to Milton's
burlesque sonnet, that Mr. Wordsworth meant on this occasion to be jocose.
But on looking the Poet steadfastly in the face while addressing his friend
Peter in the latter half of the sonnet, we could not discern the least relaxation
of feature that betrayed a latent smile, and were compelled to conclude that
he was in very sober earnest. Now, if we are right, it seems unaccountable
why the reader should be referred to Milton's sonnet at all, unless Mr.
Wordsworth, in whom we have frequently observed a sort of half-concealed
fidgetty ambition to be taken for a cousin-german of the great patriot-bard,
has really, in the simplicity of his mind, mistaken the character of that *jeu*

d'esprit. Some persons had, it seems, laughed at the Greek title of Milton's treatise, just as the public were diverted at the title of Peter Bell. Thus far the parallel holds. But we do not learn that the public laughed at Milton's book, and he could not, therefore, have been seriously hurt at the jokes passed upon 'a word on the titlepage.' It afforded him however, as he thought, a good occasion for turning the joke upon his polemical assailants, on the ground of the far more uncouth and cacophonous combination of vocables of which their names were composed. 'Gordon' is evidently brought in to supply the rhyme; but 'Colkitto, Macdonnel, or Galasp,' those rugged names 'that would have made Quintilian stare and gasp,' were at that period not yet familiarized to Southern ears; and Milton, who hated every thing Scotch, and had an exquisite ear, was no doubt unaffectedly diverted at these barbarous appellatives. And then in the close of the sonnet he has a good fling at his opponents for their dislike of Greek, which was the only sin of his title.

'Thy age, like ours, O Soul of Sir John Cheek,
Hated not learning worse than toad or asp,
When thou taught'st Cambridge, and King Edward, Greek.'

But to descend to Mr. Wordsworth. In our notice of his Peter Bell, we had occasion to remark, that his title confirmed us in the suspicion that, as he is himself devoid of any talent for humour, so he is, through a singular simplicity of mind, insusceptible of the ludicrous. Were not this the case, he would scarcely have trusted his name and that of his friend Peter, so near that of Milton, in the present instance; nor would he have blundered in his serious imitation of a burlesque poem; nor would he have called upon Peter Bell, at least in the hearing of the public, to lift up his grey-haired forehead, and rejoice in having such a poet as our Author's eccentric self, to write about him; nor, lastly, would he have been now at any loss to know why the formal annunciation of a poem with such a title, and coming from Mr. Wordsworth, should have excited more merriment than the title of the thrilling and matchless "Tam o' Shanter" of a poet who *could not* be ridiculous.

We take it, however, as a good sign, that Mr. Wordsworth has been made sensible of the fact, that the public do not wish for any more Peter Bells. How depraved soever their taste, how unjust soever their ridicule, the thing will not do again. And he seems determined to please the lovers of euphony this time by at least half of his titlepage, by the melodious names of Vaudracour and Julia. 'The River Duddon' stands boldly forward, indeed, in defiance of all ludicrous associations; but it has had this name given it, and cannot help itself. We question whether Mr. W. does not think it the most sweetly sounding title of the two.

The contents of the volume are very miscellaneous. A third part is occupied with the topographical description of the Lake country; and it forms by no means the least valuable portion. The Notes to the Sonnets contain a prose memoir of the Rev. Robert Walker, curate of Seathwaite, the abstract of whose character is given in "The Excursion." He appears to have been a man of very singularly primitive character, and incomparably more deserving of poetical honours, than most of our Author's Lakers. The reader must excuse us, if we suffer Mr. Wordsworth's prose for once to detain us from his poetry.

The subject of the memoir was born at Under Crag in Seathwaite, in 1709. He was the youngest of twelve children, born of obscure parents, who seeing him to be a sickly child, not likely to earn a livelihood by bodily labour, deemed it best to breed 'him a scholar.' He was accordingly duly initiated into the mysteries of reading, writing, and arithmetic, by the parish schoolmaster; and made sufficient progress to be qualified while yet a lad, to take upon himself the didascalic functions at Loweswater. By the assistance of 'a gentleman of the neighbourhood,' however, he managed to acquire in his leisure hours, a knowledge of the classics, and he now aspired to holy orders. The choice of two curacies was offered to him upon his ordination: the value of each was the same, viz. *five pounds per annum*; 'but the cure of Seathwaite having a cottage attached to it, *as he wished to marry*, he chose it in preference.' He got, as he expresses it, 'to the value of 40*l* for his wife's fortune,' the savings of her wages; and with this the worthy couple began housekeeping. The following letter describes his situation nineteen years after his entering upon his curacy.

> 'To Mr.——
> 'Sir, *Coniston*, July 26, 1754.
> 'I was the other day upon a party of pleasure, about five or six miles from this place, where I met with a very striking object, and of a nature not very common. Going into a clergyman's house (of whom I had frequently heard) I found him sitting at the head of a long square table, such as is commonly used in this country by the lower class of people, dressed in a coarse blue frock, trimmed with black horn buttons; a checked shirt, a leathern strap about his neck for a stock, a coarse apron, a pair of great wooden-soled shoes, plated with iron to preserve them, (what we call clogs in these parts,) with a child upon his knee eating his breakfast: his wife, and the remainder of his children, were some of them employed in waiting on each other, the rest in teazing and spinning wool, at which trade he is a great proficient; and moreover, when it is made

ready for sale, will lay it by sixteen or thirty-two pounds weight upon his back, and on foot, seven or eight miles will carry it to the market, even in the depth of winter. I was not much surprised at all this, as you may possibly be, having heard a great deal of it related before. But I must confess myself astonished with the alacrity and the good humour that appeared both in the clergyman and his wife, and more so, at the sense and ingenuity of the clergyman himself.'

Another letter, dated the following year, represents him as 'keeping the wolf from the door by frugality and good management,' without any desire after further preferment.

'He is settled among the people that are happy among themselves: and lives in the greatest unanimity and friendship with them, and, I believe, the minister and people are exceedingly satisfied with each other; and indeed how should they be dissatisfied, when they have a person of so much worth and probity for their pastor? A man who, for his candour and meekness, his sober, chaste, and virtuous conversation, his soundness in principle and practice, is an ornament to his profession, and an honour to the country he is in; and bear with me if I say, the plainness of his dress, the sanctity of his manners, the simplicity of his doctrine, and the vehemence of his expression, have a sort of resemblance to the pure practice of primitive Christianity.'

In a letter from Mr. Walker himself, it is stated that the annual income of his chapel was at this time, as near as he could compute it, about 17*l*. 10*s*. And yet, when the Bishop of the diocese recommended the joining to the curacy of Seathwaite the contiguous one of Ulpha, it was a sufficient reason for his declining the offer, that 'it might be disagreeable to his auditory at Seathwaite,' and that the inhabitants of Ulpha despaired of being able to support a schoolmaster who should not be curate there also. In a second letter to the Bishop, be writes thus:

'My Lord,
'I have the favour of yours of the 1st. instant, and am exceedingly obliged on account of the Ulpha affair: if that curacy should lapse into your Lordship's hands, I would beg leave rather to decline than embrace it; for the chapels of Seathwaite and Ulpha annexed together, would be apt to cause a general discontent among the inhabitants of both places; by either thinking themselves slighted,

being only served alternately, or neglected in the duty, *or attributing it to covetousness in me*; all which occasions of murmuring I would willingly avoid.'

The stipend attached to the curacy was subsequently augmented, but Mr. Walker's income was still extremely scanty. Nevertheless, 'the frequent offer of much better benefices, could not tempt him to quit a situation where he had been so long happy, with a consciousness of being useful.' It appears that he met with some liberal benefactors, or such as he deemed liberal, by whose assistance he was enabled to rear a numerous family, and, strange to say, to support one of his sons for some time as a student at Dublin college. The same man who was thus liberal in the education of his family, 'was even munificent,' it is added, 'in hospitality as a parish priest.'

> 'Every Sunday, were served upon the long table at which he has been described sitting with a child upon his knee, messes of broth for the refreshment of those of his congregation who came from a distance, and usually took their seats as parts of his own household. It seems scarcely possible that this custom could have commenced before the augmentation of his cure; and, what would to many have been a high price of self-denial, was paid by the pastor and his family, for this gratification; as the treat could only be provided by dressing at one time the whole, perhaps, of their weekly allowance of fresh animal food; consequently, for a succession of days, the table was covered with cold victuals only.'

The following explanatory details are requisite to shew by what means such a man as this could at his decease leave behind him no less a sum than 2000*l*.

> 'To begin with his industry; eight hours in each day, during five days in the week, and half of Saturday, except when the labours of husbandry were urgent, he was occupied in teaching. His seat was within the rails of the altar; the communion-table was his desk; and, like Shenstone's school-mistress, the master employed himself at the spinning-wheel, while the children were repeating their lessons by his side. Every evening, after school hours, if not more profitably engaged, he continued the same kind of labour, exchanging for the benefit of exercise, the small wheel at which he had sate, for the large one on which wool is spun, the spinner stepping to and fro.—Thus, was the wheel constantly in readiness to prevent the waste of a moment's time. Nor was his industry with

the pen, when occasion called for it, less eager. Entrusted with extensive management of public and private affairs, he acted in his rustic neighbourhood as scrivener, writing out petitions, deeds of conveyance, wills, covenants, &c. with pecuniary gain to himself, and to the great benefit of his employers. These labours (at all times considerable) at one period of the year, viz. between Christmas and Candlemas, when money transactions are settled in this country, were often so intense, that he passed great part of the night, and sometimes whole nights, at his desk. His garden also was tilled by his own hand; he had a right of pasturage upon the mountains for a few sheep and a couple of cows, which required his attendance; with this pastoral occupation, he joined the labours of husbandry upon a small scale, renting two or three acres in addition to his own less than one acre of glebe; and the humblest drudgery which the cultivation of these fields required was performed by himself.

'He also assisted his neighbours in hay-making and shearing their flocks, and in the performance of this latter service he was eminently dexterous. They, in their turn, complimented him with a present of a hay-cock, or a fleece; less as a recompence for this particular service than as a general acknowledgment. The Sabbath was in a strict sense kept holy; the Sunday evenings being devoted to reading the Scripture and family prayer. The principal festivals appointed by the Church were also duly observed; but through every other day in the week, through every week in the year, he was incessantly occupied in work of hand or mind; not allowing a moment for recreation, except upon a Saturday afternoon, when he indulged himself with a Newspaper, or sometimes with a Magazine. The frugality and temperance established in his house, were as admirable as the industry. Nothing to which the name of luxury could be given was there known; in the latter part of his life, indeed, when tea had been brought into almost general use, it was provided for visitors, and for such of his own family as returned occasionally to his roof, and had been accustomed to this refreshment elsewhere; but neither he nor his wife ever partook of it. The raiment worn by his family was comely and decent, but as simple as their diet; the home spun materials were made up into apparel by their own hands. At the time of the decease of this thrifty pair, their cottage contained a large store of webs of woollen and linen cloth, woven from thread of their own spinning. And it is remarkable, that the pew in the chapel in which the family used to sit, remained a few years ago neatly lined with woollen cloth spun by the pastor's own hands. It is the only pew in the chapel so distinguished; and I know of no other instance of his conformity to the delicate accommodations of modern times. The fuel of the house, like that of their neighbours, consisted of peat, procured from the mosses by their own labour. The lights by which in the winter evenings their work was performed, were of their own manufacture, such as still continue to be used in these cottages; they are made of the pith of rushes dipped in any unctuous substance that the house affords. *White* candles, as tallow candles are here called, were reserved to honour the Christmas festivals, and were perhaps produced upon no other occasions. Once a month, during the proper season, a sheep was drawn from their small mountain flock, and killed for the use of the family, and a cow, towards the close of the year, was salted and dried, for winter provision; the hide was tanned to furnish them with shoes.—By these various resources, this venerable clergyman reared a numerous family, not only preserving them, as he affectingly says, "from wanting the necessaries of life;" but afforded them an unstinted education, and the means of raising themselves in society.

'It might have been concluded that no one could thus, as it were, have converted his body into a machine of industry for the humblest uses, and kept his thoughts so frequently bent upon secular concerns, without grievous injury to the more precious parts of his nature. How could the powers of intellect thrive, or its graces be displayed, in the midst of circumstances apparently so unfavourable, and where, to the direct cultivation of the mind, so small a portion of time was allotted! But, in this extraordinary man, things in their nature adverse were reconciled; his conversation was remarkable, not only for being chaste and pure, but for the degree in which it was fervent and eloquent; his written style was correct, simple, and animated. Nor did his *affections* suffer more than his intellect; he was tenderly alive to all the duties of his pastoral office—the poor and needy "he never sent empty away,"— the stranger was fed and refreshed in passing that unfrequented vale,—the sick were visited; and the feelings of humanity found further exercise among the distresses and embarrassments in the worldly estate of his neighbours, with which his talents for business made him acquainted; and the disinterestedness, impartiality, and uprightness which he maintained in the management of all affairs confided to him, were virtues seldom separated in his own conscience from religious obligations.'

'The afternoon service in the chapel was less numerously attended than that of the morning, but by a more serious auditory: the lesson from the New Testament on those occasions was accompanied by Birkett's Commentaries. These lessons he read with impassioned emphasis, frequently drawing tears from his hearers, and leaving a lasting impression upon their minds. His devotional feelings and the powers of his own mind were further exercised, along with those of his family, in perusing the Scriptures: not only on the Sunday evenings, but on every other evening, while the rest of the household were at work, some one of the children, and in her turn the servant, for the sake of practice in reading, or for instruction, read the Bible aloud; and in this manner the whole was repeatedly gone through.'

To complete the sketch of this admirable person, we need but give the following anecdote. His wife died a few months before him, after they had been married to each other above sixty years. They were both in the ninety third year of their age. He ordered that her body should be borne to the grave by three of her daughters and one grand daughter. 'And when the corpse was lifted from the threshold, he insisted upon lending his aid, and feeling about, for he was then almost blind, took hold of a napkin fixed to the coffin; and, as a bearer of the body, entered the Chapel, a few steps from the lowly Parsonage.' Such was the sense of his various excellencies prevalent in the country, that the epithet of *Wonderful* is to this day attached to his name.

We really feel indebted to Mr. Wordsworth for having presented us with the full-length portrait of a man of such sterling and almost obsolete excellence. It shall cancel us half the defects of his poetry. And poetry after all, be it of the best quality, is exceedingly less affecting than such a simple record of unvarnished realities. The Sonnet on Seathwaite Chapel, we thought passably good, till we had read the Note which is given in illustration of it; and then we found it miserably inadequate to the theme. And this tempts us to suspect that Mr. Wordsworth is not so much to blame, after all, for the choice of many of his subjects, as for writing ballads and lyrical pieces about them, instead of throwing them into the form of honest prose. In some of his narrative poems, however, where he has adopted a free blank verse, which is the species of poetry by far the best suited to his habits of thinking and style of composition, he has risen to a very unusual height of excellence. *The Excursion*, with all its faults, assuredly contains some of the most exquisite

blank verse in the language. It is remarkable, that both his prose and his
blank verse are in general quite free from the puerilities and vulgarities
which disfigure many of his lyrical pieces. The diction of the former, as
well as that of his sonnets, is frequently, in direct opposition to his theory,
extremely elevated and richly figurative; sometimes to an excess bordering
upon affectation. The River Duddon flows through a series of thirty-three
sonnets which are for the most part of no ordinary beauty. Here and there, a
little metaphysical mud, or a *Lakish* tincture, mingles with the stream, and it
occasionally runs somewhat shallow; but the general character of the series is
that of very noble descriptive poetry. They are the growth of many years: the
following, which stands the fourteenth, was the first produced; others being
added upon occasional visits to the Stream, or as recollections of the scenes
upon its banks awakened a wish to describe them.

> 'O Mountain Stream! the Shepherd and his cot
> Are privileged inmates of deep solitude;
> Nor would the nicest anchorite exclude
> A field or two of brighter green, or plot
> Of tillage ground, that seemeth like a spot
> Of stationary sunshine:—thou hast view'd
> These only, Duddon! with their paths renew'd
> By fits and starts, yet this contents thee not.
> Thee hath some awful Spirit impelled to leave,
> Utterly to desert, the haunts of men.
> Though simple thy companions were and few;
> And through this wilderness a passage cleave
> Attended but by thy own voice, save when
> The Clouds and Fowls of the air thy way pursue!'

In thus breathing a lonely sentiment into the material elements of
picturesque beauty, no living poet has shewn greater skill and fancy than Mr.
Wordsworth. The next we shall select, is, it is true, no more than a sonnet;
but pages of description are compressed within the compass of fourteen lines,
and hours of feeling are concentered in the spirit which animates them.

> 'Child of the clouds! remote from every taint
> Of sordid industry thy lot is cast;
> Thine are the honors of the lofty waste;
> Not seldom, when with heat the valleys faint,
> Thy handmaid Frost with spangled tissue quaint
> Thy cradle decks;—to chaunt thy birth, thou hast

No meaner Poet than the whistling blast.
And Desolation is thy patron-saint!
She guards thee, ruthless Power! who would not spare
Those mighty forests, once the bison's screen,
Where stalk'd the huge deer to his shaggy lair
Through paths and alleys roofed with sombre green,
Thousand of years before the silent air
Was pierced by whizzing shaft of hunter keen!'

The following is in a different strain: it is entitled 'The Faery Chasm,' and is singularly elegant.

'No fiction was it of the antique age:
A sky-blue stone, within this sunless cleft,
Is of the very foot-marks unbereft
Which tiny Elves impress'd; on that smooth stage
Dancing with all their brilliant equipage
In secret revels—haply after theft
Of some sweet babe, flower stolen, and coarse weed left,
For the distracted mother to assuage
Her grief with, as she might!—But where, oh where
Is traceable a vestige of the notes
That ruled those dances, wild in character?
—Deep underground?—Or in the upper air,
On the shrill wind of midnight? or where floats
O'er twilight fields the autumn gossamer?'

   In the twenty first sonnet of the series, there occurs a strange catachresis, if we may not rattier term it metaphor run mad. Memory is described as breaking forth 'from her unworthy seat, the cloudy stall of Time;' the precise import of which expressions we do not quite enter into. And then to the Poet's eye, this metaphysical abstraction is embodied in a palpable form—'Her glistening tresses bound:' this would seem bold enough; yet the Author might think himself justified in venturing thus far by the exquisite line of Collins,

'And Hope enchanted smiled, and waved her golden hair.'

But Mr. Wordsworth wants just that one thing which Collins possessed in perfection—taste. The Author of the Ode on the Passions knew by instinct the precise boundary line between the sublime and the extravagant, between figure and nonsense. He never for a moment loses himself amid his own imagery, or confounds the figurative with the physical. But Mr. Wordsworth goes on to define the appearance of the glistening tresses of Memory, and to compare them to 'golden locks of birch;' and then forgetting altogether, as it should seem, the imaginary being he has conjured up, his mind fastens upon the new idea, one that relates to a simple object of perception:—

—'golden locks of birch that rise and fall
On gales that breathe too gently to recal
Aught of the fading year's inclemency.'

If these last lines have any intelligible connexion with the idea of Memory as introduced in the foregoing part of the stanza, we confess that it eludes our dull apprehensions.

Vaudracour and Julia is a tale in blank verse, which was originally intended, we presume, to form an episode in some future portion of "The Excursion." The incidents are stated to be facts, no invention having as to them been exercised. It is a touching and melancholy tale of unfortunate love, and told in Mr. Wordsworth's happiest manner. From the lyrical pieces which follow it in order, we cannot do otherwise than select the very beautiful stanza entitled

'LAMENT OF MARY QUEEN OF SCOTS,
ON THE EVE OF A NEW YEAR.
'"Smile of the Moon!—for so I name
That silent greeting from above;
A gentle flash of light that came
From Her whom drooping Captives love;
Or art them of still higher birth?
Thou that didst part the clouds of earth,
My torpor to reprove!

'"Bright boon of pitying Heaven—alas,
I may not trust thy placid cheer!
Pondering that Time to-night will pass
The threshold of another year;
For years to me are sad and dull;
My very moments are too full
Of hopelessness and fear.

'"—And yet the soul-awakening gleam,
That struck perchance the farthest cone
Of Scotland's rocky wilds, did seem
To visit me and me alone;
Me, unapproach'd by any friend,

Save those who to my sorrows lend
Tears due unto their own.

'"To-night, the church-tower bells shall ring,
Through these wide realms, a festive peal;
To the new year a welcoming;
A tuneful offering for the weal
Of happy millions lulled in sleep;
While I am forced to watch and weep,
By wounds that may not heal.

'"Born all too high, by wedlock raised
Still higher—to be cast thus low!
Would that mine eyes had never gaz'd
On aught of more ambitious show
Than the sweet flow'rets of the fields!
—It is my royal state that yields
This bitterness of woe.

'"Yet how?—for I, if there be truth
In the world's voice, was passing fair;
And beauty, for confiding youth,
Those shocks of passion can prepare
That kill the bloom before its time,
And blanch, without the Owner's crime,
The most resplendent hair.

'"Unblest distinctions! showered on me
To bind a lingering life in chains;
All that could quit my grasp or flee,
Is gone;—but not the subtle stains
Fixed in the spirit; for even here
Can I be proud that jealous fear
Of what I was remains.

'"A woman rules my prison's key;
A sister Queen, against the bent
Of law and holiest sympathy,
Detains me—doubtful of the event;
Great God, who feel'st for my distress,
My thoughts are all that I possess,
O keep them innocent!

'"Farewell for ever human aid,
Which abject mortals vainly court!
By friends deceived, by foes betrayed,
Of fears the prey, of hopes the sport,
Nought but the world-redeeming Cross
Is able to supply my loss,
My burthen to support.

'"Hark! the death-note of the year,
Sounded by the castle-clock!—
From her sunk eyes a stagnant tear
Stole forth, unsettled by the shock;
But oft the woods renewed their green,
Ere the tir'd head of Scotland's Queen
Repos'd upon the block!'

The odes are the least pleasing compositions in the volume, being for
the most part very affected and very enigmatical. There are, however, some
exceptions. The one bearing date September, 1816, merits transcription as a
varied specimen of the contents of the volume.

'The sylvan slopes with corn-clad fields
Are hung, as if with golden shields,
Bright trophies of the sun!
Like a fair sister of the sky,
Unruffled doth the blue Lake lie,
The Mountains looking on.

'And, sooth to say, yon vocal Grove
Albeit uninspired by love,
By love untaught to ring,
May well afford to mortal ear,
An impulse more profoundly dear
Than music of the Spring.
'For *that* from turbulence and heat
Proceeds, from some uneasy seat
In Nature's struggling frame,
Some region of impatient life;
And jealousy, and quivering strife,
Therein a portion claim.

'This, this is holy:—while I hear
These vespers of another year,

This hymn of thanks and praise,
My spirit seems to mount above
The anxieties of human love,
And earth's precarious days.

'But list!—though winter storms be nigh,
Unchecked is that soft harmony:
There lives Who can provide
For all his creatures; and in Him,
Even like the radiant Seraphim,
These Choristers confide.'

There is among the Inscriptions also, a short piece written in a style with which we have not been accustomed to meet in our Author's productions.

'Not seldom, clad in radiant vest,
Deceitfully goes forth the Morn;
Not seldom Evening in the west
Sinks smilingly forsworn.

'The smoothest seas will sometimes prove,
To the confiding bark, untrue;
And, if she trust the stars above,
They can be treacherous too.

'The umbrageous Oak, in pomp outspread,
Full oft, when storms the welkin rend.
Draws lightning down upon the head
It promis'd to defend.

'But Thou art true, incarnate Lord!
Who didst vouchsafe for man to die;
Thy smile is sure, thy plighted word
No change can falsify!

'I bent before thy gracious throne,
And asked for peace with suppliant knee;
And peace was given,—nor peace alone,
But faith, and hope, and extacy!'

We can make room for only two more specimens: they are in themselves sufficient to justify all the praise that has been bestowed on Mr. Wordsworth's sonnets.

'SONNET.

'The Stars are mansions built by Nature's hand;
And, haply, there the spirits of the blest
Live, clothed in radiance, their immortal vest;
Huge Ocean frames, within his yellow strand,
A habitation marvellously planned,
For life to occupy in lore and rest;
All that we see—is dome, or vault, or nest,
Or fort, erected at her sage command.
Is this a vernal thought? Even so, the Spring
Gave it while cares were weighing on my heart,
Mid song of birds and insects murmuring;
And while the youthful year's prolific art—
Of bud, leaf, blade and flower—was fashioning
Abodes, where self-disturbance hath no part.'

The other sonnet is on the death of his late Majesty.

'Ward of the Law!—dread Shadow of a King!
Whose realm had dwindled to one stately room;
Whose universe was gloom immers'd in gloom,
Darkness as thick as life o'er life could fling,
Yet haply cheered with some faint glimmering
Of Faith and Hope; if thou by nature's doom
Gently hast sunk into the quiet tomb,
Why should we bend in grief, to sorrow cling,
When thankfulness were best?—Fresh-flowing tears,
Or, where tears flow not, sigh succeeding sigh,
Yield to such after-thought the sole reply
Which justly it can claim. The Nation hears
In this deep knell—silent for threescore years,
An unexampled voice of awful memory!'

"The Prioress's Tale" from Chaucer, is a very ill-chosen subject for the experiment of exhibiting the Father of English Poetry in a modern form. The legend is so exquisitely absurd, that it must have been designed as a burlesque on the lying martyrological wonders of the Romish priesthood. It is that of a poor innocent child who had his throat cut by some wicked Jews, because he was too fond of singing Ave Maria, but who continued, by aid of the blessed Virgin, to reiterate the same articulate sounds which he had been wont to utter while living, till his corpse was found, and then, was able to give information against his murderers; but the spirit could not obtain its discharge till a grain was taken off of his tongue which the Virgin had placed there. When Chaucer wrote, such fables were not too gross for the vulgar credulity; but we know not for what purpose they are transplanted into modern poetry. To Mr. Wordsworth, indeed, we can conceive that such tales would recommend themselves by their very puerility; that he would be even melted into tears by the affected solemnity of a sly old humorist like Chaucer; and that what was meant by him for satire, might be mistaken by our Author for pathos.

We deem it quite unnecessary to repeat that our respect for Mr. Wordsworth's talents remains unaltered. The copious extracts we have given from the present volume, sufficiently evince that those talents are of a very high order. But we have so fully expressed our opinion on this point, in our reviews of the *Excursion*,[1] and of "The White Doe of Rylstone,"[2] as well as subsequently in noticing the unfortunate pair, Peter Bell and Benjamin the Waggoner,[3] that we will not run the hazard of wearying our readers by saying more upon the subject. It is certain, that while he has been as a poet ridiculously, because indiscriminately and immeasurably lauded on the one hand, he has been very ignorantly and flippantly depreciated on the other. For the latter circumstance, however, he may thank chiefly himself, and, next to himself, his friends, who have taught him to despise the warning voice of public opinion, which, however wayward and arbitrary in its first decisions, is sure to be mainly just at last. Had his judgement but been as correct as his imagination is powerful, had the purity of his taste been equal to the simplicity of his feelings, had his understanding been as sound as his heart, we hope, is warm—though we have a deeply rooted distrust of all sentimentalists and *sensationists* in this respect,—the critic's task would have been far more easy, and, to our feelings, far more pleasant. We should not then have been disposed to acquiesce in thinking that he had written enough; too much, indeed, for his permanent reputation, unless he adopts our suggestion, namely, to entrust to some competent friend the reducing of his writings, by a rigid selection, to the due compass of 'Sybilline leaves,' and to make a bonfire of the refuse—his potters, waggoners, and idiots, on the top of Skiddaw. The present volume ought, however, to do him at least this service with the public; it should be accepted as an ample atonement for his last offence, for there is a weight of sterling good poetry in it far more than adequate to turn the scale in his favour. From this time forth, therefore, it ought to be held a breach of courtesy and kindness, to say one word more of Benjamin the Waggoner or of Peter Bell.

Notes

1. E. R. N. S. Vol. III.
2. Ibid. Vol. V.
3. Ibid. Vol. XII.

—UNSIGNED, review of *The River Duddon*
volume, *Eclectic Review,* August 1820,
pp. 170–179, 183–184

THE ECCLESIASTICAL SONNETS

ABBIE FINDLAY POTTS "INTRODUCTION" (1922)

In her introduction to the *Ecclesiastical Sonnets*, Abbie Findlay Potts attempts to counter those critics who censured Wordsworth for abandoning the high ideals he expressed in the early 1790s and then criticized his work as exhibiting an attenuation of his former poetic intensity when turning to conventional themes. "In the minds of these critics," she writes, "meek doctrines have indeed blighted the transports of the bard, and withered his heroic strains." Instead, Potts maintains that there is no political or social "rupture" to be found in the late poetry and, furthermore, that in the *Ecclesiastical Sonnets*, a work published when Wordsworth was fifty-one years old, he remained consistently true to his humane and democratic beliefs. Though Wordsworth was interested in presenting in the sonnets the history of the Church of England in poetic form rather than the salutary teachings and blessings of external nature and humble people, Potts contends that he nevertheless retained a unity of purpose from his earlier days as shown in an abiding devotion to nature and his fellow humans through the medium of "a loftier theme, the spiritual history of a people." As further support of Wordsworth's unity of purpose, Potts provides commentary from Wordsworth's prose writings that demonstrate his awareness of the criticism being leveled against him and an acknowledgment that this thematic shift marked a belief that justice could only be achieved in a society aware of its history and optimistic of its future.

With respect to the evolution of this project, Potts points out that Wordsworth had always exhibited an interest in monastic ruins from his earliest travels with Dorothy. She also notes the images of church architecture garnered during a tour of continental Europe in 1820 as well as his earlier writings, such as the third essay on epitaphs and his descriptions of the English lake country. Turning to issues of literary influence, Potts stresses the importance of Scripture as well as the works of Milton, Spenser, Shakespeare, and sublime passages of the classical writers. More particularly with regard to the English sonneteers, Potts points out that Wordsworth broke new ground in English poetry by presenting a sonnet cycle that articulated a scheme of events and chose a genre typically associated with love and amorous pursuits as a vehicle for conveying ecclesiastical history instead. Finally, to further buttress the belief that Wordsworth remained inventive and experimental throughout his career, as evidenced in his prose writings, Potts quotes from these pieces to underscore Wordsworth's belief that the *Ecclesiastical Sonnets* are to be understood as an organic whole, a series of intrinsically linked poems that record the vast history of the Church of England.

⸻ ⸻ ⸻

I

The *Ecclesiastical Sonnets*, written when Wordsworth was fifty-one years old, should reveal him as a profound thinker and a powerful artist. During his career he had with more and more success labored for the perfect union of love and reason, those mutual factors in both life and art. *Laodamia* notably achieves this union in art; and the words of Protesilaus to Laodamia indicate the cost of the union in life as well: transports shall be moderated, mourning shall be meek; lofty thought embodied in act has wrought deliverance; reason and self-government are to control rebellious passion, and thus affections will be raised and solemnized.[1] But these words are the very message of the *Ecclesiastical Sonnets*, and in this very temper Wordsworth receives upon his affections the burden of institutional reason and traditional government. Has he profited by his own counsel? Is his art delivered by his lofty thought? Although in the third sonnet of the series he writes of Druid and Christianity, he might ask the question about himself, too:

> Haughty the Bard: can these meek doctrines blight
> His transports? wither his heroic strains?

Some there are, however, who feel that Wordsworth's history of the Church of England, his poetical record of a nation's love and reason, of its lofty thought embodied in act, is not a successful or characteristic poem. To many he remains chiefly the bard of external nature and of the sensations, moods, and feelings celebrated in the poem on the Wye. Even trained readers have marked those passages of his life and art which indicate that he is an ecstatic poet, an oracle rather than a builder. The first half of his life has been the more thoroughly studied by himself in *The Prelude*; by his sister in her *Journals*; by Coleridge in his critical notes; and in the recent interpretation of

Professors Legouis and Harper, to both of whom his earlier poetry is more congenial. And hence Harper's conclusion that Wordsworth's life was 'broken in the middle,'[2] and Minto's belief that 'after 1807 there is a marked falling off in the quality, though not in the quantity, of Wordsworth's poetic work,'[3] may arise somewhat from the general lack of scholarly regard for the later poetry, and somewhat from personal distaste. In the minds of these critics meek doctrines have indeed blighted the transports of the bard, and withered his heroic strains.

If the *Ecclesiastical Sonnets* are to take their rightful place in a survey of Wordsworth's art, his career must be thought of as homogeneous; and this conception would be Wordsworth's own. In the year 1815 he was anxious that the arrangement of his poems should 'correspond with the course of human life,' and should exhibit 'the three requisites of a legitimate whole, a beginning, a middle, and an end.'[4] But much earlier he had been concerned for 'the pleasure which the mind derives from the perception of similitude in dissimilitude,' and he believed that upon this perception 'depend our taste and our moral feelings.'[5] 'Homogeneous' is not a novel epithet for Wordsworth. It gave Coleridge 'great pleasure, as most accurately and happily describing him';[6] Dowden approves, and Harper quotes, the opinion of Coleridge;[7] and Christopher Wordsworth referred to the 'continuous stream of identity'[8] which flowed from the poet's earliest to his latest poems. Of the probable deviations in such a stream Wordsworth himself had given warning;[9] but he was sure that the stream advanced. In the *Character of the Happy Warrior* the combatant is one

> Who, not content that former worth stand fast,
> Looks forward, persevering to the last.

So, too, a poet would direct the orderly advance of his books:

> Go, single—yet aspiring to be joined
> With thy Forerunners that through many a year
> Have faithfully prepared each other's way.[10]

Wordsworth was not unconscious of the charges brought against him of reaction, political and literary;[11] and as well in literature as in politics did he face the accusation and answer it, asserting his fidelity to principle, and scorning the implication that with years and experience he had become less wise. His respect for the aged 'Bards of mightier grasp' grew as normally as his respect for constitutions and liturgies. He hailed ever more devotedly Ossian, 'the Son of Fingal'; Homer, 'blind Maeonides of ampler mind'; and

'Milton, to the fountain-head of glory by Urania led.'[12] He remarked in a letter to Talfourd that the great works of Chaucer, Milton, Dryden, and Cowper were composed 'when they were far advanced in life.'[13]

Since Wordsworth himself has opened the way for a comparison between the years of the artist and the nature of the work of art, additional evidence may be offered. Bede was an old man when he wrote the *Ecclesiastical History*; Alfred translated Bede and Gregory late in his career; and the *Republic* and the *Divina Commedia*, no less than the epics of Chaucer and Milton, were tasks 'hallowed by time.' More and Spenser were early productive, but Bacon's labors continued with unabated success, and Shakespeare's *Tempest* reflects the wisdom of age, not of youth. St. Augustine, the prototype for the modern world of the poet who is a builder, wrote his *De Civitate Dei* with three score of his years behind him; and according to Bryce 'it is hardly too much to say that the Holy Empire was built upon the foundation of the *De Civitate Dei*.'[14] Indeed, these works of these men are all profound studies of the spiritual history and destiny of mankind. They are contemplative and mature; they betoken judgment and long experience in the artists who produced them.

As we have noted, Wordsworth was fifty-one when he wrote the *Ecclesiastical Sonnets*. This fact of itself does not prove the excellence of his poem, but it indicates that his development was typical: the natural phenomena of his country and the humble activities of his fellow-men made way in his mind for a loftier theme, the spiritual history of a people. So Virgil had renounced *Eclogues* and *Georgics* for his *Aeneid*. Wordsworth like Dante, Spenser, and Milton, even like Augustine, Alfred, and Bede, accepted the final challenge of life and art.

II

How would Wordsworth conceive the spiritual history of a people? Here, above all, he would be like himself homogeneous. In spite of his desire to be a recluse, the advance in his art, as Minto remarks, had always come to him 'not in his seclusion, but when he was in contact with his fellow-men.'[15] 'Stand no more aloof!' is the exhortation common to *Lyrical Ballads*, the *Poems* of 1807, the *Convention of Cintra*, and the *Ecclesiastical Sonnets*, these four works being in a sense a return to the objective world from the preoccupation of *Guilt and Sorrow* and *The Borderers*; from *The Prelude*, whose theme is self; from *The White Doe*, whose 'objects ... derive their influence, not from properties inherent in them, not from what they are actually in themselves, but from such as are bestowed upon them by the minds of those who are conversant with or affected by those objects';[16] and, finally, from the unsubstantial theme of *The Recluse*.

In 1793, after a crisis evident in *Guilt and Sorrow* and *The Borderers*, Wordsworth was as one betrayed by nature and by judgment. Whether this betrayal had wrought havoc with his personal affections or his social ideals is here of little concern. The remedy lay in a rededication:

> Long have I loved what I behold,
> The night that calms, the day that cheers;
> The common growth of mother-earth
> Suffices me—her tears, her mirth,
> Her humblest mirth and tears.[17]

Out of this humility came the Prologue to Peter Bell, Peter Bell itself, and the personages in *Lyrical Ballads*. The poet recovered the simple, traditional utterance of English verse;[18] he abandoned the boat twin-sister of the crescent moon, the realm of faery, the might of magic lore, the dragon's wing.[19]

Like another Antaeus, from his contact with mother-earth Wordsworth drew both courage and refreshment, as is proved by his keen analyses in the Preface of 1800, his exact delineation in the *Poems on the Naming of Places*, and those 'present gifts of humbler industry,'[20] the first two books of *The Prelude*. In the words of his letter to Coleridge, 1809, he now sought objects 'interesting to the mind, not by its personal feelings or a strong appeal to the instincts or natural affections, but to be interesting to a meditative or imaginative mind, either from the moral importance of the pictures, or from the employment they give to the understanding affected through the imagination, and to the higher faculties.'[21] Now, too, he had found

> A hoary pathway traced between the trees,
> And winding on with such an easy line
> Along a natural opening, that I stood
> Much wondering how I could have sought in vain
> For what was now so obvious.[22]

Although this pathway led through a profound study of self, *The Prelude*, yet thence, moderated and composed, with an enthusiasm for humanity transcending his enthusiasm for external nature and his enthusiasm for his own lofty hopes, Wordsworth made his second definite return: henceforth he would exercise his skill even more devotedly,

> Not in Utopia,—subterranean fields,—
> Or some secreted island, Heaven knows where!
> But in the very world, which is the world

Of all of us,—the place where, in the end,
We find our happiness, or not at all![23]

The *Ode to Duty* and the *Character of the Happy Warrior* show the result of this adjustment. Moreover, Wordsworth had partaken of 'the very world' in certain intimate and memorable ways. After the death of John Wordsworth he could write:

A deep distress hath humanized my Soul.[24]

From his bereavement grew the sense of a holier joy, which, with the renewed yearning for seclusion, is expressed in *The White Doe*, the fairest image of one side of Wordsworth's genius, and in temper akin to the *Ecclesiastical Sonnets*. Yet the solution of *The White Doe*, as its motto implies, is meek and heroic, but not rational; and the poem itself appears as 'faintly, faintly tied to earth' as was its heroine, standing like her 'apart from human cares.'[25] Of this Wordsworth must have been aware, for again he turned his eye upon life's daily prospect; following his method in *The Happy Warrior* and in the existent sonnets, he directed his thought to 'social and civic duties, chiefly interesting to the imagination through the understanding';[26] and he restated the problems of will, duty, morality, justice, and virtue. His open-minded study of the writings of Bacon, Thomas Browne, and Weever, of geographies and books of travel, of the sources of contemporary history, gave him new power over the essay, the scientific treatise, and the political pamphlet. Nor was he a superficial student of natural and moral science; witness the Description of the Scenery of the Lakes and the *Convention of Cintra*.

Meanwhile Wordsworth's explicit purpose for *The Recluse* had undergone a change. In 1798, as we learn from a letter to James Tobin, this poem was to give pictures of 'Nature, Man, and Society';[27] in 1814, when a part was published as *The Excursion*, the whole was in conception still a poem of 'views,' but the order of the theme had been changed to 'Man, Nature, and Society,' and the author spoke through intervenient dramatic characters.

Minto has keenly analyzed *The Recluse*, Wordsworth's 'great failure,'[28] but lets fall no hint of a possible alternative for such a philosophical poem. To him the actual value even of *The Excursion* is found in the passages where Wordsworth is speaker, the record of the poet's 'own moods,' 'the harvest of his own long observation and cheerful fancy, the fortitude of his own resolute will.' But this resort to what was merely 'his own' was the same blind alley into which Wordsworth had gone on the banks of the Wye, the same tangle of phantom characters as in *The Borderers*, projections of the poet's self.

Was it not to turn the light dawning from the east into a 'steady morning'[29] that *The Prelude* was written? And is *The Excursion* not powerful because in it the poet as a dramatist has grappled with the minds of men, not the mind of Wordsworth alone? Four months after *The Excursion* was published Wordsworth wrote to R. P. Gillies: 'Our inability to catch a phantom of no value may prevent us from attempting to seize a precious substance within our reach.'[30] Phantom or substance, *The Recluse* was never completed. Presumably its author understood his own great failure as well as Minto, and at last came to realize that 'philosophy means love of wisdom—true wisdom is to let insoluble problems alone.'[31] Be that as it may, Wordsworth's explicit comment on great failures is adequate to his own circumstances: memory has too fondly hung on 'new-planned cities and unfinished towers'; self is to be annulled,

> her bondage prove
> The fetters of a dream opposed to love.[32]

So Wordsworth understood and partook of the experience of Chaucer, Virgil, Hooker, the giants of Malham Cove, and the cathedral-builders of Cologne: his mortal hopes, too, were defeated, and he did not miss

> the sole true glory
> That can belong to human story!
> At which they only shall arrive
> Who through the abyss of weakness dive.
> The very humblest are too proud of heart. . . .
> Say not that we have vanquished—but that we survive.[33]

There is no evidence that Wordsworth formally abandoned *The Recluse*; on the contrary, as late as 1824 he still hesitated before 'the task so weighty.'[34] Moreover, there is no reason to think that the *Ecclesiastical Sonnets* constitute Part 3 of the philosophical poem about 'Man, Nature, and Society.' Their theme is nature, man, and God, the 'introduction, progress, and operation of the Church in England.' Here the poet would trace man's relation to God in its actual lineaments; once more he had returned to 'mother-earth, her humblest mirth and tears,' and in so doing he was, may it be repeated, like himself, 'homogeneous.'

III

The *Ecclesiastical Sonnets* take for granted a polity, both of State and of Church, based upon Wordsworth's slowly-formed conviction that justice was not an obligation of one man or of one epoch, but the wise, brave, temperate expression of a society rooted in the past and hopeful for the future. To such a society the 'faith that elevates the just'[35] would be added like 'a breeze which springs up . . . to assist the strenuous oarsman.'[36] From the diatribes of 1793, when he regarded Burke's fidelity to compact as 'a refinement in cruelty' which would 'yoke the living to the dead,'[37] to his eulogy of Burke in *The Prelude*, Wordsworth had fixed his inward eye as relentlessly upon 'Institutes and Laws, hallowed by time,' and 'social ties endeared by Custom'[38] as ever upon a primrose by a river's brim. What he saw was as imaginatively seen as his jocund company of daffodils:

> 'The Constitution of England, which seems about to be destroyed, offers to my mind the sublimest contemplation which the history of society and government have ever presented to it; and for this cause especially, that its principles have the character of preconceived ideas, archetypes of the pure intellect, while they are, in fact, the results of a humble-minded experience.'[39]

By the same discipline he learnt 'the art of bringing words rigorously to the test of thoughts; and these again to a comparison with things, their archetypes, contemplated first in themselves, and secondly in relation to each other.'[40] He acknowledged the duty not alone of weighing 'the moral worth and intellectual power of the age in which we live,' but of determining 'what we are, compared with our ancestors.'[41] For, he believed, 'there is a spiritual community binding together the living and the dead: the good, the brave, and the wise of all ages. We would not be rejected from this community: and therefore do we hope.'[42] And therefore did Wordsworth celebrate those 'golden opportunities when the dictates of justice may be unrelentingly enforced, and the beauty of the inner mind substantiated in the outward act.'[43]

Justice was his theme, and his voice was raised for mankind.[44] This conception of justice, this idea of a spiritual State binding together the living and the dead, was for Wordsworth substantiated in the outward acts of ethical, poetical, and religious beauty as well. 'Usages of pristine mould' and 'ancient manners' seemed precious revelations of the 'far-off past.'[45] He coveted 'some Theban fragment,' or 'tender-hearted scroll of pure Simonides.'[46] And above all, perhaps, he valued the record left in stone and ritual of his country's ecclesiastical history. To churchly images, as the years went by, he had referred the most intimate associations of his life and work; he was, his nephew remarked, 'predisposed to sympathize with a form of religion which appears to afford some exercise for the imaginative faculty.'[47]

Mr. Gordon Wordsworth finds slender evidence for the poet's religious observance during boyhood;[48] but the cross, the distant spire, and the chapel-bell all take their place in the early poems.[49] Even Peter Bell knew the spire of Sarum,[50] profane rover though he was.

Not less frequently but much more appreciatively did Wordsworth and his sister in their travels look upon monastic ruin and cathedral spire. On their way to Calais in 1802 Dorothy saw St. Paul's as a significant part of the view her brother delineated in the sonnet Composed upon Westminster Bridge. In 1803 the pinnacles of Inverary recalled to her the spires of Yorkshire.[51] Then, too, Wordsworth's plans for a winter garden at Coleorton included 'a pool of water that would reflect beautifully the rocks with their hanging plants, the evergreens upon the top, and, shooting deeper than all, the naked spire of the church.'[52]

The spire of Brompton Parish Church, 'under which,' Wordsworth reminded Wrangham, 'you and I were made happy men, by the gift from Providence of excellent wives,'[53] perhaps shot deeper and pointed higher than any other in his experience; but the ecclesiastical symbol was not alien to his bleak and sorrowful days. When most anxious to repair his friendship with Coleridge, he wrote from Grasmere to Sir George Beaumont, April 8, 1808:

> 'You will deem it strange, but really some of the imagery of London
> has, since my return hither, been more present to my mind than
> that of this noble vale. I left Coleridge at seven o'clock on Sunday
> morning, and walked towards the city in a very thoughtful and
> melancholy state of mind. I had passed through Temple Bar and
> by St. Dunstan's, noticing nothing, and entirely occupied with
> my own thoughts, when, looking up, I saw before me the avenue
> of Fleet Street, silent, empty, and pure white, with a sprinkling of
> new-fallen snow, not a cart or carriage to obstruct the view, no
> noise, only a few soundless and dusky foot-passengers here and
> there. You remember the elegant line of the curve of Ludgate Hill in
> which this avenue would terminate; and beyond, towering above it,
> was the huge and majestic form of St. Paul's, solemnized by a thin
> veil of falling snow. I cannot say how much I was affected at this
> unthought-of sight in such a place, and what a blessing I felt there is
> in habits of exalted imagination. My sorrow was controlled, and my
> uneasiness of mind—not quieted and relieved altogether—seemed
> at once to receive the gift of an anchor of security.'[54]

The reader in search of a stern association of image and idea will pass the chance comments of Dorothy on churching, church-going, and christening,[55] but will not fail to note a figure in the Convention of Cintra:

'If the gentle passions of pity, love, and gratitude be porches of the temple; if the sentiments of admiration and rivalry be pillars upon which the structure is sustained; if, lastly, hatred, and anger, and vengeance, be steps which, by a mystery of nature, lead to the House of Sanctity; then was it manifest to what power the edifice was consecrated; and that the voice within was of Holiness and Truth.'[56]

And Wordsworth most effectively applies this figure in the Preface to *The Excursion*, 1814:

'The two works [*The Prelude* and *The Recluse*] have the same kind of relation to each other . . . as the antechapel has to the body of a Gothic church. Continuing this allusion, he [the author] may be permitted to add that his minor pieces, which have been long before the public, when they shall be properly arranged, will be found by the attentive reader to have such connection with the main work as may give them claim to be likened to the little cells, oratories, and sepulchral recesses ordinarily included in those edifices.'

Henceforth the poet easily and habitually referred to ecclesiastical architecture. Of the images gleaned from the tour on the Continent in 1820 many are of such origin; thus: 'the silent avenues of stateliest architecture' in the city that was 'one vast temple'; 'pinnacle and spire' and 'Convent-tower'; 'grey rocks . . . shaped like old monastic turrets'; the 'unfinished shafts' of the cathedral at Cologne; 'lurking cloistral arch'; the 'ancient Tower'; 'the firm unmoving cross'; 'the chapel far withdrawn'; the 'holy Structure'; 'shrine of the meek Virgin Mother'; 'holy enclosure' and 'sacred Pile'; 'sainted grove' and 'hallowed grot.' All these composed for one with eye and mind alike sensitive to their beauty

The venerable pageantry of Time.

Returning to the 'awful perspective' of King's College Chapel and the church to be erected by Sir George Beaumont, Wordsworth was, it may well seem to the student of his life and art, inevitably destined to write an ecclesiastical poem. Yet he

dreamt not of a perishable home
Who thus could build.[57]

Outward acts, the reverent statesmanship in ritual and cathedral of the 'perfected spirits of the just,'[58] never obscured for him 'the eternal city,' the beauty of the inner mind, whose constitution, like the Constitution of other cities, must still be the result of a humble-minded experience. Then would

come faith, to elevate the just. So in 1827 he put his own best interpretation
upon the *Ecclesiastical Sonnets*:

> For what contend the wise?—for nothing less
> Than that the Soul, freed from the bonds of Sense,
> And to her God restored by evidence
> Of things not seen, drawn forth from their recess,
> Root there, and not in forms, her holiness;—
> For Faith, which to the Patriarchs did dispense
> Sure guidance, ere a ceremonial fence
> Was needful round men thirsting to transgress;—
> For Faith, more perfect still, with which the Lord
> Of all, himself a Spirit, in the youth
> Of Christian aspiration, deigned to fill
> The temples of their hearts who, with his word
> Informed, were resolute to do his will,
> And worship him in spirit and in truth.[59]

IV

Was Wordsworth the first to present 'in verse' 'certain points in the
ecclesiastical history' of England, to use his own modest phrase? Henry
Crabb Robinson says that Thelwell in 1799 believed himself about to be a
famous epic poet, and 'thought the establishment of Christianity and the
British Constitution very appropriate subjects for his poem.'[60] Wordsworth
may have heard of Thelwell's project, directly or indirectly, but it is wiser to
refer the theme of *Ecclesiastical Sonnets* to his own habit of choice. He was not
one of those whom he reprobated in the Postscript, 1835:

> 'They who are the readiest to meddle with public affairs, whether
> in Church or State, fly to generalities, that they may be eased from
> the trouble of thinking about particulars; and thus is deputed to
> mechanical instrumentality the work which vital knowledge only
> can do well.'[61]

Moreover, he had already (in 1814) celebrated the Church and State of
England:

> Hail to the crown by Freedom shaped—to gird
> An English Sovereign's brow! and to the throne
> Whereon he sits! Whose deep foundations lie
> In veneration and the people's love;
> Whose steps are equity, whose seat is law.

—Hail to the State of England! And conjoin
With this a salutation as devout,
Made to the spiritual fabric of her Church;
Founded in truth; by blood of Martyrdom
Cemented; by the hands of Wisdom reared
In beauty of holiness, with ordered pomp,
Decent and unreproved. . . .
And O, ye swelling hills and spacious plains!
Besprent from shore to shore with steeple-towers,
And spires whose 'silent finger points to heaven';
Nor wanting, at wide intervals, the bulk
Of ancient minster lifted above the cloud
Of the dense air, which town or city breeds
To intercept the sun's glad beams may ne'er
That true succession fail of English hearts,
Who, with ancestral feeling, can perceive
What in those holy structures ye possess
Of ornamental interest, and the charm
Of pious sentiment diffused afar,
And human charity, and social love.[62]

In 1798 Wordsworth reached a conviction never afterward abandoned by him, that the materials of poetry 'are to be found in every subject which can interest the human mind.'[63] Later he confirmed and explained this statement:

'Poetry is the first and last of all knowledge it is as immortal as the heart of man. . . . If the time should ever come when what is now called science, . . . familiarized to men, shall be ready to put on, as it were, a form of flesh and blood, the poet will lend his divine spirit to aid the transfiguration, and will welcome the being thus produced, as a dear and genuine inmate of the household of man.'[64]

Thus Dante had embodied and transfigured astronomy and theology; thus Shakespeare had turned to 'glorious purpose those materials which the prepossessions of the age compelled him to make use of.'[65] In Wordsworth's conception, too, Clio, the Muse of History, must 'vindicate the majesty of truth.'[66]

If truth be essential to poetry, infinity and unity are the aspects of truth necessary to sublime poetry. 'The infinitude of truth' is a recurrent phrase in the third essay on *Epitaphs*.[67] In the letter to Pasley, 1811, Wordsworth urges 'indefinite progress ... in knowledge, in science, in civilization, in the increase of the numbers of the people, and in the augmentation of their virtue and happiness.'[68] And even more explicitly in his *Description of the Scenery of the English Lakes*, he asserts that 'sublimity will never be wanting where the sense of innumerable multitude is lost in and alternates with that of intense unity.'[69]

Poetry so conceived was in Wordsworth's opinion sublime poetry; and sublime poetry was religious poetry, as he reminded Landor in 1824:

> 'All religions owe their origin, or acceptation, to the wish of the human heart to supply in another state of existence the deficiencies of this, and to carry still nearer to perfection whatever we admire in our present condition; so that there must be many modes of expression, arising out of this coincidence, or rather identity of feeling, common to all mythologies. . . . This leads to a remark in your last, "that you are disgusted with all books that treat of religion." I am afraid it is a bad sign in me that I have little relish for any other. Even in poetry it is the imaginative only, viz., that which is conversant with, or turns upon infinity, that powerfully affects me. Perhaps I ought to explain: I mean to say that, unless in those passages where things are lost in each other, and limits vanish, and aspirations are raised, I read with something too much like indifference. But all great poets are in this view powerful religionists, and therefore among many literary pleasures lost, I have not yet to lament over that of verse as departed.'[70]

'The grand store-houses of enthusiastic and meditative imagination' were for Wordsworth 'the prophetic and lyrical parts of the Holy Scriptures,' the works of Milton and Spenser;[71] even the sublimer passages of Homer or Aeschylus.[72] He agreed with Henry Alford, however, on 'the distinction between religion in poetry and versified religion.' Writing to the latter in 1840, he defined his position:

> 'For my own part, I have been averse to frequent mention of the mysteries of Christian faith; not from a want of a due sense of their momentous nature, but the contrary. I felt it far too deeply to venture on handling the subject as familiarly as many scruple not to do. . . . Besides general reasons for diffidence in treating subjects of Holy Writ, I have some especial ones. I might err in points of faith, and I should not deem my mistakes less to be deprecated because they were expressed in metre. Even Milton, in my humble

judgment, has erred, and grievously; and what poet could hope to atone for his apprehensions [? misapprehensions] in the way in which that mighty mind has done?'[73]

The Rev. R. P. Graves has left his memorandum of a talk wherein Wordsworth indicates 'the gradual steps by which [religion as an element in poetry] . . . must advance to a power comprehensive and universally admitted.' These steps, like the steps in Wordsworth's own career, are 'defined in their order by the constitution of the human mind; and [they] . . . must proceed with vastly more slowness in the case of the progress made by collective minds than . . . in an individual soul.'[74] No clearer reason could be given for Wordsworth's renunciation of the great themes of Milton and of Dante. Not of man or 'one greater man'[75] was he to sing; he dared not celebrate 'il Valor infinito'[76] as did that brother who found himself in a forest—

Nel mezzo del cammin di nostra vita;[77]

instead he would write a memorial of the progress of religion as an element of poetry, a progress made by collective mind and traceable in ecclesiastical polity and history, in liturgy and cathedrals.

Therefore his spiritual and practical concern was unity, threatened alike by the anthropomorphism of pagan and idolatrous thought,[78] and by latitudinarianism, which 'will ever successfully lay claim to a divided worship.'[79] Political and ecclesiastical dissent were not only perilous for the statesman and priest, but perilous for the artist, to whom infinity and unity were both necessary if the work of art was to be sublime.

V
(a)

The history and description of the structure of the *Ecclesiastical Sonnets* are elsewhere given in detail. Here something must be said of its literary form in general. Wordsworth did not himself relate the series to any traditional group; and the reader is left to surmise the author's purpose. Of the classes of narrative enumerated in the Preface of 1815 the series must constitute either an epopoeia or a historic poem. On the other hand, the sonnet there is called an idyllium.[80]

An undated letter to Southey contains Wordsworth's best definition of the epic poem:

> '*Epic* poetry, of the highest class, requires in the first place an action eminently influential, an action with a grand or sublime train of consequences; it next requires the intervention and guidance of

beings superior to man, what the critics, I believe, call *machinery*; and, lastly, I think with Dennis that no subject but a religious one can answer the demand of the soul in the highest class of this species of poetry.'[81]

The first and third of these requirements are met by Wordsworth's ecclesiastical series; and the second, too, if we interpret the 'intervention and guidance' of a Superior Being in the simplest and most exalted sense.

Moreover, one may say of the series of *Ecclesiastical Sonnets* what Wordsworth said of Balbi's epitaph by Chiabrera: it is a perfect whole; there is nothing arbitrary or mechanical; it is an organized body, of which the members are bound together by a common life, and are all justly proportioned.[82] Such perfection is not accidental. Throughout the decade previous to 1821 Wordsworth frequently described the ways and means of it, as for instance in the letter to Pasley:

> 'A state ought to be governed, . . . the labors of the statesman ought to advance, upon calculations and from impulses similar to those which give motion to the hand of a great artist when he is preparing a picture, or of a mighty poet when he is determining the proportions and march of a poem; much is to be done by rule; the great outline is previously to be conceived in distinctness, but the consummation of the work must be trusted to resources that are not tangible, though known to exist.'[83]

And one may further say that the principles underlying the 'proportions' and 'march' of Wordsworth's epic, its 'great outline,' have, as he remarked of the Constitution of England, 'the character of preconceived ideas, archetypes of the pure intellect, while they are, in fact, the results of a humble-minded experience.'[84]

There were cogent artistic reasons for this not alone 'October's workmanship to rival May';[85] for from the outset of his career Wordsworth had put his faith in the 'best models of composition,'[86] including external nature. By exercise in analysis and translation and paraphrase he had sternly disciplined himself. In his own art and in the arts of painting and sculpture he was keenly aware of the cost of good work; and hence he could detect the spurious and the artificial, as with Macpherson's Ossian, or in the poetry of Scott. He could give reasons, too, for his judgments; his riper mind not only saw that an artist was deceived, but saw how he was deceived.[87] His ire at poems 'merely skin-deep as to thought and feeling, the juncture or suture of the composition not being a jot more cunning or more fitted for endurance than the first fastening together of fig-leaves in Paradise,'[88] and his enthusiasm over the exhibitions in the Jardin des Plantes[89] are symptoms of an increasing attention to organic form.

Fortunately Wordsworth's taste was catholic: his models were the best from Greece, Rome, the Middle Ages, the Renaissance, the Elizabethan and Jacobean periods, and the Eighteenth Century. His rapture over the Elgin marbles,[90] his frequent debate with Wrangham and Lonsdale and Landor on the minutiae of Latin phrases, his repeated study of the *Aeneid*, are evidence of his classical scholarship. Throughout his life he took a purely aesthetic delight in abbey and cathedral; and the final passages of the *Ecclesiastical Sonnets* display no little of the reverence of Dante in the *Paradiso*. Dante's 'fictions,' however, Wordsworth considered 'offensively grotesque and fantastic,'[91] and thus a superficial disparity prevented the English poet from that closer study of the Italian for which his temper and intelligence would seem to have fitted him.

To the bold and lofty conceptions of Michelangelo, and to Leonardo's 'intense and laborious study of scientific and mathematical details,'[92] he rendered due homage; Chaucer's 'lucid shafts of reason,'[93] and Shakespeare's judgment in the selection and ordering of his materials,[94] alike won his regard; he acknowledged Spenser's grasp of the 'highest moral truths';[95] Milton and Walton had long been the intimate companions of his thought; with Burke and Cowper, unlike as they were, he had much in common.

(b)

But no mention of models of composition would be complete without reference to the sonneteers from whom Wordsworth learned how to shape the fourteen-line stanza which he adopted for his narrative poem. Never before to the same extent had sonnets been used to carry a theme which needed march as well as proportions. Cycles of sonnets there were; groups with their parts related in mood, in subject; groups celebrating deeds which themselves formed a sequence; mild allegories of the rise and fall of passion or the growth and maturity and decay of life: but a well-articulated scheme of events originally conceived as organic parts of a whole had not before Wordsworth's experiment been attempted by an English poet in the sonnet-form.[96]

Blank verse or the Spenserian stanza would have been a dignified medium for an ecclesiastical poem. Wordsworth's reasons for disregarding them may be inferred from his letters to Southey, Lord Lonsdale, and Catherine Goodwin: he would avoid diffuseness, and he would make use of 'every possible help and attraction of sound.'[97] In his opinion Milton's sonnets had 'an energetic and varied flow of sound crowding into narrow room more of the combined effect of rhyme and blank verse than can be done by any other kind of verse.'[98] Such, then, was to be the effect of the *Ecclesiastical Sonnets*.

Hutchinson has gathered the memorable facts concerning Wordsworth and the sonnet into an Appendix to his edition (vol. 1) of the *Poems in Two Volumes*. His remarks may here be supplemented by a short statement of the formal problem that Wordsworth faced in a series of 132 sonnets whereof the transitions must be distinct, but not abrupt. The sestet, obviously, is the crucial concern.

Wordsworth was familiar with the sonnets of Michelangelo, of Shakespeare, and of Milton.[99] He was familiar, too, with the technical habit of Petrarch, Tasso, Camoens, Dante, and the Elizabethans. Of later sonneteers, Donne, Russell, Sir Egerton Brydges, Miss Williams, the Coleridges, father and son, and Southey had been the objects of his incisive comment. The way was open, then, for him to make a judicial selection from a wide range of rhyme-schemes.

He might use Shakespeare's 'heavy'[100] final couplet, the distichs of Petrarch and Dante, and the tercets of Michelangelo, in a variety of forms to suit the movement of his narrative, or the extent and relationships of his thought. He was no doubt prepared for this free adaptation by his management of rhyme in *The White Doe*. At once strict and unobtrusive, the harmony of this poem is its greatest formal beauty.

Wisely enough, Wordsworth perceived the superiority of the sonnet over any stanza reminiscent of ballad or canzone. The sonnet is an artistic invention, and as such is the proper vehicle for ecclesiastical history. Originally a love poem, it would be fitted to carry a strain of sublimated love, patriotic or religious, as Milton had discovered, and as Wordsworth through Milton had rediscovered, for, by the latter, 'style of harmony'[101] had been elevated from the serenade to the 'soul-animating' strain.[102]

In a letter to Dyce, Wordsworth sets forth his ideas about the construction of the individual sonnet:

> 'It should seem that the sonnet, like every other legitimate compo-
> sition, ought to have a beginning, a middle, and an end; in other
> words, to consist of three parts, like the three parts of a syllogism,
> if such an illustration may be used. But the frame of metre adopted
> by the Italians does not accord with this view; and, as adhered to by
> them, it seems to be, if not arbitrary, best fitted to a division of the
> sense into two parts, of eight and six lines each. Milton, however,
> has not submitted to this; in the better half of his sonnets the sense
> does not close with the rhyme at the eighth line, but overflows into
> the second portion of the metre. Now, it has struck me that this is

not done merely to gratify the ear by variety and freedom of sound, but also to aid in giving that pervading sense of intense unity in which the excellence of the sonnet has always seemed to me mainly to consist. Instead of looking at this composition as a piece of architecture, making a whole out of three parts, I have been much in the habit of preferring the image of an orbicular body a sphere, or a dewdrop. All this will appear to you a little fanciful; and I am well aware that a sonnet will often be found excellent, where the beginning, the middle, and the end are distinctly marked, and also where it is distinctly separated into two parts, to which, as I before observed, the strict Italian model, as they write it, is favorable.'[103]

Valuable as was the conception of an orbicular body if Wordsworth were to use the sonnet as a stanza, it is fortunate that he did not relinquish the traits of divisibility. For both the march and proportions of his poem, the resultant medium was a happy one, rigorous and flexible alike.

By way of summary, one may say that the *Ecclesiastical Sonnets* are related to models having dignity and beauty, and are loyally but not slavishly derived from them; furthermore, they are wrought with conscious skill by a poet at once docile and self-assured.

VI

His humility, his exalted aim, his theme, which was actual rather than fanciful, and his respect for the best traditions, made Wordsworth dependent upon his library. The ecclesiastical series is a substantial poem; it is not merely a poem on a substantial theme, but a poem whose very substance is the substance of Bede, Drayton, Daniel, Fuller, Foxe, Walton, Camden, Stow, Herbert, Donne, Whitaker, Turner, Heylin, Burnet, Stillingfleet, Dyer, Milton, the Bible, and the English Liturgy.

In selecting the best for his purpose, Wordsworth was unwilling to pervert or to blur what had been well done before him. And hence he transferred from his sources to his own work exact thoughts and exact images, and exact phrases as well. His versification of Bede is often more true to the original than is the English translation by A. M. Sellar. Such fidelity would do credit to the man of science; in the builder of a literary Church which will represent a real Church it is no less admirable. Wordsworth would give us Bede and Walton as in themselves they really are. Like Hooker, whose passion for truth he knew through Walton's *Life*, he had 'searched many books and spent many thoughtful hours.'[104] Like Milton, to whose *History of Britain* he was indebted for *Artegal and Elidure*, he could appreciate the tireless investigation underlying all genuine literary work.

The labor necessary for his substructure he did not avoid. Virgil had gone to ceremonial books of the priestly college, to Cato's *Origines*, to Varro's antiquarian treatises; perhaps to *Annales* and *Fasti*; to Naevius, Ennius, Homer and the Cyclic poems, the Greek tragedies, the *Argonautica*.[105] In the same spirit Wordsworth opened the liturgy, Stillingfleet's *Origines*, Davies' antiquarian treatises, Stow's *Chronicle*, and the works of Camden and Foxe, of Drayton, and of Bede and Milton.

It is impossible in every case to tell how conscious or how recent was Wordsworth's debt, for his memory always served him well. Bede and Turner were directly consulted; and it is probable that the histories of Fuller and Daniel lay close to his hand. From the old books that did not come amiss[106] when he was preparing an album for Lady Mary Lowther in 1819, he doubtless refreshed his knowledge of passages chosen, as Harper says, 'for solidity, elevation, and sincerity.'[107] That other books, old or new, had been recently acquired we learn from two letters to Henry Crabb Robinson, who seems to have mediated between Wordsworth and 'the bookseller near Charing Cross.' These books, which had not arrived by January 23, 1821, were in Wordsworth's possession on March 13.[108]

The poet was badly misled by his authority only in one instance, when he followed Foxe's erroneous account of the humiliation of Barbarossa by Alexander III. On the other hand, his favorable estimate of Laud has been corroborated by later historical study,[109] and was pronounced, as he told Miss Fenwick, long before the Oxford Tract Movement.

Throughout the *Ecclesiastical Sonnets* the temper of Walton rules; Fuller's condensed power has been helpful to Wordsworth in the management of vast topics like the Crusades and the wars of York and Lancaster; Daniel's style, lucid and unadorned, reappears to advantage in sestets which must be precise or final. Dyer's sensibility and Burnet's vivacity, Whitaker's zeal for circumstantial detail, all seem to live again in the sonnets they have helped to make.

Nor did Wordsworth lack skill to supplement or balance one source with another, or to discard what was specious or bigoted in his authorities. Save in dealing with the Norman Conquest, he treats people and events with sympathy and judgment; More and Cranmer, Milton and Laud, all receive unbiased praise, while Sacheverell and the dissenters are impartially rebuked. Of monasticism and reform alike the poet is a generous interpreter.

His tolerance was recognized by the eminent Roman Catholic writer Montalembert;[110] and the spirit of pure faith and humility which lay beneath his tolerance recommended him to Kenelm Henry Digby, a young English writer whose zeal had carried him farther into ritual and ecclesiastical tradition than Wordsworth was willing to go. Digby not infrequently quoted

Wordsworth in the *Mores Catholici*;[111] and between the two there later arose the friendliness of authors having a similar enthusiasm.[112]

Wordsworth's omissions are noteworthy. Caedmon, who sang out of his heart, is passed by for Bede the translator. William, Lanfranc, and Anselm are not mentioned; but Richard, the Norman become Englishman, and Henry V, point the folly of conquest. The civil wars of England are lightly touched on; enmity of class against class, sect against sect, plays no important part in the *Ecclesiastical Sonnets*; great men are not pitted against great men rather does a succession of great men illustrate the epic march of an impersonal struggle. In this way Wordsworth avoids a dramatic violence that would distort his medium, while retaining the vigor of good narrative. And he overcomes the temptation to crowd his action with persons and events. Many well-known characters are masked or lightly sketched. Aidan, Theodore, Hadrian, Wilfrid, Bernard, Thomas Bradwardine, Wolsey, Henry VIII, can be descried in passages where no names are mentioned.

As a scholar Wordsworth was astute: he found the main sources, and he did not lose his sense of proportion. Other poets of his time had been great readers and eager for research, Coleridge and Scott, for instance. Neither has so successfully reconciled his scholarship with his poetry; neither has been so modest a student, for when Wordsworth wrote to Wrangham in 1819 that his reading powers 'were never very great'[113] he did not at all imply that they had been unwisely or vainly exercised. He well knew the 'good elder writers,'[114] and to Allsop in 1821 he seemed 'almost as good a reader as Coleridge,'[115] and even more authoritative.

Nor was Wordsworth exclusive in his enthusiasms. What he studied and found good he related to what he had studied and found good. The pure faith of Walton and the celestial secrets of Milton were for him as admirable in Jacobean and Caroline times as the piety of Bede and the imagination of Gregory in the early Middle Ages. Alfred and Elizabeth he found comparable; Saxon monks and eminent reformers, of one lineage. The unity of his poem is in large part due to his unwillingness to exalt one period over another.

With scholars a pioneer, therefore; as an artist re-established in his art by study of the works of poets and cathedral builders; as a historian animated by the spirit of Bede and Alfred; as a poet linked with Virgil, with Dante, with Milton, and with Spenser by the nature of his theme, Wordsworth wrote the *Ecclesiastical Sonnets*.

Notes

1. *Laod.* 77, 137–8, 140, 73–4, 144.
2. *William Wordsworth*, 1916, 1.6.

3. *Enc. Brit.*, eleventh ed., 28.830.

4. Preface to the edition of 1815, *Poetical Works*, Oxford ed., 1909, pp. 954–5.

5. Preface to the second edition of *Lyrical Ballads*, *Prose Works*, ed. by Knight, 1896, 1.68.

6. *Letters of Samuel Taylor Coleridge*, ed. by E. H. Coleridge, 1895, 1.373. The letter quoted was written July 13, 1802.

7. Dowden's *Memoir*, P. W., Aldine ed., 1892–3, i.xxii; and Harper's *William Wordsworth* 2.44.

8. *Memoirs of William Wordsworth*, ed. by Reed, 1851, 1.4–5. 2

9. *Reply to the Letter of Mathetes*, *Prose Works* 1.90.

10. *In desultory* 17–19, *Prelude to the Poems Chiefly of Early and Late Years.*

11. *Letters of the Wordsworth Family*, ed. by Knight, 1907, 2.162.

12. *Ossian* 53, 79–82.

13. *Letters* 3.115.

14. *The Holy Roman Empire*, 1904, p. 94, note.

15. *Wordsworth's Great Failure*, *Nineteenth Century* for September, 1889, p. 449.

16. *Letters* 2.68.

17. *P. B.* 131–5.

18. Cf. Barstow, *Wordsworth's Theory of Poetic Diction*, 1917.

19. *P. B.* 80, 101, no. 136.

20. *Prelude* 1.133–4.

21. *Letters* 3.473.

22. *When, to* 47–52.

23. *Prelude* ll. 139–43.

24. *Peele Castle* 36.

25. *White Doe* 1864–5, 1859.

26. *Letters* 3473–4.

27. *Letters* 1.115.

28. *Op. cit.* in the *Nineteenth Century*, pp. 435–51.

29. *Prelude* 1.127.

30. *Letters* 2.39.

31. *Op. cit.* in the Nineteenth Century, p. 443.

32. *Laod.* 132, 149–50.

33. *Ode: Thanks.* 83–7, 91. Cf. also *Malham*, and the *Journals of Dorothy Wordsworth*, ed. by Knight, 1897, 2.178–9.

34. *Letters* 2.237.

35. *Primrose* 51.

36. *Convention of Cintra*, *Prose Works* 1.211.

37. *Letter to the Bishop of Llandaff, Prose Works* 1.25.

38. *Prelude* 7.526–8.

39. *Memoirs*, ed. by Reed, 2.259.

40. *Epitaphs* 2, *Prose Works* 2.164.

41. *Prose Works* 1.85.

42. *Prose Works* 1.272.

43. *Prose Works* 1.215.

44. *Prose Works* 1.213.

45. Dedication to *The River Duddon*, The minstrels 59, 55, 72.

46. *Departing summer* 52–4.

47. *Memoirs*, ed. by Reed, 2.151.

48. *The Boyhood of Wordsworth*, in *Cornhill Magazine*, N.S. 48 (1920). 419.

49. *Descr. Sk.* Quarto 70; *Guilt* 21; *Bord.* 1651.

50. *P. B.* 212.

51. *Journals* 2.25.

52. *Letters* 1.279.

53. *Letters* 1.429.

54. *Letters*, 1.34.9.

55. Harper, *William Wordsworth* 2.51; and *Letters* 1.298, 2.5.

56. *Prose Works* 1.205.

57. *Eccl. Son.* 3.45.1–2.

58. *Eccl. Son.* 3.47.14.

59. *Eccl. Son.* 2.30, added to the series in 1827.

60. *Diary*, ed. by Sadler, 1869, 1.37.

61. *P. W.*, Oxford ed., p. 963.

62. *Excursion* 6.1–12, 17–29.

63. *Advertisement to Lyrical Ballads, Prose Works* 1.31.

64. Preface to *Lyrical Ballads*, 1800, *P. W.*, Oxford ed., p. 939.

65. *Essay Supplementary to the Preface, P. W.*, Oxford ed., p. 946.

66. *Plea: Hist.* 8.

67. *Prose Works* 2.176, 181.

68. *Prose Works* 1.316.

69. *Prose Works* 2.80; and cf. Henry Crabb Robinson, *Diary*, September 10, 1816:

> '[Wordsworth] represented . . . much as, unknown to him, the German philosophers have done, that by the imagination the mere fact is exhibited as connected with that infinity without which there is no poetry.'

70. *Letters* 2.214–5.

71. Preface to the edition of 1815, *P. W.*, Oxford ed., p. 957.

72. *Letters* 2.250–1.

73. *Memoirs*, ed. by Reed, 2.368–9.

74. *Memoirs*, ed. by Reed, 2.370.

75. *Paradise Lost* 1.1, 4.

76. Dante, *Paradiso* 33.81.

77. Dante, *Inferno* 1.1.

78. Preface to the edition of 1815, *P. W.*, Oxford ed., p. 957.

79. *Postscript*, 1835, *P. W.*, Oxford ed., p. 965.

80. *P. W.*, Oxford ed., p. 954.

81. *Memoirs*, ed. by Reed, 2.62.

82. *Prose Works* 2.183.

83. *Prose Works* 1.318.

84. *Memoirs*, ed. by Reed, 2.259.

85. *Trosachs* 1.1.

86. Advertisement to *Lyrical Ballads*, 1798, *Prose Works* 1.32.

87. Reply to the Letter of Mathetes, *Prose Works* 1.102.

88. *Letters* 2.80–1.

89. *Memoirs*, ed. by Reed, 2.106.

90. *Letters* 2.63; and cf. the *Diary* of Henry Crabb Robinson, November 20, 1820.

91. *Letters* 2.216.

92. Cf. his translations of the sonnets of Michael Angelo, *P. W.*, Oxford ed., pp. 256–7; cf. also Robinson's *Diary* 1.360.

93. *Eccl. Son.* 2.31.13.

94. *Essay Supplementary to the Preface, P. W.*, Oxford ed., p. 947.

95. Preface to the edition of 1815, *P. W.*, Oxford ed., p. 957.

96. Cf. chap. 4 of the Introduction in Dr. John S. Smart's recent edition of *The Sonnets of Milton*, 1921.

97. *Memoirs*, ed. by Reed, 2.70. Cf. also *ibid.* 2.60, 62.

98. *Memoirs*, ed. by Reed, 1.286, note.

99. *Letters* 1.173; *Essay Supplementary*, 1815, *P. W.*, Oxford ed., p. 947.

100. *Memoirs*, ed. by Reed, 2.258.

101. *Letters* 2.180.

102. *Misc. Son.* 2.1.14.

103. *Memoirs*, ed. by Reed, 2.281–2. Cf. also Smart, op. cit., pp. 14–38.

104. Walton, *The Lives of Donne, Wotton, Hooker, Herbert, and Sanderson*, 2 vols., Boston, 1832, 2.78.

105. Sellar, *Virgil*, p. 310.

106. Undated letter to Wrangham, *Letters* 2.128.

107. *William Wordsworth* 2.310.

108. *Letters* 2.141, 143.

109. Gardiner, *The Great Civil War*, 1889, 2.50–1.

110. *Monks of the West*, 1861, Introduction, 1.96, note.

111. London, 1844, 1.1.7, 17; 1–545; 1.8.87.

112. *Letters* 2.441; cf. also an article in the *Athenaum* 3579.714, May 30, 1896.

113. *Letters* 2.125.

114. *Letters* 1.468–9.

115. Knight, *The Life of William Wordsworth*, 1889, 3.52.

—ABBIE FINDLAY POTTS, "Introduction"
from *The Ecclesiastical Sonnets of
William Wordsworth*, 1922, pp. 1–27

PETER BELL

Wordsworth's ballad *Peter Bell* was ridiculed before it was even published in 1819. Peter Bell is a selfish rustic who is given over to immoral behavior and temptations. During a struggle with an unattended ass, which he intends to steal, he discovers the drowned owner. When Peter rides on the ass carrying the drowned man, a fierce struggle ensues between his unregenerate nature and the new spirit of benevolence within him. Salvation looms when he hears the Wesleyans, an orthodox Christian appeal.

PERCY BYSSHE SHELLEY
"PETER BELL THE THIRD" (1819)

In the following excerpt from "Peter Bell the Third," Percy Bysshe Shelley satirizes Wordsworth's poem. While Peter Bell tells the story of an immoral and superstitious itinerant potter who transforms after witnessing the touching and devoted response of an ass that remained faithful to its deceased owner, Shelley's Peter is a Methodist who will pay for his sins. Here, Shelley pokes fun at Wordsworth's imagination, calling him a "pint-pot," a reference to one who sells beer. In the context of the quote from Shelley's poem, this can be interpreted as a jab. Shelley is here measuring Wordsworth's poetic skills in *Peter Bell* and comparing them to a pint pot, a drinking vessel that holds little. Shelley finds that Wordsworth's creative skills in the poem are equally as scant. Shelley's pint pot is also a reference to Peter Bell's former profligate ways as he passes an inn: "And now is passing by an inn / Brim-full of a carousing crew, / That make, with curses not a few,

/ An uproar and a drunken din. / I cannot well express the thoughts / Which Peter in those noises found." Beyond the obvious parody of Wordsworth's poem, scholars have said that Shelley's poem was intended as a critique of Wordsworth's career and shifting political alliances, from his former radical days of the early 1790s to his conservatism from approximately 1795 on. Shelley's poem was not published until 1839, when Mary Shelley added it to the second edition of her late husband's *Poetical Works*. Apparently, Mary was uncomfortable with the fact that the poem made fun of Wordsworth and went so far as to include a favorable comment on Wordsworth's poem: "Much of it is beautifully written—. . . it has so much of himself in it, that it cannot fail to interest greatly. . . ."

He had a mind which was somehow
At once circumference and centre
Of all he might or feel or know;
Nothing went ever out, although
Something did ever enter.
He had as much imagination
As a pint-pot;—he never could
Fancy another situation,
From which to dart his contemplation,
Than that wherein he stood.
Yet his was individual mind,
And new created all he saw
In a new manner, and refined
Those new creations, and combined
Them, by a master-spirit's law.
Thus—though unimaginative—
An apprehension clear, intense,
Of his mind's work, had made alive
The things it wrought on; I believe
Wakening a sort of thought in sense.

—PERCY BYSSHE SHELLEY, "Peter Bell
the Third," 1819, part 4, stanzas 7–10

WILLIAM WORDSWORTH (1819)

In his letter to Robert Southey, Wordsworth explains his wish that *Peter Bell* be taken seriously and earn its place in English literature. Wordsworth also reminds Southey, as expressed in the prologue to the poem, of his belief that the humblest of men can be reformed through the exercise of their imagination, a faculty that does not require the intervention of a supernatural agency. Rather the imagination can be summoned simply, during the course of performing "the humblest departments of daily life."

TO ROBERT SOUTHEY, ESQ., P.L., ETC. ETC.
MY DEAR FRIEND,

The Tale of Peter Bell, which I now introduce to your notice, and to that of the Public, has, in its Manuscript state, nearly survived its 'minority':—for it first saw the light in the summer of 1798. During this long interval, pains have been taken at different times to make the production less unworthy of a favourable reception; or, rather, to fit it for filling 'permanently' a station, however humble, in the Literature of our Country. This has, indeed, been the aim of all my endeavours in Poetry, which, you know, have been sufficiently laborious to prove that I deem the Art not lightly to be approached; and that the attainment of excellence in it may laudably be made the principal object of intellectual pursuit by any man, who, with reasonable consideration of circumstances, has faith in his own impulses. The Poem of Peter Bell, as the Prologue will show, was composed under a belief that the Imagination not only does not require for its exercise the intervention of supernatural agency, but that, though such agency be excluded, the faculty may be called forth as imperiously and for kindred results of pleasure, by incidents, within the compass of poetic probability, in the humblest departments of daily life. Since that Prologue was written, 'you' have exhibited most splendid effects of judicious daring, in the opposite and usual course. Let this acknowledgment make my peace with the lovers of the supernatural; and I am persuaded it will be admitted, that to you, as a Master in that province of the Art, the following Tale, whether from contrast or congruity, is not an unappropriate offering. Accept it, then, as a public testimony of affectionate admiration from one with whose name yours has been often coupled (to use your own words) for evil and for good; and believe me to be, with earnest wishes that life and health may be granted you to complete the many important works in which you are engaged, and with high respect,

Most faithfully yours,
WILLIAM WORDSWORTH.
Rydal Mount, April 7, 1819.

—WILLIAM WORDSWORTH, letter to
Robert Southey, April 7, 1819

Chronology

1770	Born April 7 at Cockermouth in Cumberland.
1778	Death of mother, Ann Wordsworth.
1779	Enters school near Esthwaite Lake in the lake country.
1783	Death of father, John Wordsworth.
1787–1791	Attends St. John's College, Cambridge University.
1790	Walking tour of France, Germany, and Switzerland.
1791	Walking tour of North Wales, where he ascends Mount Snowdon.
1791–1792	Residence in France, where he associated with moderate faction of the revolutionists. Love affair with Annette Vallon. Birth of their daughter, Anne Caroline.
1793	Publication of *An Evening Walk* and *Descriptive Sketches.*
1795	Death of college friend Raisley Calvert, whose legacy enables Wordsworth to devote himself to poetry.
1795–1798	Settles with his sister, Dorothy, first at Racedown, then at Alfoxden. In 1797–1798, he is constantly in the company of Samuel Taylor Coleridge.
1798	In September, *Lyrical Ballads* is published.
1798–1799	Winters with Dorothy at Goslar in Germany.
1799	Moves with Dorothy to Dove Cottage, Grasmere, where he writes *The Prelude* in its first version, in two parts.
1800	Second edition of *Lyrical Ballads*, with "Preface" added.
1802	Marries Mary Hutchinson.
1805	Death of his brother John Wordsworth in a shipwreck in February. *The Prelude,* in thirteen books, is finished, but the poet chooses not to publish it.

1807	Publishes *Poems in Two Volumes.*
1810–1812	Rift with Coleridge; subsequent friendship is never the same.
1813–1842	Becomes a government tax collector for Westmoreland. Lives at Rydal Mount, near Ambleside.
1814	Publishes *The Excursion.*
1843	Becomes poet laureate.
1850	Dies April 23 at Rydal Mount. *The Prelude,* in fourteen books, is published posthumously.

Index

A

Addresses to the Freeholders of
   Westmorland, 105–106
Adonais (Shelley), 100
Aeschylus, 229, 310
Affliction of Margaret,The, 113
Alastor (Shelley), 95–96, 99, 101
Alford, Henry, 310
Alforden, Somerset, 1
Alice du Clos (Coleridge), 159, 164–
   165, 167
Alice Fell or Poverty, 109, 111, 115
alien element, 176, 177
America, 17–19, 74
analogy, 235
Ancient Mariner, Rime of the
   (Coleridge), 12, 93, 137, 159, 160,
   161, 162, 163, 164, 166, 167
Anecdote for Fathers, 111
angels, 16–17, 178, 249
anima mundi, 183
"Animal Tranquility and Decay," 136
antithetic poets, 92
Aristotle, 125, 226
Arnold, Matthew, 31, 101, 109, 111,
   112, 141–142, 160, 187
     "Memorial Verses," 76–77
     "Preface," 83–85
art, 141, 144, 227, 312
     famous painters, 177, 243, 244, 313
     poetry and, 131, 143, 176, 186

Artegal and Elidure, 157
artistic partnership, 1
asceticism, 26
Augustine, St., 301
austerity, 25, 26, 67
autobiographical poem. See Prelude,
   The
Autobiography, 267
Axiologus signature, 55

B

Bacon, Francis, 11, 227, 303
Bagehot, Walter, 154
Bailly, Nicholas, 53
balance/equilibrium, 11, 89, 90
ballads, 84, 111, 150–169
     Eighteenth-Century style, 155,
       158, 159
     inversion/alliteration in, 158,
       166–167
     marked qualities of, 158
     repetition in, 166
     simplicity of style of, 151
     types of influence from, 154–157
     See also Lyrical Ballads
"Banks of the Wye," 65
bathos, 155
Beaumont, Lady, 268–274
Beaumont, Sir George, 274, 306, 307
Beaupuy, Capt. Michel, 29, 31, 32,
   35–36

beauty, 82, 101, 107–108, 143, 195, 239
   Hymn to Intellectual Beauty,
     95–98
   of outer world/nature, 67, 75, 92,
     149, 170, 186, 248, 281, 290
Bede, 301, 315, 316, 317
"Beggars, The," 145
Bell, Peter, 75, 297, 306
Benjamin the Waggoner, 297
Besserve (apothecary), 47, 48
biographers, 25, 32, 45
Biographia Literaria (Coleridge), 103,
   151, 195
biography, 1–2
   birth, 1
   career, 83, 104
   childhood, 89
   death, 2, 23
   education, 1, 24, 25, 96, 124
   health, 21–22
   marriage/family, 1, 2, 30, 37
   mistress, 1, 30. *See also* Vallon,
     Annette
   politics/sympathies, 42, 57, 85,
     175, 275, 277, 278
   residences, 1, 6, 55. *See also* Lake
     District
   supreme period, 121–122, 123
Blake, William, 137, 143, 153, 159
blank verse, 153, 289–290, 292, 313
Blois, France, 28, 29, 34, 39, 43, 50, 54
   Vallon sisters at, 49, 53
   Wordsworth's stay at, 35, 36–37
boldness, speculative, 183–184
Bolton Priory, 209–210
Bonaparte, Napoleon, 50
Borderers, The, 44, 122, 136, 157, 301,
   302, 303
Botanical Garden, The (Darwin), 121,
   130–131
Bourdon, Léonard, 45–46, 47, 48, 57
Bradley, A.C., 108–117
Brothers, The, 87, 113, 155, 157, 257
Brown, T.E., 268
Browne, Thomas, 303

Browning, Elizabeth Barrett, 72–74
Browning, Robert, 14–15, 137
   Lost Leader, 275
Burke, Edmund, 305, 313
Burney, Charles, 61
Burns, Robert, 17, 68, 70, 71, 84, 130,
   143, 145–146, 229
Byron, Lord, 2, 62, 67, 76, 77, 79, 80,
   86, 90–91, 92–94, 95, 108, 111,
   236, 241, 245, 247, 248, 257
   "Byronic gloom," 121, 126
   Childe Harold, 93
   Don Juan, 93
   verses of, 250–251
   Wordsworth compared to, 73, 85

C

Cadoudal, Georges, 52, 54
Calais, France, 24, 306
Cambridge, England, 1, 24, 25, 26,
   124
Candide (Voltaire), 254
Carlyle, Thomas, 17, 18, 19, 20, 21–
   23, 43, 137
Caroline. *See* Wordsworth, Anne
   Caroline
Catholic Emancipation, 276
Cenci, The (Shelley), 94, 101
character, 11, 16, 73, 177, 260
   appearance and, 7, 8–9, 10, 14
   demeanor, 7, 8, 9, 15–16, 23, 43,
     89
   familial kindness, 7, 8, 9, 10
Chateaubriand, François-René, 177
Chaucer, Geoffrey, 91, 243, 275, 296–
   297, 301, 304, 313
Childe Harold (Byron), 93, 125
childhood, 137, 145, 182, 192, 197,
   205, 247–248, 250, 256
Childless Father, The, 155, 158
children, 63, 64, 145, 213, 217, 233–
   234
Chouans, 51, 52, 53–54
Christabel (Coleridge), 94, 158, 165,
   167

Christianity, 29, 73, 235, 299, 308
Christmas/Candlemas, 287, 288
Church of England, 298, 299, 304, 308–309
classical ideal, 108, 141, 239
Cloud, The (Shelley), 101, 102
Coleridge, Ernest Hartley, 196
Coleridge, Hartley, 197, 199, 200
Coleridge, Samuel Taylor, 1, 6, 57, 84, 86, 90, 111, 123, 128, 130, 133, 136, 140, 158, 159–161, 162, 167, 194–195, 268, 273, 299, 300, 317
   Alice du Clos, 159, 164–165, 167
   ballads, influence on, 150–169
   Biographia Literaria, 103, 151, 195, 200
   Christabel, 94, 158, 165, 167
   The Dark Ladie, 159, 160, 164, 167
   Dejection, 161, 165
   on *The Excursion*, 221–236
   Kubla Khan, 165, 167
   Love, 94, 164
   on *The Prelude*, 169–173
   Rime of the Ancient Mariner, 12, 93, 137, 159, 160, 161, 162, 163, 164, 166, 167
   The Three Graves, 159, 161, 166, 167
   Wordsworth and, 10–12, 306
   See also *Lyrical Ballads*
Collected Works, 2
community, poet of, 116
"Complaint," 65
"Composed upon Westminster Bridge," 306
composition, 124, 125, 140, 312, 313
   in ballads, 157–158
   metrical, 135, 143, 144
Comptroller of Stamps, 104
Concordat, the, 29
contemplative life, 86, 140, 149, 168, 181, 182, 185, 242, 247, 248, 258. *See also* tranquility/solitude
Convention, the, 29, 37, 46, 47, 48

Convention of Cintra, 275, 303, 306
conversation, 6, 7, 9, 10
Council of the Five Hundred, 48
Cowley, Abraham, 225
Cowper, William, 144, 213, 215, 301, 313
Crabbe, George, 144
Cromwell, Oliver, 225
Cumberland, 1, 215, 230

D
Daffodil stanzas, 111, 114, 184, 232, 273
Dafour, André Augustin, 37
Dalton's atomic theory, 20
d'Anglas, Boissy, 48
Dante Alighieri, 243, 301, 309, 311, 313, 314, 317
Dark Ladie, The (Coleridge), 159, 160, 164, 166, 167
Darwin, Erasmus, 121, 130–131, 133
Darwin/Darwinian theories, 73, 247
Dawson, W.J., 274–281
de Carbonnières, Ramond, 131
de la Rochemouhet, Chevalier, 53
de Montlivault, Guyon, 50, 52
De Quincey, Thomas, 13–14, 26, 89, 159, 266
de Rancogne, Charles, 52
De Vere, Aubrey, 86–87, 124–125, 139, 147
Décadi, Toussaint, 54
Defoe, Daniel, 230
Della Cruscans, 151, 159
Description of the Scenery of English Lakes, 303, 310
Descriptive Sketches, 1, 37
   H.W. Garrod on, 121–133
diction, 143, 175, 183, 184, 187, 208, 219, 231, 233, 237, 290
didactic poetry/motive, 76, 94–95, 130
Digby, Kenelm Henry, 316–317
divinity, 148, 191, 204, 249, 253, 264, 265, 266, 270

Don Juan (Byron), 93, 236
Dove Cottage, 2, 197
Dowden, Edward, 88–90, 196, 275, 300
Drachenfels, 11, 12
Dryden, John, 91, 243, 301
duality, 176
Duddon River sonnets, 281–298
Dufort, Comte de Cheverny, 50, 51–52

E

Ecclesiastical Sonnets, 94, 298–321
    architectural references in, 307
    history/structure of, 311
    interpretation upon, 308
    well-known characters in, 317
Edinburgh Review, 64
"efficacious spirit," 178
egotism, 73, 106, 188, 213
Egyptian Maid, The, 157
Eliot, George, 72
Elizabethans, 91, 92, 184, 313, 314
Ellen Irwin, 155, 158
Emerson, Ralph Waldo, 17–20, 139
Endymion (Keats), 102, 103, 106
energy, 140, 176
England, 18–19, 25, 38, 92, 308–309
    Constitution of, 305, 312
    English Channel, 43
    "First Visit to England," 17–20
    modern poetry in, 85–86
    patriotism in, 278, 279
    Reform Bill in, 19, 276
    to Toussaint l'Overtue, 277
    See also Church of England;
        Lake District; specific city
English poetry/poets, 130, 153, 169, 187, 296
Enragés (maddened ones), 48
Epicurean poets, 250
Epitaphs, 309
Epithalamium, 91–92
Evangelicals, 25
Evening Voluntaries, 204

Evening Walk, An, 1, 122, 123–124, 126
    passage from, 56–57
Excursion, The, 6–7, 20, 45, 65, 67, 80, 83, 94, 100, 105, 116, 130, 187, 210–268, 289–290, 292, 297, 303, 304
    four speakers in, 211, 213, 218, 227, 230, 246, 254
    Francis Jeffrey on, 213–220
    Henry Crabb Robinson on, 220–221
    Margaret/Wanderer in, 110, 113, 148
    passages from, 110, 113, 115, 117, 229
    preface to, 307
    Robert Southey on, 221
    Samuel Taylor Coleridge on, 221–236
    sixth book of, 232
    William Hazlitt on, 211–213

F

Faerie Queene (Spenser), 91
"Faery Chasm, The," 291
famous lines/poems, 113
"Farewell, A," 87
Fate of the Nortons. See White Doe of Rhylstone
Faust, 183
Federation, eve of, 24
feeling, 75, 95, 139, 146, 187, 192, 223, 236, 244–245
    expression of, 72, 73, 79, 135, 142, 222, 239–240
    freedom of, 70–71
    in profound maxim, 26, 36
    states of, poetry and, 80–81
    See also sentiment/
        sentimentalism; sympathy
"Female Vagrant, The," 136
Fenwick Notes, 192, 194, 198
Fidelity, 157, 223–224
Field, Barren, 151

Fielding, Henry, 16, 17, 230
Fingal's Cave, 18, 19
Force of Prayer, The, 155, 166
Fountain, The, 155
Fournier, the American, 46
Fourquier-Tinville, 48, 49
Fox, Charles James, 111
France, 1, 38, 88, 124, 127. *See also* specific city
French language, knowledge of, 24, 28, 31
French Revolution, 29, 40, 43, 45, 50, 55–56, 85, 121, 122–123, 127, 135, 170, 173, 188, 276
    commitment to, 23, 24, 88, 89
    September massacres/ *septembrisseurs*, 37, 46, 56
    spiritual father of, 130
    See also Girondins; Reign of Terror
French writers/poetry, 184, 244
Fuller, Margaret, 74–76, 80

G
Garrod, H.W., 121–133
    "The 'Immortal Ode,'" 196–206
Gellet-Duvivier, 47, 48, 49
genius, 26, 44, 63, 65, 66, 68, 71, 74, 75, 104, 124, 151, 153, 159, 180, 187, 207, 208, 214, 217, 223, 224, 225, 229, 243, 245–246, 280
    characterization of, 85, 216
    recognition of, 70, 244, 245
George and Sarah Green, 157
Georgian (a romantic), 23, 25
Gillies, R. P., 304
Girondins, 1, 38, 43, 48, 57. *See also* Reign of Terror
Gleim, Johann Wilhelm Ludwig, 234–235
Godwin, William, 23, 44
    Political Justice, 122
Godwinism, 123, 131
Goethe, Johann Wolfgang von, 77, 79, 85, 86

Wilhelm Meister, 18, 19
Goodwin, Catherine, 313
Goody Blake and Harry Gill, 111, 158
Gordon, George, 62. *See also* Byron, Lord
Grasmere, England, 2, 197, 241, 306
Graves, Rev. R. P., 311
Gray, John, 84, 108, 243
Greece, 92, 93, 94, 313
Greeks, 84, 141, 174, 283
Growth of a Poet's Mind. See Prelude, The
guardians, 24, 38, 42
Guilt and Sorrow, 44, 122, 301, 302

H
happiness, 5, 6, 149
"Happy Warrior, The," 87, 193, 205, 248, 252, 262, 264, 280, 300, 303
Harper, George McLean
    "The Intimations Ode," 190–196
Harper, Professor, 32, 56, 125, 126, 127, 300
Hart-Leap Well, 65, 155, 157
Hawkshead, 98
Haydon, 102–103, 104, 105
Hazlitt, William, 2, 16, 64–65, 133, 156
    on *The Excursion*, 211–213
    "Mr. Wordsworth," 236–246
healing/paliative powers, 77, 79–81, 236–237, 249
Hébertists, 48
Heine, Heinrich, 84, 85, 86
Her Eyes are Wild, 158
heroism, 1, 156, 263, 274, 280–281. *See also* patriotism
Herrick, Robert, 143, 250
Highland Boy, The, 157
Homer, 229, 238, 300, 310, 316
Horace, 230
Horn of Egremont Castle, The, 155
Hugo, Victor, 177, 181
humanity, 101, 137, 178, 238, 240
    destiny of Man, 100, 112–113, 114

in famous lines, 113
See also peasantry/country
　　people
Hunt, Leigh, 15–17, 76–77, 105
Hutchinson, Mary (wife), 2
Hymn to Intellectual Beauty (Shelley),
　　95–98

I

"I heard a thousand blended notes,"
　　87
idealism/ideality, 99, 102, 149
"Idiot Boy, The," 1, 111, 155, 158
imagery, 81, 154, 178, 226, 233, 256
　　scenery, 102, 188, 210, 212, 240–
　　　241, 247
imagination, 86, 89, 92, 96, 141, 147,
　　149, 151, 204, 223, 227, 229, 239
　　nature and, 11, 213
　　power of, 129, 173, 183, 297
　　reminiscence doctrine and,
　　　200–201
　　speculative boldness and,
　　　183–184
immortality/eternity, 150, 190–191
individuality, 111, 122, 169, 230
inferior short pieces, 83, 84, 87
infinity, 149
inspiration, 83
intellect, 44–45, 75, 87, 89, 101, 121,
　　139, 146, 179, 198, 201, 236, 312
"Intimations of Immortality." *See*
　　Ode: Intimations of Immortality
"invisible world," 116
"iron age," 77
Isle of Wight, 43
Italy, 180

J

Jacobins, 36, 46, 47, 48, 52, 188, 234–
　　235. *See also* Reign of Terror
Jeffrey, Francis, 63, 207–208, 263
　　on *The Excursion*, 213–220
Johnson, Dr. Samuel, 243
Jones, 124, 127, 132

joy, 114, 123, 149, 204, 232, 258
justice, 71

K

Keats, John, 2, 82, 84, 90, 102–107,
　　136, 148
　　"Addressed to Haydon," 64
　　Endymion, 102, 103, 106
　　Hyperion, 106
　　Lamia, 103, 107
　　Ode to Melancholy, 106
　　Saint Agnes' Eve, 178
"Khan of Tartary," 9, 10
Knight, W., 187
　　Life of Wordsworth, 55

L

Lake District, 1, 2, 12, 24, 105, 148,
　　174, 180, 189, 190, 197, 201, 214,
　　215, 229, 284, 298
"Lake Poets: William Wordsworth,
　　The," 13–14
Lake Poets/Lakists, 2, 90, 103, 284
"Lake School," 180, 207
Lalla Rookh (Moore), 103
Lamb, Charles, 16, 63–64, 90, 98,
　　103, 104, 111, 163, 220
"Lament of Mary Queen of Scots, on
　　the Eve of a New Year," 292–294
Lamia (Keats), 103
Landor, Walter Savage, 310, 313
landscape poets, 90, 92
language, 134–135, 145, 158, 184,
　　223, 229, 230, 242
　　of common parlance, 174, 181,
　　　184, 237
　　metre and, 143, 144, 195, 225–226
　　modes of, 222
　　phraseology, 98, 214, 217, 220
　　wordiness, 208, 218, 220
"Laodamia," 87, 141, 157, 241, 248,
　　263, 299
Larochejaquelin, 52
"Leech-Gatherer, The," 65, 116, 141,
　　145, 174, 178, 228, 248, 263

as most characteristic poem, 146
     passage from, 252
Legendre, 48
Legouis, Émile, 23–58, 123, 126, 127,
     130, 131, 300
     criticism from, 33
Lessing, Gotthold Ephraim, 234–235
letters
     Annette/Dorothy, 39, 40–41,
          41–42, 45, 50–51, 56
     Annette to Wordsworth, 49, 56
     by Wordsworth, 268–274, 306,
          311
Liberalism, 85
liberty, 44, 70, 93–94, 156, 277
     Civil Liberty, 269, 271
     See also patriotism
Life of Wordsworth (Knight), 55
"Lines Left upon a Seat in a Yew-
     tree," 69–70, 87, 98
lionism/lion-dinners, 21, 22
Llandaff, Bishop of, 43
Lockhart, John Gibson, 7–9
London, England, 5, 22, 39, 269
Longfellow, Henry Wadsworth,
     66–67
Lonsdale, Lord, 313
Lost Leader (Browning), 275
"Lost Leader, The" (Browning),
     14–15
Lucretius, 19
Lucy Gray, or Solitude, 100, 115–116,
     144, 155, 158
Lyrical Ballads, 1, 64–65, 67, 91, 153,
     156, 162, 208, 215, 238, 240, 301,
     302
     narrative style of, 154
     preface to, 124, 132, 133–135, 151
lyricism, 76–77

M

Macaulay, Thomas Babington, 67,
     188
Macpherson, James, 18
Manzoni, Alessandro, 84

Marlowe, Christopher, 144
marriage, 40–41, 42, 44, 57
Martineau, Harriet, 81–82
Matthew group, 100
mediocrity, 155, 174
"Memorial Verses" (Arnold), 76–77
Meredith, George, 79–81
metaphor, 160, 164, 234
metaphysics, 1, 11, 143, 175, 188, 194,
     208, 209
meter, 144, 145–146, 167, 184
Michael, 100, 113, 155, 181, 248, 263
Michelangelo, sonnets of, 314
Mill, John Stuart, 79–81
Milton, John, 6, 15, 92, 93, 104, 105,
     144, 154, 161, 213, 215, 227, 241,
     243, 268, 274, 279, 282, 299, 300,
     310–311, 313–314, 315, 316, 317
     national affairs and, 275
     Paradise Lost, 16, 230
     Wordsworth compared to, 7,
          108, 117
Miscellaneous Poems, 79, 281
"Modern British Poets" (Fuller),
     74–76
modern poetry, 85–86, 136, 174, 177,
     243
monarchy, suppression of, 56
Monkhouse, 103, 104
Montmorency-Laval, Vicomte de, 53
"Moods of my own Mind," 271
morals/moralist, 25, 26, 66, 74, 76,
     86, 185–186, 189, 217, 228, 249,
     254, 256, 259, 263
     "moral being," 265
     moral poet, 106, 261
     morality/non-morality, 107, 112,
          265
Morley, John, 276
Mountain, the (parliamentary
     faction), 47, 48, 57
mountains, poet of, 114
Muses, 66, 238, 239, 309
musicality, 76–77
Myers, F.W.H., 146, 188–190

Myers, Tom, 26
mysticism, 149, 161, 184, 208, 214, 216, 218, 253

N

narcissism, 151
nature, 24, 65, 68, 75, 79, 99, 100, 130, 132, 139, 148, 149, 170, 254, 256
  idolatry of, 12, 26, 29, 67, 193
  passion for, 11, 13, 86, 92, 147, 246, 247–248
  return to, 66, 237
  spirituality of, 98, 178–179
Neo-Platonists, 199
Newton, Isaac, 20
Ninth Thermidor, 29, 48, 50

O

octosyllabic couplets, 153
Ode composed upon an Evening of extraordinary Splendour and Beauty, 203
Ode: Intimations of Immortality From Recollections of Early Childhood, 2, 80, 81, 98, 105, 149, 161, 182, 184, 190–206, 247, 249, 264
  George McLean Harper on, 190–196
  motto/germ of poem, 191–192
  passage from, 200
"Ode to Duty," 87, 193, 205, 252, 303
Ode to Melancholy (Keats), 106
Ode to the West Wind (Shelley), 102, 251
Olivier, Charles, 29
"On the Feelings of a Highminded Spaniard," 20
originality, 65, 74, 76, 108, 109, 214, 216, 240, 245
Orléans, France, 23, 24, 27, 34, 36–37, 46
  "Civic Feast" at, 56
  the Terror at, 45, 46–47, 48, 49
  Wordsworth in, 30
ornamentation, 237, 239

Oxford Tract Movement, 316

P

paganism, 102, 107
pantheism, 128, 177, 234, 253, 255
Paradise Lost (Milton), 5, 16, 91
paradoxes, 109–110, 217, 235, 258
parallelism, 107, 166
Pardessus, Jean Marie, 52, 53
Pardessus the younger, 50, 52
Paris, France, 37, 48, 50, 54
Parnassus, 66
passions, 89, 134, 138, 142, 147, 186, 187, 212, 255
Pater, Walter, 173–188
pathos, 65, 154, 218, 239
patriotism, 85, 108. *See also* heroism
  sonnets on, 268–281
Peacock, Thomas Love
  "Four Ages of Poetry," 66
peasantry/country people, 10, 63, 133, 136, 153, 180–181, 213–214
People's Society, 46
Percy, Thomas, 153, 154, 169, 206
Peter Bell, 2, 105, 155, 281, 282, 283, 302, 321–323
"Peter Bell the Third" (Shelley), 321–322
"Phaedo" (Plato), 195
philosophic writer, 68–69, 76, 101, 197, 198, 253, 258, 263
piety, 73, 95, 192, 194, 196, 198, 205
Pindaric poet, 218, 229, 238
plagiarism, 93
Plato, 190, 197, 199
  "Phaedo," 195
Platonists, 182, 197, 213, 253
Poe, Edgar Allan, 159, 167
Poems in Two Volumes, 2, 79, 80, 232, 314
Poems of 1807, 301
"Poems of the Affections," 86, 87
"Poems of the Fancy," 86, 87
"Poems of the Imagination," 87, 201
Poems on the Naming of Places, 302

poet laureate, 2, 14
poetic belief, famous declaration of, 133–134
poetry, 44, 65, 67, 73, 84, 105, 135, 141, 142, 161, 252, 309, 310
    best of, 83, 87, 105, 110, 183–184, 193
    blank verse, 142, 153, 289–290, 292
    defects of, 225–234, 289
    epic poetry, 311–312
    lyrical poetry, 280, 281
    pastoral poems, 178, 181, 212
    personal character of, 86–87
    poetical philosophy, 69, 71–72, 182
    publication, first poems, 39
    theories of, 151, 152, 154, 221
    See also modern poetry
"Poet's Epitaph, A," 87, 114
point of view, 255
Political Justice (Godwin), 122
politics, 14, 25, 42, 85, 275–276, 278
    abstract political rights, 261
    of the age, 66
    sonnets on, 268–281
    See also French Revolution
Pollard, Jane, 42
"Poor Susan," 65
Pope, Alexander, 91, 143, 154, 243
Potts, Abbie Findlay, 298–321
poverty, 38, 44, 50, 111
preexistence, doctrine/notion, 197, 200–201, 247, 249, 252–253
Preface, 160, 302
"Preface" (Arnold), 1, 83–85
prefaces, famous, 142
Prelude, The, 29, 35, 43, 83, 95, 122, 124, 130, 138, 142, 183, 193, 299, 301, 302–303, 304, 305, 307
    French Revolution and, 37
    ninth book of, 31, 32
    passage from, 115, 123, 202–203, 267–268
    Samuel Taylor Coleridge on, 169–173

second book of, 123
sixth book of, 125, 126, 128
profound maxim, 26
prolixity/wordiness, 216, 219, 222
Prometheus Unbound (Shelley), 94
prose, 141, 144
Protestantism, 92
provincialism, 145
Puritanism, 92, 279

R
Racedown in Dorset, 1
Radicalism, new, 93
"Rainbow, The," 192, 194, 197, 198, 205
Rannie, David Watson, 90–108
ratiocination, 69
Recluse, The, 2, 174, 178, 187, 189, 210, 280–281, 301, 303, 304, 307
"recognitions," 192
recollections, 234, 239, 240, 250, 256
Reign of Terror, 23, 24, 42, 43, 45, 49, 52, 57. *See also* French Revolution; Jacobins
religion, 94, 127–128, 180, 217. *See also* divinity; piety; spirituality
Reliques (Percy), 152, 153, 206
reminiscence doctrine, 200–201
"Resolution and Independence," 2, 178
Restoration, the, 53
Reverie of Poor Susan, The, 155, 158
Revolt of Islam (Shelley), 101
Revolutionary poets, 132
Reynolds, John Hamilton, 105
rhythmical power, 184
Rising in the North, The, 156
River Duddon sonnets, 281–298
    Inscriptions, 195
    odes, 292–295
Rob Roy's Grave, 156
Robespierre, Maximilien, 48, 50
Robinson, Henry Crabb, 5–6, 103, 308, 316, 319
    on *The Excursion*, 220–221

Robinson Crusoe (Defoe), 244
Rogers, Samuel, 269, 270–271
romanticism, 90–108, 136, 169
    essence of, 94
    Romantic Revival, 91, 92, 108
Rousseau, Jean Jacques, 122, 131, 151,
    177
    French Revolution and, 130
    nature/sensibility, worship of,
      29
    original goodness doctrine, 193
royalists, 50, 54
royalty, fall of, 56
rural/natural objects, 80, 181
    rustic life, 134, 174–175
    as soothing subjects, 79
"Ruth," 87, 113, 155, 181
Rydal Mount, 2, 9, 17, 18, 105
    Lake of Rydale, 5

S

Sailor's Mother, The, 111, 113
Saint Agnes' Eve (Keats), 178
Sand, George, 181
Savoy, annexation of, 130
scenery, 100, 188, 213, 249, 254, 257.
    See also imagery
Scherer, Edmond, 85–86
science, 142, 248, 249–250, 260, 266,
    309
Scotland, 28, 94, 156, 229, 292–294
Scott, Sir Walter, 64, 65, 66, 67, 90,
    108, 164–165, 206, 312, 317
Scudder, Vida D., 135–138
Seathwaite, 284–285, 289
seclusion. *See* tranquility/solitude
self-analysis, 137, 206. See also
    Prelude, The
self-consciousness, 91, 222
self-dependence, 116
self-indulgence, 207, 216
self-perfection, 75
senses, 27, 89, 129, 148, 227
sensibility, innate, 177–178
sensuality, 27

"Sentiment and Reflection," 87
sentiment/sentimentalism, 65, 92,
    150, 151, 181, 228, 229, 230–231,
    241, 257, 297
    of justice, 71–72
    See also feeling; sympathy
Seven Sisters, The, 155, 158
Shaftesbury, Anthony Ashley
    Cooper, 253
Shairp, John Campbell, 208–210
Shakespeare, William, 17, 62, 68, 75,
    83, 92, 106, 109, 184, 243, 299, 301,
    314
    Wordsworth compared to, 74, 76
"She dwelt among the untrodden
    ways," 87
"She was a phantom of delight," 87
Shelley, Mary, 322
Shelley, Percy Bysshe, 2, 76, 82, 89,
    90, 91, 94, 95, 95–98, 100, 101, 102,
    103, 111, 136, 177, 247, 251
    "Peter Bell the Third," 321–322
similes, 164
"Simon Lee," 145, 259
simplicity, 74, 86, 137, 145, 150, 207,
    212, 214, 220, 237, 238, 245, 276
Sir Patrick Spence (ballad), 154, 161,
    163, 165
sister, 8, 9, 10, 299. *See also*
    Wordsworth, Dorothy
Skiddaw (mountain), 221, 241, 297
"slumber did my spirit seal, A," 87
Smith, Adam, 261
Smith, Sydney, 63, 64
socialism, 100, 188
Solitary Reaper, The, 156
Song at the Feast of Brougham Castle,
    258
    Lord Clifford in, 156, 157, 163
"songs of despair," 86
sonnets, 20, 30, 65, 142, 243, 314
    patriotic and political, 268–274
    River Duddon sonnets, 281–298
    to Toussaint l'Overtue, 277–278
    Venetian Republic and, 85

Sonnets Dedicated to National Independence and Liberty, 100

sorrow, 112, 148, 181, 258
    futility of, 248, 263, 265
    strength and, 261–262

soul, 114, 178, 182, 190
    journey of, 149–150, 190, 192
    prior existence of, 195
    See also spirituality

Southey, Robert, 2, 6–7, 9, 14, 62, 108, 221, 311, 313, 322–323

specialism, 260

Spenser, Edmund, 93, 157, 299, 301, 310, 313, 317
    Faerie Queene, 91
    Shephearde's Calendar, 91

Spinozism, 73, 113, 234

Spirit of the Age, 237

spirituality, 73, 74, 90, 98, 179, 235, 247. *See also* religion; soul

"Stanzas on Peele Castle," 96, 263

Stephen, Leslie, 247–268

"Stepping Westward," 174, 178, 267

Stoicism, 131

Stork, Charles Wharton, 150–169

sublimity, 109, 117, 217, 246, 257

suffering, 114, 156, 260. *See also* sorrow

Swinburne, Algernon Charles, 111, 160, 165

Switzerland, 27, 85, 93, 94, 180
    Swiss tour, 124, 125, 126, 127–129, 132

symbolism, 156, 249, 257
    divine possession, 257
    of fundamental feelings, 266

Symons, Arthur, 138–150

sympathy, 73, 111, 116, 236, 256, 259, 261, 262, 263

T

Taylor, Sir Henry, 67–72, 237

Tennyson, Alfred (Lord), 82

Terror, the/Terrorists. *See* Reign of Terror

"Thanksgiving Ode, The," 281

The Sensitive Plant (Shelley), 101, 102

Thomson, James, 144

Thorn, The, 111, 113, 158

Three Graves, The (Coleridge), 159, 161, 162, 166, 167

"Three years she grew in sun and shower," 87

Ticknor, George, 9–10

"Tintern Abbey," 1, 20, 61, 87, 94, 95, 105, 136, 142, 182, 193, 252, 267

"To a Daisy," 65

"To the Cuckoo," 65, 156, 192, 197–198, 256

Tobin, James, 303

Tories and Whigs, 14, 276

tranquility/solitude, 61, 68, 85, 111, 114–116, 124, 137, 139, 146, 149, 211, 214, 216, 237, 240, 254–255, 275, 303
    "emotion recollected in," 147
    See also contemplative life; Lake District

transcendent spirit, 169, 170, 197

truth, 218–219, 236, 237, 245
    moral truth, 74
    nature and, 129, 238
    of observation, 229
    philosophic perceptions of, 69
    revealing aspects of, 68

"Two April Mornings, The," 184

Two Sisters, The, 158

"Two Voices," 20

U

unity of all things, 90, 99

universality, 147

unpoetical natures, 80

V

Vallon, Annette (Marie Anne), 1, 23, 24, 28, 29, 34–35, 36, 38–39, 45, 51–52, 53–54, 121, 127
    daughter of, 23, 30, 37–38
    marriage hopes of, 40–41

See also letters

Vallon, Charles Henry, 28, 36, 49, 52, 54

Vallon, Françoise, 54

Vallon, Jean Jacques, 28, 36, 49

Vallon, Paul, 28, 30, 37, 45, 47–48, 49, 53, 55

Vallon family, 28–29, 35, 45, 49

Vallon sisters, 51, 52, 53

vanity, 11

"Vaudracour and Julia," 23, 31, 32–34, 35, 283, 292

    lettres de cachet in, 31, 32

    passages from, 33, 34, 35

    Wordsworth's story and, 32, 55

Vendémiaire insurrection, 50–51

verisimilitude, 231

versification, 124

Victoria (Queen), 23, 25

Victorian era, 26, 137

Virgil, 19, 301, 304, 316, 317

visions/visionary power, 89, 114, 149–150, 174, 197, 199, 201, 202, 204, 205, 212

Voltaire, 103, 255

W

Waggoner, The, 2, 124, 281

Walker, Rev. Robert, 284–286

Watson, William

    "Wordsworth's Grave," 87–88

Watts, Alaric, 43

"We Are Seven," 136, 137, 153, 158, 235

Welt-Schmerz, 126

Wesleyans, 321

Westmoreland, England, 25, 182, 183

Westmoreland Girl, The, 157

Wharfdale, 209–210

Whigs and Tories, 276

White Doe of Rylstone, The, 2, 113, 156, 158, 163, 206–210, 248, 262–263, 297, 301, 303, 314

    Emily Norton in, 152, 157, 163, 206

    Francis Jeffrey on, 207–208

    John Campbell Shairp on, 208–210

    John Wilson on, 206–207

wife, 9, 10. *See also* Hutchinson, Mary

Wilhelm Meister (Goethe), 18, 19

Wilson, John, 206–207, 246

"Wisdom and Spirit of the universe," 193

Wordsworth, Anne Caroline (daughter), 23, 37–38, 39, 41, 42, 49, 56

Wordsworth, Bishop, 131

Wordsworth, Christopher, 103, 300

Wordsworth, Dorothy (sister), 5, 24, 26, 27, 39, 49, 146, 197, 298, 306. *See also* letters

Wordsworth, Gordon, 196, 305

Wordsworth, John (brother), 280

Wordsworth, John (father), 1, 303

Wordsworthians, 196

"Wordsworth's Grave" (Watson), 87–88

Wordworth, Anne Cookson (mother), 1

Wordworth, Bishop (nephew), 45

Y

Yarnall, Ellis, 35, 55

Young, Charles Mayne, 10–13

youth, 80, 99, 136, 264, 265